Best Dog Hikes Colorado

HELP US KEEP THIS GUIDE UP TO DATE

Every effort has been made by the authors and editors to make this guide as accurate and useful as possible. However, many things can change after a guide is published—trails are rerouted, regulations change, techniques evolve, facilities come under new management, and so on.

We would appreciate hearing from you concerning your experiences with this guide and how you feel it could be improved and kept up to date. While we may not be able to respond to all comments and suggestions, we'll take them to heart, and we'll also make certain to share them with the authors. Please send your comments and suggestions to the following address:

Globe Pequot Press
Reader Response/Editorial Department
PO Box 480
Guilford, CT 06437

Or you may e-mail us at: editorial@GlobePequot.com

Thanks for your input, and happy trails!

Best Dog Hikes Colorado

edited by FalconGuides

FALCON GUIDES

GUILFORD, CONNECTICUT
HELENA, MONTANA

AN IMPRINT OF GLOBE PEQUOT PRESS

FALCONGUIDES®

Text contributed by Bob D'Antonio, Maryann Gaug, Stewart Green, Linda B. Mullally, and Tracy Salcedo-Chourré.

FalconGuides is an imprint of Globe Pequot Press.
Falcon, FalconGuides, and Outfit Your Mind are registered trademarks of Morris Book Publishing, LLC.

Illustrations by Todd Telander and Diane Blasius.

All photos by Maryann Gaug except: pp. 4, 6, 9, 21, 39, and 85 by Stephen Gorman and Eli Burakian; p. 17 by David S. Mullally; pp. 69, 73, 77, 79, 84, 90, and 283 by Bob D'Antonio; p. 77 © istockphoto.

Overview map on p. vi © Morris Book Publishing, LLC. All hike maps by Mapping Specialists except: pp. 63, 67, 70, 74, 76, 80, 83, 86, and 89 by Trailhead Graphics, Inc. © Morris Book Publishing, LLC; pp. 53, 168, 176, 184, 193, 200, and 204 by Design Maps, Inc. © Morris Book Publishing, LLC.

Project editor: Meredith Dias
Layout artist: Mary Ballachino

Library of Congress Cataloging-in-Publication Data
Best dog hikes Colorado / edited by FalconGuides.
pages cm
ISBN 978-0-7627-8369-4
1. Hiking with dogs—Colorado—Guidebooks. 2. Colorado—Guidebooks.
I. FalconGuides (Publisher)
SF427.4574.C6B45 2013
796.5109788—dc23

2012050356

Printed in the United States of America

10 9 8 7 6 5 4 3 2

Contents

Map Legend ..... **viii**
Introduction **1**
Why Hike with Your Dog? 1
Preparing for Fido to Hit the Trail 2
What to Expect on the Trail 11
How to Use This Guide 15
Trail Finder **18**

The Hikes

Eastern Plains **21**
1. Homestead Trail 22
2. Picket Wire Canyonlands 28
3. Dawson Butte Ranch Open Space 34
4. Rocky Mountain Arsenal National Wildlife Refuge 40
5. Pawnee Buttes 46
6. Edna Mae Bennett Nature Trail 51

Front Range **55**
7. Lory State Park Loop 56
8. Dome Mountain Trail 63
9. Devil's Backbone Nature Trail 66
10. Mount Audubon 69
11. Blue Lake 72
12. Heil Valley Ranch/Lichen Loop 75
13. Bear Peak 78
14. Walker Ranch 82
15. Marshall Mesa 85
16. Eldorado Canyon Trail 88

North-Central Mountains **91**
17. Wheeler Trail 92
18. North Mount Elbert Trail 97
19. Notch Mountain 102
20. Mount Thomas Trail 108
21. Granite Lakes Trail 112
22. Silver Creek Trail 118
23. Kelly Lake 125
24. Seven Lakes 129

Overview

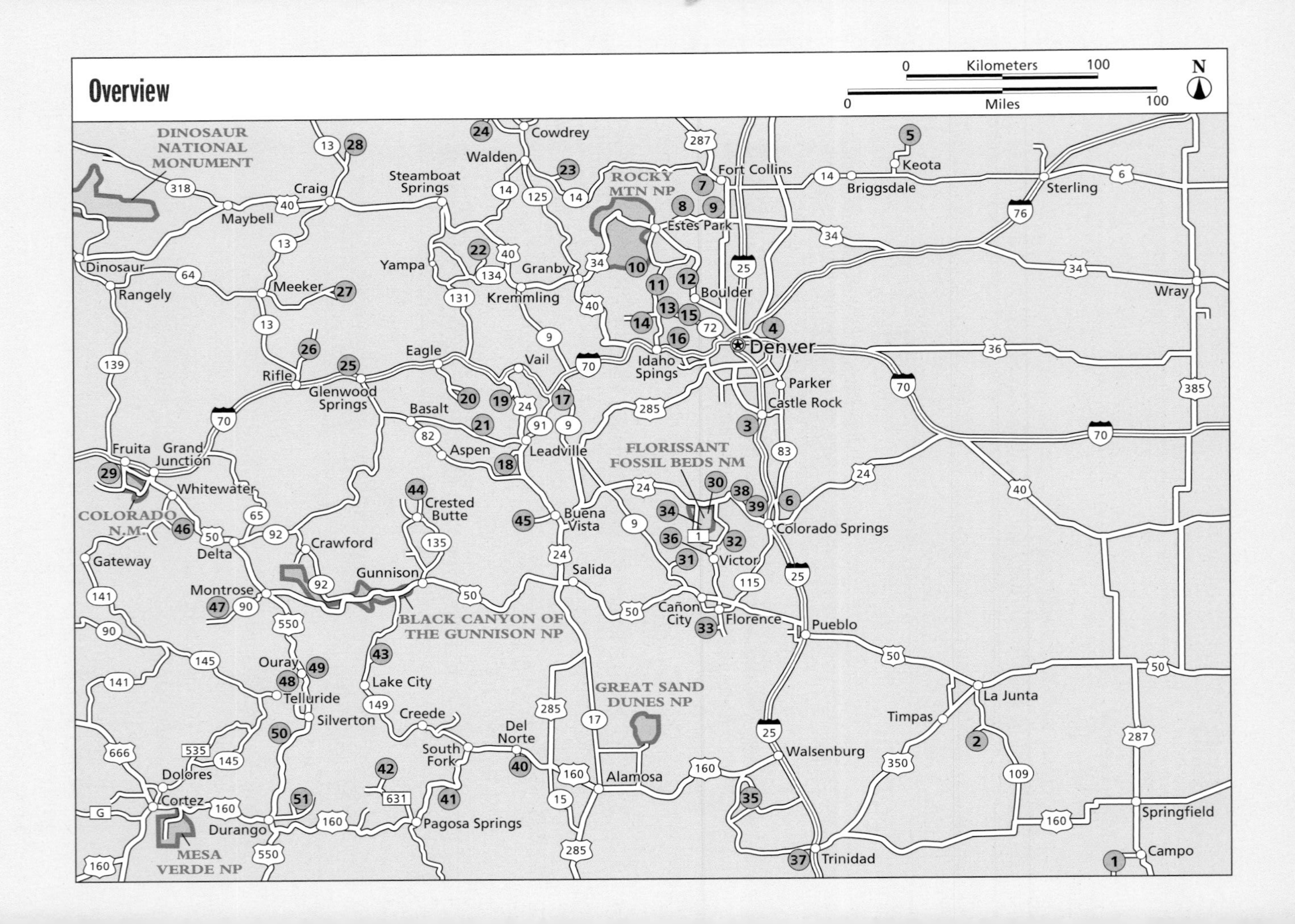
Overview
Kilometers
Miles
0
100
N
DINOSAUR NATIONAL MONUMENT
ROCKY MTN NP
FLORISSANT FOSSIL BEDS NM
COLORADO N.M.
BLACK CANYON OF THE GUNNISON NP
GREAT SAND DUNES NP
MESA VERDE NP
Cowdrey
Walden
Steamboat Springs
Craig
Maybell
Dinosaur
Rangely
Meeker
Yampa
Granby
Kremmling
Fort Collins
Estes Park
Boulder
Denver
Idaho Spings
Parker
Castle Rock
Keota
Briggsdale
Sterling
Wray
Eagle
Vail
Rifle
Glenwood Springs
Basalt
Aspen
Leadville
Fruita
Grand Junction
Whitewater
Delta
Gateway
Crawford
Crested Butte
Buena Vista
Gunnison
Montrose
Salida
Colorado Springs
Victor
Cañon City
Florence
Pueblo
Ouray
Telluride
Silverton
Lake City
Creede
Del Norte
South Fork
Alamosa
Walsenburg
La Junta
Timpas
Springfield
Campo
Trinidad
Pagosa Springs
Dolores
Cortez
Durango

Northwest......135
25. Storm King Fourteen Memorial Trail 137
26. Coyote and Squirrel Trails...... 143
27. Marvine Loop 148
28. Black Mountain (West Summit) Trail 154
29. Devils Canyon...... 159

Southeast Mountains......165
30. Susan G. Bretag/Palmer Loop 166
31. Thompson Mountain...... 170
32. Mount Cutler Trail 175
33. Newlin Creek Trail...... 178
34. The Crags Trail 183
35. Spanish Peaks Traverse 187
36. Horsethief Falls...... 192
37. Reilly and Levsa Canyons 195
38. Lower Barr Trail 199
39. Red Rock Canyon Trail 202

South-Central Mountains 205
40. Middle Frisco Trail 206
41. Alberta Peak: Continental Divide National Scenic Trail 211
42. Williams Creek Trail 215
43. Devils Creek and Lake...... 220
44. Washington Gulch Trail...... 225
45. Ptarmigan Lake 230

Southwest 235
46. Big Dominguez Canyon 236
47. Upper Roubideau Area Loop 241
48. Jud Wiebe Memorial Trail...... 247
49. Cascade and Portland Loop 251
50. Pass and Coal Creek Loop 257
51. First Fork and Red Creek Loop...... 263

Appendix A: Hiking Gear 268

Appendix B: Medical Emergencies and Treatment......279

Appendix C: Wildlife Conflicts 282

Hike Index......286

Map Legend

70	Interstate Highway
34	U.S. Highway
72	State Highway
FR 2361	County/Forest Road
	Local Road
	Unpaved Road
	Jeep Trail
	Railroad Tracks
	Paved Trail
	Featured Trail
	Trail
	Off-Trail Hike
	Continental Divide
	State Line
	Body of Water
	Marsh/Swamp
	River/Creek
	Intermittent Streams
	National Park/National Forest
	National Monument/ Wilderness Area
	Local/State Park/Wildlife Refuge
	Miscellaneous Fill

	Appalachian Trail
	Bridge
	Campground
	Capital
	Cavern/Cave/Natural Bridge
	Radio Tower
	Gate
	Horse Trail
	Mountain Peak/Summit
P	Parking
	Pass
	Picnic Area
	Point of Interest/Structure
	Ranger District Office
	Restroom
	Spring
	Town
7	Trailhead
	Tunnel
	Water
	Waterfall
	Viewpoint/Overlook
?	Visitor/Information Center
	Wheelchair Accessible

Introduction

Colorado! The word conjures images of rugged peaks, cascading mountain streams, and crystal clear alpine lakes. Indeed, the state's middle section lives up to those expectations, but the state as a whole offers so much more. Colorado's western canyon country, carved by raging torrents, is rich in dinosaur graveyards and the artifacts and ruins of Ancestral Puebloan and Fremont Indians, all well worth exploring. The Eastern Plains, long thought too flat to be scenic, have plenty of natural delights tucked away for the hiker. Buttes rise above the plains, providing a haven for hawks and falcons, while southeastern canyons cache signs of ancient inhabitants including American Indian petroglyphs and North America's largest known dinosaur tracksite.

About 355 million years ago, Colorado sat near the equator. Little crustaceans in shallow seas died and were compressed into limestone. The Ancestral Rockies were uplifted from the seas and formed part of the supercontinent Pangaea. As time progressed, the mountains eroded, and coastal dunes became today's magnificent sandstone cliffs. The present Rocky Mountains were uplifted starting 70 million years ago. Volcanic activity 25 million years ago created plateaus and several mountain ranges. Then, from 25 million to 5 million years ago, the entire region rose 5,000 feet to its present elevation. Ice ages took hold of Colorado (by that time located north of the equator around the thirty-ninth parallel), and from 1.8 million to 12,000 years ago, glaciers carved the magnificent craggy peaks and U-shaped valleys we see today.

Human history in Colorado started with hunter-gatherers, followed by the Ancestral Puebloan culture that, from 500 BC to AD 1300, farmed and then built pueblos and magnificent cliff dwellings in the southwest corner of the state. After AD 1300 other Native Americans moved into the Eastern Plains and mountain valleys. Spanish explorers arrived in the late 1500s, followed by trappers and traders. The gold rush of 1859 was perhaps the most significant event in the state's history, bringing settlers, fortune seekers, and improved transportation. The railroad companies performed engineering miracles to conquer impassable mountains, hastening both the transportation of ore and the state's development. Later, equally impressive roads were built for the automobile.

Today these roads provide us with relatively easy travel to hiking trails. Hiking is one of the best ways to explore Colorado, and there's no better companion for your outing than your dog. Dogs are often members of the family, and you wouldn't want to hit the trail without them. With a little bit of effort, strong legs and lungs, and your dog by your side, you can experience the natural world of Colorado's vast hiking trails. We hope this book will help get you there.

Why Hike with Your Dog?

Hiking is a healthy, noncompetitive, and inexpensive form of outdoor recreation. As a dog owner you have the privilege of having a live-in hiking companion who will enhance the experience in a way no other best friend can. Your dog's innate curiosity will make you notice and appreciate more of the natural world around you. His alertness and intuition can give you an added sense of security.

Hiking also provides time for quality bonding between owner and dog. And dog owners with busy schedules find that hiking is a convenient opportunity to combine their own and their dog's need for exercise and play in a safe, natural setting.

Hiking can be very beneficial to your dog physically and mentally. In addition to the opportunity for physical exercise, the natural smells, sights, and sounds off the beaten track are invigorating and rejuvenating. Hiking and the training regimen to keep your dog in good form can be excellent prevention for several physical and behavioral disorders and in some cases may help reduce the symptoms of other ailments.

According to statistics, one in three dogs in America is overweight, which is usually a result of feeding too much (often the wrong foods) and moving too little. As in humans, obesity can trigger more serious health problems including heart attack, high blood pressure, diabetes, or even arthritis. To determine how fit your dog is, use this simple rule: You should be able to feel your dog's ribs when you run your hands along her sides (feel them, not see them).

The stress on your dog's joints from carrying extra weight can also exacerbate preexisting conditions such as hip dysplasia. The exercise from hiking can help keep your dog trimmer and strengthen muscles that support the hips.

Hiking can also help dogs that suffer from boredom, which can result in depressive lethargy or destructive behaviors. Regular exercise in the great outdoors can help mellow out high-strung dogs and dogs prone to overt dominance and aggression.

Hiking is a natural and enjoyable way for people and dogs to stay fit. Running up a dirt trail, leaping over streams, climbing on boulders, negotiating fallen limbs in the forest, and paddling circles in a lake keep a dog's spirit soaring and her body agile, trim, and toned.

Preparing for Fido to Hit the Trail

If you plan to bring your dog, you need to consider a few things other than just the area's land management regulations concerning dogs. Preparing your dog for hiking is like coaching an athlete for an Olympic decathlon. You must get her in good physical condition (muscular and cardiovascular) to enjoy the hike safely. Certain parts of your dog's body will require special care and attention before hiking to prevent injury or discomfort. Mental conditioning includes

Conditioning will enhance your dog's fitness for the trail.

familiarizing her with hiking equipment and the trail environment, as well as basic commands.

Obedience

One of the gratifying aspects of obedience classes and hiking is that they complement each other. The drills prepare your dog, and the trail becomes a most enjoyable arena to practice and reinforce the classroom lessons. Obedience is especially important for a hiking dog because the nuisance and hazard of a few uncontrolled dogs can result in all dogs being banned from the trail.

DOES YOUR DOG NEED OBEDIENCE TRAINING?

If the fact that basic obedience facilitates and enhances your relationship with your dog isn't motivation enough, realize that once you step out of your yard and onto the trail, everything your dog is and isn't reflects on you and affects other people, animals, and the surrounding environment. Basic obedience skills are essential on the trail.

Vital aspects of your dog's trail education include:

1. **Learning appropriate behavior around people and animals on the trail.**
2. **Learning to respond to commands in spite of the naturally seductive sights, sounds, and smells of the trail.**
3. **Learning a repertoire of commands, including, at a minimum, come, sit, down, stay or wait, heel, no, and leave it.**

Basic Commands

Use the word "off" when training your dog not to jump on people and dance on furniture. "Down" should be used strictly for lying down. It is unrealistic to expect an exuberant pup to respond to the down command under highly excitable circumstances. The best you can expect is for your dog to learn to display her excitement with all four paws touching the ground and stay "off." That drill, repeated over time, will prove to be one of your most challenging and rewarding accomplishments. Consistency and follow-through in your drills, reinforced by praise and food reward, are essential.

Teach your dog that when you say "stay" or "wait" in the car, he should remain in the open vehicle until his leash is on and you've given the command that it's okay to jump out. The same thing applies to wanting your dog to learn impulse control—he should wait for your okay before sprinting and dashing off after you unleash him. The day may come when that simple command might save your dog's life.

Training Options

You can train your dog yourself. Several good training books are available; find them at the library and at bookstores and pet supply stores. The two main advantages of training your dog yourself are control of the training schedule and the minimal cost. The "do-it-yourself" method works best if you know and understand how a dog thinks and have the self-discipline to set aside about 15 minutes twice a day to work with your dog.

Successful training is not measured just by the achievement of a dog's sitting, staying, and coming. The objective is to have your dog respond to commands with respectful but enthusiastic immediacy, rather than cowering compliance. Be careful with your dog's psyche. A novice dog owner with a well-intentioned trial-and-error approach can damage a dog's psyche just as easily as an experienced trainer who doesn't realize his methods are breaking the dog's spirit.

Calling your dog over to give him a reprimand is as counterproductive to fostering reliable off-leash recalls as sticking your pup's nose in his business is to housebreaking.

In teaching your dog commands for the trail, tone and verbal and body language can give a dog mixed or vague messages that confuse the dog, frustrate the owner, and undermine hiker/dog team spirit. In this case you might opt to enroll your dog in a group obedience class or hire a private trainer. A good trainer can quickly get the desired response from the dog (sitting, lying down, heeling). The trainer can teach the owner to communicate clearly, confidently, and in some cases assertively what he or she wants from the dog, all the while using humane, reward-based techniques.

Other hikers may yield to you as you pass with your dog. If you encounter a large group of hikers, you should be the one to step off the trail and yield to the group as it passes.

A qualified trainer can also help you work with and around your dog's natural instincts and breed characteristics so that traits like dominance, guarding and chasing instincts, independence, hyperalertness, or roaming do not become problems. A trainer can instruct you in the appropriate use of tools such as the head halter, which is widely preferred over the less humane choke collar.

Group classes are often offered for a reasonable fee through local kennel clubs, pet supply stores, and veterinary clinics. Consider a puppy class or adult obedience class one of the best investments in your dog's and your relationship on the trail. Regardless of whether you are an experienced or first-time dog owner, the controlled but buzzing environment of a group class makes an excellent training ground for dogs to work on their social interaction with other dogs and humans, while learning to ignore distractions. Puppy classes have the advantage of training both pup and owner right out of the starting gate.

Private sessions can be more effective with dogs (especially adult dogs) and owners whose training needs require more one-on-one attention.

How Soon Should You Start Training Your Dog?

Although dogs are not admitted to puppy classes until they have had at least their first two DHLP-P (distemper/parvo) vaccinations (at about ten weeks), you should start working with your puppy on your own before that.

Basic training should start from the time the pup is born. Puppies that are handled by human hands earlier on bond more easily and accept human touch more readily. Practice enthusiastically calling your puppy to come and rewarding him with praise, petting, and a treat. This is the first step in many months of work toward every dog owner's ultimate goal—a reliable recall off-leash. Never use your dog's name to reprimand, punish, or administer anything she views as unpleasant. The more pleasant the experience, the more reason she'll have to come quickly when you call her name.

Communicating with Your Dog

Your dog's two ways of communicating with you are through body language and vocal sounds. Listen to what he is trying to tell you by paying attention to his changes in demeanor on the trail. He is giving you important information about how he feels physically and his concerns about what awaits around the bend.

Body language: When everything is okay, your dog will have a light, relaxed sway and an energetic bounce in his step. Ears suddenly forward and tail up or raised hackles (hair standing up on the back of his neck or base of the tail) indicate tension and alertness triggered by a smell, sound, or sight.

Vocal communication: If your dog appears uneasy, hyperactive, and alert and begins to bark, growl, or whine, she could be sensing a possible threat. The unusual smell, sound, or sight may not be visible to you, but you should respect her concern. Stop, listen, and look around. Pat your dog and speak to her reassuringly while keeping your wits about you. Make sure your dog is leashed and proceed cautiously until you identify the source of her concern, which can be as simple as another hiker around the bend or the presence of a rodent in the bushes.

Be sensitive: Tail down, stiff gait, and a lethargic pace may indicate a tightening of your dog's back or hip muscles from straining or bruising of soft tissue. Examine him carefully, checking his paws and between the toes for cuts or foreign bodies that could be causing him discomfort or pain. If he appears okay, stop and rest and make sure he gets water. He may need a snack to boost his energy.

If your dog looks drained, demoralized, or sick; is injured; or you cannot explain his odd behavior, trust that something is wrong. Dogs in general have an almost misplaced desire to please, even when in pain. Be considerate of your best friend's needs and limitations. Do not push him and jeopardize his well-being to meet your expectations and goals. On the trail you are a team and your teammate depends on you. Alter the route, and when in doubt cut the excursion short. In the unfortunate event that there is something serious going on with your dog, you may have to carry him out. You want to share safe, positive experiences that will nurture his and your enthusiasm for hiking.

On the other hand, fatigue at the end of the day is normal. A mellow dog after a solid day's work and play on the trail is a good thing. After a meal and a good night's rest, your dog should emerge refreshed in the morning. If he's dragging, take it easy by hiking a shorter distance to your next campsite or making extra rest stops on the way to the car if this is the end of the trip.

Building Confidence

Exposure to the trail environment at an early age (preferably before twelve weeks) will help build your dog's confidence. Dogs get comfortable with sounds, sights, and experiences by early and constant exposure as pups (ideally before sixteen weeks old). Beyond four months of age, new experiences are met with a degree of natural apprehension and caution. If your dog has already developed a fear of certain situations, you will need to recondition her by introducing the threatening stimuli gradually and in small doses. This is often typical of the more primitive breeds and particularly hybrids, whose acute survival instincts prevent them from taking the new and unusual in stride.

On the other hand, this kind of environmental hyperawareness can become an asset on the trail. Such a dog may sense and communicate real dangers to you before you even see, hear, or feel the hint of a threat. She may be the one to smell or see the bear, hear the landslide, or feel a precarious situation developing.

Doggie backpacks are available for every size dog, and most dogs love to have a purpose.

Let your dog get used to seeing backpacks, walking sticks, tents, and other hiking equipment around the house. Simulate trail circumstances by having friends with backpacks, walking sticks, and fishing rods stroll around the yard or come around the corner while you are on a walk with your dog. By the time you head for the trail, strangers waddling toward your dog in full backcountry outfits will not cause retreat or barking. There may be horses, pack stock, and cyclists on the trail, so introduce your dog to these ahead of time too.

Building Stamina

Puppies Eight to Sixteen Weeks Old

Even a big backyard can be full of adventures and exploration possibilities for a pup. It's a good idea to introduce your pup to the natural hiking setting as early as possible, but you must be sensible about her vulnerability to infectious diseases. Pups get their initial immunity from their mother's milk, but they need protection through inoculation after they stop nursing.

By twelve weeks your pup should have had the first of three DHLP-P vaccinations. Although it may be reasonably safe to socialize and romp around other pups on the same vaccination schedule, hold off on the great outdoors until she has had her final series of DHLP-P and rabies vaccinations (four to six months). Try to take her to a park, beach, or neighborhood trail for exercise and sensory stimulation (20- to 30-minute sessions) in addition to playtime and at least two leash walks daily. Use good sense and don't expose your pup to strange dogs or other animals until she has been vaccinated against rabies.

Puppies Four to Six Months Old

By now your puppy should be fully immunized and can safely venture away from the grassy greenbelts of civilization and closer to nature. Fields, meadows, or nearby forested trails will be more stimulating for your pup, although the distractions will make training more challenging for both of you.

Use a long rope or expandable leash (20 to 30 feet) so your pup can romp and explore under controlled conditions. Practice *sit, stay, down,* and *come* at the end of the rope several times. Let him off leash in a safe area of the trail and practice calling him enthusiastically during these pre-hike drills, rewarding him with a "good dog," a pat, and treats. Always use verbal praise and a pat, and when the desired behavior becomes consistent, use food rewards only some of the time.

Tell your dog to go play, and do not call him unless you have eye contact or know you have his attention. When he is busy smelling, listening, or digging for creatures, he does not hear you. Do not compete and set yourselves up for failure. Never call him to you for a reprimand, no matter how frustrated you may be with his behavior.

These introductory training excursions (30 minutes to 1 hour) will leave an overactive puppy calm and sleepy for his indoor life. Remember that during the first several months (six for small dogs, nine to twelve for larger dogs), most of the dog's energy is going into the growth of his young body. Do not stress the healthy development of your dog's muscles and bones with long distances and hills. With giant breeds, until twelve to eighteen months, keep the excursions short (under an hour) and on mostly flat terrain.

Take frequent rest stops and water breaks. In warm weather, stop every 20 minutes for your puppy to rest and drink water.

Adult Dogs

Gradual conditioning principles also apply to adult dogs that are just being introduced to the fun of hiking. If your dog's arena of physical activity has been primarily in the yard, begin by planning a walking route that allows you to be out 30 minutes twice daily (morning and evening). Follow your lifestyle and your dog's fitness level. Consult your physician and your veterinarian before making any changes to your and your dog's physical activity level. See the sidebar below for a sample training plan.

SAMPLE TRAINING REGIME

Week 1

Morning and Evening

15-minute sniff and stroll (warm-up)

10-minute brisk walk (cardiovascular workout)

5-minute sniff and stroll (cooldown)

Weeks 2 and 3

Morning and Evening

15-minute sniff and stroll (warm-up)

20-minute brisk walk (cardiovascular workout)

5-minute sniff and stroll (cooldown)

Week 4

Morning and Evening

15-minute sniff and stroll (warm-up)

30-minute brisk walk (cardiovascular workout)

10-minute stroll and sniff (cooldown)

Week 5

Morning and Evening

15-minute sniff and stroll (warm-up)

30-minute brisk walk (cardiovascular workout)

10-minute sniff and stroll (cooldown)

One additional longer walk at end of week (about 1.5 hours)

The suggested longer walk at the end of week 5 is about increasing distance, not speed. Consider using this week 5 regimen as a guideline for maintaining your dog's conditioning between hikes.

Once you both feel reasonably fit, incorporate some stairs or a hill to train for the up-and-down of backcountry trails. Ideally, your dog should be getting at least two hours of outdoor exercise daily, including walks and off-leash playtime. Make sure she always has drinking water, shade, and rest as needed.

During the summer months, shade from trees or cooling off in surface water helps dogs regulate their body temperature. If your dog decides to lounge in a mud puddle, let her.

A dirty dog is the least of your worries.

Pacing

A person of average physical fitness walks about 3 miles per hour on a paved, level path. To get a better idea of your and your dog's average stride and pace, time yourself walking around the local high school running track with your dog on leash. (Tracks are 0.25 mile per lap.) Keep in mind that on a hike, the terrain, weather, and elevation will affect your pace. In the mountains, for every 1,000 feet of elevation gain you can add 1 extra mile to the original length of the hike. Contrary to what many people think, hiking downhill is not twice as fast as hiking uphill. It takes about three-quarters of the time to hike the same distance downhill.

Let your dog's pace determine the pace of the hike. When hiking an off-leash trail, keep her on leash during the first few minutes of the hike. If she's off-leash fresh out of the starting gate, she may run around in a burst of energy and tucker herself out too soon because she doesn't know how to pace herself.

Health Considerations

Seriously and realistically consider your dog's age and current physical condition. This is not to say that if your dog is older, overweight, or has a medical condition she cannot hike. But if common sense precludes a human couch potato from sprinting a mile or driving to 8,000 feet for a 5-mile hike, the same applies to a dog who divides his time between the yard and his dog bed.

Some dogs are able, once trained, to carry part or all of their food on the trail. Carry water for your dog when you are hiking between water sources.

Consult your veterinarian to help evaluate your dog's health and discuss under what conditions hiking would be beneficial.

Training with Dog Packs

Day hikes should be carefree, travel-light fun. Overnight trips require significantly more gear, which is an opportunity to give fit, medium-to-large adult dogs (more than thirty-five pounds) the sense of purpose so many thrive on. With patient and proper training, these enthusiastic bundles of dog muscle power can learn to carry food and backpacking accessories.

It is important to emphasize that loaded packs should only be carried by adult dogs that have reached full physical maturity. The total weight on your dog's back should not exceed a quarter to a third of his weight (a forty-pound dog should not carry more than ten to thirteen pounds of evenly distributed weight). Begin by placing a face cloth or small towel on your dog's back to introduce your dog to the feel of weight on his back. Leave the pack around the house near his bed or crate for a few days and in the car when you take him for a ride.

Dog pack

Feed him little treats while you try the pack on him (empty), and praise him for having the pack on. Take it off and repeat the exercise twice a day for about a week.

The next step is to put the pack on when going on a leash walk. Give him the treat while you are putting the pack on, and then put his leash on as you would on a regular walk.

Put the pack on for short hikes with only treats in the pouches, so you can give your dog the treats from his pack on snack breaks. The idea is to create positive associations with the pack so that eventually the sight of the pack evokes an enthusiastic response from your dog.

Packs should conform to your dog's build.

Pre-Hike Care

Dewclaws: All dogs are born with front dewclaws, and many have rear dewclaws. This fifth digit on the inside of the leg is very prone to tearing and ideally should be removed by a veterinarian within a few days after birth. If dewclaws have not been removed, consider having this surgery done at the same time your dog is spayed or neutered.

Nails: Nails should be comfortably short without sacrificing traction. Even dogs that are active enough outdoors to keep their nails naturally worn need to have the nail on the dewclaw trimmed. Consult a groomer or your veterinarian on the proper use of dog nail clippers and nail file for maintenance between clips.

Feet: Dog footpads get toughened (light sandpaper texture) by regular and gradual extended walks and runs on rough and varied surfaces (pavement, sand, and rocks). Booties should be worn to alleviate tenderness and protect footpads from cuts on ice and sharp rocks.

Spaying and neutering: Your dog will be just as smart, loving, and trim after he or she is altered. Altering does not make dogs fat. Too much food and too little exercise do. Besides some of the social and medical benefits of altering, which include a reduced incidence of mammary gland cancer in females and prostate cancer in males, a decreased sexual drive will make your pet less apt to roam or tangle with other dogs. The trail advantage of neutering is a male dog that is more congenial and less preoccupied with competition around other males.

Vaccinations: Your dog should be current on all vaccinations (DHLP-P, rabies, and a vaccination against Lyme disease are advisable). The veterinary community's thinking on annual vaccines has evolved over the last few years, and many veterinarians now customize vaccine regimens to the individual dog, taking into account age and lifestyle. Discuss these changes with your veterinarian. Also ask him or her about the recent vaccine against rattlesnake venom.

Heartworm: Mosquitoes carry this parasite. Consult your veterinarian about heartworm preventive medication.

West Nile virus: Mosquitoes carry this virus. At this time there have been no reports of noticeable symptoms or fatal infections in canines. No vaccine or specific treatment exists.

Fleas and ticks: Dogs can be infected with tapeworms by ingesting fleas that are carriers of tapeworm eggs. Some types of ticks are carriers of disease. There is a bigger arsenal of flea and tick products on the market than ever. Consult your veterinarian on the treatment of choice for your dog and his hiking needs.

Grooming: Long coats should be trimmed (not shaved), particularly under the belly and behind the legs during the summer. Trimming hair between the toes prevents foxtails (invasive grasses found primarily in the western United States) from going undetected while they burrow, puncture, and infect. In the winter, less hair between the toes prevents the formation of icicles around the pads, decreasing the chance for frostbite.

What to Expect on the Trail

Every hike shares routine preparations, but some destinations require more specific planning. Always get information ahead of time about the area where you want to hike.

Are dogs allowed? Determine which agency regulates the area (national, state, regional, or other), call ahead for its restrictions about dogs on the trails, and abide by the rules.

Do you need a permit? Call the managing agency about its regulations.

What kind of weather can you expect? The high country is subject to more variable and extreme weather. Check the weather forecast and fire danger advisory at a ranger station. Afternoon thunderstorms in the summer are common, and it is best to be below the timberline and off exposed ridges. In the spring and fall, pay attention to sudden drops in temperature and clouds moving in announcing snowfall.

What are the trail conditions? Advisories about fast water, high streams, and trail damage are commonly posted at ranger stations or visitor centers. If nothing is posted, ask anyway.

What is the terrain like? A topographic map is an indispensable tool in planning your hike. Learn to read the information. A topographic map indicates boundaries between public lands and private lands and clearly shows marked trails and campgrounds. It shows you the elevation changes and how hilly or flat the surrounding terrain may be, so you can anticipate the difficulty of the trail and pace yourself appropriately. Every 1,000 feet of elevation equals about 1 extra mile of hiking. The map shows you if there is surface water (lakes, streams, and rivers) along the way. Studying the topographic map of the region beforehand allows you to choose the most appropriate trail for your dog's comfort and safety and to pack accordingly. Forests mean more shade; open ridge trails mean potential exposure to the elements (heat of the day, wind, and lightning); meadows mean mosquitoes; streams, rivers, and lakes indicate cooling stops.

GPS (global positioning system) technology gives your current and precise location. GPS allows you to map out distance and elevation changes, view the route from a flyover perspective, and store and print the data.

What wildlife can you expect? You will want to know about bears, mountain lions, rattlesnakes, or other creatures that may be a safety concern to you and your dog.

What if something happens to you? Leave a copy of your itinerary with a friend or family member. Use their name and contact number on your dog's temporary ID and the lost dog flyer.

Trail Hazards

Foxtails

The arrowlike grasses are at their worst in late summer and early fall, when the grasses are dry, sharp, and just waiting to burrow in some dog's fuzzy coat. The dry foxtail can be inhaled by a dog, lodge itself in the ear canal or between the toes, and camouflage itself in the dog's undercoat, puncturing the skin and causing infection. Foxtails have the potential to cause damage to vital organs.

Inspect your dog's ears and toes and run your hands through his coat, inspecting under the belly, legs, and tail. Brush out his coat after excursions where there were even hints of foxtails. Violent sneezing and snorting is an indication he may have inhaled a foxtail. Even if the sneezing or shaking decreases in intensity or frequency, the foxtail can still be tucked where it irritates only occasionally while it travels deeper, causing more serious damage. Take your dog to a vet as soon as possible. He may have to be anesthetized to remove the foxtail.

Poison Ivy, Oak, and Sumac

These three-leaved, low-growing plants (poison oak has shiny leaves) can cause topical irritations on hairless areas of your dog's body. (You can apply cortisone cream to the affected area to relieve the discomfort.) Find out if there is poison ivy (usually in the eastern states), poison oak (mainly in the western states), or poison sumac where you plan to hike, and make sure you wash your hands with soap after handling your dog. The resin can rub off your dog onto you, your sleeping bag, your car seat, and your furniture at home. If you are very sensitive to these rashes, bathe your dog after

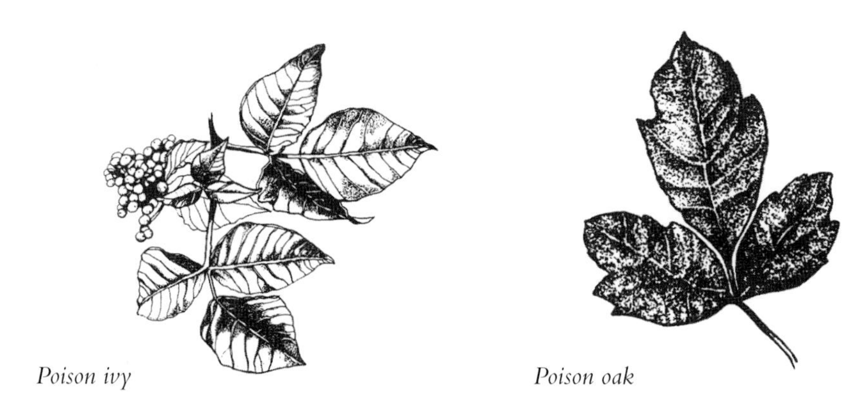

Poison ivy *Poison oak*

the hike and sponge your arms and legs with diluted chlorine bleach or Tecnu soap, an outdoor cleanser that removes plant oil from your skin. Tecnu soap also can be used on your laundry.

Other Poisonous Plants

Unfortunately, your dog may be one that is tempted to chew and taste hazardous plants. This includes plants found in your backyard, like rhubarb. In the wilderness, however, there are similar dangers—plants such as rhododendrons and Japanese yew may cause considerable sickness and discomfort for your pet. If you suspect poisoning, take note of what your dog ate and head back to the car. Once out of the woods, call your vet or an animal poison control center.

Mosquitoes

Avon's Skin-So-Soft is a less toxic and more pleasant-smelling mosquito repellent, than—though not as effective as—repellents containing DEET. Mix one cap of the oil with one pint of water in a spray bottle. Spray your dog and run your hands through her coat from head to toe and tail to cover her with a light film of the mixture. Be careful to avoid her eyes and nostrils, but do not miss the outer ear areas. Organic solutions containing eucalyptus can also be used as a mosquito repellent.

Besides being annoying, mosquitoes carry heartworm. Consult your veterinarian about preventive medication.

Fleas and Ticks

Fleas are uncomfortable for your dog and carry tapeworm eggs, and ticks are one of nature's most painfully potent and tenacious creatures for their size. Some ticks cause uncomfortable red, swollen irritation to the area of the skin where they attach or inflict temporary paralysis. Other types of ticks carry Rocky Mountain spotted fever and Lyme disease, the latter of which is reported to be the most common tick-carried disease in the United States.

Where Do Dogs Get Ticks?

Ticks thrive on wild hosts (deer are the most common). They're found around lakes, streams, meadows, and some wooded areas, hiding out in grasses or plants until climbing on and clinging to an unsuspecting hiker or dog. On dogs, they crawl out of the fur and attach to the skin around the neck, face, ears, stomach, or any soft, fleshy cavity. They attach to their hosts by sticking their mouthparts into the skin to feed on the host's blood.

Removing a Tick

1. Try not to break off any mouthparts (remaining parts can cause infection), and avoid getting tick fluids on you through crushing or puncturing the tick.
2. Grasp the tick as close to the skin as possible with blunt forceps or tweezers, or with your fingers in rubber gloves, tissue, or any barrier to shield your skin from possible tick fluids.
3. Remove the tick with a steady pull.
4. After removing the tick, disinfect the skin with alcohol and wash your hands with soap and water.

There is an abundance of chemical and natural flea and tick products on the market, including collars, dips, sprays, powders, pills, and oils. Some products have the advantages of being effective on both fleas and ticks, remain effective on wet dogs, and require an easy once-a-month topical application. Consult your veterinarian about a safe and appropriate product.

Seasonal Considerations

Summer heat can be taxing on your dog. The dry heat of the West, however, is more tolerable than the humidity of the South and East.

Minimizing Dehydration and Heat Stroke Risk

1. Hike in the early morning or late afternoon.
2. Carry at least eight ounces of water per dog for each hour on the trail or 3 miles of hiking.
3. Rest in a shaded area during the intensity of midday.
4. Take frequent rest stops and offer your dog water.
5. Let him take a plunge in the lake or lie belly-down in a stream or mud puddle to cool off.

Winter conditions will affect your dog's feet, her endurance, and her body warmth. Crusty snow can chafe and cut her pads, and walking in deep snow is very taxing and can put a short-haired dog at risk of hypothermia and frostbite.

Snow Safety

1. Carry booties for icy conditions and use them on dogs not accustomed to winter conditions. Take a couple of extras as replacements for the ones lost in the snow. Keeping your dog on leash while she is in booties makes it easier to know when to adjust them or to retrieve any that drop off.
2. Consider a wool or polypropylene sweater for a short-haired dog.
3. Encourage your dog to walk behind you in your tracks. It is less strenuous.

4. Take a small sled or snow disk with an insulated foam pad so your dog can rest off the frozen ground.
5. Keep your outings short in winter, and carry snacks like liver or jerky treats and warm drinking water.

Spring, in some parts of the country, means heavy rain, mosquitoes, fleas, ticks, and a new crop of poison oak and poison ivy. Find out what you are in for so you can be prepared.

Fall announces hunting season in many parts of the backcountry. Check the hunting regulations and dates for the hiking area you have in mind. Most important, you and your dog should wear bright colors when hiking anywhere in the fall. Orange hunting vests are available for dogs, and colorful harnesses and bandannas are a good idea. When in doubt about hunting, keep your dog on a leash on forested trails.

How to Use This Guide

The fifty-one featured hikes in this guide offer a sample of Colorado's beautiful and varied terrain and its fascinating geology, flora and fauna, and human history. Hikes range from easy to strenuous, but your dog can go with you on every hike in this book, either on leash or under voice control.

Please realize that trail locations and conditions, roads, and signage are subject to change over time. Trail mileage is as much an art as a science, even for land managers. Times change and so do trail conditions. Remember to check with the appropriate land management agency for current fees, regulations, and trail information before heading out, then have a great hike!

Dogs Under Control

Under Canine Compatibility in the hike specs, the words "Dogs must be under control" mean dogs can be off leash but must be under immediate voice control. If you cannot control your dog by voice command, regulations typically require the dog be leashed. According to the Colorado Division of Wildlife, harassment of wildlife (even chasing squirrels) by dogs and humans is illegal in Colorado.

Leave No Trace

Going into a wild area is like visiting a famous museum. You obviously do not want to leave your mark on an art treasure in the museum. If everybody going through the museum left one little mark, the piece of art would be quickly destroyed—and of what value is a big building full of trashed art? The same goes for pristine wildlands. If we all left just one little mark on the landscape, the backcountry would soon be spoiled.

A wilderness can accommodate human use as long as everybody behaves. But a few thoughtless or uninformed visitors can ruin it for everybody who follows. All backcountry users have a responsibility to follow the rules of zero-impact camping.

Nowadays most wilderness users want to walk softly, but some aren't aware that they have poor manners. Often their actions are dictated by the outdated habits of a past generation of campers, who cut green boughs for evening shelters, built campfires with fire rings, and dug trenches around tents. In the 1950s these practices may have been acceptable. But they leave long-lasting scars, and today such behavior is absolutely unacceptable.

Because wild places are becoming rare and the number of users is mushrooming, a code of ethics has grown out of the necessity of coping with the unending waves of people who want a perfect backcountry experience. Today we all must leave no clues that we were there. Enjoy the wild, but don't leave any trace of your visit.

More people competing for the use of limited recreation areas leaves dog owners vulnerable to criticism. So, when hiking with Fido, remember:

- Pack out everything you pack in.
- Do not leave dog scat on the trail. Bury it away from the trail and surface water. Or, better yet, carry plastic bags for removal.
- Hike only where dogs are permitted and abide by the regulations posted.
- Stay on the trail and in designated campsites in heavily used or developed areas.
- Step lightly in more remote, pristine areas.
- Do not let your dog chase wildlife.
- Do not let your dog charge other dogs or hikers, regardless of his harmless exuberance and friendly intentions. A leash is a great pacifier around people who may not be comfortable with dogs.
- Dogs can spook horses and pack stock, putting riders in a precarious situation. Step off the trail and wait with your dog at a sit position until the traffic has passed. Always leash your dog when passing other hikers, cyclists, horseback riders, or anyone with whom you are sharing the trail.
- Don't let your dog bark at hikers, pack animals, wildlife, or the moon. It is intrusive to those who choose hiking as an escape to quiet and serenity.
- Some hikers have strong opinions about why dogs should not be allowed in the backcountry. Avoid debating the issue with other hikers. Be courteous and use this opportunity to influence other hikers positively by keeping your dog on his best backcountry behavior.

Leave no trace—and put your ear to the ground and listen carefully. Thousands of people coming behind you are thanking you for your courtesy and good sense.

Levels of Difficulty

This hike rating system was developed from several sources and personal experience. These difficulty levels are meant as guidelines; the trails may prove easier or harder depending on ability and physical fitness. Hikes are rated by having one or more of the noted characteristics.

Easy—4 miles or less total trip distance in one day; elevation gain less than 600 feet; paved or smooth-surfaced dirt trail; less than a 6 percent grade average

Moderate—Up to 8 miles total trip distance in one day; elevation gain of 600 to 1,200 feet; a 6 to 8 percent grade average

Difficult—Up to 12 miles total trip distance in one day; elevation gain of 1,200 to 2,500 feet; an 8 to 10 percent grade average

Most difficult—Up to 16 miles total trip distance in one day; elevation gain of 2,500 to 3,500 feet; trail not well defined in places; a 10 to 15 percent grade average

Strenuous—Mainly reserved for peak climbs or canyon descents; greater than 15 percent grade average

Trail Finder

Easy/Moderate Hikes

1. Homestead Trail
3. Dawson Butte Ranch Open Space
4. Rocky Mountain Arsenal National Wildlife Refuge
5. Pawnee Buttes
6. Edna Mae Bennett Nature Trail
9. Devil's Backbone Nature Trail
11. Blue Lake
12. Heil Valley Ranch/Lichen Loop
14. Walker Ranch
15. Marshall Mesa
16. Eldorado Canyon Trail
26. Coyote and Squirrel Trails
29. Devils Canyon
30. Susan G. Bretag/Palmer Loop
32. Mount Cutler Trail
34. The Crags Trail
36. Horsethief Falls
37. Reilly and Levsa Canyon
38. Lower Barr Trail
39. Red Rock Canyon Trail
41. Alberta Peak: Continental Divide National Scenic Trail
42. Williams Creek Trail

Difficult/Strenuous Hikes

2. Picket Wire Canyonlands
7. Lory State Park Loop
8. Dome Mountain Trail
10. Mount Audubon
13. Bear Peak
17. Wheeler Trail
18. North Mount Elbert Trail
19. Notch Mountain
20. Mount Thomas Trail
21. Granite Lakes Trail
22. Silver Creek Trail
23. Kelly Lake
24 Seven Lakes
25. Storm King Fourteen Memorial Trail
27. Marvine Loop
28. Black Mountain (West Summit) Trail
31. Thompson Mountain
33. Newlin Creek Trail
35. Spanish Peaks Traverse
40. Middle Frisco Trail
43. Devils Creek and Lake
44. Washington Gulch Trail
45. Ptarmigan Lake
46. Big Dominguez Canyon
47. Upper Roubideau Area Loop
48. Jud Wiebe Memorial Trail
49. Cascade and Portland Loop
50. Pass and Coal Creek Loop
51. First Fork and Red Creek Loop

Less than 5 Miles

5. Pawnee Buttes
6. Edna Mae Bennett Nature Trail
9. Devil's Backbone Nature Trail
12. Heil Valley Ranch/Lichen Loop
15. Marshall Mesa
25. Storm King Fourteen Memorial Trail
26. Coyote and Squirrel Trails
30. Susan G. Bretag/Palmer Loop
32. Mount Cutler Trail
34. The Crags Trail
36. Horsethief Tralls
39. Red Rock Canyon Trail
44. Washington Gulch Trail
48. Jud Wiebe Memorial Trail

5–10 Miles

1. Homestead Trail
3. Dawson Butte Ranch Open Space

4. Rocky Mountain Arsenal National Wildlife Refuge
7. Lory State Park Loop
8. Dome Mountain Trail
10. Mount Audubon
11. Blue Lake
13. Bear Peak
14. Walker Ranch
16. Eldorado Canyon Trail
17. Wheeler Trail
18. North Mount Elbert Trail
20. Mount Thomas Trail
28. Black Mountain (West Summit) Trail
29. Devils Canyon
31. Thompson Mountain
33. Newlin Creek Trail
37. Reilly and Levsa Canyons
38. Lower Barr Trail
41. Alberta Peak: Continental Divide National Scenic Trail
42. Williams Creek Trail
45. Ptarmigan Lake
47. Upper Roubideau Area Loop
49. Cascade and Portland Loop
50. Pass and Coal Creek Loop
51. First Fork and Red Creek Loop

More than 10 Miles

2. Picket Wire Canyonlands
19. Notch Mountain
21. Granite Lakes Trail
22. Silver Creek Trail
23. Kelly Lake
24. Seven Lakes
27. Marvine Loop
35. Spanish Peaks Traverse
40. Middle Frisco Trail
43. Devils Creek and Lake
46. Big Dominguez Canyon

On Leash

3. Dawson Butte Ranch Open Space
5. Pawnee Buttes
6. Edna Mae Bennett Nature Trail
7. Lory State Park Loop
9. Devil's Backbone Nature Trail
10. Mount Audubon
11. Blue Lake
12. Heil Valley/Lichen Loop
13. Bear Peak
14. Walker Ranch
15. Marshall Mesa
16. Eldorado Canyon Trail
19. Notch Mountain
21. Granite Lakes Trail
23. Kelly Lake
24. Seven Lakes
25. Storm King Fourteen Memorial Trail
26. Coyote and Squirrel Trails
28. Black Mountain (West Summit) Trail
30. Susan G. Bretag/Palmer Loop
32. Mount Cutler Trail
34. The Crags Trail
36. Horsethief Falls
37. Reilly and Levsa Canyons
38. Lower Barr Trail
39. Red Rock Canyon Trail
44. Washington Gulch Trail
48. Jud Wiebe Memorial Trail

Off Leash/Under Control

1. Homestead Trail
2. Picket Wire Canyonlands
8. Dome Mountain Trail
17. Wheeler Trail
18. North Mount Elbert Trail
20. Mount Thomas Trail
22. Silver Creek Trail
27. Marvine Loop
29. Devils Canyon
31. Thompson Mountain
33. Newlin Creek Trail
35. Spanish Peaks Traverse

40. Middle Frisco Trail
41. Alberta Peak: Continental Divide National Scenic Trail
42. Williams Creek Trail
43. Devils Creek and Lake
45. Ptarmigan Lake
46. Big Dominguez Canyon
47. Upper Roubidea Area Loop
49. Cascade and Portland Loop
50. Pass and Coal Creek Loop
51. First Fork and Red Creek Loop

EASTERN PLAINS

Almost half of Colorado lies on the Great Plains where they bump into the Rocky Mountains. Even the lowest point in Colorado, at 3,337 feet near the Nebraska border east of Wray, is lofty compared to most of the nation. The Dust Bowl of the 1930s ended many dreams, yet it created the situation that ultimately resulted in the formation of the Pawnee National Grassland and Comanche National Grassland. The latter contains not only remains of pioneer settlements but also those of Native American inhabitants who left rock carvings and an equinox marker tucked away in a cave.

Most hikers ignore the plains, thinking they are flat and boring, not to mention that most of the land is private. But the plains have special hidden spots every hiker should take time to explore. And with most people dismissing the plains as a good hiking destination, what a great place to go for solitude!

If on a trail that allows dogs to be off leash, be sure that your dog is able to respond to voice commands.

1 Homestead Trail

The Homestead and Arch Rock Trails travel across a variety of landforms and through human history. Rock art from 2,000 years ago to the modern era is pecked and painted onto canyon walls. An equinox carving exists in a crack on a canyon wall. Remains of homesteads from the late 1800s and early 1900s dot the landscape. Hells Half Acre, a rock arch, numerous little canyons, springs, a forlorn windmill, wind-blown plains, prairie flowers, and juniper trees are just some of the sights you'll see as you hike this loop. Watch for great horned owls!

Start: From the Picture Canyon Picnic Area
Distance: 8.5-mile loop (9.5 miles if you include three spur trails)
Approximate hiking time: 3 to 5 hours
Difficulty: Moderate due to length
Elevation gain: 570 feet (280 feet plus another 290 feet in undulations)
Seasons: Best in spring and fall. Summer can be very hot, and winter can bring blizzards and snow.
Trail surface: Dirt trail, forest roads, short-grass prairie
Other trail users: Equestrians, mountain bikers, motorists (in a few places), hunters (in season)
Canine compatibility: Dogs must be under control. Water is scarce along the trail, so bring your own.
Fees and permits: None
Maps: USGS Campo SW and Tubs Springs
Trail contacts: Comanche National Grassland, Carrizo Unit, Springfield; (719) 523-6591; www.fs.usda.gov/psicc
Other: You can camp in the parking lot. There are three covered picnic tables and one vault toilet. It's a very pleasant area next to canyon cliffs. There's no garbage service available here—pack it out!

Finding the trailhead: From the junction of US 287/385 and US 160 in Springfield, drive south on US 287/385 for 16.4 miles to just south of mile marker 13. Turn right onto Baca CR M. The road is wide and well-graded dirt, but it can have washboards. The rest of the drive to the trailhead in the Picture Canyon Picnic Area is on maintained dirt roads. Drive 9 miles west to BCR 18 and turn left (south). Drive another 7.9 miles to the entrance to Picture Canyon Picnic Area and turn right onto FR 2361. The road splits in 0.6 mile; take the left branch. The picnic area is another 1.4 miles south. **GPS:** N37 00.73' / W102 44.66'

The Hike

Most people think of eastern Colorado as a flat, uninspiring expanse, but the south-eastern corner bordering Oklahoma is full of interesting canyons, rock formations, wildlife, reptiles, birds, and human history.

There's evidence of people dwelling in Picture Canyon as far back as 2,000 years ago. The canyons provided their inhabitants with abundant wildlife and shelter from the elements, and supported wet bottomlands and running streams and springs, which made life in the canyons even more attractive. The first inhabitants were hunter-gatherers. By AD 1000, farming enabled a more settled lifestyle. In Crack Cave within

Picture Canyon, ancient residents carved lines onto the wall. Experts surmise the markings may have been used to help with crop planting and harvesting, or to indicate ceremonies. During spring and fall equinox, the sun's rays illuminate these lines at sunrise. Because of vandalism, a locked gate now prevents the casual visitor from entering the cave, but festivals held in spring and fall allow a limited number of people to see the sunrise illumination.

About 0.4 mile from the trailhead on a side spur, numerous petroglyphs and pictographs are displayed on the canyon wall. A sea that covered much of Colorado back in Cretaceous times (about 100 million years ago) deposited these sandstone cliffs. Depictions of horses (which were introduced to North America by the Spanish) indicate that some of the artwork was done as recently as 500 years ago. Sadly, in more recent times, visitors have carved or painted initials and drawings over preexisting artwork. It's sometimes hard to tell what is old and what is new. In one large opening, look for parallel lines carved in the rock. Some people believe these lines to be related to *ohgam* writing, an alphabet used in the British Isles from about AD 0 to 500. Some of the drawings have been interpreted as compasses and sundials, as well as equinox indicators.

The Antiquities Act of 1906 and the Archaeological Resources Act of 1979 protect rock art and homestead ruins. Please respect the rock art by not touching it. Others arriving after you want to see original, not scarred, rock art. Touching rock art with hands, chalk, or even paper can hasten deterioration, plus it can interfere with new archaeological dating techniques.

The Jicarilla Apache are known to have inhabited this area since the early 1600s, and the Comanches arrived around 1700. In 1541 the conquistador Coronado claimed this land for Spain during his search for the legendary cities of gold. By 1846 the United States declared ownership of the region. Cattle barons grazed their herds on the endless grasslands in the 1870s and 1880s. Homesteaders arrived between 1890 and 1926 in search of a new life. But making a living was tough in the arid climate. A continuous water supply was of utmost importance, and visitors today can still see the remains of rock houses close to the springs at Crack Cave and Cave Springs.

Unfamiliar with the dry climate, settlers practiced ranching and farming methods they had brought from wetter homelands. Overgrazing and plowing methods combined to damage the fragile land. Several drought years, in conjunction with the normally windy weather, blew away the topsoil in the Dust Bowl of the 1930s. By 1938 farmers and ranchers were broke and begged the federal government for relief. A federal land purchase program was created, and between 1938 and 1942 the government bought thousands of farms, totaling 11.3 million acres of land. The USDA Forest Service was assigned to manage 5.5 million of these acres, and in 1960, 4 million acres were designated a national grasslands, where restoration efforts continue today.

Arch Rock on spur trail

Presently 200 grazing allotments are managed by the Forest Service in Comanche National Grassland.

The prairies also attract diverse wildlife, including approximately 275 species of birds, 40 of reptiles, 9 of amphibians, 11 of fish, and 60 of different mammals, including bear, mountain lion, bobcat, coyote, deer, and antelope. (***Caution:*** Watch for rattlesnakes in the grass, rock crevices, and ruins. Keep your dog on leash in these areas.)

Although the trail is decently marked, this hike is often an exercise in *Where's the next trail marker?* Occasionally markers have fallen over or are farther apart. Trail markers consist of juniper logs with white paint on top, rock cairns, and carsonite posts (like highway reflector posts, but brown). Some trail sections follow forest roads. Three spurs are included in the hike description: one to rock art, one to homestead ruins and Crack Cave (closed), and the other to a rock arch and rock molar.

Miles and Directions

0.0 Start at the trail register box by the Picture Canyon Picnic Area after checking out the big interpretive sign with the trail map and three smaller signs. The Homestead Trail quickly joins a nonmotorized two-track road—turn left. Elevation: 4,300 feet.

0.4 A faint trail heads left near a sign about protecting Indian pictures and carvings. (***Side trip:*** You can turn left here to see the rock art on the canyon walls. It's about 0.4 mile out-and-back. Return the way you came and turn left onto the road to continue on Homestead Trail.)

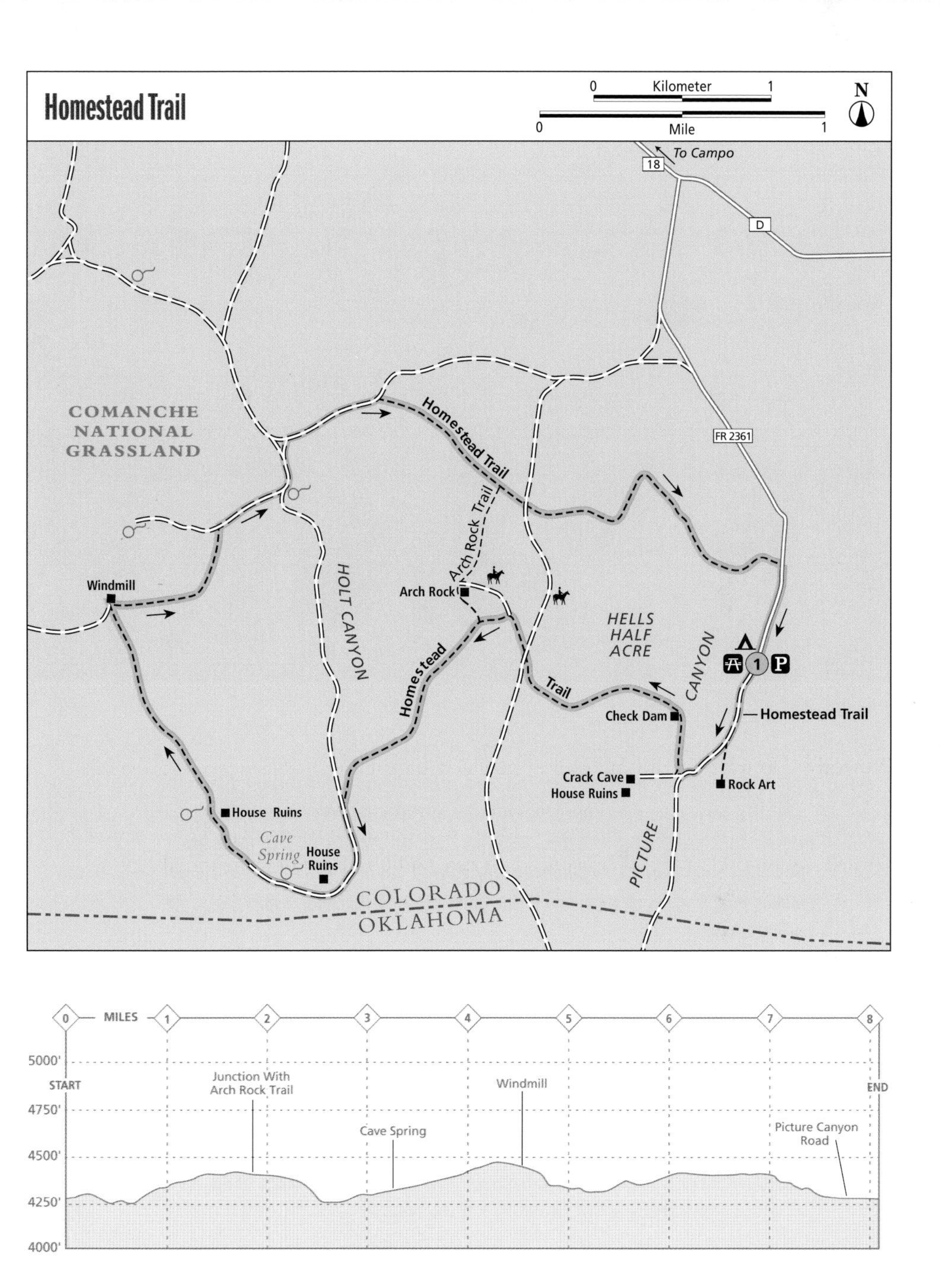
Homestead Trail
0 Kilometer 1
0 Mile 1
N
To Campo
18
D
FR 2361
COMANCHE
NATIONAL
GRASSLAND
Homestead Trail
Arch Rock Trail
Windmill
Arch Rock
HOLT CANYON
HELLS
HALF
ACRE
CANYON
Homestead
Trail
Check Dam
Homestead Trail
1
Crack Cave
House Ruins
Rock Art
House Ruins
Cave
Spring
House
Ruins
PICTURE
COLORADO
OKLAHOMA
MILES
0
1
2
3
4
5
6
7
8
5000'
4750'
4500'
4250'
4000'
START
END
Junction With
Arch Rock Trail
Windmill
Cave Spring
Picture Canyon
Road

Posts showing route at mile 7

0.6 Arrive at a trail and road junction. The road goes left and the Homestead Trail makes a very sharp right onto a singletrack trail. Take the Homestead Trail, following the wooden posts with white tops. GPS: N37 00.40' / W102 45.01'. (***Side trip:*** You can continue on the two-track road slightly to the right to the base of the cliff, where you'll see house ruins and Crack Cave [closed]. This spur is about 0.3 mile out and back.)

0.8 Arrive at a check dam and the HOMESTEAD TRAIL AND ARCH ROCK TRAIL sign with a left arrow. Turn left and walk across the check dam, continuing to curve left to the next post. Turn right and walk up the trail. Some juniper trees almost cover the trail, and it crisscrosses a little dry creek several times. Keep following the wooden posts.

1.1 The trail forks. The right fork is a hiker bypass trail and offers an interesting glimpse of Hells Half Acre. The Homestead Trail goes left and is better marked. Turn left onto this trail, which soon makes a left turn to climb up out of the canyon. Continue following wooden posts. (***Note:*** Watch out for yucca plants—members of the lily family—as their pointy leaves tend to hurt if you bump into them.)

1.3 Reach the ridgetop. The trail tread disappears, so follow the white-topped posts. GPS: N37 00.55' / W102 45.39'.

1.7 Cross a doubletrack trail just before the next wooden post. At the post a sign indicates the horse trail goes right and the hiker bypass goes left. GPS: N37 00.85' / W102 45.61'. Turn left and follow the cairns down into a little slickrock canyon, following more cairns and the rock-lined trail. (***Note:*** Toward the bottom, if there's water in a pond, look for little frogs. You'll also see Indian marbles on the nearby rocks.)

1.9 Arrive at the junction where the Homestead Trail and Arch Rock Trail split. Turn left onto Homestead Trail. (***Side trip:*** It's worth the 0.25-mile out-and-back hike on Arch Rock Trail (the right fork) to see the arch and molar [as in tooth] rock.)

2.8 The trail intersects a road (FR 2361.E). Turn left and walk down the road.

3.25 An old rock house is on the right. GPS: N37 00.03' / W102 46.36'. OKLAHOMA STATE LINE sign is on the left.

3.5 Cave Spring is on your right. (***Note:*** Although the water comes from a spring, the Forest Service suggests treating it as a safety precaution.) Continue walking down the road, which turns into a singletrack soon after Cave Spring. The trail heads through a wonderful cottonwood grove, then across a lush grassy area.

3.9 Arrive at the ruins of an old homestead. Look for the wooden post at the top of the slickrock. The trail goes up the slickrock.

4.75 Arrive at a broken windmill. GPS: N37 00.94' / W102 47.23'. Elevation: 4,473 feet. The trail turns right. The trail tread disappears. Follow the white-topped trail posts.

5.25 The trail leads to a post at the canyon edge. GPS: N37 01.06' / W102 46.80'. Look for rock cairns as the trail drops down into the next canyon. Walk a little right, follow the water line down the slickrock, and then turn a little left. You'll see some big cairns. Follow them down to the canyon bottom.

5.4 Arrive at a dirt road (FR 2361.L) and turn right, walking on the road, which is the Homestead Trail.

5.7 The road forks. Take the left fork (FR 2361.E).

5.8 The road forks. Take the right fork (FR 2361.E).

6.25 The Homestead Trail turns right off FR 2361.E at a sign. Follow the trail right, up a little canyon of sorts and past some interesting rock formations. Continue following wooden posts. As you reach the high area, head to the post on the right. The trail curves right here as the tread disappears.

6.8 Reach the junction of Arch Rock and Homestead Trails. GPS: N37 01.28' / W102 45.67'. Go straight (southeast); do not turn right. Continue on Arch Rock (also Homestead) Trail, ignoring any doubletrack trails.

7.3 Turn left up an open area, following the posts. GPS: N37 01.17' / W102 45.21'. Once up on the ridge, turn right, and walk along the high area for a while, heading generally southeast.

8.0 At the post, the trail starts heading downhill to FR 2361 (the road to the picnic area). Follow the cairns down a little slickrock area.

8.2 Reach FR 2361. Turn right and walk down the dirt road.

8.5 Arrive back at the trailhead.

2 Picket Wire Canyonlands

Picket Wire Canyonlands is a trip back in time, visiting early homesteads, a mission, and traveling even farther back to dinosaurs. It is a beautiful rimrock canyon with junipers, cacti, grasses, cottonwoods, and the Purgatoire River. Once down in the wide canyon, the hike is mostly gentle with a few hills. Intricately carved headstones in an old cemetery, and dinosaur tracks from 150 million years ago, are the highlights of this hike. The dinosaur tracksite is the largest documented in North America.

Start: From the Withers Canyon Trailhead
Distance: 10.8 miles out and back
Approximate hiking time: 5.5 to 7 hours
Difficulty: Difficult due to distance
Elevation gain/loss: 150-foot gain/415-foot loss, including undulations
Seasons: Best in spring and fall
Trail surface: Dirt road, mainly doubletrack, sometimes rocky, with one steep section
Other trail users: Equestrians, mountain bikers, hunters (in season), 4WDs during tours
Canine compatibility: Dogs must be under control
Fees and permits: None
Maps: USGS Riley Canyon and Beaty Canyon; USDA Forest Service Comanche National Grassland
Trail contacts: Comanche National Grassland, La Junta; (719) 384-2181; www.fs.usda.gov/psicc
Other: No camping allowed in the canyon. Primitive camping is allowed on top of the canyon near Withers Canyon Trailhead. A vault toilet, pullouts, and fire grates are available year-round. Camping is also available at Picket Wire Corrals, along with a vault toilet. Visiting equestrians may use the corrals for their horses. Only day use is allowed in the canyon itself, and a dusk-to-dawn closure order is in effect. Bring water. If you want to cross the river to explore more of the tracksite, bring old shoes with you. Be careful crossing, because dinosaur tracks create drops in the streambed.

Finding the trailhead: From La Junta, drive south on CO 109 for 13.6 miles (past mile marker 43) to FR 2200, with a sign to Vogel and Picket Wire Canyons. Turn right onto FR 2200 and drive about 8 miles to Otero CR 25, also with a sign for Picket Wire Canyonlands. Turn left and continue for 6 miles to FR 2185. Turn left at Picket Wire Corrals. FR 2185 is to the left of the vault toilet. Drive 3.3 miles to Withers Canyon Trailhead and park. **GPS:** N37 39.59' / W103 34.22'

The Hike

Although people often visualize eastern Colorado as endless and uninteresting plains, the southeastern part of the state is punctuated by canyons and juniper forests. Established in 1960, Comanche National Grassland is one of the exclamation points within the text of this land. The Forest Service manages some 435,000 acres here in Comanche National Grassland, and has since the US government gave it the charge of rehabilitating the area in 1954. The government bailed out Dust Bowl victims whose property had been rendered virtually worthless due to poor farming techniques and overgrazing. Thanks to revegetation efforts and the protection of natural grasses—still

Remains of the Dolores Mission and its cemetery

ongoing—the grassland today serves as both a wildlife habitat and a playground for human recreation. Conservation and control methods have also allowed for the reintroduction of livestock grazing.

Humans have lived in the Purgatoire Valley for perhaps as long as 10,000 years. Experts place rock art in the canyonlands between 375 and 4,500 years old. Spanish explorers first came to the area in the 1500s, when the Purgatoire Valley was verdant and full of wildlife. Legend has it that a group of early Spanish military explorers met their deaths in the Purgatoire Valley, either due to exposure or conflict with the Native Americans. Either way, the men were said to have died before having their last rites administered, thus the river that courses through the canyon was named El Rio de las Animas Perdidas en Purgatorio (the River of Lost Souls in Purgatory). French trappers who wandered into the canyon during the eighteenth century shortened the name to Purgatoire. Settlers struggled with the French pronunciation, and the river became known as Picket Wire. (By the way, Purgatoire is pronounced "purgatory" in these parts.)

Jicarilla Apaches hunted and farmed the area for about a century, between 1620 and 1720, after which the Comanches took control. French traders and trappers arrived prior to 1800 and hunted the plentiful beaver down to very low levels. Without a healthy beaver population to build and maintain dams, the pools and marshes of the Purgatoire River disappeared. Today you see a small river meandering along a broad valley between rimrock walls.

Leave the parking area by the bulletin board, pass through a wide opening in a fence, sign the trail register, and descend to a pipe gate. Please close any gates behind you. From the gate, the trail drops steeply through the rimrock layer of Withers Canyon, losing 250 feet in the next 0.25 mile. Right after the trail joins another double-track road in Purgatoire Canyon, ruins of an old homestead appear on the right. The trail goes up and over a few side ridges, bringing you close to the cliffs. Farther upstream, remains of adobe walls rise from the ground just past the RIVER WATER sign. (Remember to treat any river water before drinking it.)

Just a little farther down the trail are the remains of the Dolores Mission, with its small cemetery. In 1871 Damacio Lopez led twelve families here, where they remained for two generations. The little headstones are intricately carved with a variety of symbols (like hearts) and inscribed with dates between 1896 and 1900. They are fragile and several are broken, so avoid touching them. A vehicle turnaround for guided tours is located here. A smoother dirt road takes you to the dinosaur tracksite another 1.6 miles upstream.

Envision yourself here 150 million years ago. Imagine a large lake of about 6 miles in diameter, set in a semiarid region. Algae, snails, minute crustaceans, fish, and horsetail plants live in and along the lake. Watch as a group of brontosaurs walk along the shore, side by side. Come another time, as brontosaurs and two-legged dinosaurs use the area heavily, trampling anything underfoot. Visit yet another time to see three-toed carnivorous dinosaurs, perhaps allosaurus, walk near the lake. Today interpretive signs explain the fossil footprints.

By the river the three-toed footprints jump out at you. Compare your foot size with theirs. Depending on the river flows, tracks can sometimes be filled with mud. The brontosaur tracks lie on the south side of the river. They extend for 0.25 mile and contain about one hundred different trackways with 1,300 visible footprints. Dinosaur science has not progressed enough to verify which dinosaurs created the tracks; however, current speculation includes members of the brontosaur order (large terrestrial plant eaters) such as brachiosaurid, camarasaurid, and diplodocid families, and the theropod order (terrestrial carnivores) such as allosaurus. Take care while here—help preserve the tracks for future generations. If you wander off trail, remember the US Army's Pinyon Canyon Maneuver Site is just north of Picket Wire Canyonlands and is off-limits, besides being dangerous.

Miles and Directions

0.0 Start at the Withers Canyon Trailhead. Elevation: 4,630 feet.

0.05 Arrive at the trail register. Turn left onto Picket Wire Trail.

0.2 Reach a pipe gate and walk around it.

0.9 Reach the intersection with a nonmotorized dirt road (doubletrack) in Purgatoire Canyon and turn right. GPS: N37 39.73' / W103 33.70'

◄ *Dinosaur Trackway in Picket Wire Canyon*

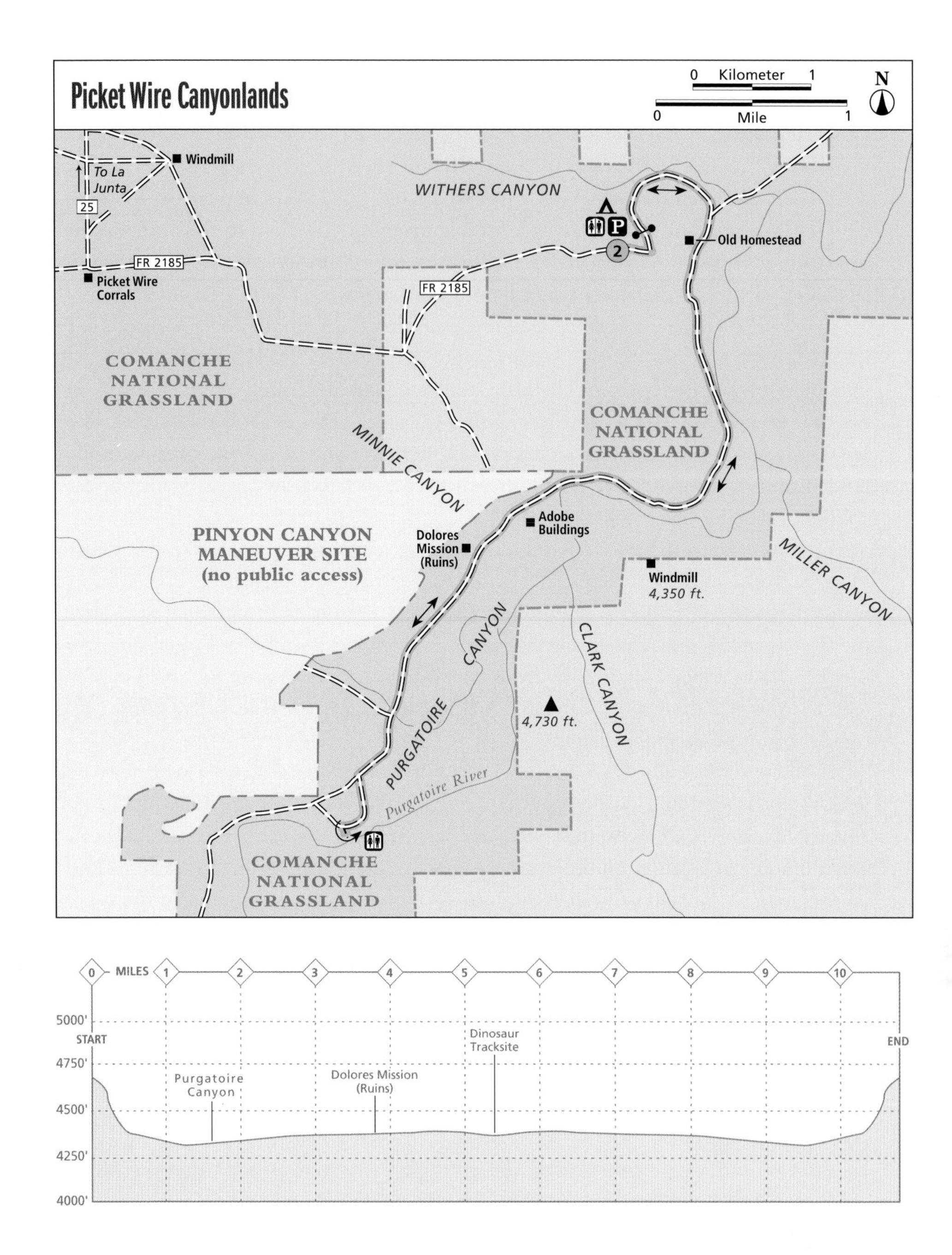

1.1 Reach the remains of an old homestead.

3.5 Reach the remains of old adobe buildings.

3.8 Reach the Dolores Mission ruins and cemetery.

IF YOU MEET A RATTLESNAKE

Rattlesnakes tend to avoid humans. They will strike if surprised, threatened, or hassled, so be extra alert with your dog. Watch where you step or where you put your hands on rocks or ledges. If it's really hot, snakes rest in shaded areas. In spring and fall they try to warm up in sunny areas. If you see or hear a rattlesnake, *freeze!* Make sure your dog is under control or on leash. That may be hard to do, but rattlesnakes strike at motion and heat. Stand still and look for the snake. Be quiet until the snake calms down, uncoils, and slithers away. If you see the snake 4 to 5 feet or more from you, back away slowly, bringing your dog with you.

5.1 The road forks. Take the left road branch to reach the vault toilet and the trail to the dinosaur tracksite. Turn left.

5.4 Stop and read the interpretive signs before looking for tracks along the riverbank (both sides). Elevation: 4,360 feet. GPS: N37 37.05' / W103 35.78'. Return the way you came.

10.8 Arrive back at the trailhead.

Purgatoire River and trail about 2.8 miles

3 Dawson Butte Ranch Open Space

The loop trail in Dawson Butte Ranch Open Space winds gently through ponderosa pine and Gambel oak (oakbrush) forest and across several meadows on the south side of Dawson Butte. Occasionally you get glimpses of the tops of Pikes Peak and Devils Head, along with the ridge of the Rampart Range to the west. This open space features separate bridle trails complete with over sixty horse jumps. The area is excellent wildlife habitat with a good diversity of birds. With a picnic table almost halfway around the loop, this trail provides for a leisurely hike.

Start: From the Dawson Butte Ranch Trailhead on the north side of the parking lot
Distance: 5.0-mile loop
Approximate hiking time: 1.5 to 2.5 hours
Difficulty: Moderate due to distance
Elevation gain: 320 feet (including undulations)
Seasons: Best Apr through Nov—you can cross-country ski or snowshoe when there's enough snow
Trail surface: Natural surface trail
Other trail users: Equestrians and mountain bikers
Canine compatibility: Dogs must be on leash
Fees and permits: None
Maps: USGS Dawson Butte; Douglas County Open Space Dawson Butte Ranch Trail map at www.douglas.co.us/openspace/Dawson_Butte_Ranch.html
Trail contacts: Douglas County Open Space, 100 Third St., Castle Rock; (303) 663-7495; www.dcoutdoors.org

Finding the trailhead: From Castle Rock, head south on I-25 to exit 181, Plum Creek. At the traffic light, go straight ahead on the Frontage Road. Drive south 5.3 miles to Tomah Road. Turn right (west) onto Tomah Road, cross the railroad tracks (coal trains may take a long time to clear the crossing), and drive 1.6 miles to the Dawson Butte Ranch entrance on the right. A portable toilet and picnic tables are located by the parking lot. Bring your own water as none is available along the trail. There is no access or trail to the top of Dawson Butte, both to protect wildlife and because part of the top is private property. Please stay on established trails. **GPS:** N39 17.70' / W104 55.23'

The Hike

In June 1820 Major Stephen H. Long set out from the area around Council Bluffs, Iowa, with a group of nineteen men under orders from the Secretary of War to explore the Platte River and its tributaries. His expedition included a naturalist, a landscape painter, a zoologist, and a physician with a background in geology and botany. Doctor James, the physician, kept a detailed diary of the trip, describing vegetation, climate, fauna, geology, and geography. On July 10 the group arrived at and described Dawson Butte. On July 13 Doctor James and two others started to ascend Pikes Peak. They arrived on the summit at 4 p.m. on July 14.

Trail and Dawson Butte 

Dawson Butte framed by ponderosa pine

Some forty years later, Thomas Dawson established squatters' rights on the area below the butte that now bears his name. He became the first postmaster at nearby Bear Canyon.

Dawson's name also became attached to the sandstone formation that makes up a good portion of the buttes and cliffs east of the foothills in Douglas County. About 70 million years ago, the Rocky Mountains started slowly rising, and Pikes Peak, a huge block of granite, emerged. While the mountains rose, erosion wore them down, creating large alluvial fans at their bases. No buttes existed back in those early times. Instead, dinosaurs like triceratops, as well as crocodiles and turtles, roamed what is now the plains. In the temperate climate fig trees, palms, magnolias, willows, and maples grew instead of today's ponderosa pines. The coarse eroded granite from Pikes Peak became the 55-million-year-old white-and-buff rock (mostly quartz and feldspar) called "Dawson Arkose." Petrified wood is the most common fossil found in this formation. Some layers erode very easily, leaving behind the many buttes along I-25, such as Castle Rock and Dawson Butte, as well as hoodoos (rock columns weathered into interesting shapes). The caps on the buttes are held together by a harder, iron-containing rock layer that covered the looser rocks, pebbles, and sand. Imagine this area 50 million years ago when no buttes existed—only a high plain at the base of the mountains.

Today Gambel oak (oakbrush) and ponderosa pines have replaced palms and magnolias. Oakbrush produces small acorns, about 1 inch long. Native Americans shelled the nuts and soaked them in water to release the bitter tannic acid. Then they ground the nuts into acorn meal that became bread, mush, and pancakes. Deer enjoy browsing oakbrush, while birds and bears eat the acorns. Oakbrush only grows roughly south of Morrison (CO 74) on the eastern slope of the Colorado Rockies, but on the western slope it grows in most locations between 5,500 to 10,000 feet.

Ponderosa pines live in dry, warm places between 5,500 and 9,000 feet elevation. Trees can grow 150 feet tall and 3 to 4 feet in diameter. Bigger trees may live 300 to 500 years. Their needles are long and grow in packets of two or three. Some people say the bark smells like butterscotch. The bark of a mature ponderosa is fairly thick and fire-resistant. However, if the fire reaches the tree's crown, then the tree will burn. Douglas County thinned the ponderosa forest in 2009 to provide more space between the trees to suppress potential wildfires.

The Chapman Young family owned the Dawson Butte Ranch between 1950 and 2004. Douglas County purchased 828 acres of land from the family between 2004 and 2007, with help from Great Outdoors Colorado, the Douglas County Open Space fund, and some private donations. The land is protected by a conservation easement, meaning it cannot be developed or subdivided. Douglas Land Conservancy holds the conservation easement, while Douglas County owns the land. A little piece of private property exists in the middle of this open space area, so please respect the property owners' rights. The Youngs designed and created many horse paths and jumps on their property. The county selected sixty of the jumps and kept them for local equestrians to enjoy with their horses.

Douglas County was especially interested in the Dawson Butte Ranch because of the good wildlife habitat. The land also supports a diversity of birds. Some that come to nest at Dawson Butte Ranch include prairie falcons, ovenbirds, western tanagers, and black-headed grosbeaks. The Audubon Society sponsors a Christmas Bird Count over about a three-week period starting in mid-December each year, and Dawson Butte Ranch Open Space is one of their locations. Results are used to study the status of wintering bird populations across North America and to create strategies for habitat protection and resolution of any environmental threats.

Dawson Butte Ranch Open Space is a wonderful little area to escape from the crowded city and enjoy a day in the rolling woodlands with your family (both two- and four-legged members). Come often to see what changes the different seasons bring to this special place.

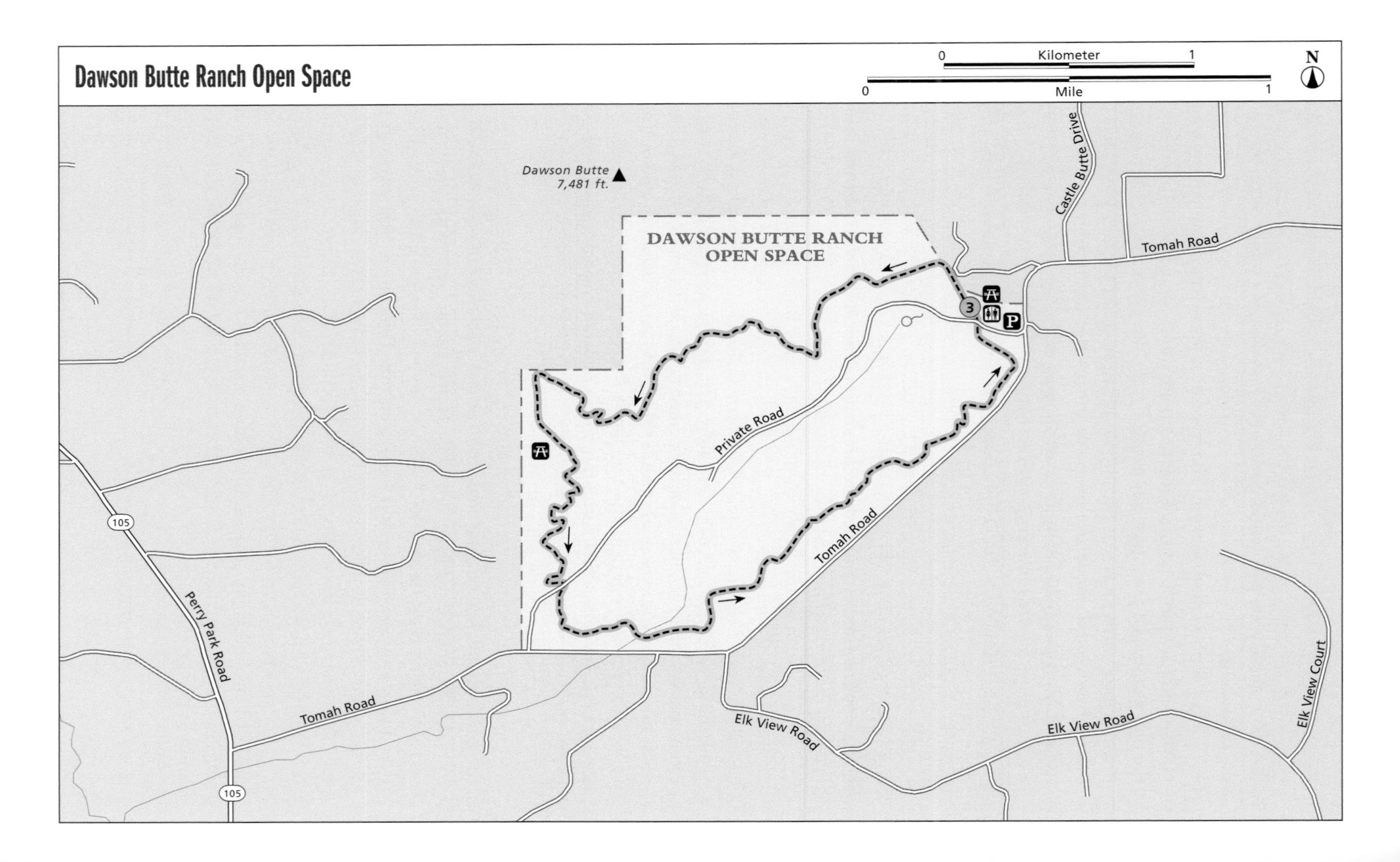
Dawson Butte Ranch Open Space
0
Kilometer
1
0
Mile
1
N
Dawson Butte
7,481 ft.
DAWSON BUTTE RANCH
OPEN SPACE
Castle Butte Drive
Tomah Road
3
P
Private Road
Tomah Road
105
Perry Park Road
Tomah Road
Elk View Road
Elk View Road
Elk View Court
105

Miles and Directions

0.0 Start at the trailhead on the north side of the parking lot. Elevation: 6,815 feet. The loop is described here in a counterclockwise direction. You can also start at the trailhead on the south side.

0.9 Reach the junction with Manger Meadow Trail, one of the many bridle paths with horse jumps. Continue straight ahead.

1.4 Over the next 0.5 mile, you'll come to junctions with several bridle paths. All are well marked. Stay on the main trail for hikers and mountain bikers.

2.0 Look to the right—you'll see a picnic table down Picnic Tree Trail. This is a good place for lunch if you'd like to take this spur trail. GPS: N39 17.41' / W104 56.40'

2.8 Reach the junction with the private road. Continue straight ahead on the trail.

3.3 Cross a little creek, which is the low point of the hike.

3.5 At the junction with Tomah Meadow Path, continue straight ahead.

4.4 Reach the four-way junction of the Dawson Butte Trail, Tomah Meadow Path, and Play Pen Path. Continue straight ahead.

5.0 Pass three picnic tables to the right. Play Pen Path comes in from the left. Arrive back at the parking lot.

Many dogs, such as this Newfoundland, are at home in the mountains.

4 Rocky Mountain Arsenal National Wildlife Refuge

Created in 1992, Rocky Mountain Arsenal National Wildlife Refuge (RMANWR) is a serene wildlife oasis near a bustling urban area. Over the years the mile-wide buffer around the former chemical weapons plant provided a refuge for prairie animals and birds as the Denver metro area expanded. White-tailed and mule deer, eagles, prairie dogs, hawks, waterfowl, burrowing owls, and more thrive here, so close to millions of people. Enjoy watching wildlife on your hike through shortgrass prairie, woodlands, and wetlands rich in farming and military history.

Please note that only assistance dogs are allowed on the trail. No other dogs allowed.

Start: From the trailhead by interpretive signs southwest of the contact station
Distance: 5.9-mile loop with spur
Approximate hiking time: 1.75 to 2.75 hours
Difficulty: Moderate due to distance; easy loop available
Elevation gain: 40 feet
Seasons: Year-round except after big snowstorms; summer can be very hot
Trail surface: Natural surface and crushed rock trail, dirt road, boardwalk
Other trail users: Hikers only, anglers around Lakes Mary and Ladora
Canine compatibility: Assistance dogs only
Fees and permits: None, except for catch-and-release fishing
Map: USGS Montbello
Trail contacts: US Fish & Wildlife Service, Rocky Mountain Arsenal National Wildlife Refuge, 6550 Gateway Rd., Commerce City; (303) 289-0930; www.fws.gov/rockymountainarsenal
Other: RMANWR offers many different wildlife-viewing tours and nature programs, including an auto tour route. Visit the website for more information. Please remain on the trails and obey all posted signs. Alcohol and firearms are prohibited.

Finding the trailhead: From I-70 in Commerce City, take exit 278, Northfield/Quebec Street and head north on Quebec 2.5 miles to Prairie Parkway. Turn right onto Prairie Parkway and drive 0.6 mile to Gateway Road. Turn left onto Gateway Road and continue 1 mile to the visitor center. Be sure to stop at the visitor center, where water, restrooms, exhibits, and a bookstore are available. Then drive 1.7 miles to the contact station and park by the trailhead, or you can walk about 1 mile on the Legacy Trail from the east side of the visitor center to the Lake Mary Trail by the contact station. **GPS:** N39 49.27' / W104 51.84'

The Hike

Originally shortgrass prairie, RMANWR was home to antelope, deer, gray wolves, black-footed ferrets, and bison. The Arapaho and Cheyenne made their living here before homesteaders arrived in the late 1800s. The new residents built houses, grew crops, dug irrigation ditches, and planted nonnative trees. The bombing of Pearl Harbor in 1941 changed the fate of these 27 square miles (17,000 acres). The US Army purchased the land from the farmers and built a chemical weapons manufacturing complex, the Rocky Mountain Arsenal.

After World War II, the army leased some of the facilities to private companies to offset operational costs and maintain the complex for national security. One company

Lake Mary

manufactured agricultural pesticides. Although waste generated during production years was disposed of according to accepted practices in those days, part of the arsenal became contaminated. It was declared a Superfund site in 1987. The cleanup program was completed in 2010.

As a result of the buffer zone established around the manufacturing facilities, over the years a large animal population began to thrive in the arsenal. With the discovery of a communal roost of bald eagles, the U.S. Fish & Wildlife Service (USFWS) became involved in the area. In 1992 Congress designated the Rocky Mountain Arsenal National Wildlife Refuge, which at 15,000 acres, is one of the largest urban wildlife refuges in the country. Exhibits in the visitor center and interpretive signs at several trail junctions relate more historical and natural history details.

The USFWS offers numerous environmental education programs to schoolchildren. During one class, teachers and students gathered near a prairie dog town to observe these little critters. While they watched, a young badger grabbed a prairie dog for its lunch. Nothing like seeing nature in action!

During your first visit, take a wildlife viewing bus tour that gives a great overview of the refuge. Then take a hike! The featured loop takes you on a tour of the various facets of RMANWR.

Swallow boxes line the shore of Lake Mary, while ducks and geese enjoy the water. Partway around the lake, watch for the Prairie Trail to the right. This trail switchbacks out of a little gully, then heads across the plains. Listen for the prairie dogs' warning yips as you approach. They scurry about and are vigilant for hawks. Sometimes when a hawk catches a prairie dog, an eagle will come along and steal the hawk's catch. On a clear day you can see forever, from the downtown Denver skyline to the majestic Front Range beyond.

Woodland Trail goes through an old homestead area. Cottonwoods line abandoned lanes, and elm, fruit trees, white poplar, New Mexico locust, and even a ponderosa pine reveal a human touch. White-tailed deer, a woodland species, roam freely here. They bound away as you approach, white tails held high. Refuge staff revegetated the old lanes and fields to restore the native shortgrass prairie. Native grass seed is purchased, but the native wildflower seeds must be collected from similar sites in eastern Colorado or other states.

A viewing blind down a spur trail off Rod and Gun Club Trail overlooks a wetland area, where the vegetation is very different from that along Prairie Trail. Red-winged blackbirds sing a symphony, with other birds joining the chorus. Ladora Loop Trail presents opportunities to watch ducks, great blue herons, various shorebirds, and other waterfowl enjoying Lake Ladora—watch for cormorants with their outspread wings. Deer wander around, browsing the grasses, casting a glance toward hikers.

The RMANWR is an oasis in a bustling urban area. Check the website frequently for new interpretive programs and tours as well as any sudden closures. Visit

HOME WHERE THE BISON ROAM

March 17, 2007, was a very special day at Rocky Mountain Arsenal National Wildlife Refuge. Sixteen bison from the National Bison Range (NBR) in Montana arrived at their new home here. The U.S. Fish & Wildlife Service will allow the herd to expand to approximately 250 animals. Bison once roamed the shortgrass prairie where the Denver metro area now lies. This small herd will help the USFWS evaluate the bison's impact on RMANWR's native shortgrass ecosystem. The USFWS operates a bison conservation program that includes the NBR, established in 1908 to conserve the American bison.

Some bison have been crossbred with domestic cattle. The DNA of the bison chosen for RMANWR was tested, and the results showed no cattle genes in their ancestry. By moving pure bison to different appropriate wildlife refuges in at least five states, the USFWS hopes to ensure the long-term conservation of the species.

You can take a tour by reservation only to see these original natives of Colorado's Eastern Plains.

Deer near Lake Ladora

often when you have a little time. Watch the seasons change and take advantage of the many nature programs, kids' programs, and tours that are offered throughout the year.

Miles and Directions

(***Note:*** These directions assume you drive from the visitor center to the contact station (old visitor center) to start your hike. You can start hiking from the interpretive signs east of the visitor center to reach the trailhead by the contact station. That will add 2 miles out and back to your hike.)

0.0 Start at the trailhead by the interpretive signs southwest of the contact station. Elevation: 5,210 feet. After 500 feet, reach a T intersection with the Prairie Switchback Trail. Turn left and head to Lake Mary.

0.15 Reach a Y intersection by interpretive signs. Turn right (west) onto the Lake Mary Trail.

0.2 Reach the junction with Prairie Switchback Trail. Continue straight ahead. The little birdhouses on poles along the trail are for tree swallows.

0.4 Arrive at the junction with the Prairie Trail. Turn right. At the top of the switchbacks, enjoy the antics of the prairie dogs.

0.9 Reach a junction with a road from the contact station. Turn right and walk down the road.

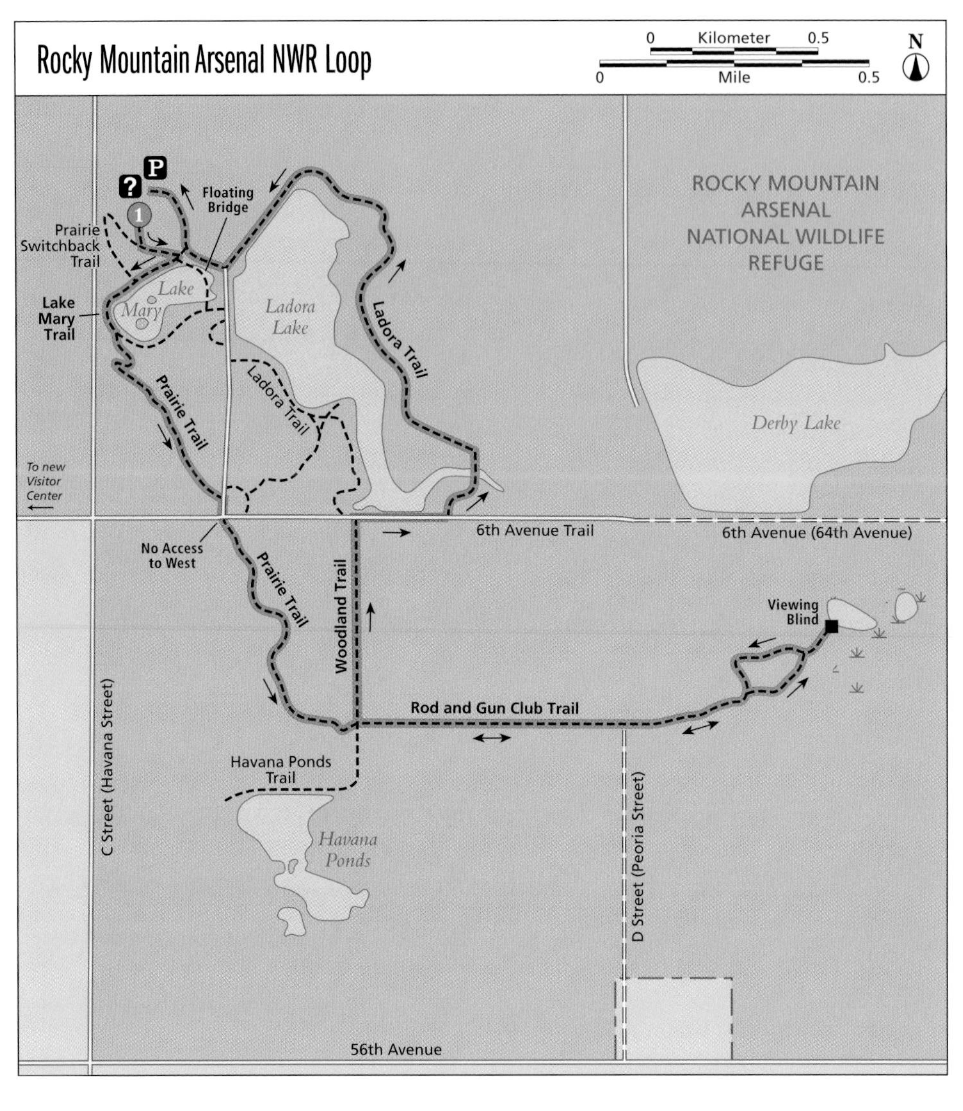
Rocky Mountain Arsenal NWR Loop
0 Kilometer 0.5
0 Mile 0.5
N
ROCKY MOUNTAIN ARSENAL NATIONAL WILDLIFE REFUGE
Floating Bridge
Prairie Switchback Trail
Lake Mary
Lake Mary Trail
Ladora Lake
Ladora Trail
Prairie Trail
Derby Lake
To new Visitor Center
No Access to West
6th Avenue Trail
6th Avenue (64th Avenue)
Woodland Trail
Viewing Blind
Rod and Gun Club Trail
Havana Ponds Trail
Havana Ponds
C Street (Havana Street)
D Street (Peoria Street)
56th Avenue

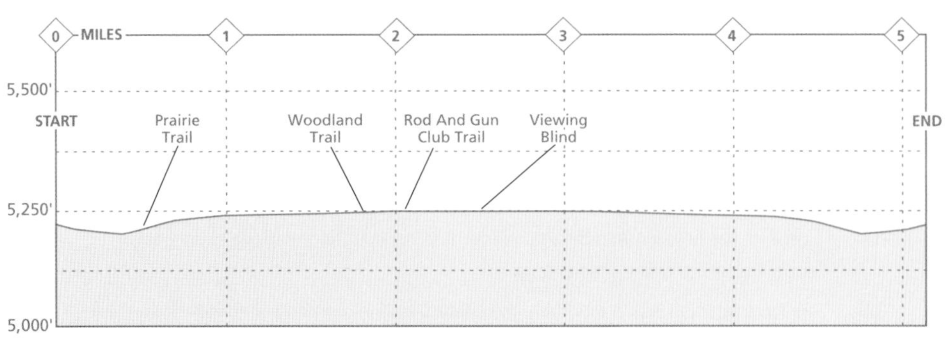
0 MILES
1
2
3
4
5
5,500'
5,250'
5,000'
START
END
Prairie Trail
Woodland Trail
Rod And Gun Club Trail
Viewing Blind

1.0 At the junction with the 6th Avenue Trail, go across the road to the continuation of Prairie Trail. GPS: N39 48.78' / W104 51.64'

1.6 Reach the four-way junction with the Havana Ponds Trail and Woodland Trail. Go a tad left to continue the hike, heading east to the Rod and Gun Club Trail loop.

2.4 Arrive at the start/end of the Rod and Gun Club Trail loop. Turn right. There's a bench here.

2.5 At the spur trail to the Rod and Gun Club viewing blind, turn right onto the spur.

2.6 Arrive at the viewing blind, with interpretive signs and views of the wetland. GPS: N39 48.60' / W104 50.35'. Return on the spur.

2.7 Arrive back to the Rod and Gun Club Trail and turn right to complete the loop.

2.9 Reach the end of the loop. Turn right to continue on the Rod and Gun Trail.

3.1 Continue west on the Rod and Gun Club Trail.

3.9 Reach the junction of the Havana Ponds and Woodland Trails. Turn right onto Woodland Trail and continue north.

4.3 Turn right onto 6th Avenue Trail.

4.5 Reach the Ladora Loop Trail and turn left. Cross the arm of Ladora Lake on a boardwalk.

5.4 The trail curves over the Lake Ladora dam.

5.7 Turn right to return to the contact station. GPS: N39 49.18' / W104 51.63'

5.8 Head to the left and walk through the picnic area to the contact station.

5.9 Arrive back at the contact station.

Options

1. For a very short and easy hike with your dog, walk the 0.9-mile lollipop from the contact station around Lake Mary and back.

2. For a 1.9-mile loop, start as in the featured hike, but at mile 0.9 turn left and walk across the old parking area to a trail. Walk 0.25 mile to Ladora Loop Trail; turn left. At the paved road turn right, then in about 200 feet turn left onto the trail that switchbacks down to Lake Mary. Turn left at the next junction, then right to walk on the floating bridge on the east side of Lake Mary. Follow the instructions from the 0.15-mile mark in the Miles and Directions in reverse back to the contact station.

5 Pawnee Buttes

The Pawnee Buttes protrude 200 to 250 feet above this trail like upside-down vases. The surrounding shortgrass prairie is home to many birds, including great horned owls, American kestrels, eagles, hawks, swallows, and mountain plover, to mention a few of the 296 species that have been spotted in Pawnee National Grassland. Coyotes, foxes, deer, mountain lions, pronghorns, rattlesnakes, and an assortment of mice, voles, jackrabbits, and prairie dogs call this special place home. Spring fills the prairie with colorful wildflowers and is a great time for bird watching.

Start: From the Pawnee Buttes (Trail 840) Trailhead
Distance: 3.6 miles out and back
Approximate hiking time: 1.5 to 2.5 hours
Difficulty: Easy
Elevation gain/loss: 30-foot gain/290-foot loss
Seasons: Year-round except after big snowstorms; summer can be very hot. Spring and fall are best for hiking.
Trail surface: Dirt trail
Other trail users: Equestrians
Canine compatibility: Dogs must be on leash
Fees and permits: None for hiking, except for groups larger than 75 people
Maps: USGS Grover SE and Pawnee Buttes
Trail contacts: Pawnee National Grassland, Greeley; (970) 346-5000; www.fs.usda.gov/arp
Other: Please obey any seasonal closures and avoid disturbing nesting birds. Hawks and falcons nest in the cliffs while others nest in the grasses. Rattlesnakes live in this area too, so keep an eye and ear open for them, and a watchful eye on your dog.

Finding the trailhead: From I-25 east of Fort Collins, take exit 269A (Ault). Drive 50.4 miles east on CO 14, through Briggsdale, to the sign for Keota at Weld CR 103, just east of mile marker 189. Turn left and drive 4 miles to where the road curves right onto WCR 98. In another 0.8 mile, you're at Keota. Head northeast on WCR 98½. In another 0.3 mile, turn left onto WCR 105. The road turns a few times, but follow the signs for Pawnee Buttes. In 2.9 miles, turn right onto WCR 104 and drive another 3 miles to WCR 111. Turn left. When you reach WCR 110 in 3 miles, continue straight ahead. Drive another 1.2 miles to FR 685, which heads north from a left curve. Turn right and you'll reach the trailhead in 1.2 miles. Turn left into the parking lot. There are no facilities or water at the trailhead or the overlook, another 0.5 mile past the parking lot. Bring water with you. **GPS:** N40 48.83' / W104 00.00'

The Hike

Driving from Ault to the Keota turnoff on CO 14, the world around you is a far cry from the nonstop traffic of I-25 and the congestion of the Denver/Boulder/Fort Collins metro areas. Rolling hills of grass stretch to the horizon on each side of the road, punctuated with a lone tree here and there. A ranch house may appear in the distance. A few rows of little trees have been planted on the north side of the highway, probably for a windbreak, if the trees can survive the dry, windy climate of Colorado's high plains.

Pawnee Buttes and surrounding area

Before you turn into the trailhead parking lot, you'll pass an old-time windmill still used to pump water for cattle. Listen to it creak and groan; watch the tail and vane keep the wheel into the wind. To the north you'll see the Cedar Creek wind farm, its 274 turbines generating 300 megawatts of electricity. Located on private land, the wind farm began operation in October 2007. The old and the new are quite a contrast, but each serves its purpose. Unfortunately, large birds, raptors in particular, can't see the rotating turbine blades and a collision always results in the bird's death.

Colorado was covered by the Cretaceous Seaway from 114 million to 65 million years ago. After the dinosaurs disappeared 65 million years ago, the Rockies were uplifted and volcanoes ejected ash high into the sky. The inland sea receded, but sediments eroded from the mountains to the west covered the old seabed. For more than 10 million years sandstone, siltstone, and ashy claystone were deposited on the plains, eventually becoming the White River Formation.

The opening acts of the Age of Mammals starred camels, rhinoceros, three-toed horses, and hippopotamus-like animals grazing on the grasslands and woodlands that had developed. Erosion continued to wear down the Rockies, and the deposits on the plains became the Arikaree Formation and the Ogallala Formation, the latter comprising sandstone and conglomerate (rocks and stones cemented together).

Trail and juniper trees

Around 5 million years ago the whole area was uplifted about 5,000 feet. Rivers increased in speed and volume, sometimes fed by melting mountain glaciers. Water eroded through the sediment layers on the plains, especially the softer White River Formation. Some of the harder Ogallala Formation remained, protecting the underlying materials. The Pawnee Buttes are remnants of those early plains, as are the Chalk Bluffs to the north. The White River Formation in the Pawnee Buttes area contains one of the prime deposits of vertebrate fossils in the world. Please remember fossils are protected by law and must not be removed from the area.

Erosion continues today, creating the badlands features found along the trail as it drops down a little gully between the trailhead area and Lips Bluff. Just enough moisture allows junipers to grow, with an occasional piñon pine or limber pine for good measure. Prickly pear cactus blooms brightly in mid-June, along with purple locoweed, white yucca, and white prairie phlox. While hiking, you might notice tufted sandwort, a pincushion-like plant that grows on the siltstone barrens in the area. One general aspect of shortgrass prairie is that vegetation covers less than 50 percent of it.

Bison once roamed this area in herds as large as 60 million. Blue grama and buffalo grass satiated these large animals, which moved constantly in search of new food.

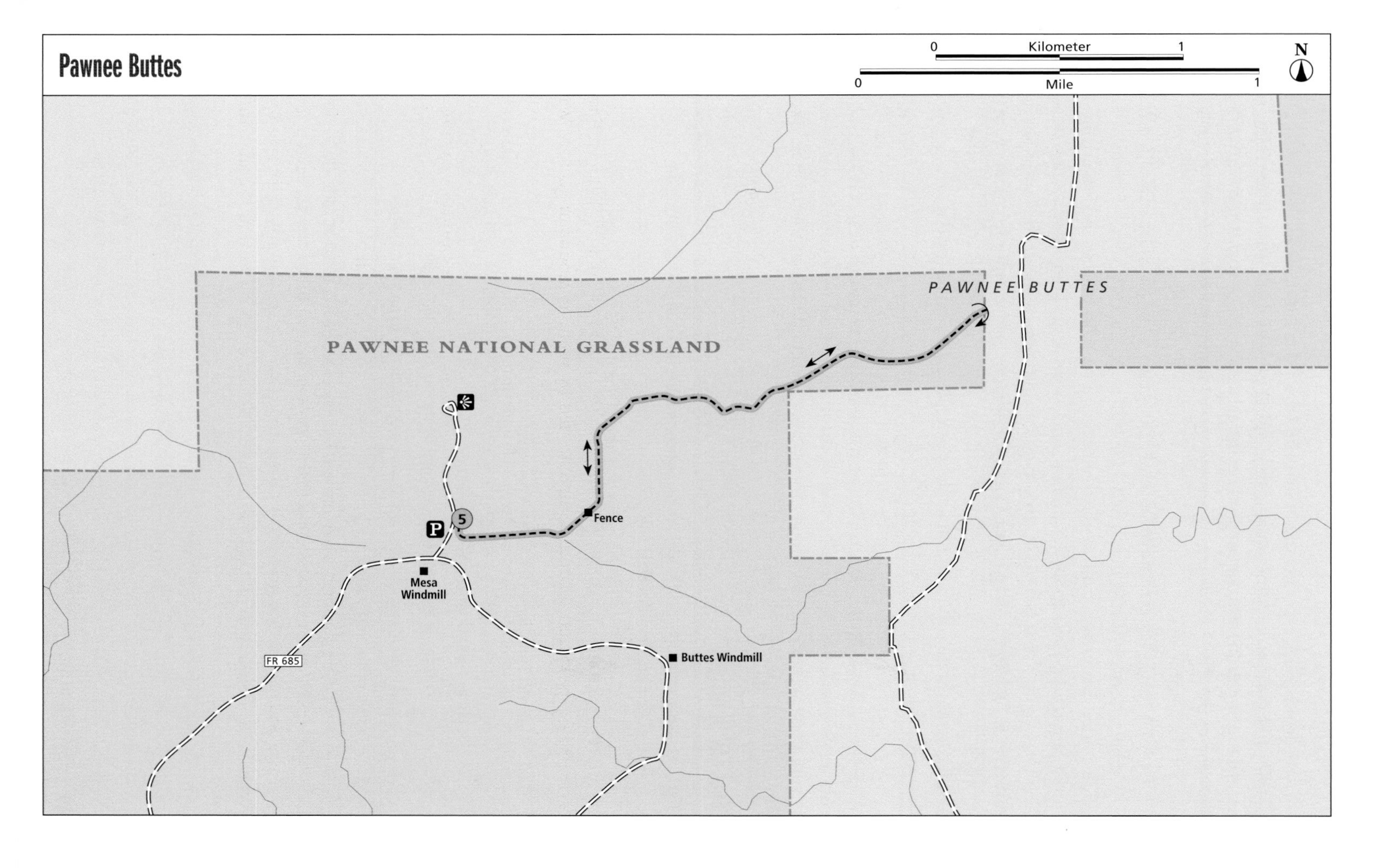
Pawnee Buttes
0
Kilometer
1
0
Mile
1
N
PAWNEE BUTTES
PAWNEE NATIONAL GRASSLAND
5
P
Fence
Mesa Windmill
Buttes Windmill
FR 685

The grasslands and bison adapted to each other. As settlers moved west to homestead, they turned the sod, exposing the prairie soil to wind erosion. Unlike the bison, cattle continually grazed the same area, giving the grasses no time to recover. With low annual precipitation rates, farming was marginal at best. High winds accompanied the drought of the 1930s, blowing loose soil everywhere. Many people left their farms during this Dust Bowl.

In 1934 the US government created a program to purchase marginal lands. By 1946 the government had purchased 11.3 million acres, of which 5.5 million acres came under the jurisdiction of the Department of Agriculture and eventually the Forest Service. In 1960 about 3.8 million acres were designated as national grasslands. The Pawnee National Grassland consists of 193,060 acres. One of the Forest Service's duties is to manage national grasslands for forage and recreation resources, while another is to manage the resources to "maintain and improve soil and vegetative cover and to demonstrate sound and practical principles of land use for the areas in which they are located."

Because the buttes are crumbling sandstone, please refrain from climbing them. While you hike, keep an eye out for prairie residents: antelope, deer, rabbits, and, of course, the myriad birds. (And be sure to maintain control over your dog at all times during these wildlife observations.) Enjoy some peaceful time in this unique section of Colorado's Eastern Plains.

Miles and Directions

0.0 Start at the interpretive signs in the parking lot. The trail is to the right. Elevation: 5,420 feet. Hike down the little gully.

0.4 Reach a fence and bulletin board. Just beyond, the trail branches. Go left on the main Pawnee Buttes Trail. The right branch goes to Lips Bluff, which is closed Mar 1 to June 30 to protect nesting birds.

0.6 The trail winds through a little juniper forest.

1.0 An overgrown doubletrack comes in from the right (also closed Mar 1 to June 30). Continue on the main trail to the left.

1.1 A trail comes in from the right. Continue on the main trail to the left.

1.4 A faint trail crosses the main trail. Continue straight ahead on the main trail.

1.5 Arrive at the west butte.

1.8 Arrive at the grassland/private property boundary. Elevation: 5,160 feet. GPS: 40 49.32' / W103 58.48'. You're in between the west and east buttes. Turn around and return the way you came.

3.6 Arrive back at the trailhead.

6 Edna Mae Bennett Nature Trail

This excellent loop trail threads across colorful sandstone bluffs at Palmer Park in northeast Colorado Springs. Gorgeous vistas also come with lots of wildlife, such as squirrels, birds, rabbits, and red foxes, so be sure to keep your dog on leash.

Start: From the trailhead at the North Cañon parking lot
Distance: 2.6-mile loop
Approximate hiking time: 1 to 2 hours
Difficulty: Moderate
Elevation gain: 130 feet
Seasons: Year-round
Trail surface: Single- and doubletrack dirt path
Other trail users: Runners, cyclists, equestrians
Canine compatibility: Dogs must be on leash
Fees and permits: None
Map: USGS Pikeview
Trail contacts: Colorado Springs Parks, Recreation, and Cultural Services, 1401 Recreation Way, Colorado Springs, CO 80905-1975; (719) 385-5940; www.springsgov.com
Other: Colorado Springs city parks rules apply

Finding the trailhead: From I-25, take the Fillmore Street exit (exit 145). Drive east on Fillmore Street, which becomes North Circle Drive beyond the Union Boulevard intersection, for 2.5 miles to Paseo Road. Take a left onto Paseo Road and drive 0.8 mile northwest past the Colorado Springs Country Club golf course. Turn left immediately after passing the park entrance; park in the lot at the North Cañon trailhead. **GPS:** N38 52.661' / W104 46.655'

The Hike

The Edna Mae Bennett Nature Trail is a lovely hike through the ravines and rocky bluffs of expansive Palmer Park in the urban heart of Colorado Springs. The rustic trail climbs high above the houses, affording excellent views and exploring shallow canyons, crumbling rock buttresses, and fanciful hoodoos shaped like primitive sculptures. While most Palmer Park trails are multiuse, you won't compete with mountain bikers on most of the Bennett Trail—it's too darn rocky. The trail is easy to follow, with trail markers and metal posts with arrows pointing the way.

Palmer Park, a 730-acre city park, is a rocky little wilderness surrounded by urban sprawl. This park, a wooded enclave of ponderosa pine and scrub oak, offers grand vistas of the city and the Front Range peaks.

Begin at the North Cañon parking lot on the left (north) just past the park entrance. A trail map is located on the left side of the parking area. Begin from the trailhead on the right side. Cross a wooden bridge and walk left past restrooms to a trail junction. Go right (north) on a narrow trail marked with a post on the left designating the Edna Mae Bennett Nature Trail. Hike through a copse of scrub oak and then northeast through a meadow. After 400 feet you reach a trail junction. Go left onto the marked Bennett Trail.

Hike northwest and then north along the eastern edge of North Cañon, dipping through shady groves of scrub oak and passing tall pines. Across the valley to the west is the Mark Reyner Stables. After 0.5 mile the trail reaches a four-way junction at a flat area that was once a parking lot. Go right onto the Bennett Trail.

A large sign here dedicates the trail to the memory of Edna Mae Bennett, a schoolteacher who developed a nature-based curriculum for local children. She particularly loved to hike in the North Cañon area, so after her death in 1972, her friends built the trail to honor Bennett's legacy. Past the sign the gently climbing path rambles along rustic split-rail fences and through a mixed woodland of ponderosa pine, juniper, and scrub oak. Climb the steepening trail, which bends east up a rocky ravine, to a switchback to the right. Just ahead is a three-way junction. Templeton Trail steps left. Go straight on the main trail.

The Bennett Trail continues slowly climbing over stone steps and timber risers as it swings across the western side of a hill above North Cañon. Above is the rocky rim of a plateau. After 0.3 mile you reach another three-way trail junction. Yucca Trail heads left. Keep straight on the Bennett Trail. Continue hiking south and then southeast. As the trail contours onto the sunny south-facing slopes, the forest thins and more views open up. Look for spectacular scenic vistas of downtown Colorado Springs to the southwest and Pikes Peak, lifting its bulky shoulders above the Front Range.

As you hike, keep alert for birds, including magpies, ravens, hawks, chickadees, pygmy nuthatches, and towhees. Palmer Park is a good bird-watching area. You'll see few animals here, however, since the city has slowly engulfed the park. You might, however, spot squirrels, rabbits, red foxes, coyotes, and an occasional rattlesnake.

After skirting the edge of North Cañon, the trail reaches its high point. Stop here and enjoy the spacious views. Pale cliffs spill down the slope below, while the city spreads west to the mountains. The trail heads southeast and begins a gentle descent as it switchbacks and traverses across the hillside. After dipping across a shallow ravine, the trail bends south and reaches a fork. Templeton Trail goes left, while the Bennett Trail heads right. Take the right fork and descend the stony trail to a short scrambling section.

A pastel-painted sandstone outcrop and amphitheater soon appears to the left, providing an excellent opportunity to catch a rest. Enjoy the scenic view from the broad ledge below the cliffs, then peer into an interesting cave to the south. The small grotto corkscrews up into the cliff, forming a unique chamber that kids love to explore. This sandstone, deposited by ancient streams that flowed from the Rockies, has a rough, granular texture. The rock formation, called Dawson arkose, is soft and erodes fast.

From the trail at the north end of the amphitheater, make a sharp right hairpin turn to stay on the route. Look carefully so that you don't miss the trail and end up in the brush below. The trail rapidly descends stone stairs and steep grades in a ravine before leveling out at the base of a craggy white bluff at a three-way trail junction. Recognize the junction? You should, this is where the Edna Mae Bennett Trail splits. Take the left fork and hike 400 feet back to the trailhead.

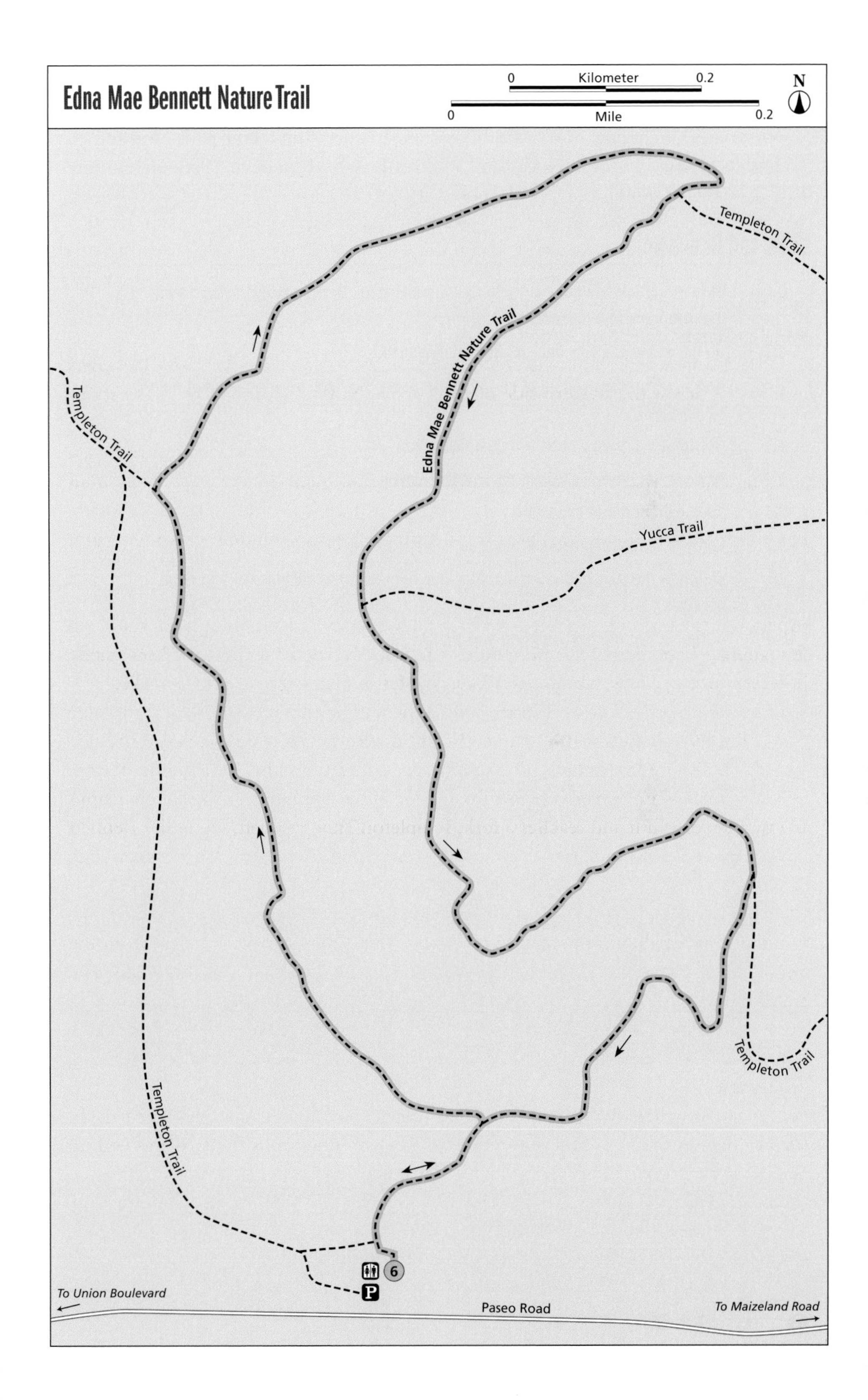

Edna Mae Bennett Nature Trail
0
Kilometer
0.2
0
Mile
0.2
N
Templeton Trail
Edna Mae Bennett Nature Trail
Templeton Trail
Yucca Trail
Templeton Trail
Templeton Trail
6
P
To Union Boulevard
Paseo Road
To Maizeland Road

Options

Palmer Park boasts an extensive trail system (see the map at the parking lot) and other opportunities, including mountain biking and nature study. The park, donated to Colorado Springs by founder General William Jackson Palmer in 1902, offers more than 25 miles of trails.

Miles and Directions

0.0	Start at the trailhead at the North Cañon parking lot. Cross a bridge and go past the restrooms to a junction.
0.1	Go left at the junction with the Bennett Trail loop.
0.5	Reach a four-way junction at an old parking area. Go right, past the Bennett dedication sign.
1.2	Go straight at the junction with Templeton Trail.
1.7	Arrive at the trail's high point above North Cañon.
2.1	Keep right at the trail junction.
2.2	Come to an amphitheater and a cave to the left of the trail.
2.5	Return to the start of the Bennett Trail loop. Turn left at a trail junction and head downhill.
2.6	Arrive back at the trailhead and parking lot.

FRONT RANGE

The easternmost spine of mountains in Colorado, running from the Wyoming border to Colorado Springs, is known as the Front Range. Rising first in foothills, then into high mountains, they provided a formidable barrier and foreboding of what was yet to come for any explorer or pioneer trying to cross the North American continent. Five of Colorado's fifty-four peaks over 14,000 feet, including Longs Peak and Mount Evans, are located in this region. Another famous Front Range peak, Pikes Peak, can be seen from several hikes in this guide.

The Front Range foothills contain fun hiking trails and interesting geology. A rock feature known as the Flatirons protrudes like a row of standing irons from the foothills in the Boulder area. Another great example of these tilted rocks, created from the Fountain Formation, can be seen in Red Rocks Park and Roxborough State Park. A real gem, Roxborough has received numerous state and national designations for its tilted geology and rich natural and human history. Dinosaur Ridge, a National Natural Landmark west of Denver, preserves dinosaur tracks from eons ago in the Dakota Hogback. Foothills canyon topography creates a perfect funnel for flash floods.

About 80 percent of Colorado's population lives in the metropolitan areas just east of the Front Range. Within a short driving distance, recreational opportunities abound. With altitudes between 5,000 and 14,264 feet, hikers can enjoy their sport nearly year-round. As summer temperatures rise beyond 90° F in the foothills, backcountry trails to mountain peaks and lakes offer a great respite.

Rocky Mountain National Park is one of the crown jewels of the national park system, with its glacially sculpted peaks and high alpine lakes. Trail Ridge Road, the highest continuous automobile road in the United States, takes you to the "land above the trees," the alpine tundra. An interesting land of small microclimates, the ecosystem is very fragile. The Rocky Mountain Nature Association offers great classes in all aspects of the region's natural history, including this remarkable ecosystem. Rocky, as locals call the park, contains an incredible number of hiking trails to lakes, historic sites, mountaintops, and even across the Continental Divide.

When going on long hikes with Fido, you'll need to take enough water for drinking (for you and the dog) and cooking. If you are sure of the availability of water, consider carrying less and boiling, filtering, or chemically treating the water in camp. There are several water purification systems available at outdoor recreation stores, but be aware that some dogs will not drink chemically treated water.

7 Lory State Park Loop

Lory State Park is a hiker's dream, with many trails designated for "foot only." Situated next to Horsetooth Reservoir, trails climb into the nearby montane foothills with ponderosa pine and Douglas fir forests. Wild turkeys hide, mule deer browse, and Abert's squirrels and cottontail rabbits frolic. Lory even has six backcountry campsites available by permit. At a lower elevation, this is a perfect place to satisfy early-season hiking and camping urges. Arthur's Rock protrudes above the park, providing views of the Fort Collins area. This hike makes a loop using sections of six different trails.

Start: From the Well Gulch Nature Trailhead by the South Eltuck Picnic Area
Distance: 6.6-mile loop
Approximate hiking time: 2.5 to 4 hours
Difficulty: Difficult due to elevation gain and some steep spots
Elevation gain: 1,670 feet (including three elevation gains/losses)
Seasons: Year-round, except after big snowstorms
Trail surface: Dirt trail, sometimes steep and rocky, sometimes gentle
Other trail users: Some trail sections open to mountain bikers and equestrians, others are hiker only; hunters in season
Canine compatibility: Dogs must be on leash. There is little to no water along the trail.
Fees and permits: Daily fee or annual parks pass required. Permit required (with fee) for backpacking (overnight camping at designated campsites only). Campfires are not allowed in the backcountry.
Maps: USGS Horsetooth Reservoir; Latitude 40° Colorado Front Range
Trail contacts: Lory State Park, 708 Lodgepole Drive, Bellvue; (970) 493-1623; http://parks.state.co.us/parks/lory
Other: Vault toilets but no water. Bring water with you.

Finding the trailhead: From Fort Collins, take US 287 north. Just past mile marker 350, US 287 turns right. Continue straight ahead onto Larimer CR 54G. Drive 2.7 miles through Laporte, then turn left to Rist Canyon (LCR 52E). Turn left after 1 mile onto LCR 23N in Bellvue, drive 1.4 miles south, and then turn right onto CR 25G. Drive another 1.7 miles to the park entrance and turn left. Pay the entrance fee and stop in the visitor center to check out the interpretive displays. Restrooms and water are available at the visitor center. Drive 0.9 mile south to the South Eltuck Picnic Area, across from the Well Gulch Nature Trail kiosk. **GPS:** N40 34.70' / W105 10.70'

The Hike

Human activity around present-day Fort Collins can be traced back about 11,000 years. The largest Folsom culture campsite is located north of town. The term "Folsom culture" comes from archaeological evidence first found in 1926 near Folsom, New Mexico, that distinguished this group's tools and culture from those of other ancient Native Americans. More modern tribes of the area included the Arapaho, Cheyenne, and Ute.

In the early 1800s fur traders came to the area in search of pelts. In 1836 a party of trappers climbed into the foothills west of the Fort Collins area. Their supplies

Hikers on Arthur's Rock Trail and view

became too heavy and they decided to hide them. The supposed location of this cache was near today's Bellvue. Because the cache included gunpowder, the river near their cache became known as the Cache la Poudre.

One of the party members, Antoine Janise, returned a few years later to settle down. Janise saw his opportunity for success after gold was discovered near Denver. Near present-day Laporte, he established a settlement called Colona in 1859, after receiving permission from the local Arapaho tribe. Prospectors began combing all the tributaries of the South Platte River, including the Cache la Poudre. Settlers continued to arrive, establishing farms to feed themselves and the miners.

One settler was John Kimmons, who homesteaded 160 acres in the area of today's Lory State Park. In 1897 he exchanged his land for John Howard's family ranch in North Park. The Howards appreciated the milder winters near Fort Collins, plus the nearby schools for their children. They grew hay, raised cattle, and harvested timber in the foothills. Purchasing adjacent lands over the years, their ranch expanded to 3,600 acres. Stop by Homestead Picnic Area to see the three cedar trees and sandstone slabs where the Howards' house used to stand.

The plains and foothills of Colorado are known to be dry, and early farmers looked to the Cache la Poudre River for relief. G. R. Sanderson built the first irrigation

ditch in northern Colorado, diverting water from the Poudre above Bellvue. By 1933 irrigation took much water from the Poudre and the Big Thompson River to the south. The U.S. Bureau of Reclamation started the Colorado–Big Thompson Project, to divert west-slope water to the thirsty farms and growing population of the east. A 9.75-foot-diameter tunnel, up to 3,600 feet underground, was drilled under the Continental Divide. The Alva B. Adams Tunnel transports water from Grand Lake on the west side of the Continental Divide to Marys Lake near Estes Park on the east. Water from Marys Lake flows through various reservoirs and ultimately to Horsetooth Reservoir, which was completed in 1949.

By 1967, after three generations, ranching became unprofitable for the Howard family. Part of the land was sold and developed into Soldier Canyon Estates, which you drive past to reach the park. The State of Colorado procured the remaining land for the park, which opened in May 1975. A later land purchase added about 100 acres, and presently Lory State Park consists of 2,591 acres. The park is named in honor of Dr. Charles A. Lory, a former president of Colorado Agricultural College (today's Colorado State University) and an early settler. As Fort Collins and the surrounding area quickly expanded, Lory State Park's role in wildlife preservation became very important. Recreational opportunities within Lory State Park, Horsetooth Mountain Open Space, and Horsetooth Reservoir also provide welcome relief from the fast pace of the modern world.

This hike starts at the Well Gulch Nature Trailhead near the South Eltuck Picnic Area. Following Well Gulch through yucca, wooly mullein, and shortgrass prairie, the trail enters ponderosa pine and Douglas fir forests. Watch out for poison ivy along this trail. It then joins the Timber Trail and climbs steadily and sometimes steeply to a ridge. As the trail turns from south- to north-facing slopes, notice how the vegetation changes in response to a slightly cooler and wetter climate on the north faces. At various points check out the excellent views of the Eastern Plains and Fort Collins.

At the ridgeline, numbered poles mark campsites. Near campsites 1 and 2, look straight ahead to see Arthur's Rock. A short trail scrambles to its top for even better views. Return to the main trail and head downhill on the Arthur's Rock Trail, which drops and twists below granite cliffs to the Overlook Trail. This trail travels the edge of forest and plains, climbing and dropping across drainages below Arthur's Rock before finally emerging onto the prairie for the last leg of the loop.

Miles and Directions

0.0 Start at Well Gulch Nature Trailhead by South Eltuck Picnic Area. Elevation: 5,480 feet. Stop at the kiosk for information and a *Well Gulch Self-Guided Nature Trail* brochure.

0.1 Reach the intersection with West Valley Trail. Cross the bridge and turn right onto Well Gulch Nature Trail.

◀ *Little waterfall on Well Gulch Nature Trail*

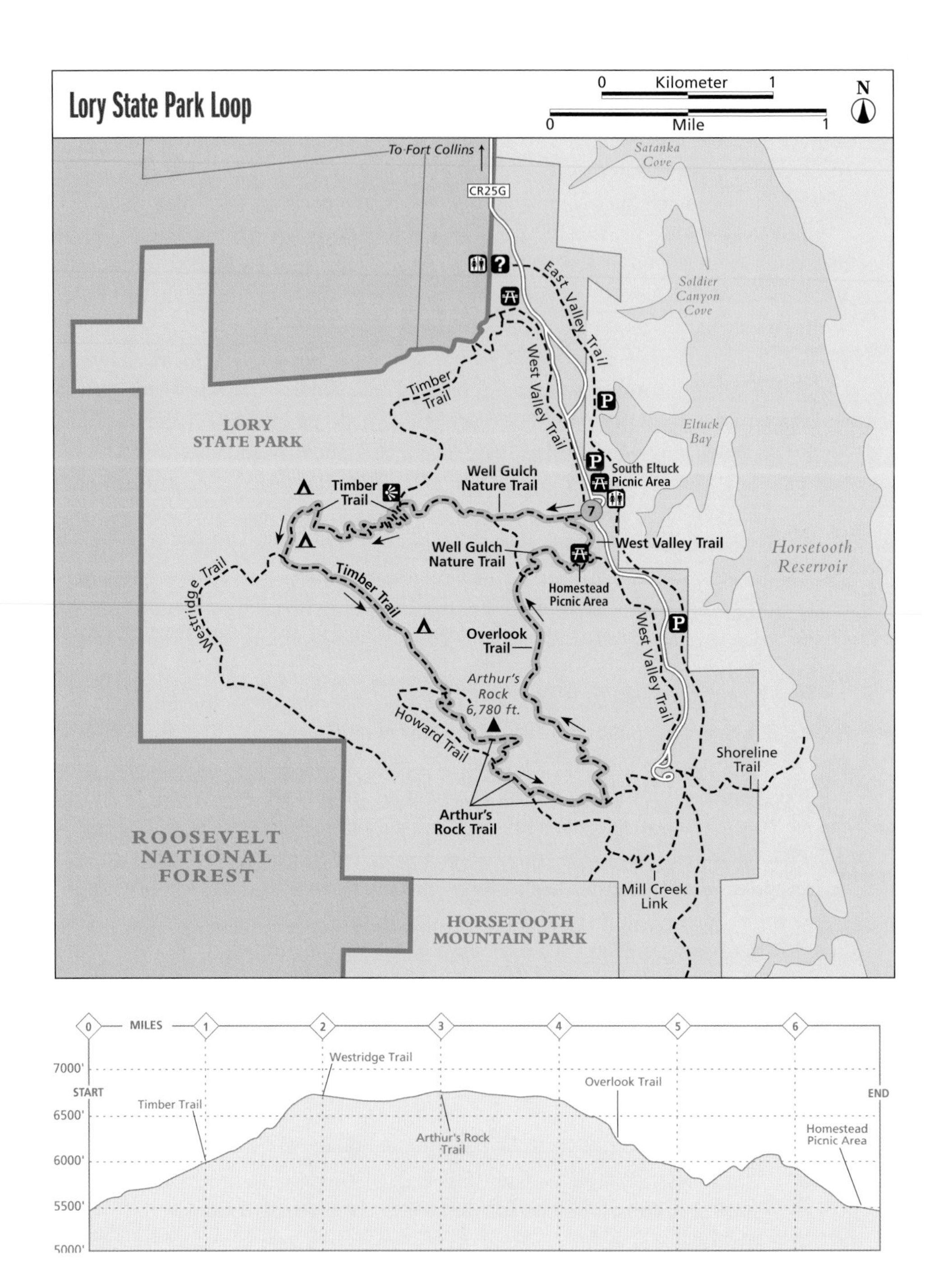

Lory State Park Loop
Kilometer
Mile
N
To Fort Collins
CR25G
Satanka Cove
East Valley Trail
Soldier Canyon Cove
Timber Trail
West Valley Trail
LORY STATE PARK
Eltuck Bay
South Eltuck Picnic Area
Timber Trail
Well Gulch Nature Trail
7
Well Gulch Nature Trail
West Valley Trail
Horsetooth Reservoir
Westridge Trail
Timber Trail
Homestead Picnic Area
Overlook Trail
West Valley Trail
Arthur's Rock 6,780 ft.
Howard Trail
Shoreline Trail
Arthur's Rock Trail
ROOSEVELT NATIONAL FOREST
Mill Creek Link
HORSETOOTH MOUNTAIN PARK
MILES
START
END
Timber Trail
Westridge Trail
Arthur's Rock Trail
Overlook Trail
Homestead Picnic Area
7000'
6500'
6000'
5500'
5000'

THE WOOD TICK

Colorado has relatively few poisonous or irritating plants, insects, and reptiles. Be aware, however, of the wood tick, *Dermacentor andersoni.* The small insect is about ⅛ inch long, with a flat body. Ticks are active from late March into early July and live in grassy, woody, or brushy areas, waiting for a warm-blooded body. Humans and dogs can easily pick up ticks by brushing against vegetation. The tick embeds itself head first into your flesh, with its body sticking out. Unlike mosquitoes, ticks feed on the host's blood for hours. An anchor below their mouths keeps them attached.

The wood tick may carry one of two infections that are threatening to human hosts. If the tick bite goes undetected, a person may develop the virus Colorado tick fever. Symptoms appear within three to six days after the bite and include head and body aches, lethargy, nausea, vomiting, and abdominal pain. The illness lasts for five to ten days. These wood ticks also carry the bacterium that causes Rocky Mountain spotted fever. Symptoms appear in two to four days, including fever, spotted rash, headache, nausea, vomiting, and abdominal and muscle pain. If Rocky Mountain spotted fever is suspected, seek medical attention immediately as this illness can be life threatening.

When hiking during tick season, check yourself (skin, hair, clothes) and your dog often to remove any ticks before they can transmit disease. Applying DEET- and permethrin-based repellents on skin and clothes can help. Wear light-colored clothing so you can see ticks more easily. Tuck loose clothing into your socks and pants. If you find a tick embedded in your skin, grasp the skin as close as possible to the tick with a pair of tweezers and gently pull it straight out. Remove the tick intact. Do *not* leave the head and neck in your skin. Other removal methods, such as covering the insect with alcohol, fingernail polish, or oil, may cause the tick to regurgitate and pass infection on to its host. If you cannot effectively remove the tick, seek medical attention.

For more on how to remove ticks from your dog, see our step-by-step guide on page 14.

0.5 Come to the intersection of Well Gulch Nature Trail and the access trail to Timber Trail. Continue straight ahead on the access trail to reach Timber Trail.

1.0 Reach a T intersection with Timber Trail. GPS: N40 34.71' / W105 11.51'. Turn left onto the Timber Trail and head uphill. The trail switchbacks up an open, south-facing slope.

1.3 The trail swings left, from a south-facing to a north-facing slope. (***Note:*** Check out the change in vegetation with the change in slope aspect.)

2.3 Westridge Trail comes in from the right. Curve left on Timber Trail. (***Note:*** The flat ponderosa-filled area is a nice place for a little break. You'll be passing by the designated campsites on this section.)

3.0 Reach the Campsite 1 sign on the left and Campsite 2 sign on the right. As you continue along the trail, Arthur's Rock is ahead.

3.1 Arrive at the three-way junction with Howard, Arthur's Rock, and Timber Trails. Turn left onto Arthur's Rock Trail.

3.2 Come to the intersection with the spur trail to Arthur's Rock summit. GPS: N40 34.09' / W105 11.30'. (***Side trip:*** Turn left to scramble to the top of Arthur's Rock [6,780 feet] for great views. It's 0.1 mile out and back to the saddle between rock lumps.) Curve right and head downhill on Arthur's Rock Trail. The trail switchbacks and drops down along the side of Arthur's Rock. (***Note:*** You'll get a good view of what 1.7-billion-year-old rock looks like.)

3.8 The trail curves right as it drops below the ridge at the end of Arthur's Rock.

4.0 An access trail to a bouldering area is on your right. Continue downhill to the left on Arthur's Rock Trail.

4.3 Reach the intersection with the Mill Creek Link. Turn left at this fork, staying on Arthur's Rock Trail.

4.6 Reach the intersection with Overlook Trail. GPS: N40 33.81' / W105 10.66'. Turn left and follow Overlook toward Well Gulch Nature Trail. Overlook Trail meanders up and down at the edge of the forest but eventually levels out.

5.8 Arrive at the intersection of Overlook Trail and Well Gulch Nature Trail. Turn right and follow the nature trail downhill toward Homestead Picnic Area.

6.3 Reach the intersection of Well Gulch Nature and West Valley Trails. Turn left and walk on West Valley Trail, past Homestead Picnic Area, heading mostly north.

6.5 Reach the intersection of West Valley Trail and Well Gulch Nature Trail. Turn right, cross the bridge, turn right, and return to South Eltuck Picnic Area.

6.6 Arrive back at the Well Gulch Nature Trail kiosk.

8 Dome Mountain Trail

This is a strenuous hike that climbs up to the summit of Sheep Mountain (8,450 feet), high above the Big Thompson River and Canyon. The trail is well marked with mileage markers and informative signs pointing out information on plant life, erosions, and geology. Be sure your dog is in good health and physical shape for this hike (see workout recommendations on page 8).

Start: From the Dome Mountain Trailhead near the kiosk
Distance: 9.0 miles out and back
Approximate hiking time: 4 to 5 hours
Difficulty: Moderate to strenuous
Elevation gain: About 3,000 feet
Seasons: Apr to Nov
Trail surface: Varies between very smooth in some sections to extremely rocky in others
Other trail users: None
Canine compatibility: Dogs must be under control
Map: Nat Geo Trails Illustrated 101 Cache la Poudre-Big Thompson
Trail contacts: Roosevelt National Forest and the city of Loveland; (970) 295-6600; www.fs.usda.gov/contactus/arp/about-forest/contactus

Finding the trailhead: From the junction of US 287 and US 34 in Loveland, travel west on US 34 for 14 miles into Big Thompson Canyon, to the Dome Mountain Trailhead on the left. The hike starts at a gate near the restrooms. **GPS:** N40 25.28' / W105 17.21'

The Hike

From the parking area, follow the road up past a gate to a sign pointing to the summit trail. Make a quick left and go up to a second sign near a large pipe on the left. Go left again here; the trail becomes narrow as it clings to the side of a steep hill.

Begin a steep climb to where the trail cuts across a talus slope. Read the first of many informative signs that are located along the trail. This section of the trail travels through a forest of beautiful ponderosa pines and the occasional Douglas fir. Along the trail pointed yuccas and prickly pear cacti grow alongside delicate blooming wildflowers.

The trail switches back steeply in a west-to-east direction, with nice views in both directions. Soon you arrive at the 1-mile marker, with open views to the east. The trail becomes quite steep as you continue to climb high above a narrow gulch to the left.

The terrain stays rocky and continues to switchback up and up. Arrive at the 2-mile marker and begin the steepest section of the hike. The trail becomes quite narrow and very rocky as it travels through a beautiful forest of mature ponderosa pines and weird rock formations. Slide through a natural rock corridor and begin a slight descent to a spring, on the right just before the 3-mile marker. This is a good spot for a rest.

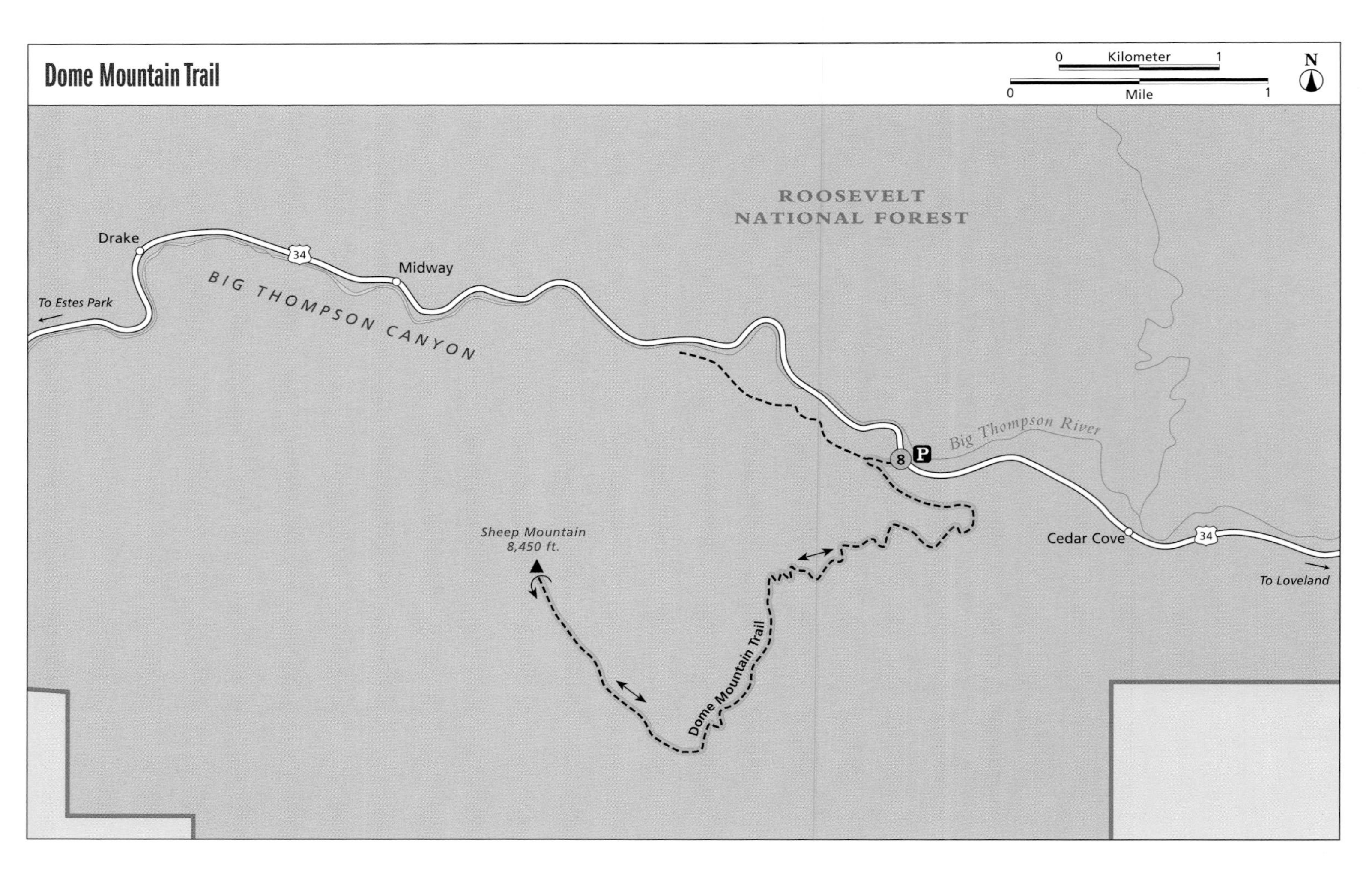
Dome Mountain Trail
0
Kilometer
1
0
Mile
1
N
ROOSEVELT
NATIONAL FOREST
Drake
34
Midway
To Estes Park
BIG THOMPSON CANYON
Big Thompson River
8
P
Sheep Mountain
8,450 ft.
Cedar Cove
To Loveland
Dome Mountain Trail

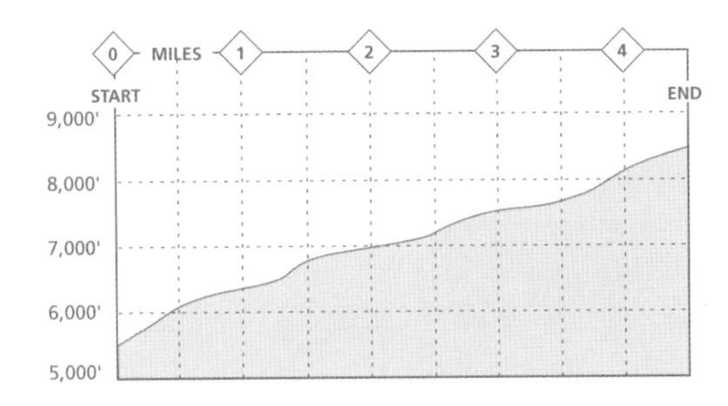

At the 3-mile marker the trail stays fairly level and actually drops a bit into a beautiful aspen forest with a small drainage. What a relief from all that climbing! Enjoy nice hiking through the aspen, with views of Sheep Mountain to the north and west.

Arrive at the 4-mile marker and cruise up through the rocks to the summit of Sheep Mountain. Enjoy views to the north, and of Loveland and the plains to the east.

After a well-deserved rest, retrace your route back to the trailhead.

Miles and Directions

0.0	Start by passing the gate.
0.2	Go left up a narrow trail.
0.4	Go left, climbing up a steep hill.
0.6	Cross a talus slope.
1.0	Pass a mile marker.
2.0	Pass a mile marker.
2.5	Pass through a natural rock corridor.
2.9	Reach the spring.
3.0	Pass a mile marker.
3.5	Reach the aspen forest.
4.0	Pass a mile marker.
4.5	Arrive at the summit of Sheep Mountain. Retrace your steps.
9.0	Arrive back at the trailhead.

9 Devil's Backbone Nature Trail

This nice family hike follows along the base of the Devil's Backbone, just west of Loveland. This is a great hike for the whole family—both two- and four-legged members. When hiking with both dogs and kids, be sure you have snacks and waters—even on shorter, easy hikes. Kids will tire often, so stopping for a snack break for both Fido and your child will be much appreciated.

Start: From the Devil's Backbone Nature Trailhead
Distance: 2.7-mile loop
Approximate hiking time: 1.5 to 2.5 hours
Difficulty: Easy
Elevation gain: 200 feet
Trail surface: Smooth
Seasons: Year-round
Other trail users: Mountain bikers and equestrians
Canine compatibility: Dogs must be on leash
Maps: USGS Larimer County CO; Larimer County Open Space/Devil's Backbone map
Trail contacts: Larimer County Parks and Open Lands; (970) 498-7000; www.larimer.org/naturalresources

Finding the trailhead: From the intersection of US 287 and US 34 in Loveland, go west on US 34 for 4.8 miles to Glade Road. Turn right onto Glade Road and make an immediate right turn onto Wild Lane. Travel 0.3 mile on Wild Lane to the Devil's Backbone Trailhead and parking area. **GPS:** N40 24.42' / W105 09.08'

The Hike

From the parking area, walk north on a road up to the trailhead kiosk. Grab a Devil's Backbone Nature Trail map. The map explains local history, geology, flora, and wildlife surrounding the Devil's Backbone area.

Past the kiosk the trail follows a road leading to the Wild Lane Bed and Breakfast. Go right just before the bed-and-breakfast, following the sign for the Devil's Backbone Trail, up to a gate. Stay right of the gate and curve around the side of a small hill, with an irrigation ditch on your left and a house down to the right.

Cross two wooden footbridges at the 0.3-mile point and climb a small hill toward a trail junction. There are good views to the north, and in the early summer months yuccas, lupines, and other wildflowers bloom on the east-facing hill. Continue north.

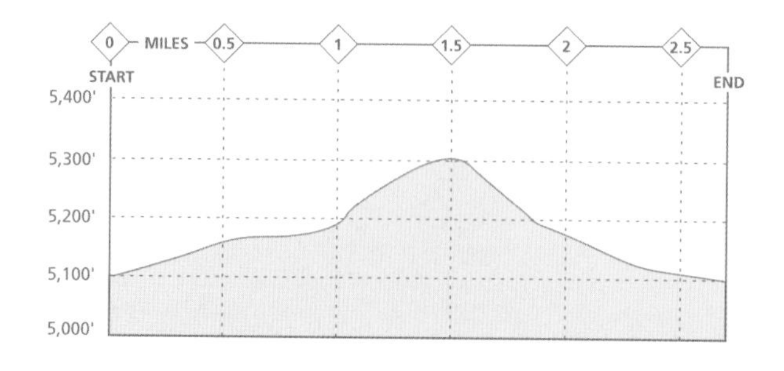

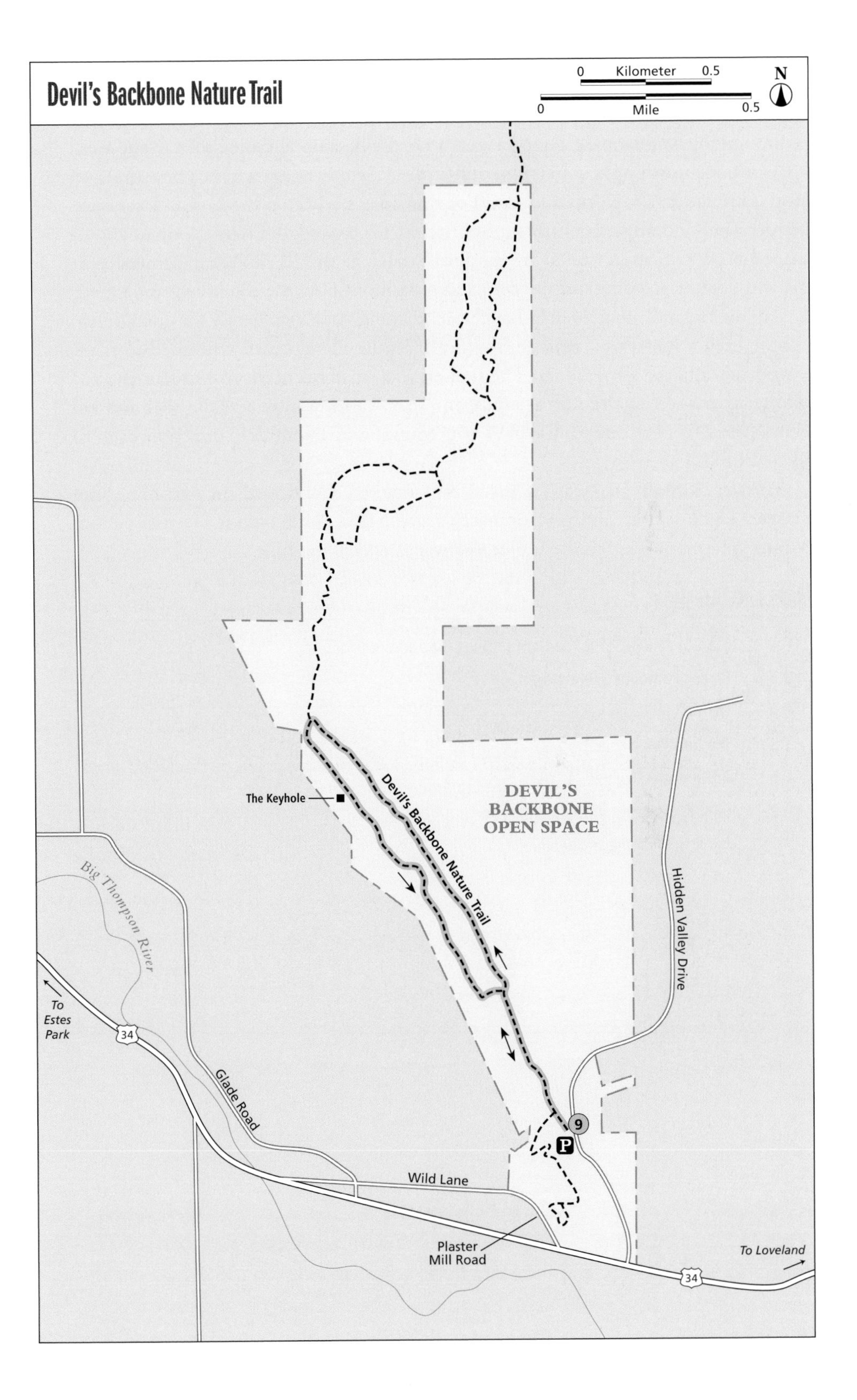
Devil's Backbone Nature Trail
0 Kilometer 0.5
0 Mile 0.5
N
DEVIL'S BACKBONE OPEN SPACE
Devil's Backbone Nature Trail
The Keyhole
Big Thompson River
Hidden Valley Drive
To Estes Park
34
Glade Road
Wild Lane
Plaster Mill Road
To Loveland
34
9
P

Arrive at a trail junction; for this hike go right. The Devil's Backbone Nature Trail travels through a nice area of mahogany oak, cacti, and hills filled with yuccas. At around the 1-mile mark a good view of Devil's Backbone can be seen to the west.

Continue north up to a trail junction at the 1.3-mile mark, where a new trail and loop continue to the north and east. For this hike, go left on the Devil's Backbone Nature Trail and angle back to the south and up toward the Keyhole (a keyhole-shaped rock formation caused by erosion). Arrive at the Keyhole and a metal post marked 6. Time to bring out the map and read about how the Keyhole was formed.

Follow the trail along Devil's Backbone, keeping your map handy for quick reference. Reach a metal post marked 5 at the 1.7-mile mark. Learn who used to roam these lands millions of years ago. The trail crests a small hill at the 1.8-mile mark and offers great views to the north, south, and east. Large yuccas line the trail and tall prairie grass fills the open hillsides as you continue in a southerly direction back to the trailhead.

At the 2-mile mark, reach a metal post marked 3 and read the map. The trail makes a slight decline, and you soon arrive at the first trail junction. Go straight and retrace your route back to the trailhead and the end of the hike.

Miles and Directions

0.0	Start by following the road toward the bed-and-breakfast.
0.3	Cross two wooden footbridges.
0.5	The trail forks; go right.
1.3	The trail forks; go left.
1.5	Arrive at the Keyhole.
2.2	Continue straight at the trail junction.
2.7	Arrive back at the trailhead.

10 Mount Audubon

A wonderful day hike leads up to the beautiful alpine summit of Mount Audubon (13,223 feet). Wildflowers, panoramic high alpine views, and alpine lakes make this hike well worth the effort. This is a very strenuous hike with a lot of altitude gain in a long, 4-mile march to the summit. There are stunning views of Pawnee Peak, Mount Toll, Paiute Peak, Sawtooth Mountain, and Rocky Mountain National Park to the north. This is a very popular trail that sees a fair amount of traffic in the summer months. Your best bet to avoid the crowds would be to do the hike midweek.

Start: From the Beaver Creek Trailhead
Distance: 8.0 miles out and back
Approximate hiking time: 4 to 6 hours
Difficulty: Strenuous
Elevation gain: About 3,200 feet
Seasons: Late June to early Oct
Trail surface: Well-traveled trail on the lower section, with very loose, rocky tread to the summit
Other trail users: None
Canine compatibility: Dogs must be on leash
Map: Nat Geo Trails Illustrated 102 Indian Peaks/Gold Hill
Trail contacts: Boulder Ranger District, USDA Forest Service; (970) 295-6600; www.fs.usda.gov/contactus/arp/about-forest/contactus
Other: Camping is available at Brainard Lake Recreation Area.

Finding the trailhead: From the junction of CO 93 (Broadway) and CO 119 (Canyon) in downtown Boulder, go west on CO 119 for 18 miles to Nederland and the junction with CO 72. Go west on CO 72 for 10 miles to CR 102. Turn left onto CR 102 to the Brainard Lake Recreation Area and the Mitchell Creek Trailhead parking area. **GPS:** N40 04.60' / W105 34.52'

Nala, the Super Lab near the summit

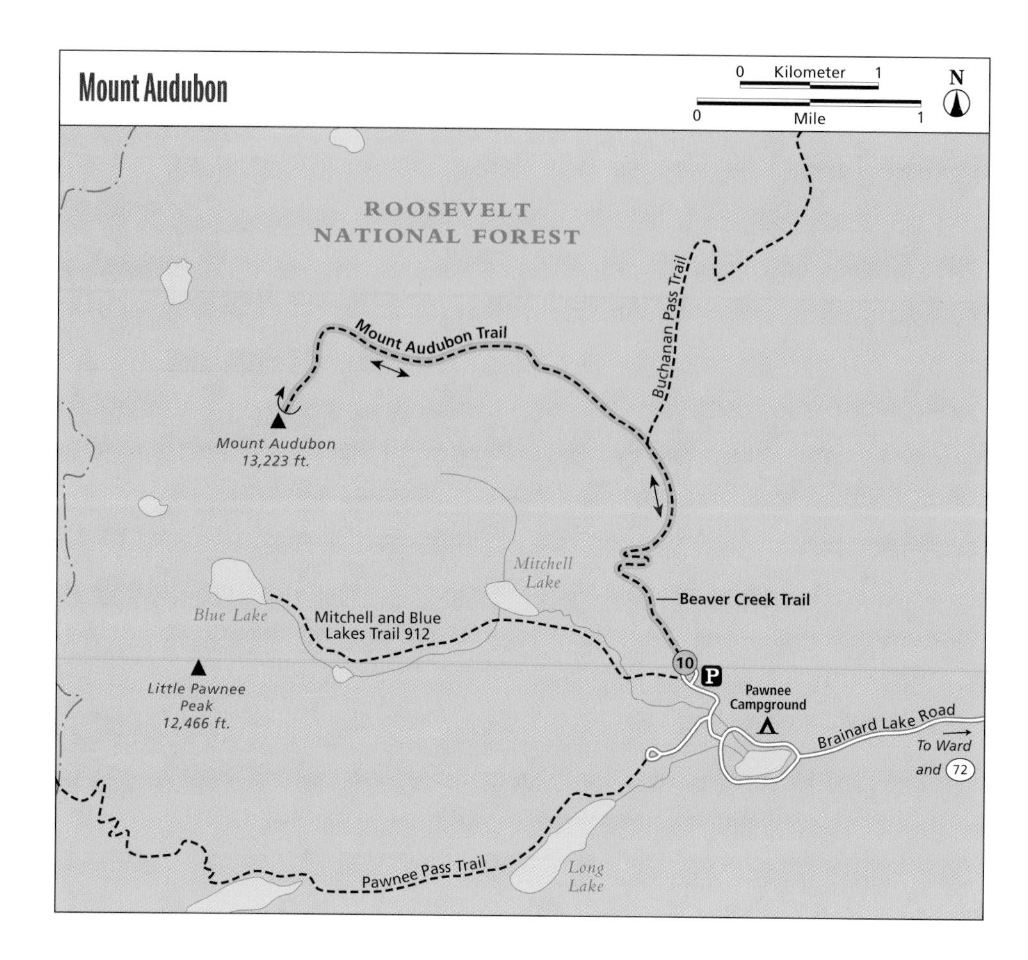

The Hike

The hike starts at the Beaver Creek Trailhead, located at the Mitchell Creek Trailhead parking area above Brainard Lake. Access the well-marked Beaver Creek Trail on the north side of the parking area. The trail is well maintained and makes a gradual climb to a shelf and the Mount Audubon Trail. After about 0.5 mile of easy hiking through a dense spruce forest, the trail makes a sharp right turn up a steep switchback, with views out to the east.

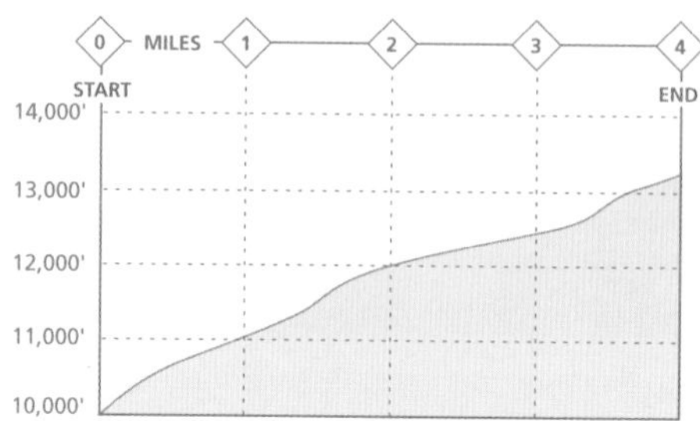

At 1.3 miles the Beaver Creek Trail goes right down to Coney Flats Road. The Mount Audubon Trail continues straight. The trail takes a tight line up through a stand of twisted krummholz and a small boulder field. You are gaining

considerable altitude at this point, as the pine trees disappear behind you. The trail cuts over a small, beautiful stream and up through a stunning alpine meadow to a snowfield.

At 2.5 miles the trail makes a sharp right away from a snowfield and climbs steeply through a boulder field to a broad, flat ridge with excellent views of the surrounding alpine peaks. At 3.5 miles the trail goes left, up a steep, rocky trail to the summit. There are a number of side trails that shoot off from the main trail and take a steep scramble to the summit. Follow the cairns and stay on the main trail. It is easier to gain the summit following the main trail, and less intrusive to the surrounding alpine environment. At 4 miles you arrive at the summit of Mount Audubon.

The last section of the hike lies above timberline and is exposed to violent lightning storms. Get an early start and try to be off the summit by noon during the thunderstorm season. The last mile of the trail gains 1,000 feet and can be very strenuous for those not acclimated to altitude. Take a break at one of the many rock shelters on the summit and enjoy the spectacular alpine scenery from this beautiful peak.

C. C. Parry, a botanist, and zoologist J. W. Velie climbed the mountain in 1864 and named the peak after the famous naturalist, who never set foot in Colorado.

After you've summited, retrace your steps to the trailhead.

Miles and Directions

0.0 Start from the parking area and access the signed Beaver Creek Trail.

0.4 The trail cuts right up a steep switchback.

1.3 At the junction with the Beaver Creek Trail, continue straight on the Mount Audubon Trail 913.

1.9 Enjoy great views of the surrounding peaks and Blue Lake.

2.5 Climb steep switchbacks to a ridge.

3.5 Climb steep switchbacks to the summit.

4.0 Arrive on the Mount Audubon summit. Retrace your steps.

8.0 Arrive back at the trailhead.

11 Blue Lake

A wonderful day hike leads to Blue Lake in the Indian Peaks Wilderness area. This short hike takes you up to a beautiful alpine lake surrounded by stunning alpine peaks. Due to the rocky and sometimes wet and snowy conditions of the trail, you may want to consider outfitting your pooch with weather-appropriate booties for his sensitive paws.

Start: From the Mitchell Creek Trailhead
Distance: 5.0 miles out and back
Approximate hiking time: 2.5 to 4 hours
Difficulty: Moderate
Elevation gain: About 1,000 feet
Seasons: June to Oct
Trail surface: Well-traveled and rocky on the lower section, with loose, rocky, and wet conditions up to Blue Lake. Expect to find snow on the upper section of the trail well into June.
Other trail users: Equestrians
Canine compatibility: Dogs must be on leash
Map: Nat Geo Trails Illustrated 102 Indian Peaks/Gold Hill
Trail contacts: Boulder Ranger District, USDA Forest Service; (970) 295-6600; www.fs.usda.gov/contactus/arp/about-forest/contactus
Other: Camping is available at Brainard Lake Recreation Area

Finding the trailhead: From the junction of CO 93 (Broadway) and CO 119 (Canyon) in Boulder, go west on CO 119 for 18 miles to Nederland and the junction with CO 72. Go west on CO 72 for 10 miles to CR 102. Turn left onto CR 102 to the Brainard Lake Recreation Area and the Mitchell Lake Trailhead parking area. **GPS:** N40 04.60' / W105 34.52'

The Hike

This is one of my favorite hikes in the Indian Peaks Wilderness area, and you get a lot of bang for the buck on this hike. Beautiful views, spectacular wildflowers, lovely alpine lakes; this hike has it all. If you are planning to hike up to Blue Lake during the weekend in the summer months, arrive early to secure a parking space. The parking lot fills up quickly in summer and finding a space after early morning can be a problem.

The hike begins at the Mitchell Lake Trailhead, located near the restrooms at the Mitchell Lake Trailhead parking area. The Mitchell Lake Trail begins at an elevation of 10,472 feet and climbs to 11,352 feet (at Blue Lake) in just under 2.5 miles. The start of the trail is wide, level, and somewhat rocky. At the 0.2-mile mark you enter the boundary of the wilderness area, and the trail wanders through dense, tall spruce trees.

At around the 0.3-mile mark, cross over Mitchell Creek on a wooden footbridge. After the footbridge the trail climbs gently to Mitchell Lake, with wildflowers and spectacular views of Mount Audubon (13,223 feet), Little Pawnee Peak, Mount Toll, and Paiute Peak. Mitchell Lake is a shallow, fourteen-acre lake that is stocked with cutthroat trout and is quite popular with anglers. The meadow around the lake is

Laurel D'Antonio enjoying a beautiful summer day in the Indian Peaks

filled with wildflowers that grow profusely in the moist, fertile soil. Blanketflowers, alpine primrose, mountain lupines, mountain-avers, goldenbanner, and globeflowers are just a few of the flowers that blossom around Mitchell Creek and Mitchell Lake.

At the 1-mile mark the trail crosses over Mitchell Creek again, on a makeshift bridge of logs and fallen trees. After Mitchell Creek the trail climbs on log steps to a meadow with good views of the surrounding peaks. This is another place to stop and enjoy the views and the wildflowers. Wooden walkways guide you through the marshy area of the meadow and up to the drier, rocky section of the trail.

At around the 2-mile mark the trail cuts across a snowfield, following rock cairns, with Mitchell Creek and Little Pawnee Peak on the left. At the 2.5-mile mark, Blue Lake appears in a cirque below the towering summits of Mount Toll and Paiute Peak. Blue Lake covers almost twenty-three acres, is almost 100 feet deep, and is stocked with cutthroat trout.

Take a lunch break and enjoy the panoramic views and alpine splendor, then retrace your steps to the trailhead.

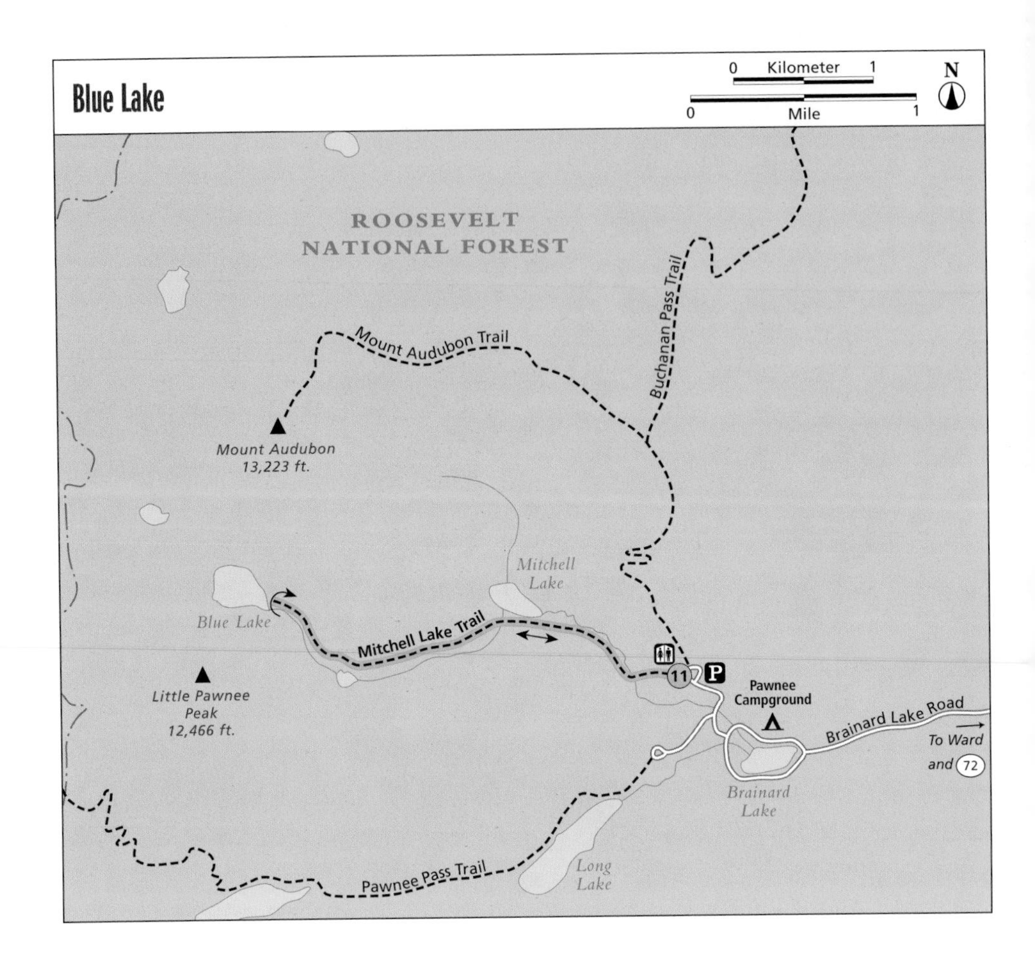

Miles and Directions

0.0 Start on the Mitchell Lake Trail.

0.2 Arrive at the Indian Peaks Wilderness boundary.

0.8 Arrive at beautiful Mitchell Lake.

1.0 Cross over Mitchell Creek.

1.5 Alpine meadow and ponds.

2.5 Arrive at Blue Lake. Retrace your steps.

5.0 Arrive back at the trailhead.

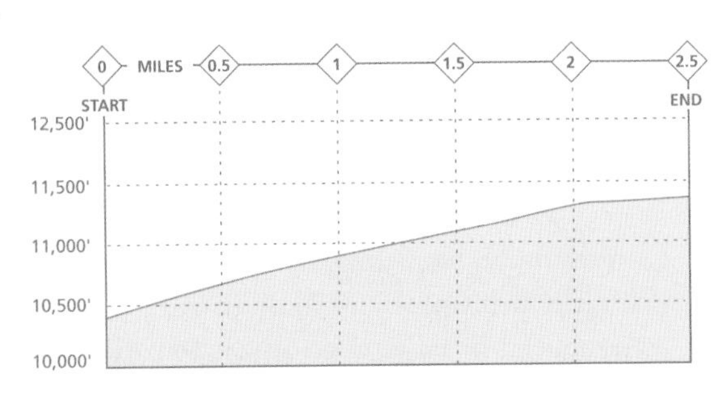

12 Heil Valley Ranch/Lichen Loop

This great family hike is in Boulder County's newest open space area. It is a great way to get the kids out into the woods on a short, scenic loop through stands of beautiful ponderosa pines and open meadows. Heil Valley Ranch is an excellent spot for wildlife viewing, so keep an eye on your dog for this hike.

Start: From the Lichen Loop Trailhead
Distance: 1.3-mile loop
Approximate hiking time: 1 to 2 hours
Difficulty: Easy
Elevation gain: About 5,900 feet
Seasons: Year-round
Trail surface: Smooth and well maintained by volunteers and open space rangers
Other trail users: Equestrians
Canine compatibility: Dogs must be on leash or voice control
Map: Boulder County Open Space/Heil Valley Ranch map
Trail contacts: Boulder County Open Space; (303) 678-6200; www.bouldercounty.org/government/dept/pages/pos.aspx

Finding the trailhead: From Boulder, follow US 36 north toward the town of Lyons to Lefthand Canyon Road. Turn left onto Lefthand Canyon Road for 0.5 mile to Geer Canyon Road. Turn right onto Geer Canyon Road for 1.3 miles to the signed trailhead and parking area. **GPS:** N40 08.57' / W105 18.02'

The Hike

From the trailhead/picnic area, pass the information kiosk and follow the signs for the Lichen Loop. The trail goes over a wooden bridge and heads left, up to the start of the loop portion of the hike.

Travel through stands of beautiful ponderosa pines and a meadow filled with tall grasses, yuccas, and cacti. Views to the north up the valley are spectacular, with sharp-cut canyons and open meadows. Reach a trail junction at around the 0.5-mile mark and go right, switchbacking up through the ponderosas. Past several large lichen-covered boulders, the trail breaks out into an open meadow with tall prairie grass and the occasional ponderosa tree. Views open to the south and east at upturned sedimentary rock along a ridgeline. The trail cuts through the open meadow and begins a gentle descent back toward the trailhead.

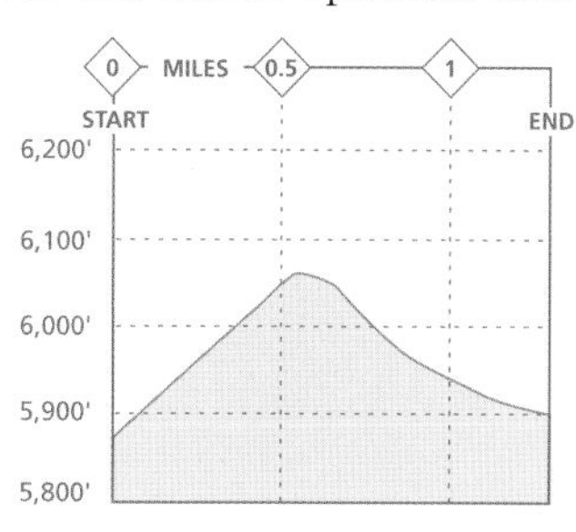

Enjoy the pleasant hiking through the meadow, close the loop, and retrace your steps back to the trailhead. Picnic tables are located near the trailhead, so bring a lunch and enjoy spending an afternoon with the family at this beautiful open space area.

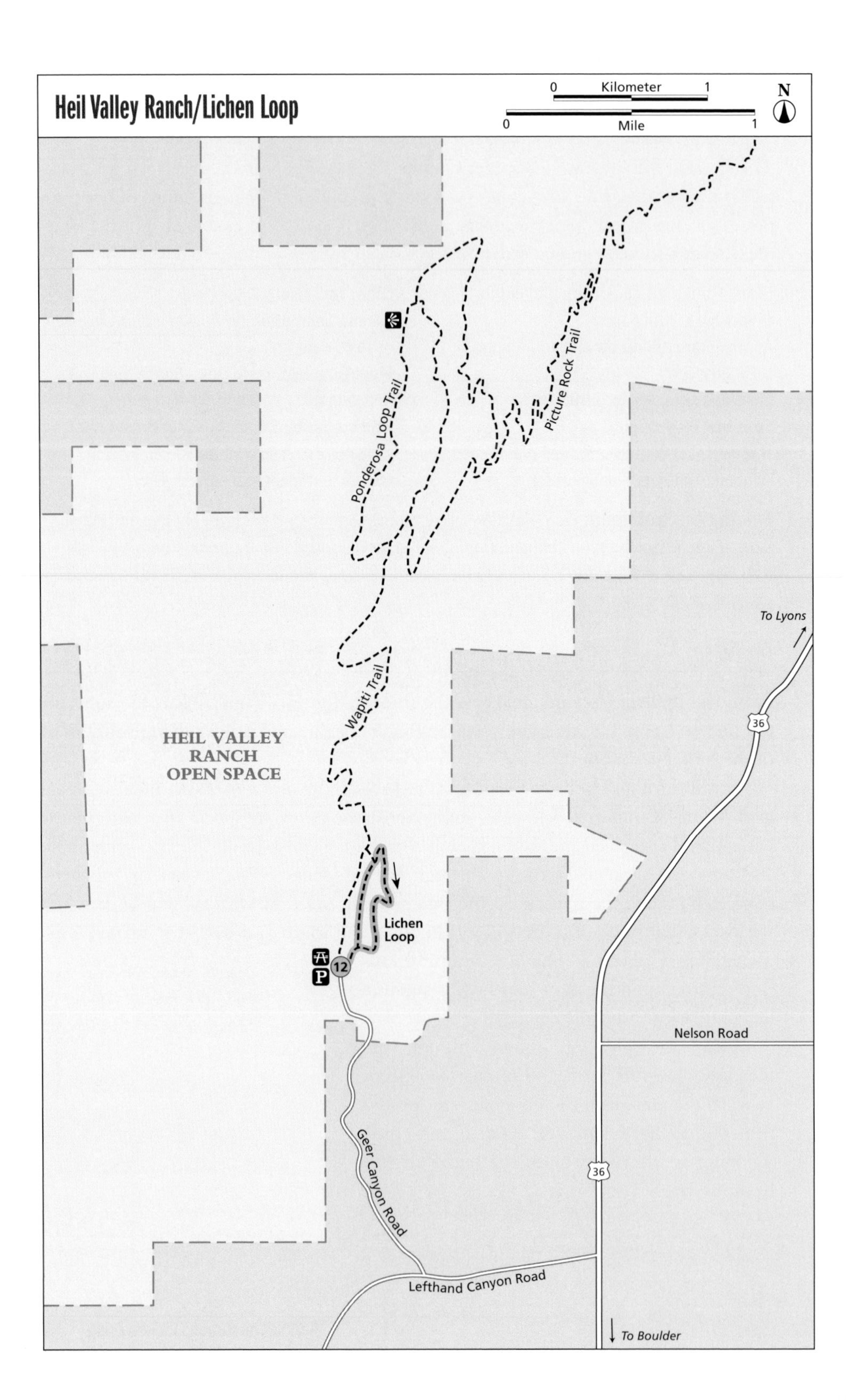

Heil Valley Ranch/Lichen Loop
0
Kilometer
1
0
Mile
1
N
Ponderosa Loop Trail
Picture Rock Trail
Wapiti Trail
HEIL VALLEY
RANCH
OPEN SPACE
Lichen
Loop
12
P
To Lyons
36
Nelson Road
Geer Canyon Road
Lefthand Canyon Road
To Boulder

Hiking with the dog is a family-friendly activity. Be sure everyone in the family—dog included—has ample supplies for the length of your hike.

Miles and Directions

0.0 Start by passing the information kiosk and picking up the Lichen Loop.

0.5 Arrive at a trail junction.

1.3 Arrive back at the trailhead.

13 Bear Peak

This is a strenuous but great hike up to the summit of Bear Peak (8,461 feet), one of Boulder's most visible landmarks. The Bear Peak Trail follows Bear Creek up beautiful Bear Canyon, then makes a steep ascent up the Bear Peak West Ridge Trail to the summit. Expect beautiful vistas and blooming wildflowers during the summer months.

Start: From the Walter Orr-Roberts Trailhead
Distance: 7.4-mile loop
Approximate hiking time: 4 to 5 hours
Difficulty: Strenuous
Elevation gain: About 2,000 feet
Seasons: Year-round
Trail surface: Well-traveled and smooth up to the Bear Canyon Trail. From there on, the trail is rocky and steep.
Other trail users: Equestrians
Canine compatibility: Dogs must be on leash
Map: USGS Eldorado Springs CO
Trail contacts: City of Boulder Mountain Parks and Open Space; (303) 441-3440; www.bouldercolorado.gov

Finding the trailhead: From the junction of Broadway and Table Mesa Road in Boulder, go west on Table Mesa for 2.4 miles to the National Center for Atmospheric Research (NCAR), where you'll find parking and the trailhead. **GPS:** N39 58.45' / W105 16.28'

The Hike

From the parking area, access the Walter Orr-Roberts Weather Trail on the west side of NCAR. Follow this informative trail for a short 0.2 mile to a kiosk and a sign pointing to the Mesa Trail. Drop a short distance, then climb steeply to a water tower.

From the water tower follow signs for the Mesa Trail, staying left at all trail junctions. At the 1.2-mile mark you arrive at the junction of the Mesa Trail and Bear Creek. Go left up the steep, wide road to a junction with Mesa Trail and the Bear Canyon Trail on the right.

Turn right onto the Bear Canyon Trail, passing a utility tower and power lines. The trail becomes rockier and begins to climb steeply. It crosses Bear Creek several times and winds through several patches of aspens, willows, and cottonwoods. Wildflowers grow profusely along the creek, as do ferns and other flowering shrubs.

At the 3.1-mile mark you arrive at a beautiful, small meadow and a trail junction. The Green-Bear Trail goes to the right. You go left and up on the Bear Peak West Ridge Trail into the pines. The trail climbs steeply through the pines to an open area at an old fence line. The trail cuts to the left and away from private property. Here views open to the west to Walker Ranch Open Space, the Indian Peaks, and Mount Meeker (13,911 feet) to the north.

The trail begins to climb a steep hillside with numerous granite boulders. At around the 4.2-mile mark the trail forks to the left, climbing a series of steep, granite

Awesome views from the summit of Bear Peak

steps. Before you know it you are standing below the pointed summit of Bear Peak. Follow the trail through the rocks to the north ridge, past the Fern Canyon Trail, and scramble up the north ridge to the summit proper. Take a long rest and enjoy the spectacular views in all directions.

After your rest and photo session, go back down the ridge to the Fern Canyon Trail. Go right and down the very steep Fern Canyon Trail to a saddle. The trail is loose and rocky and drops over 2,000 feet in 1.4 miles, a real knee tweaker. Fern Canyon is a narrow, densely vegetated canyon filled with spectacular rock formations, aspens, and pine trees. The trail in several sections is made of steep steps and wood stairs.

The trail breaks out of the narrow canyon and you arrive at a junction with Shanahan North Trail. Continue straight on the Fern Canyon Trail, dropping to the Mesa Trail. Wildflowers bloom along the trail and in the open areas. Go left on the Mesa Trail, down to Bear Creek. From here, retrace your route back to NCAR and the parking area.

Miles and Directions

0.0 Start behind NCAR on the Walter Orr-Roberts Trail.

0.2 Arrive at a kiosk and sign for the Mesa Trail.

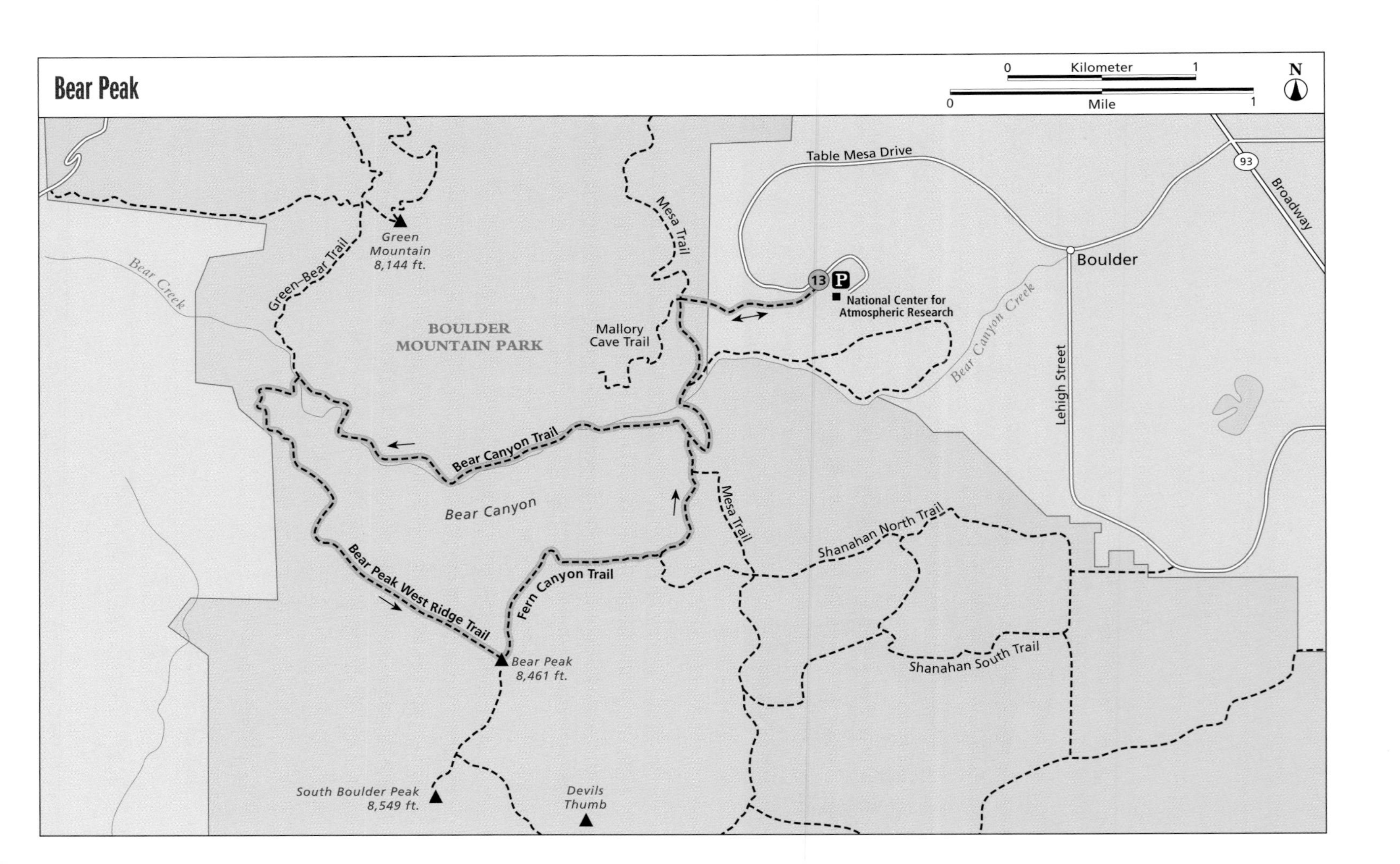
Bear Peak
0
Kilometer
1
0
Mile
1
N
Green
Mountain
8,144 ft.
Green–Bear Trail
Bear Creek
BOULDER
MOUNTAIN PARK
Mesa Trail
Mallory
Cave Trail
Table Mesa Drive
93
Broadway
Boulder
13
P
National Center for
Atmospheric Research
Bear Canyon Creek
Lehigh Street
Bear Canyon Trail
Bear Canyon
Mesa Trail
Shanahan North Trail
Bear Peak West Ridge Trail
Fern Canyon Trail
Bear Peak
8,461 ft.
Shanahan South Trail
South Boulder Peak
8,549 ft.
Devils
Thumb

0.7	Pass a very large water tank.
1.2	Arrive at a junction with the Mesa Trail and Bear Creek.
1.4	Arrive at a junction with Bear Canyon Trail.
3.1	Arrive at a junction with Green-Bear Trail.
4.7	Arrive at the spectacular summit of Bear Peak.
4.8	Arrive at a junction with Fern Canyon Trail.
5.6	Arrive at a junction with Shanahan North Trail.
6.0	Arrive back at a junction with Mesa Trail.
7.4	Arrive back at NCAR, the trailhead, and the parking area.

14 Walker Ranch

This popular hike leads around the old homestead of James Walker. Beautiful views, excellent wildflowers, and good fishing along South Boulder Creek are the main attractions on this hike. Fly fishing is excellent along several sections of South Boulder Creek.

Start: From the South Boulder Creek Trailhead and parking area
Distance: 7.4-mile loop
Approximate hiking time: 3 to 4.5 hours
Difficulty: Moderate
Elevation gain: Minimal
Seasons: Year-round
Trail surface: Extremely rocky in places
Other trail users: Mountain bikers and equestrians
Canine compatibility: Dogs must be on leash
Maps: USGS Boulder County; Boulder County Open Space/Walker Ranch map
Trail contacts: Boulder County Open Space; (303) 678-6200; www.bouldercounty.org/government/dept/pages/pos.aspx

Finding the trailhead: From the intersection of Broadway and Baseline Road in Boulder, travel 7.5 miles west on Baseline, which becomes Flagstaff Road and climbs up past Flagstaff Mountain. Turn left into the South Boulder Creek trailhead and parking area at Walker Ranch. **GPS:** N39 57.05' / W105 20.15'

The Hike

From the trailhead, go through the gate and begin a nice descent to South Boulder Creek. The Walker Ranch Loop Trail follows an old road and passes several rock formations on the right. At the bottom of the hill, cross a small stream and then go right along beautiful South Boulder Creek.

The trail goes upstream to a bridge. Cross the bridge and go left up the steep hill. Crest the steep part of the hill, where the trail bends to the right, and enjoy excellent views to the west. This trail is extremely popular with mountain bikers, so be aware of their presence, especially on weekends.

The trail becomes level just past a small rock garden and travels past a gate and down through a beautiful forested area. Climb up a hill and through another gate, where the trail drops you onto Reservoir Road. Go left up the road for 0.1 mile to a trail on the left. Go left up the trail and arrive at Crescent Meadows. Turn left onto the Walker Ranch Loop Trail, heading to the east and through the open meadow. There are great views to the west, and wildflowers light up the meadow in late spring and early summer.

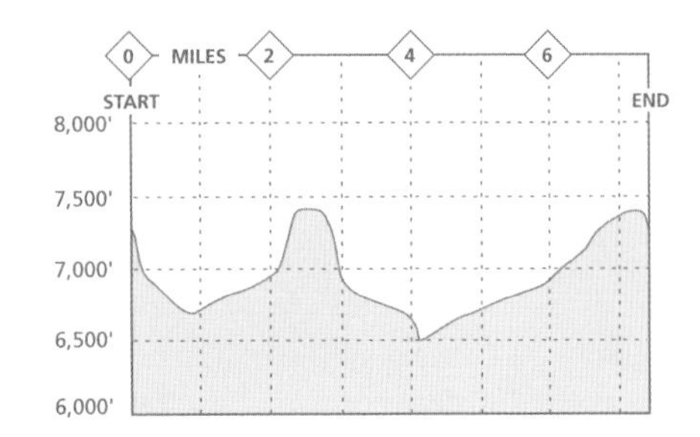

At around the 3.5-mile mark the trail leads you into a dense forest and starts to

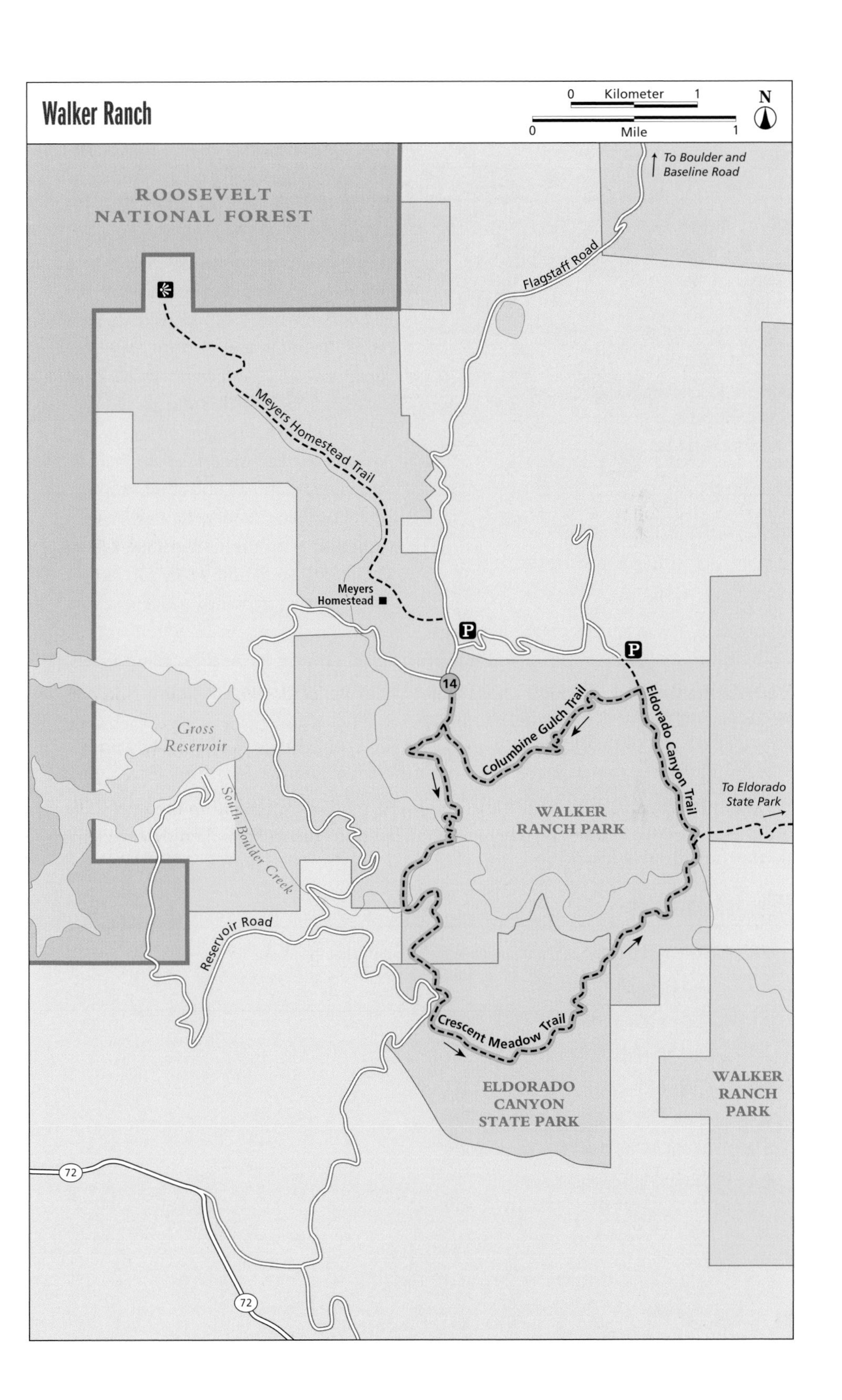
Walker Ranch
0 Kilometer 1
0 Mile 1
N
To Boulder and Baseline Road
ROOSEVELT NATIONAL FOREST
Flagstaff Road
Meyers Homestead Trail
Meyers Homestead
14
Gross Reservoir
South Boulder Creek
Columbine Gulch Trail
Eldorado Canyon Trail
To Eldorado State Park
WALKER RANCH PARK
Reservoir Road
Crescent Meadow Trail
ELDORADO CANYON STATE PARK
WALKER RANCH PARK
72
72

A young deer getting its new antlers

drop in elevation. Travel past several rocky sections and through a small, open meadow. Arrive at a sign warning mountain bikers to dismount. Follow rock-and-log steps steeply down to South Boulder Creek and a bridge. This is a good spot to take a break with your dog and admire the scenery. South Boulder Creek runs wild through this section, and the deep pools of water are crystal clear and excellent for fly fishing.

Cross the bridge and turn left, passing the Eldorado Canyon Trail on the right. Begin a good climb through the ponderosa and spruce trees to a junction with the Columbine Gulch Trail at the 5.8-mile mark. Go left on this narrow trail into a narrow, forested gulch. Pass a small stream, then begin a steep ascent past several switchbacks. A beautiful stretch brings you up and out of the gulch to a ridge and excellent views. Go right and up a gentle grade, following the Columbine Gulch Trail past a recent burn area and back to the trailhead.

Once the site of the largest cattle ranch on the Front Range, Walker Ranch is now a beautiful piece of open space land that provides a glimpse into Boulder County history. James Walker first came to the area for health reasons, and thrived in the fresh mountain air and peaceful setting of open meadows and mountain terrain. Hope you do the same on this hike.

Miles and Directions

0.0 Start from the parking area and pass through a gate at the kiosk.

1.0 Cross over a small stream.

1.5 Cross a bridge over South Boulder Creek.

2.4 Pass Reservoir Road.

4.5 Begin a serious steep, rocky descent.

4.7 Cross a bridge over South Boulder Creek.

5.8 Go left on the Columbine Gulch Trail.

7.4 Arrive back at the trailhead.

15 Marshall Mesa

Kids, dogs—the entire family—will enjoy this beautiful Front Range hike on a great trail system with wonderful vistas in a parklike setting.

Start: From the Marshall Valley Trailhead parking area
Distance: 3.3-mile loop
Approximately hiking time: 1.5 to 3 hours
Difficulty: Moderate
Elevation gain: About 150 feet
Seasons: Year-round; can be snow packed in winter months
Trail surface: Smooth and hard packed with short rocky sections
Other trail users: Mountain bikers and equestrians
Canine compatibility: Dogs must be on leash or voice control
Map: Boulder County Open Space/Marshall Mesa
Trail contacts: Boulder County Open Space; (303) 678-6200; www.bouldercounty.org/government/dept/pages/pos.aspx

Finding the trailhead: From Boulder, access Broadway (CO 93) south to the intersection with Marshall Road (CO 170). Turn left onto Marshall Road and make a quick right into the trailhead parking area. **GPS:** N39 57.18' / W105 13.89'

The Hike

Start from the trailhead parking area and walk south into an open field on the Marshall Valley Trail. Hike through cactus, prairie grass and yucca to a trail junction at a wooden bridge. Follow the Community Ditch Trail up a short hill with great views to the east, west, and north. Arrive at the top of the hill and panoramic views. Go right, following the Community Ditch Trail and enjoying more great views. The trail follows the ditch on your left. This is a great place to let your dog swim on hot summer days. Pass several trail junctions, staying on the Community Ditch Trail to a junction with the Coal Seam Trail. Turn right onto this beautiful trail; wildflowers are profuse here during the spring and summer months. Arrive back at the trailhead and parking area.

A dog's natural gait is usually faster than ours, so it can be difficult for them to adjust to our slower pace, particularly on narrow or steeper trails.

This is a very popular hiking and biking trail in the Boulder area. It can be extremely busy

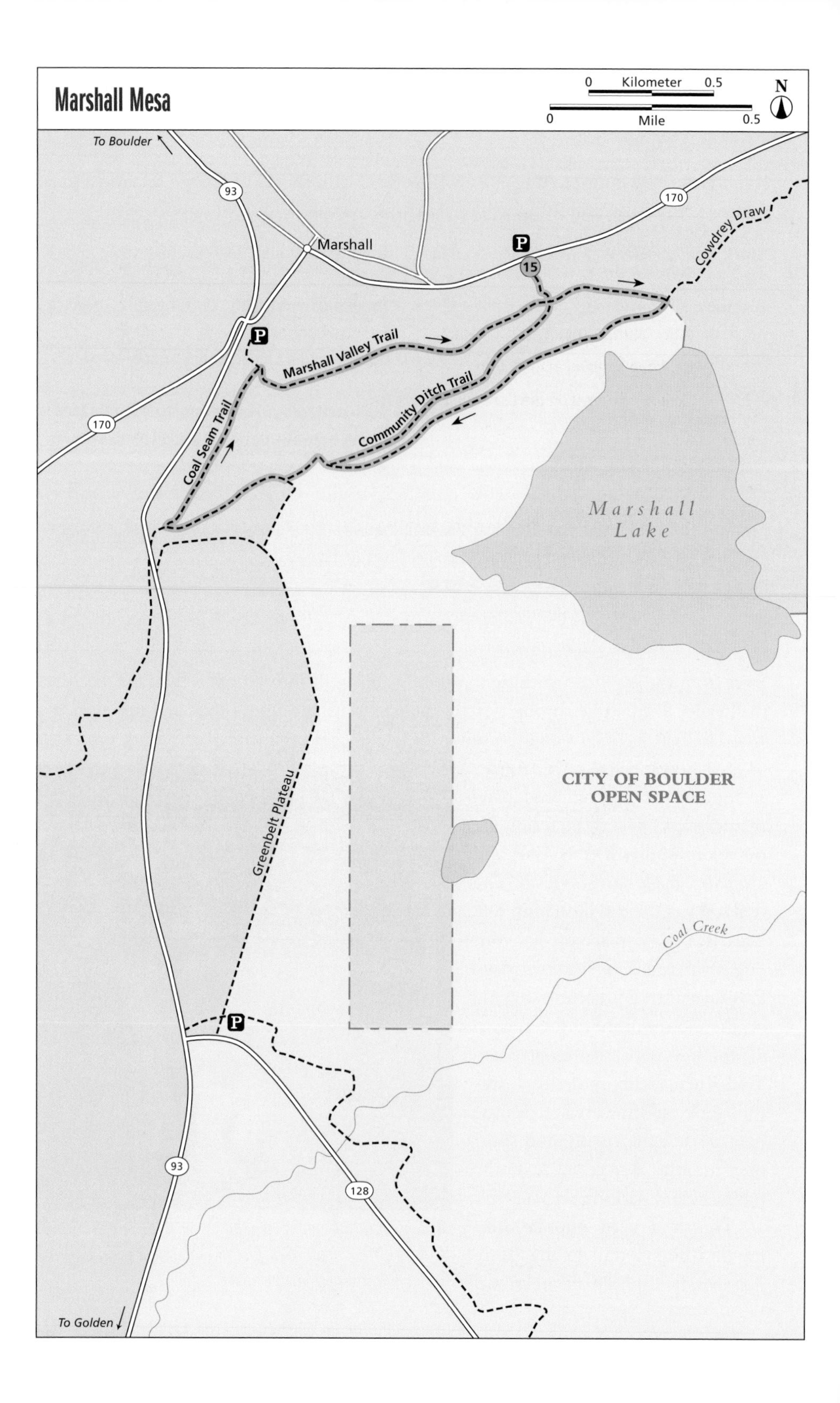
Marshall Mesa
0
Kilometer
0.5
0
Mile
0.5
N
To Boulder
93
170
Marshall
P
15
Cowdrey Draw
Marshall Valley Trail
Community Ditch Trail
Coal Seam Trail
170
Marshall Lake
CITY OF BOULDER
OPEN SPACE
Greenbelt Plateau
Coal Creek
93
128
To Golden

during the weekends. Get to the parking early and be respectful of other trail users. Share the trail and be courteous; a smile to fellow users goes a long way.

Miles and Directions

0.0 From the parking area, head south and access the Marshall Valley Trail. Follow the Marshall Valley Trail left into an open field.

0.9 Reach a junction with the Community Ditch Trail just past a bridge. Veer right on the Community Ditch Trail and climb a hill to a trail junction.

1.2 Arrive at a trail junction; turn right, following the Community Ditch Trail.

1.4 Continue straight on the Community Ditch Trail.

2.2 Continue straight on the Community Ditch Trail.

2.3 Arrive at a junction with the Greenbelt Trail. Continue straight on the Community Ditch Trail.

2.7 Arrive at a junction with the Coal Seam Trail. Turn right onto the Coal Seam Trail.

3.3 Arrive back at the trailhead parking area.

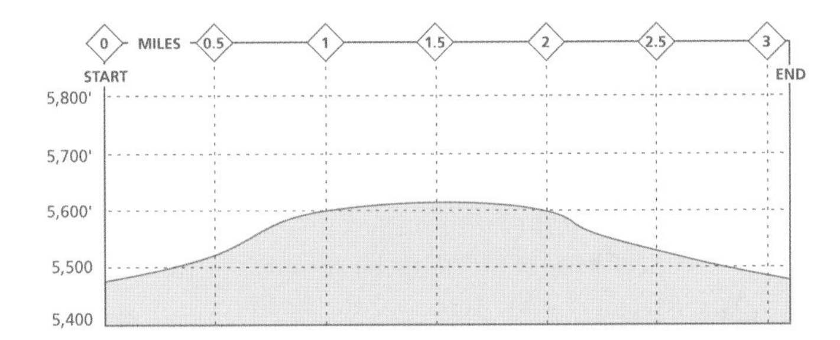

16 Eldorado Canyon Trail

This beautiful hike leads along towering rock walls. The trail travels up a south- and west-facing hillside through North Draw, with spectacular views of the Indian Peaks, the Continental Divide, Denver, and towering, sheer rock walls.

Start: From the Eldorado Canyon Trailhead, just north of the parking area
Distance: 5.8 miles out and back
Approximate hiking time: 2.5 to 3.5 hours
Difficulty: Moderate
Elevation gain: 1,000 feet
Seasons: Year-round
Trail surface: Smooth in parts, extremely rocky in others
Other trail users: Equestrians
Canine compatibility: Dogs must be on leash
Maps: USGS Boulder County; Colorado State Parks/Eldorado Canyon State Park map
Trail contacts: Colorado State Parks; (303) 866-3437; www.parks.state.co.us

Finding the trailhead: From the intersection of Broadway and Baseline in Boulder, travel south on Broadway (CO 93) to CO 170. Go right on CO 170 for 4.4 miles to the entrance/fee station and parking area for Eldorado Canyon State Park. Pay the day-use fee and follow the dirt road up to the ranger station, parking area, and trailhead. **GPS:** N39 55.49' / W105 17.37'

The Hike

From the parking area at the ranger station, walk north up some steps and cross the road to access the Eldorado Canyon Trailhead. Begin a steep climb into North Draw on the Eldorado Canyon Trail. Much work has been done on the lower section of the trail to eliminate cutting switchbacks, so stay on the main trail.

You gain altitude quickly as the trail climbs up into North Draw. Great views open to the north, of Shirttail Peak and towering rock walls that are popular with rock climbers from around the world. Eldorado Canyon has been a popular spot for rock climbers since the 1950s, and has been at the forefront of Colorado rock climbing.

At around the 0.4-mile mark, the trail climbs through a series of steep switchbacks across a steep hillside. At the top of the switchbacks, a climbers' trail on the right leads to the Rincon Wall. Continue straight on the Eldorado Canyon Trail.

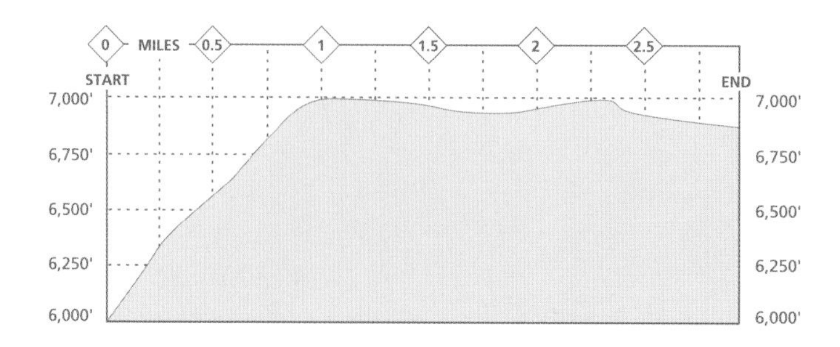

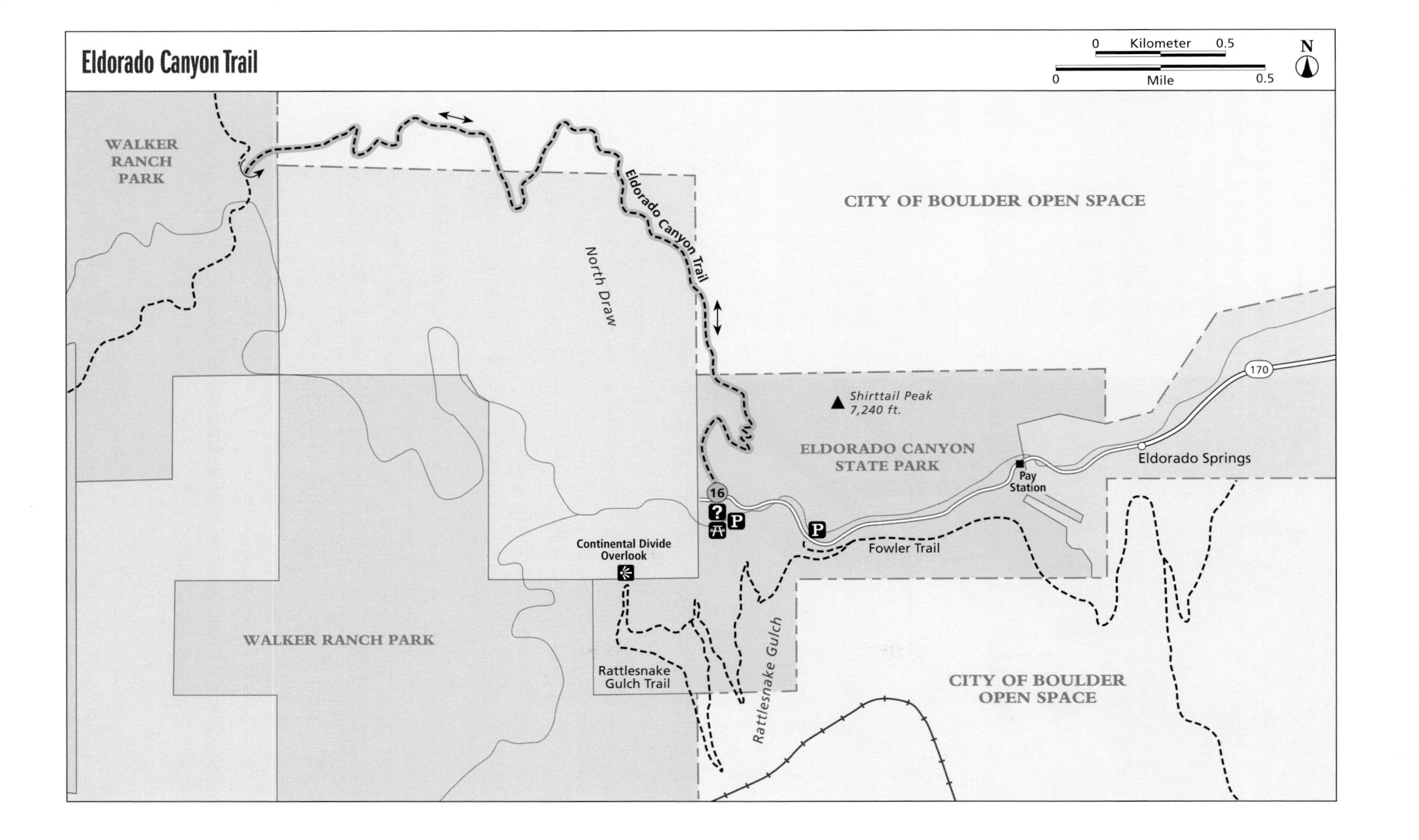
Eldorado Canyon Trail
0 Kilometer 0.5
0 Mile 0.5
N
WALKER RANCH PARK
CITY OF BOULDER OPEN SPACE
Eldorado Canyon Trail
North Draw
Shirttail Peak 7,240 ft.
ELDORADO CANYON STATE PARK
170
Eldorado Springs
Pay Station
16
Fowler Trail
Continental Divide Overlook
WALKER RANCH PARK
Rattlesnake Gulch Trail
Rattlesnake Gulch
CITY OF BOULDER OPEN SPACE

Summer hiking at its best on the lower section of the trail

The trail becomes level and views open to the west, onto the Indian Peaks and the Continental Divide. Cacti, yuccas, and other sun-loving plants grow on the west-facing hillside, which becomes quite colorful with blooming flowers and cacti during the late spring and early summer months.

At around the 1.3-mile mark, the trail climbs five steep switchbacks and enters a dense pine forest. Large, colorful boulders line the trail; look for a small spring that seeps out from one of the boulders, just to the right of the trail. The trail curves to the west and crosses over a small seasonal drainage via a wooden footbridge.

Beyond the footbridge the trail begins a modest climb up through the pines to an open meadow filled with yuccas and small ponderosas, with great views to the east, south, and west. South Boulder Peak (8,549 feet) looms high above to the northeast. The trail cuts a straight line across the meadow and climbs a short, rocky section, gaining a small ridge and high point with great views south to Eldorado Mountain.

At around the 2.9-mile mark, the trail begins to drop and goes right, down into Walker Ranch Open Space. This is the turnaround point of this hike. Feel free to drop down to Walker Ranch and South Boulder Creek for more mileage and views. Otherwise, retrace your steps to the trailhead.

Miles and Directions

0.0 Start by heading up into North Draw on the Eldorado Canyon Trail.

0.5 A climbers' trail to Rincon Wall goes right.

1.3 Arrive at a series of steep switchbacks.

2.9 Arrive at the turnaround point and great views to the west.

5.8 Arrive back at the trailhead.

NORTH-CENTRAL MOUNTAINS

North-central Colorado is a land of sharp social and landscape contrasts. The northern half is still steeped in ranching, with only one great ski area in the region, while the southern half contains numerous world-class ski (now year-round) resorts. All or parts of fourteen wilderness areas, plus trails throughout national forest lands, can keep you in new hiking terrain for many years. Fifteen of Colorado's fifty-four peaks over 14,000 feet are located in the area.

Ranching still provides the livelihood in most of the northern half of this region. From North Park—a huge valley between the Medicine Bow, Rabbit Ears, and Park mountain ranges—the North Platte River begins its journey to the Missouri River, then on to the Gulf of Mexico via the Mississippi. Bison once grazed here; now cattle and wildlife munch the tall grasses. Walden is the main town and the gateway to less-used areas of the Mount Zirkel Wilderness and Colorado State Forest State Park. North Park hides interesting treasures including sand dunes, Colorado's largest herd of moose, great hiking, and a yurt system. The Arapaho National Wildlife Refuge provides nesting habitat for waterfowl and other migratory birds. Moose were reintroduced to the area in the late 1970s. Elk, pronghorn, mule deer, and sage grouse also take advantage of the refuge's shrubland.

The Yampa River and its tributaries also support the ranching community, keeping the Old West spirit alive and well. Steamboat Springs keeps one foot on each side of the cultural divide—one with ranching, the other with tourists, a ski resort, and hot springs.

The western part of Rocky Mountain National Park, in the eastern part of this section, holds the headwaters of the Colorado River and offers wonderful wildlife viewing.

The southern half of the region contains the highest peaks in the state, along with much of the high-priced mountain real estate. The state's two highest peaks, Mount Elbert and Mount Massive, raise their lofty heads above Leadville.

17 Wheeler Trail

This trail to the top of Wheeler Pass (the unofficial name) is part of both the Wheeler National Recreational Trail and the Colorado Trail. It climbs steadily through spruce-fir and lodgepole forests on the western slope of the Tenmile Range. Views of the Gore Range, Copper Mountain, Breckenridge, French Gulch, and the Front Range are fabulous! Because this trail goes to a ridge above tree line, be sure to get an early start to avoid afternoon thunder and lightning storms.

Start: From the Wheeler Flats Trailhead
Distance: 8.6 miles out and back (6.6 miles after trailhead is relocated)
Approximate hiking time: 5 to 6 hours
Difficulty: Most difficult due to elevation gain
Elevation gain: 2,730 feet
Seasons: Best from late June to mid-Oct
Trail surface: Dirt trail with some small creek crossings, rocks, and roots
Other trail users: Equestrians, mountain bikers, hunters (in season)
Canine compatibility: Dogs must be under control
Fees and permits: None
Maps: USGS Breckenridge, Copper Mountain, and Vail Pass; Nat Geo Trails Illustrated 109 Breckenridge/Tennessee Pass and 108 Vail/Frisco/Dillon; Latitude 40° Summit County
Trail contacts: White River National Forest, Dillon Ranger District, Silverthorne; (970) 468-5400; www.fs.usda.gov/whiteriver
Other: This trail crosses several avalanche chutes in the winter. It is neither maintained nor marked for winter use.

Finding the trailhead: From Frisco, head west on I-70 to exit 195 (for Copper Mountain and Leadville/CO 91). Exit and take CO 91 over I-70. The entrance to Copper Mountain Resort is on the right; turn left here onto an unnamed road and drive past the gas station (with restrooms, food, and water). It's 0.4 mile to the parking lot at Wheeler Flats Trailhead. **GPS:** N39 30.55' / W106 08.50'.

The Hike

Many summer moons ago Ute Indians camped in this area and hunted bison, deer, elk, antelope, and mountain sheep in the surrounding high open areas. In 1879 Judge John Wheeler purchased 320 acres, now part of Copper Mountain Resort, and started a hay ranch. The next year silver miners arrived, and the ranch became a town known by various names: Wheeler's Ranch, Wheeler Station, Wheeler's, Wheeler, and Wheeler Junction. Wheeler prospered with a hotel, saloons, and a post office. Several sawmills provided lumber for the numerous mines along Tenmile Creek from Frisco to the top of Fremont Pass.

Despite its status as a mining town, tourists also came to Wheeler for the beautiful scenery and excellent fishing. In 1884 the Colorado & Southern Railroad finished laying tracks to Wheeler on the east side of Tenmile Creek. The railroad station at Wheeler was named Solitude Station. On the other side of the creek, the Denver &

View from pass to east down Sawmill Gulch

Rio Grande Railroad built a line with a station called Wheeler's. The Denver & Rio Grande serviced this area from 1880 to 1911. The Colorado & Southern ended its rail service around 1937.

The trail is mostly flat for the first mile, as it follows part of the old Colorado & Southern Railroad route, now covering a gas pipeline. In one place the trail seems lower than the creek! After 1 mile you reach a junction with a post. Turn left, up the trail, to access Wheeler Pass. After the trailhead is relocated, you will cross a bridge to reach this post, eliminating 2 miles round-trip from your hike. Judge Wheeler used this trail to take his stock from Wheeler to his ranch in South Park. The trail now ends near Hoosier Pass, south of Breckenridge. It was designated a National Recreational Trail in 1979.

In about 3.4 miles the trail exits the forest for a view of Climax Molybdenum Mine's settling ponds. Several prosperous mining towns, including Robinson and Kokomo of Wheeler's era, are buried under the ponds. Watch and listen for marmots. As the trail contours left into another drainage, you can see the ridge of the Tenmile Range and cairns marking the trail. From here the trail winds in and out of forest, meadow, and willows. Colorful wildflowers line the route. Trees become twisted krummholz near tree line, and finally give up. The trail is sometimes smothered by

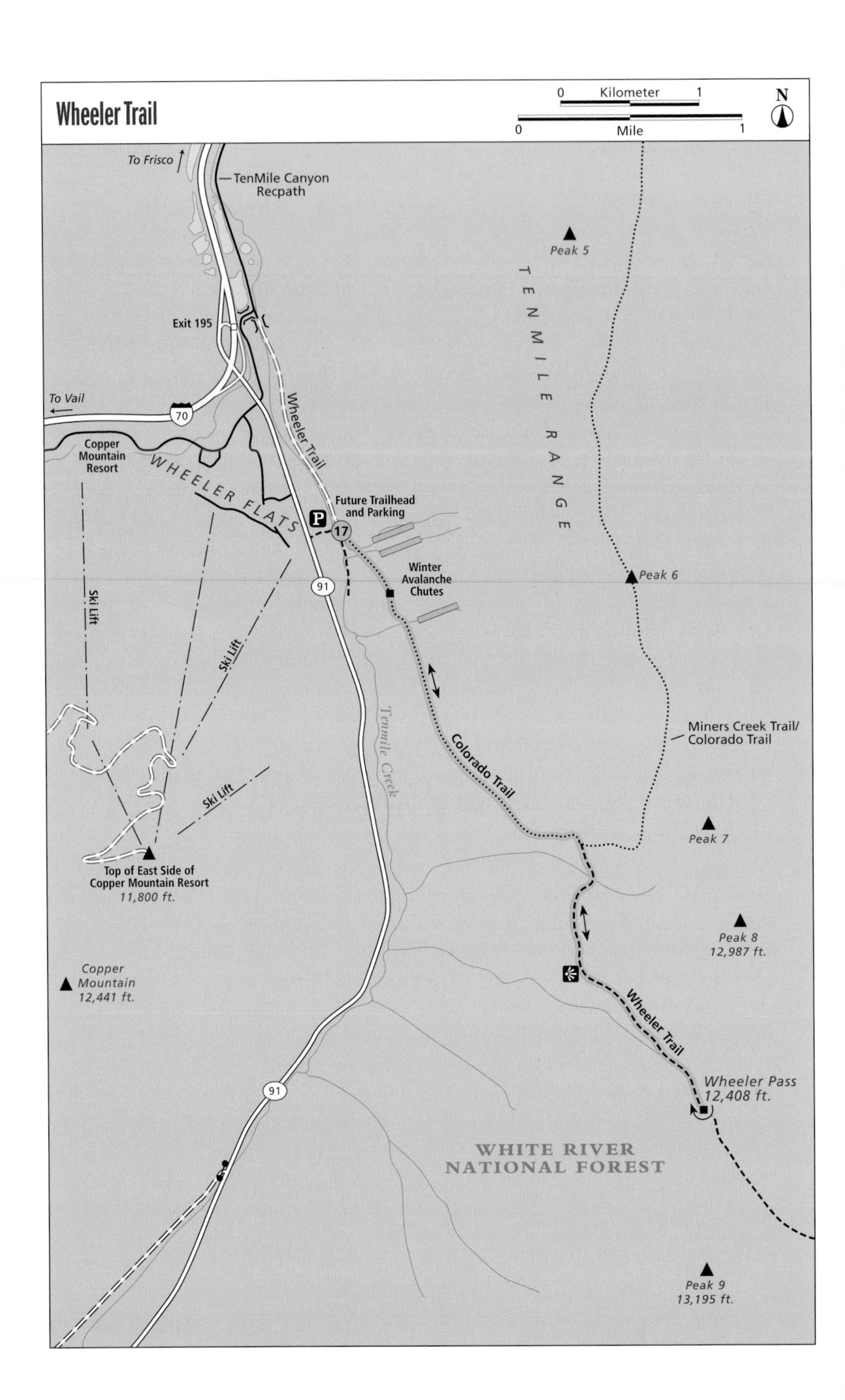
Wheeler Trail
0
Kilometer
1
0
Mile
1
N
To Frisco
TenMile Canyon Recpath
Peak 5
TENMILE RANGE
Exit 195
To Vail
70
Wheeler Trail
Copper Mountain Resort
WHEELER FLATS
Future Trailhead and Parking
17
Winter Avalanche Chutes
Peak 6
91
Ski Lift
Ski Lift
Tenmile Creek
Colorado Trail
Miners Creek Trail/ Colorado Trail
Ski Lift
Peak 7
Top of East Side of Copper Mountain Resort
11,800 ft.
Peak 8
12,987 ft.
Copper Mountain
12,441 ft.
Wheeler Trail
Wheeler Pass
12,408 ft.
91
WHITE RIVER NATIONAL FOREST
Peak 9
13,195 ft.

willows, but is passable. Three cairns built of good-size logs mark the way; the second one, however, is not on the trail, so stay alert. Finally, when your breath is short from elevation and the steep trail, the summit cairn comes into view.

That is, until you reach it and realize the trail continues farther up. Notice the vegetation along the trail. Willows and little red elephants grow in shallow depressions containing snow and water. The drier areas contain sedges and grasses, old-man-of-the-mountain, paintbrush, American bistort, chickweed, and alpine avens. The tundra is fragile. If you must go off trail, step on rocks as much as possible. When in a group, spread out.

The sign at the top of Wheeler Pass reports an elevation of 12,460 feet, but the topo map clearly indicates it's just under 12,400 feet. Be sure to hike to the little rocky knob on the left (12,408 feet) for the best easterly views. Breckenridge, French Gulch, and part of the Breckenridge ski area are on the east side; Copper Mountain and the Gore Range are to the northwest.

Founded in 1859 by General George E. Spencer, Breckenridge was named after US vice president John Cabell Breckinridge to ensure the new town would receive a post office. During the Civil War, John Breckinridge joined the Confederate Army. Upset Breckinridge residents changed the "i" to "e," spelling the name "Breckenridge." Other stories indicate the town was named after Thomas E. Breckenridge, a member of the original mining party. At one time, men panning gold in the Blue River and French Gulch could earn as much as $12 to $20 a day each! Dredge boats came later to scoop up more gold, and mines were burrowed into the hills. The largest gold nugget ever found in Colorado came from this area. At thirteen pounds it was called "Tom's Baby" (after Tom Groves, its finder).

Today both Breckenridge and Copper Mountain are known for their popular ski areas. Ski lifts at each area can be seen from various points along the trail. Skiing, other forms of outdoor recreation, and vacation homes have replaced mining in a new "gold rush" to the Rockies.

Miles and Directions

0.0 Start in the parking lot. Elevation: 9,680 feet. Cross the wooden bridge over West Tenmile Creek, turn right down the paved bike path, and in less than 0.1 mile come to a second bridge over Tenmile Creek. Veer right and walk across the gravel-topped bridge.

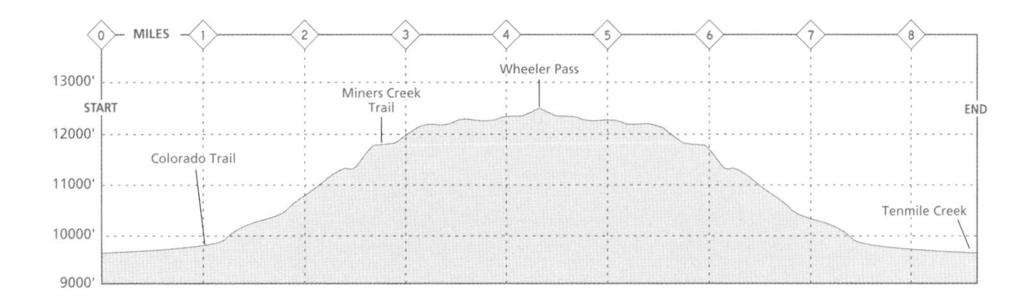

1.0 Reach a junction with the Colorado Trail and turn left, heading uphill on the Colorado Trail, marked with a post. GPS: N39 29.83' / W106 08.08' (***Note:*** One trail [along the gas pipeline] goes straight along the creek and the other, the Colorado Trail, goes right to CO 91.)

2.8 Reach the trail junction with Miners Creek Trail. GPS: N39 28.63' / W106 06.93'. Go right on Wheeler Trail.

4.3 Arrive at the top of Wheeler Pass and the rocky knob viewpoint. Elevation: 12,408 feet. GPS: N39 27.67' / W106 06.32'. Return the way you came.

8.6 Arrive back at the trailhead.

18 North Mount Elbert Trail

Mount Elbert is the highest point in Colorado and second highest in the Lower 48. The North Mount Elbert Trail climbs steeply through lodgepole, then spruce-fir forest and across alpine tundra. The worst parts of hiking Mount Elbert are its false summits and wind. The best parts include tremendous views and a feeling of great accomplishment. It's imperative to leave no later than 6:30 a.m. to avoid thunderstorms and lightning. Allow at least four to six hours for the hike to the top. Bring plenty of water and energy food, for yourself and your dog.

Start: From the Mount Elbert Trailhead near Elbert Creek Campground
Distance: 9.8 miles out and back
Approximate hiking time: 7 to 11 hours
Difficulty: Strenuous due to steepness and elevation
Elevation gain: 4,473 feet (including undulations)
Seasons: Best from July through Sept
Trail surface: Dirt trail, mostly steep, rocky in a few areas
Other trail users: Equestrians, mountain bikers, hunters (in season) on the Colorado Trail section only
Canine compatibility: Dogs must be under control, preferably on leash to avoid conflicts with other hikers and/or their dogs (very high volume of people/dogs on the trail)
Fees and permits: Groups of 10 or more people must get a permit from the Forest Service in Leadville
Maps: USGS Mount Elbert and Mount Massive; USFS San Isabel National Forest map; Nat Geo Trails Illustrated 127 Aspen/Independence Pass; Latitude 40° Summit County
Trail contacts: San Isabel National Forest, Leadville Ranger District, Leadville; (719) 486-0749; www.fs.usda.gov/psicc
Other: FR 110/CR 11, the dirt road to the trailhead, is less than two cars wide, so be watchful for oncoming cars, especially around curves. It's passable by most vehicles, the worst problems being a few potholes and washboard sections. There is a vault toilet but no water at the trailhead. Make sure to bring a lot of water for you and your dog, as none is available along the trail.

Finding the trailhead: From Leadville, drive south on US 24 (Harrison Avenue in Leadville) for about 4 miles. Turn right onto CO 300 West, a well-marked road at mile marker 180. In 0.7 mile, turn left onto Lake CR 11 (Halfmoon Road), again well-signed. In another 1.3 miles, stay on LCR 11, which turns right and becomes dirt. In 2.2 miles this road becomes FR 110. Continue for about 3 miles to the Mount Elbert Trailhead parking lot on the left. The trailhead is 0.1 mile off FR 110. **GPS:** N39 09.10' / W106 24.72'

The Hike

When first seeing Mount Elbert from afar, you might wonder about its "highest in Colorado" status. Looming above the Arkansas Valley, which already lies at 10,000 feet, the elevation gain does not seem dramatic. North of Mount Elbert across Halfmoon Creek, the aptly named Mount Massive (14,421 feet) stands a mere 12 feet lower.

Mt. Elbert from just below treeline

Mount Elbert's long, smooth ridges make it a good first fourteener (peak over 14,000 feet in elevation) to climb. The magnificent views are reason enough to return.

French Mountain, Casco Peak, and Frasco form the foreground for summits to the west. Five of Colorado's fourteeners pierce the western sky: Capitol Peak (14,130 feet) with its distinctive knife-edge ridge, white-faced Snowmass Mountain (14,092 feet), the Maroon Bells with Maroon Peak (14,156 feet) and North Maroon Peak (14,014 feet), and Pyramid Peak (14,018 feet). To the south lies La Plata Peak (14,336 feet) in the Sawatch Range. To the north, Mount Massive, Mount of the Holy Cross (14,005 feet), and Notch Mountain (13,237 feet) dominate, with the Gore Range in the distance. The mighty Mosquito Range, which made Leadville a mining center, rises to the east. You can see all the way to Pikes Peak (14,115 feet) and the Sangre de Cristo Range. Down below lie the South Halfmoon and Arkansas Valleys and Twin Lakes.

When the current Rocky Mountains arose from the earth about 65 million years ago, mineral-rich liquid oozed into faults and cracks in the stressed rock. As the liquid cooled, rich ores formed. The Leadville area, located at the north end of the Arkansas Valley, has produced more than $500 million in silver, lead, zinc, gold, and other minerals. The Arkansas Valley is actually part of the Rio Grande Rift, a slice of land that stayed in place when the rest of Colorado rose about 5,000 feet, between 28 million and 5 million years ago. Glaciers later formed the cirque on Elbert's east side, while glacial moraines dammed Lake Creek, creating Twin Lakes. Mount Elbert itself is formed of 1.7-billion-year-old gneiss and schist.

Mount Elbert stood guardian as Leadville boomed first with gold, then with silver. In 1860, Abe Lee hit the first major gold strike. In 1874, as the gold dwindled, miners extracted silver-rich lead carbonate. The silver rush started, turning Leadville and surroundings into a large city, second to Denver. Enjoying prosperity, Leadville built a magnificent ice palace during the winter of 1896. It covered over three acres, with two 90-foot Norman towers. Inside, lighted dining rooms and an ice rink provided hours of entertainment. Ice sculptures of miners and prospectors decorated the palace.

The Hayden Survey of 1874 recorded the first ascent of Mount Elbert. The peak was named after Samuel Hitt Elbert, who first held the position of territorial secretary until the governor seized the state seal from him. Elbert resigned and left Colorado in 1866, only to return in 1873 as territorial governor. He held this post for one year before being appointed to the Colorado Supreme Court. Elbert was instrumental in formulating visionary conservation and irrigation concepts.

Hiking Mount Elbert is invariably an adventure. Snow falls at any time of year, and the temperature seldom exceeds 50°F. The wind always seems to blow. Plan ahead and be prepared for adverse conditions. Weekends find the trail filled with people. Yet there is nothing like standing at the top of Colorado, beholding an endless horizon of mountains.

The first section follows part of the Colorado Trail, which traverses almost 500 miles of the state. About 1.2 miles into the hike you come to a juncture. Turn right onto the North Mount Elbert Trail. In the next trail section, small groups of skinny lodgepole pines stand right in the middle of the trail, reminiscent of pictures with ski tracks each going on opposite sides of a tree. From here the trail climbs steeply to a ridge. The Forest Service rerouted this section in 1992, a great improvement over the old trail. Along the ridge a glimpse of the top comes into view. But it's really a false summit at about 13,880 feet—the real summit rises 550 feet higher.

Once above tree line, around 11,900 feet, the trail climbs through beautiful alpine tundra. The tiny plants are extremely fragile, so please stay on the trail. Yellow alpine avens, old-man-of-the-mountain with its large sunflower head, various paintbrushes, and blue-purple sky pilot brighten the surroundings. If stopping for a break on the tundra, watch out for marmots that might try to swipe your snack.

The trail is steepest along the right side of the false summit. Loose rocks and some big rock steps make this section challenging. After this part the trail becomes gentler. The summit lies beyond the next rock hump. The last 0.1 mile crosses a somewhat skinny ridge where the wind can blast with fury. Finally the summit appears, complete with short rock walls to shelter hikers from the winds. Remember to sign the peak register. Enjoy the view and the top of Colorado!

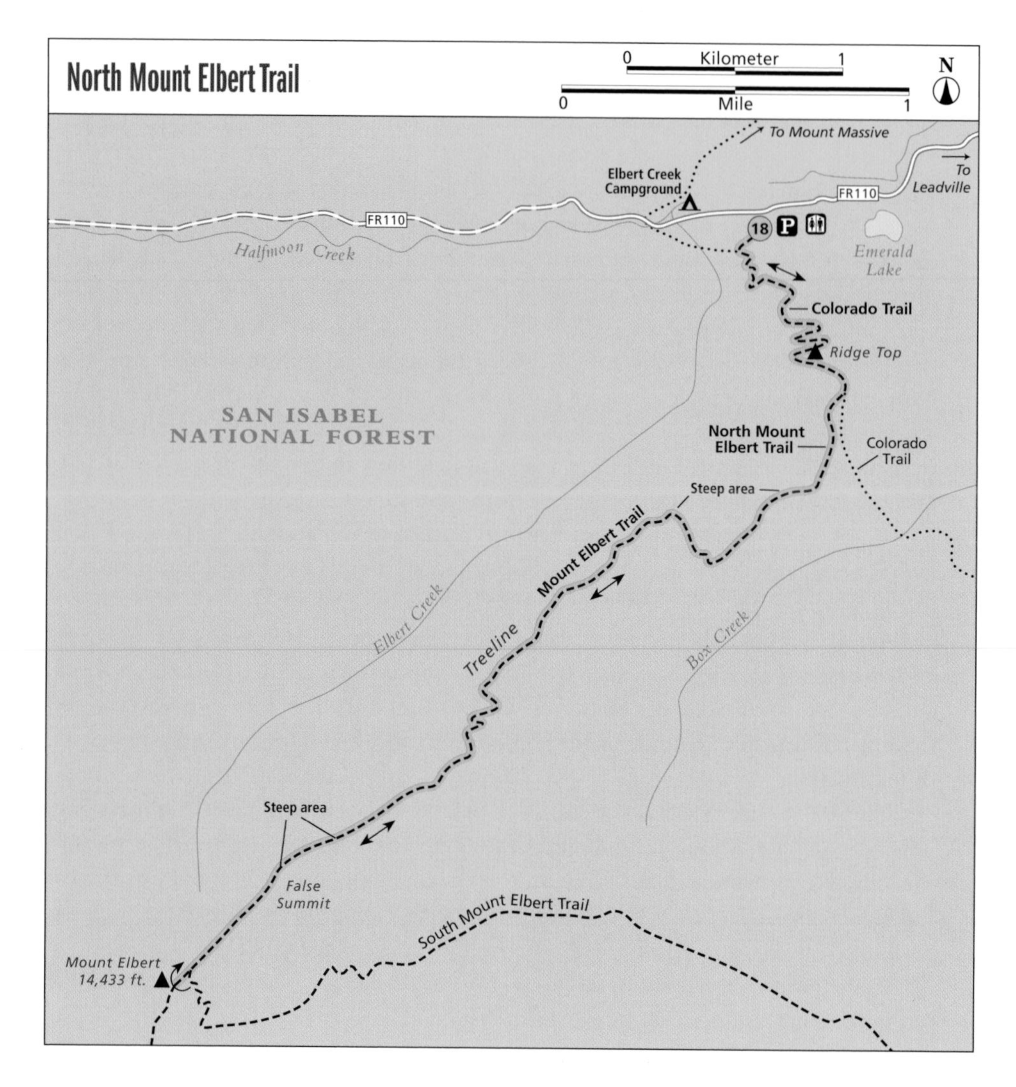

Miles and Directions

0.0 Start at Mount Elbert Trailhead near Elbert Creek Campground. Elevation: 10,040 feet.

0.1 Reach the junction with the Colorado Trail. Turn left onto the Colorado Trail.

0.9 Reach the top of a little ridge and descend slightly.

1.2 Reach the junction of the Colorado Trail and the North Mount Elbert Trail. GPS: N39 08.65' / W106 24.45'. Turn right to climb Mount Elbert.

2.2 Reach the northeast ridge.

2.9 Reach the tree line.

View of Elk Mountains from summit

4.4	Arrive at a false summit. GPS: N39 07.34' / W106 26.34'. Now there are two smaller false summits to go.
4.8	Reach the junction with the South Mount Elbert Trail, which comes in from the left. Continue straight ahead along the ridge.
4.9	You're on top! Elevation: 14,433 feet. GPS: N39 07.06' / W106 26.69'. Return the way you came.
9.8	Arrive back at the trailhead.

The Colorado Fourteeners Initiative (CFI) started in 1994 when people realized the damage being caused by the alarming popularity of climbing Colorado's fourteeners. An estimated 200,000 people climbed fourteeners annually by 2002, a 300 percent increase in ten years. By 2010 that number had risen to 500,000 hikers annually. CFI forms partnerships with land agencies, hiking groups, and companies to protect and preserve both natural and recreational resources.

19 Notch Mountain

This hike takes you to the historic stone shelter on Notch Mountain for a fantastic view of Mount of the Holy Cross. The trail starts gently, passing through spruce-fir forest with occasional glimpses of the notch in Notch Mountain. Eventually the trail climbs to tree line, then through tundra and boulder fields via switchbacks. Watch for pikas, white-tailed ptarmigans, marmots, and beautiful alpine wildflowers. The switchbacks make the hike easier than most trails up 13,000-foot peaks. Remember to leave early to reach the summit by 11 a.m. so you can head back by noon and avoid thunderstorms.

Start: From the Fall Creek Trailhead
Distance: 10.8 miles out and back
Approximate hiking time: 5 to 7 hours
Difficulty: Most difficult due to length and elevation gain
Elevation gain: 2,763 feet, plus about 120 feet in undulations
Seasons: Best from late June to mid-Oct
Trail surface: Dirt trail, very rocky in spots
Other trail users: Equestrians (Fall Creek Trail section) and hunters (in season)
Canine compatibility: Dogs must be on leash
Fees and permits: None. A free self-issued Wilderness Use Permit is required year-round for all users. One person in each group must carry a permit. Call the Holy Cross Ranger District for details. Group size limit: No more than 15 people per group with a maximum combination of 25 people and pack or saddle animals in any one group.
Maps: USGS Mount of the Holy Cross and Minturn; Nat Geo Trails Illustrated 126 Holy Cross/Ruedi Reservoir; Latitude 40° Vail & Eagle
Trail contacts: White River National Forest, Holy Cross Ranger District, Minturn; (970) 827-5715; www.fs.usda.gov/whiteriver
Other: The dirt access road may be bumpy with rocks and potholes. Most passenger cars can make the trip with care. The road is narrow, so be careful when rounding curves. The parking lot gets crowded early as the trailhead for Mount of the Holy Cross is also here. Half Moon Campground near the trailhead has seven campsites. Bring plenty of water with you.

Finding the trailhead: From Minturn, drive south on US 24 toward Leadville for about 3 miles (5 miles from the junction of I-70 and US 24). Just past mile marker 148, turn right onto Tigiwon Road (FR 707), which provides national forest access. Drive 8.1 miles up this dirt road to the trailhead. **GPS:** N39 30.02' / W106 25.94'

The Hike

In the 1800s various stories about a mountain with a "snowy cross" circulated around Colorado. In 1869 William H. Brewer reported seeing Mount of the Holy Cross (14,005 feet) from the summit of Grays Peak (14,269 feet). As part of the Hayden Survey in the 1870s, William Henry Jackson photographed various areas of Colorado. The Hayden Survey was one of four great surveys of the West sponsored by the US government between 1867 and 1878. From 1873 to 1875, expedition leader Ferdinand V. Hayden concentrated on Colorado.

Historic shelter and Mt. of the Holy Cross

The 1873 survey set a goal to find this mysterious peak. Jackson climbed Grays Peak and also spotted the cross from the summit. By August the survey group arrived near present-day Minturn. For three days they attempted in vain to find a route on Notch Mountain (13,237 feet) from which to view and photograph the "cross." Fallen trees and thick willows made the going too rough for pack animals, and the group ended up carrying Jackson's one hundred pounds of photographic gear on foot. Jackson used a wet glass plate camera. Not only was the "film" made of glass, which had to be handled carefully, but also it needed to be developed soon after exposure. Jackson carried a portable darkroom tent and all necessary chemicals and supplies with him. Finally finding an approach, the still-difficult hike took two days, with little food and no shelter. (The surveyors thought they could do it in one day.) Finally atop Notch Mountain, fog decreased visibility to a few feet. Luckily, the fog broke briefly, giving Jackson a glimpse of the infamous cross across the valley. The next morning dawned clear and still, giving him a beautiful shot of the cross. He took several pictures, which caused a sensation across the country as people believed the snow-filled cross to be a sign from God.

The devout began to make annual pilgrimages to Mount of the Holy Cross in 1927. The USDA Forest Service issued a special-use permit in 1928 to the Mount of the Holy Cross Pilgrimage Association, allowing the construction and maintenance of community houses and a semipublic campground. President Herbert Hoover proclaimed 1,392 acres around Mount of the Holy Cross as a national monument in 1929. Survey crews laid out an automobile route from US 24 to Tigiwon, and with help from citizens, the Eagle County government, and F. G. Bonfils, a road was completed to Tigiwon in 1932.

The Civilian Conservation Corps (CCC) improved the road in 1933, extending it to the present trailhead. The CCC also constructed the Notch Mountain Trail, the

WILDLIFE WATCHING ON NOTCH MOUNTAIN

Notch Mountain is a good area to see alpine animals and birds, particularly marmots, pikas, and white-tailed ptarmigan.

In summer ptarmigan blend in perfectly with the mottled rocks, making them hard to see. Members of the grouse family, the males live in the alpine tundra all year. Ptarmigan blend in to the landscape so well, it's possible to almost step on one before noticing it's there.

Ptarmigan mate for life, although after breeding the couple goes their separate ways until the next spring. In summer tiny chicks line up to follow around after mom. When threatened, the mother will fake a broken wing to draw predators away from her offspring.

In winter ptarmigan plumage turns white, with feet and legs heavily feathered for warmth and flotation on the snow. Willows, which produce next year's buds in the fall, provide food for ptarmigan during long, cold winters. The birds might dive into a snowdrift, especially around willows, to stay warm on cold nights—a ptarmigan version of an igloo. Look for piles of ptarmigan droppings near willows while hiking.

The pika lives in rock piles in the alpine and subalpine zones year-round. The pika alert reverberates through the rocks. Active during winter as well as summer, the pika eats hay piles it busily collects during the summer. The small, mouselike creature with the short tail belongs to the rabbit order. Look closely or you might miss the busy critter as it scurries among the rocks. A mouthful of grass and flowers whizzes by as the pika stores its hay. Researchers have discovered that pikas will steal each other's piles.

Watch for big white splotches on boulders along the trail. The splotches indicate pika restrooms. Bright orange lichen often grows near the splotches, energized by the nitrogen-rich fertilizer.

Please remember to keep your dog on leash to avoid confrontation with or disruption of the wildlife.

large community house at Tigiwon, and the stone shelter on Notch Mountain. The present Notch Mountain Trail, with its many switchbacks, stands as testimony to the excellent work done by the CCC. This trail was originally used by packhorses as well as hikers. Pilgrimages ceased in the early 1940s, presumably because of World War II. The US Army actually controlled much of this area between 1938 and 1950. Nearby Camp Hale was a training ground for the famous 10th Mountain Division troops.

The cross is created by a 1,500-foot vertical gully and a 750-foot horizontal rock bench on the mountain's eastern face. Collected snow causes the formation to stand out against the mountainside. The right arm later deteriorated due to rockslides, and access remained difficult even after the CCC's work. In 1950 President Harry Truman retracted national monument status and returned the land to the Forest Service. Even slightly damaged, a cross of snow still forms today. The Tigiwon Community House, after years of disrepair, has been mostly restored and is occasionally used for weddings. The Forest Service maintains the historic Notch Mountain stone shelter and its lightning rods to provide protection for hikers in case a thunderstorm moves in. Overnight camping is not allowed in the shelter.

Make sure to start on the Fall Creek Trail, not the Half Moon Trail. Just beyond the trailhead and creek crossing, take the right trail and head south, entering the Holy Cross Wilderness. The first mile is fairly gentle, but rocky. The trail then climbs, with occasional small elevation drops. The terrain drops steeply to the left, to Fall Creek below. After 2.4 miles the trail widens, with a scattering of boulders providing a perfect spot for a break before turning right up the Notch Mountain Trail.

From the rest spot it's another 3 miles to the shelter and viewpoint. After a few switchbacks the trail begins to pass through tree line and zigzags across the slope to the summit. More than twenty-seven switchbacks help you ascend the last 780 feet. Avoid the temptation to shortcut the switchbacks, as they keep the trail at a reasonable grade (which makes for easier hiking in the thinning air) and protect the terrain. Marmots and pikas zip around this area with amusing antics. Watch for white-tailed ptarmigan moms followed by a line of little chicks.

Once you reach the ridge and stone shelter, Mount of the Holy Cross looms large directly ahead. The alpine wildflowers grow thick and beautiful in July and early August. White arctic gentians signal summer's end. Please walk carefully on the fragile tundra, using rocks for steps as much as possible. And if you must camp, do it below tree line.

Miles and Directions

0.0 Start at the Fall Creek Trailhead (versus the Half Moon Trailhead). Elevation: 10,314 feet. Cross a creek on a bridge and take the right fork in the trail (heading south).

1.4 The trail traverses a landslide area.

1.6 Cross a wide creek on boulders. (***Note:*** The crossing may be easier or harder depending on water volume. Be careful.)

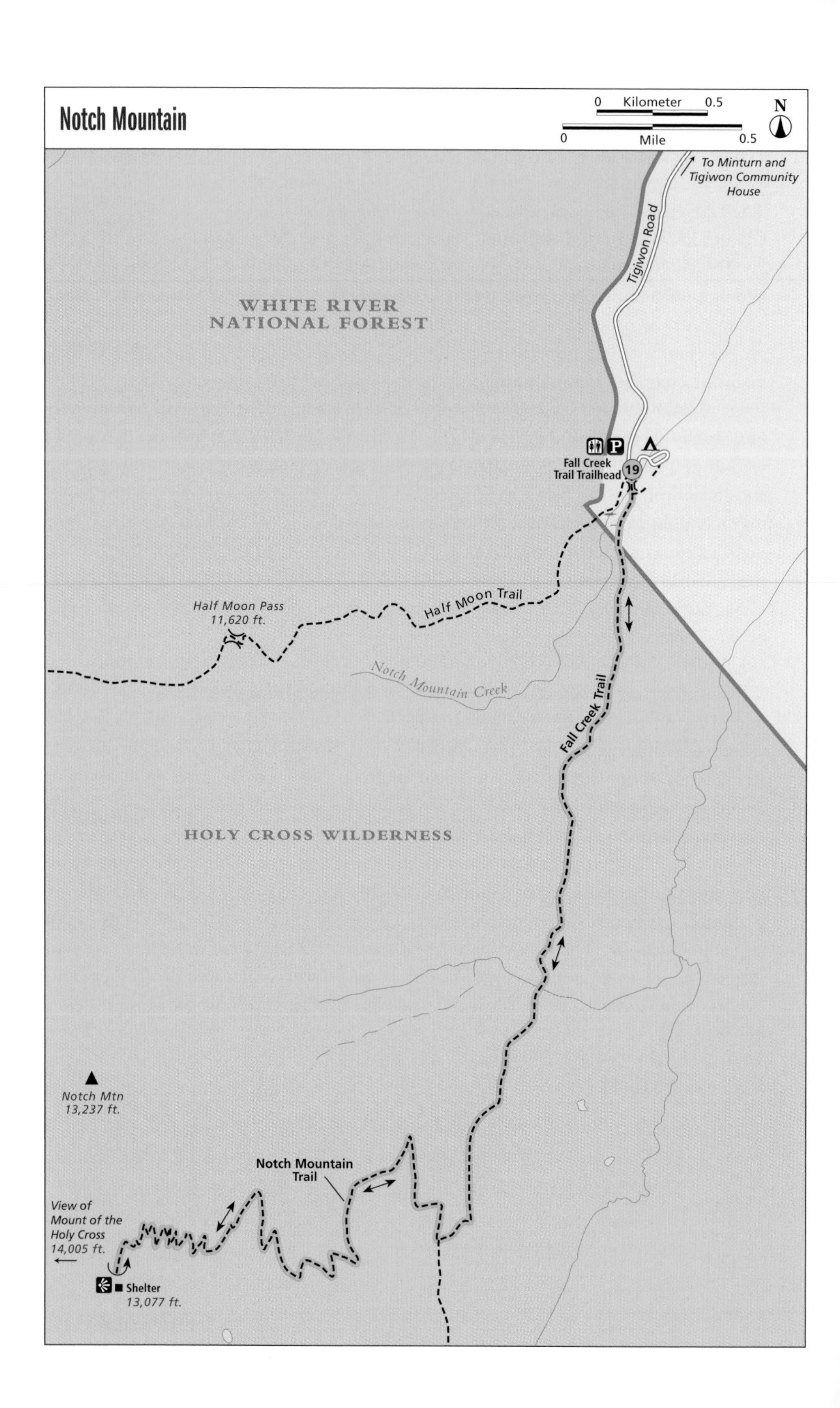
Notch Mountain
0 Kilometer 0.5
0 Mile 0.5
N
To Minturn and Tigiwon Community House
Tigiwon Road
WHITE RIVER NATIONAL FOREST
Fall Creek Trail Trailhead
19
Half Moon Pass 11,620 ft.
Half Moon Trail
Notch Mountain Creek
Fall Creek Trail
HOLY CROSS WILDERNESS
Notch Mtn 13,237 ft.
Notch Mountain Trail
View of Mount of the Holy Cross 14,005 ft.
Shelter 13,077 ft.

BENEFITS OF LEASHING YOUR DOG

Keeping dogs leashed on the trail benefits you, your pet, other visitors, and wildlife. Dogs will surely come out the losers in a bout with the porcupines and mountain lions that live in these areas. Bears have also been known to chase dogs back to their owners. Freely roaming dogs can cause serious damage to delicate ecosystems. A leashed dog can also help you become more aware of wildlife, as dogs can easily detect smells and movement that would go unnoticed by humans.

2.4 Reach the trail intersection with Notch Mountain and Fall Creek Trails. GPS: N39 28.26' / W106 26.52'. This is a good place for a break. Turn right onto Notch Mountain Trail.

3.5 Start to enter the land above the trees. (***Note:*** Turn back if thunderstorms are imminent.)

4.2 Switchbacks increase in number up to the ridge. Depending on where you start counting, you'll zigzag up more than twenty switchbacks in 780 feet. (***Note:*** Please do not shortcut the switchbacks. Shortcutting causes environmental damage and erosion that does not heal quickly at this elevation. Also, don't attempt this trail during whiteouts or low visibility. If you miss any of four particular switchbacks, you'll be freefalling over a cliff.)

5.4 Reach the stone shelter on Notch Mountain, with a breathtaking view of Mount of the Holy Cross. Elevation: 13,077 feet. GPS: N39 28.17' / W106 27.52'. (***Note:*** The shelter is meant for protection from lightning. Overnight camping is prohibited.) Return the way you came.

10.8 Arrive back at the trailhead.

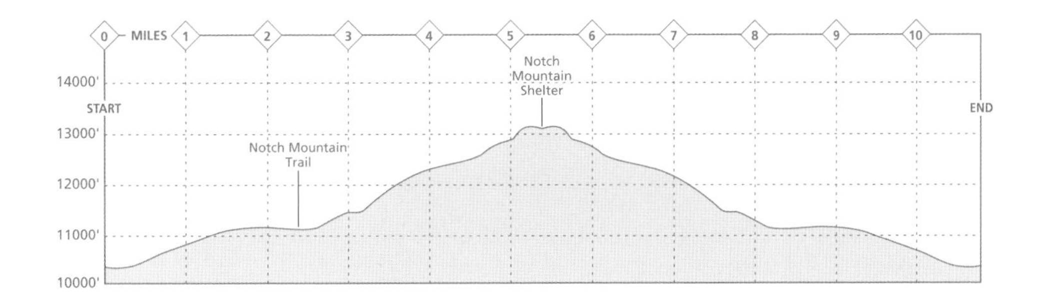

20 Mount Thomas Trail

The Mount Thomas summit, a bump on Red Table Mountain, offers spectacular 360-degree views of the central Colorado Rockies! Overwhelming views stretch from the Maroon Bells and Elk Mountains in the southwest, circling northwest to the Flat Tops, then I-70 north of Eagle. The Gore Range rises in the northeast, with the Sawatch Mountains towering in the east and southeast. Cattle still graze on some of the grassy southern slopes. Beautiful alpine wildflowers decorate the upper ridges. The trail traverses an open ridge for about 1.6 miles, so be sure to make the summit and be heading down before thunderstorms hit.

Start: 0.5 mile from the top of Crooked Creek Pass at the junction with FR 431
Distance: 9.2 miles out and back
Approximate hiking time: 4 to 7 hours
Difficulty: Difficult due to elevation gain and distance
Elevation gain/loss: 1,197-foot gain/370-foot loss
Seasons: Best from late June to mid-Oct
Trail surface: Dirt road and dirt trail with some steep sections and a boulder field
Other trail users: Equestrians and hunters (in season)
Canine compatibility: Dogs must be under control
Fees and permits: None
Maps: USGS Crooked Creek Pass; Nat Geo Trails Illustrated 126 Holy Cross/Ruedi Reservoir; Latitude 40° Vail & Eagle
Trail contacts: White River National Forest, Eagle Ranger District, Eagle; (970) 328-6388. White River National Forest, Sopris Ranger District, Aspen; (970) 963-2266; www.fs.usda.gov/whiteriver
Other: In winter the access road is closed by snow just past Sylvan Lake State Park, 5.5 miles from the trailhead. The road is used by snowmobilers and cross-country skiers. The trail is neither maintained nor marked for winter use.

Finding the trailhead: From I-70 (exit 147) in Eagle, head south about 0.3 mile to US 6 and turn right in the traffic circle. Drive 1 mile, following the SYLVAN LAKE signs to a second traffic circle just past mile marker 149. You basically turn left via the traffic circle onto Sylvan Lakes Road. Continue 1.7 miles and turn right onto Brush Creek Road (Eagle CR 307). Drive about 8.8 miles to the fork in the road. Take the right branch, West Brush Creek (smooth dirt road), again to Sylvan Lake. Drive another 10 miles to the top of Crooked Creek Pass. The dirt road narrows and becomes FR 400 past Sylvan Lake State Park. You can park in the dirt area to the right at the top of the pass (add 1 mile round-trip to the hike mileage). Or, at the top of the pass, turn right onto an unmarked dirt road and drive 0.5 mile to the junction with FR 431. Park on the flat grassy area at the junction. **GPS:** N39 26.34' / W106 41.10'. With a 4WD you can drive 0.2 mile from the junction with FR 431 to the actual trailhead and park under the power lines.

The Hike

Mount Thomas (11,977 feet) was named after the head of the St. Louis & Colorado Smelting Company. Thomas (the rest of his name apparently lost to history) started a smelter along the Colorado Midland Railroad in the Fryingpan Valley around 1890.

Summit cairn on Mt. Thomas

The town that grew nearby, Thomasville, also bears his name. He became involved in some mining ventures north of town in the Lime Creek drainage. He did not have much luck—the mines produced little ore and his unprofitable smelter closed in 1892. A little peak on the ridge between Lime and Brush Creeks commemorates his involvement in the area. The ridge itself is known as Red Table Mountain.

Grassy meadows provide good grazing for cattle in the Lime Creek drainage. When settlers arrived in Colorado in the late 1800s, cattle and sheep grazed freely on public lands. Ranchers and sheepherders ran as much stock as possible, damaging many acres across the West through overgrazing. The Taylor Grazing Act of 1934 created grazing districts to minimize the degradation of public lands. Today the USDA Forest Service grants grazing permits on the lands under its management. A rancher may hold several grazing allotments in an area. With guidance from the Forest Service, the rancher moves his herd at designated times, rotating cattle to different areas. Rotation has several benefits: The cattle continue to have fresh grass to eat; the grass in any given area is not totally consumed and has time to recover and stay healthy; and fences help keep cattle in designated areas. The rancher holding the grazing allotments is responsible for maintaining the fences. In the Lime Creek area, "lay down" fences are common. After the cattle leave the high country in the fall, the rancher lets the fences down. This practice prevents snow damage. In spring trees downed by winter snows and winds are removed from the fence line, the fences are set up again, and cattle are brought back to the grassy slopes. The rancher also helps maintain the hiking and other trails, which his cattle use.

During the hike you may come across herds of cattle. They will not bother you and will just move up or off the trail as you approach. Please restrain dogs and do not harass the herd. Part of this area is currently (as of late 2010) being managed as a recommended wilderness area.

From the junction with FR 431, the hike follows a rough 4WD road, climbing steadily up to the trailhead located under some power lines. The turnoff to the trailhead is not marked, so follow the cues in the Miles and Directions carefully. A deep, thick, spruce-fir forest surrounds the trail, creating a dark primeval atmosphere where the appearance of elves and gnomes would hardly be surprising. Slip past the forest spirits into an open meadow with an airy view of the Lime Creek drainage. The trail winds between small stands of conifers and open, flower-covered meadows.

The trail continues up to a ridge and follows the north side. Below, the town of Eagle sits in the distance, with Sylvan Lake in the foreground. Catch a breather on a level area in the trees before negotiating an interesting skinny ridge. Red boulder fields drape the ridge to the north and south. The trail is tricky here, with a slippery climb up the next ridge. As the trail enters open meadow at tree line, the views are incredible. The Maroon Bells (Maroon Peak and North Maroon Peak), Pyramid, Snowmass, and Capitol peaks rear their 14,000-foot heads to the southwest.

The trail traverses below the ridge to the south side. After attaining the ridge again, turn right and hike to the red rock Mount Thomas summit. The rocks are the Maroon Formation, the same rocks that comprise the famous Maroon Bells near Aspen. This formation eroded from the Ancestral Rockies in western Colorado. As sediments were buried by streams, a rustlike stain formed, creating the red color. There is no official trail to the top, but it's easy to find the way. Views in every direction include the Gore Range, the Flat Tops, Mount Sopris near Carbondale, the Holy Cross Wilderness, and the peaks mentioned above.

Keep an eye out for thunderstorms. The ridge is no place to be if lightning is flashing or approaching. Enjoy a picnic lunch and return the way you came.

Miles and Directions

0.0 Start at the junction with FR 431. Walk uphill on the rough 4WD road to the left. Elevation: 10,150 feet.

0.2 A side road heads to the right by some power lines. Turn right here and walk uphill. Follow the road as it curves left. The Mount Thomas (Trail 1870) Trailhead is on the right. GPS: N39 26.18' / W106 41.00'.

0.6 The trail enters a meadow. (***Note:*** Beautiful views of the Lime Creek drainage.)

1.3 The trail starts to switchback up the ridge.

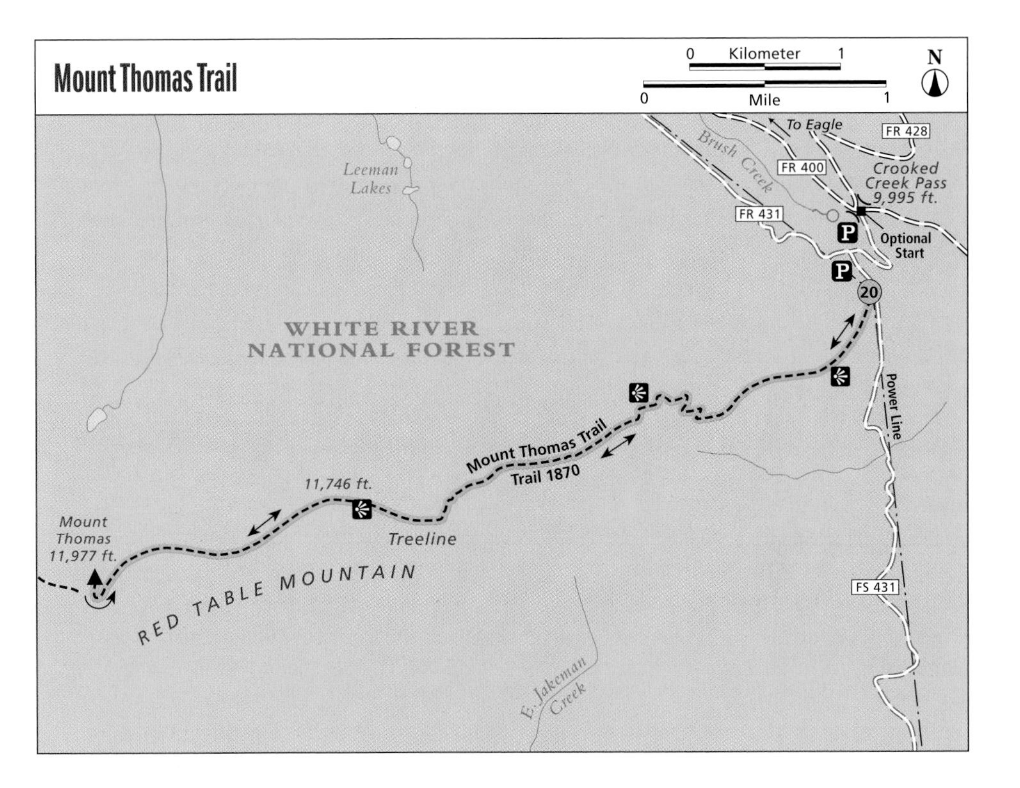

2.0 The trail crosses some meadows. Cairns mark the route.

2.6 Pass a sign at the boundary of the recommended wilderness area. GPS: N39 25.51' / W106 42.85'. The trail climbs steeply up the ridge. Red boulder fields lie on both sides of the trail.

3.0 The trail is now above tree line. It is fairly easy to find and is marked by cairns.

3.2 The trail crosses a hump on Red Table Mountain and descends a little from here. (***Note:*** Awesome views of the Maroon Bells are to the southwest.)

4.0 The trail leaves the ridge to traverse along the south side through a boulder field.

4.5 At a big cairn, turn right up the ridge to the summit of Mount Thomas. GPS: N39 25.12' / W106 44.59'. There's no trail, but there are some open areas between the krummholz (stunted trees) to walk on. Continue up a boulder field to the top.

4.6 Reach the Mount Thomas summit. Elevation: 11,977 feet. GPS: N39 25.19' / W106 44.58' Return the way you came.

9.2 Arrive back at the trailhead.

21 Granite Lakes Trail

The Granite Lakes Trail first wanders along the Fryingpan River, meandering up and down through thick forest and around some interesting granitic formations. The first 3.3 miles are fairly gentle. Turning up the Granite Creek drainage, the trail climbs steadily, and often steeply, to Lower Granite Lake, tucked in a bench above Granite Creek. Upper Granite Lake is about 0.75 mile farther along a fairly gentle path. Once in the subalpine zone, the wildflowers and views are beautiful. Backpack in—don't forget supplies for your dog—and take an extra day or two to explore this beautiful and quiet area.

Start: From the Granite Lakes (Trail 1922) Trailhead
Distance: 13.6-miles out and back
Approximate hiking time: 8 to 12 hours (recommended 2- to 3-day backpack)
Difficulty: Most difficult due to elevation gain, length, and altitude
Elevation gain: 2,930 feet, plus some small undulations
Seasons: Best from late June to mid-Oct
Trail surface: Dirt trail, sometimes steep
Other trail users: Equestrians, anglers, hunters (in season)
Canine compatibility: Dogs must be on leash
Fees and permits: None. Group size limit: No more than 15 people per group with a maximum combination of 25 people and pack or saddle animals in any one group.
Maps: USGS Nast and Mount Champion; Nat Geo Trails Illustrated 126 Holy Cross/Ruedi Reservoir and 127 Aspen/Independence Pass; Latitude 40° Crested Butte, Aspen, Gunnison
Trail contacts: White River National Forest, Sopris Ranger District, Carbondale; (970) 963-2266; www.fs.usda.gov/whiteriver
Other: Water from streams and lakes must be treated.

Finding the trailhead: From Basalt, drive east on Fryingpan River Road (FS 105) about 31 miles (paved all the way) to a sign on the right that says NAST LAKE, GRANITE LAKES TRAIL TRAILHEAD. Turn right and drive down a dirt road about 0.9 mile and cross the Fryingpan River bridge. On the other side of the bridge to the right is a parking area and the trailhead. Be sure to park here and not drive any farther. There are no facilities here. Walk down the road to the Fryingpan River Ranch–the trail continues on the left past the mailboxes. Please stay on the trail and respect private property.
GPS: N39 17.88' / W106 36.31'

The Hike

Several stories recount the naming of the Fryingpan River. In one version several miners ran across the mountains from a river drainage to escape angry Utes, only to find more Utes camped on the other side. One miner commented that it was like "jumping from the frying pan into the fire." The river from which they ran became known as the Fryingpan. Another account reports trappers being attacked by Utes, with only two trappers surviving. One left his wounded companion in a nearby cave and hung a frying pan in a tree so he could find his buddy when he returned with help. Henry Gannet, one of the leaders of the Hayden Survey, officially named the river.

Upper Granite Lake

For many years the Ute Indians hunted game in the Fryingpan and Roaring Fork River valleys. As miners swarmed over the area and homesteaders established ranches and farms, the Utes were forced from their cherished homelands. Mines were located near Meredith and Thomasville around 1882, but the ore soon played out. Other mines near Aspen were booming, but transportation proved to be an expensive nightmare. A race developed between railroad companies to provide rail service to Aspen and Glenwood Springs. The Colorado Midland Railway Company decided to build a railroad from Colorado Springs through Leadville and on to Aspen. The route tunneled through the Sawatch Range and down the Fryingpan River to its intersection with the Roaring Fork River. By November 1887 the railroad arrived at Aspen Junction, presently the town of Basalt.

As settlers moved into the area, they harvested its many resources. Some people provided elk and deer meat to the railroad workers and miners. By 1890 eight sawmills reportedly operated along the Fryingpan River, supplying lumber for building railroads, homes, buildings, and mine tunnels.

Even back in the 1890s, the Fryingpan valley had earned a reputation as a sportsman's paradise, with large herds of elk and deer and abundant trout in lakes and streams. In the early 1900s Arthur Hanthorn and James Morris built a tourist resort with a large lodge and several other buildings near the Nast railroad siding.

The mountains in the Fryingpan valley area became part of the Holy Cross Forest Reserve in 1905. Len Shoemaker served as a forest ranger in the area for about twenty years and in 1958 wrote a book, *Roaring Fork Valley,* in which he relates interesting historical tidbits. In 1918 the last Colorado Midland Railway train ran the Fryingpan route. The sawmills closed soon thereafter, and the Fryingpan River valley returned to a quieter existence.

In 1978 Congress designated the Hunter-Fryingpan Wilderness, named after two of its drainages. When the area around Mount Massive (14,421 feet) was considered for wilderness designation, Congress intended to include it in the Hunter-Fryingpan. An oversight, however, created a separate Mount Massive Wilderness in 1980. The Spruce Creek drainage was added to the Hunter-Fryingpan in 1993, for a total of 82,729 acres.

The first part of the hike crosses Mountain Nast Community, home to the private Fryingpan River Ranch and several summer cabins. Please respect the rights of property owners by staying on the trail. You'll pass through a few meadows, sometimes close to the creek, then enter thick forest. The trail crosses many small creeks while weaving up and down around various granitic formations. The Forest Service has worked on the trail with the help of Colorado Rocky Mountain School and others. Take time to appreciate their work in boggy areas. Part of the task of keeping an area pristine involves maintaining trails to avoid environmental damage. Volunteer and youth groups play an important role by helping the Forest Service with trail projects.

In about 3.3 miles the trail intersects the Fryingpan Lakes Trail. Taking a right turn, the Granite Lakes Trail climbs steeply out of the valley. The trail occasionally levels out, giving you a chance for a breather. Granite Creek cascades nearby, forming small waterfalls and interesting waterslides. At 5 miles the trail enters a beautiful meadow with sweeping views up the valley. After crossing Granite Creek twice, you begin climbing again.

Granite Lakes are nestled on a bench above Granite Creek. Trout jump and swim in the clear waters of Lower Granite Lake. The trail to the upper lake crosses flower-filled meadows. If you're backpacking, remember to camp at least 100 feet away from the lakes, streams, and trail. By making yourself less obvious, you and others can fully enjoy the peace and solitude.

Miles and Directions

0.0 Start at the Granite Lakes (Trail 1922) Trailhead by Nast Lake. Elevation: 8,700 feet. Please sign the trailhead register and read up-to-date regulations on the bulletin board.

0.2 Arrive at Fryingpan River Ranch. Walk on the road to the left past the mailboxes for Mountain Nast Community.

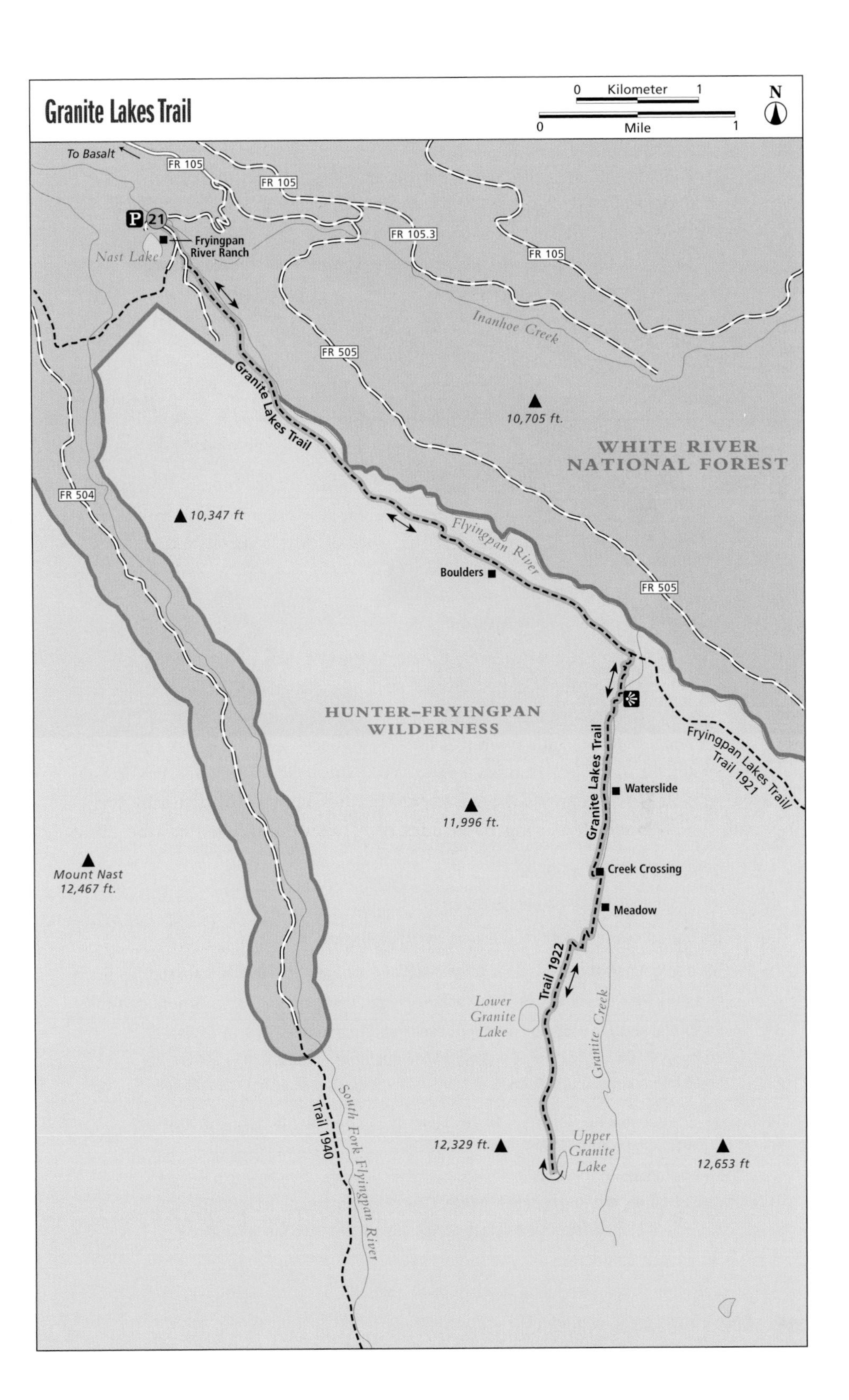

Granite Lakes Trail
0 Kilometer 1
0 Mile 1
N
To Basalt
FR 105
FR 105
FR 105.3
FR 105
FR 505
FR 505
FR 504
21
P
Fryingpan River Ranch
Nast Lake
Inanhoe Creek
Granite Lakes Trail
10,705 ft.
WHITE RIVER NATIONAL FOREST
10,347 ft
Flyingpan River
Boulders
HUNTER–FRYINGPAN WILDERNESS
Fryingpan Lakes Trail/ Trail 1921
Granite Lakes Trail
Waterslide
11,996 ft.
Mount Nast 12,467 ft.
Creek Crossing
Meadow
Trail 1922
Lower Granite Lake
Granite Creek
Trail 1940
South Fork Flyingpan River
12,329 ft.
Upper Granite Lake
12,653 ft

Waterslide in Granite Creek

0.3 Granite Lakes Trail turns left off the road. Follow the trail to the left along the river. GPS: N39 17.70' / W106 36.15'

1.2 Reach the wilderness area boundary sign.

1.5 The trail comes very close to a U-curve on the Fryingpan River.

2.3 The trail wanders through various granitic boulders and rock formations. Watch out for cairns marking the trail in rocky areas.

3.3 Reach the junction with the Fryingpan Lakes Trail. Elevation: 9,480 feet. GPS: N39 16.05' / W106 33.73'. This is a good place for a break. Turn right onto the Granite Lakes Trail and head uphill. The trail starts to switchback steeply not too far from here.

4.3 To the left is a waterslide down smooth granite.

5.0 The trail comes to a beautiful meadow and goes downstream a little to a Granite Creek crossing over big boulders. (***Note:*** Creek crossing can be tricky.) GPS: N39 15.10' / W106 33.88'. In a few feet you'll cross another little creek. Continue across the meadow, staying right of a big boulder in the meadow. There's a cairn near the trees.

5.1 Cross Granite Creek again. You now leave Granite Creek and climb uphill to a bench above the drainage. The trail switchbacks steeply in spots (again).

5.7 The trail climbs more gently through some wetter areas and more open areas.

6.0 The trail crosses a little creek. Turn right at the cairn. (***Note:*** Remember this spot on the way back as it's easy to miss.) Reach Lower Granite Lake. Elevation: about 11,400 feet. GPS: N39 14.50' / W106 34.22'

6.2 Come to a meadow with a view. Cross a little flat area.

6.4 Come to a creek crossing with lots of tree stumps. The trail is a little hard to find, but there are some cairns. Keep heading across the open area, slightly uphill. (***Note:*** Look behind for a good view of the Sawatch Range.) Come to a little flat area. The trail will drop down to the upper lake.

6.8 Reach Upper Granite Lake. Elevation: 11,600 feet. GPS: N39 13.87' / W106 34.15'. Return the way you came.

13.6 Arrive back at the trailhead.

When camping with your dog, be ready and willing to clean up after Fido. Bury his fecal matter as you bury yours. Plan where your dog will sleep. Most backpackers keep their dogs in the tent at night. Be sure your dog wears a tag that allows a finder of a lost dog to be a returner.

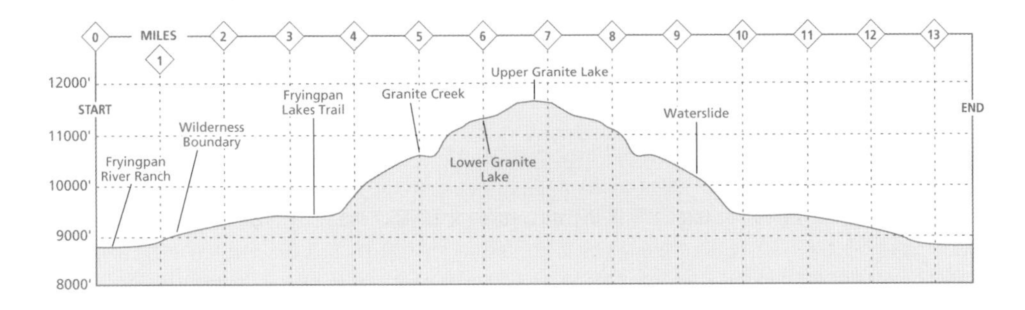

22 Silver Creek Trail

Silver Creek Trail starts out on closed logging roads, rising slightly to the Sarvis Creek Wilderness boundary. From here the trail mostly heads downhill, with a few uphills for variety. Silver Creek is a sparkling, crystal-clear stream, very worthy of its name. Interesting granitic formations appear occasionally on the north side of the trail. Lodgepole pine, Engelmann spruce, subalpine fir, aspen, and eventually ponderosa pine trees line the trail. This area is great for a quiet getaway, except during hunting season, which starts at the end of August.

Start: From the east Silver Creek (Trail 1106) Trailhead on Red Dirt Road
Distance: 12.4 miles point to point (with opportunities for camping and an out-and-back return)
Approximate hiking time: 5 to 8 hours
Difficulty: Difficult due to length
Elevation gain/loss: About 300-foot gain/2,060-foot loss (plus little undulations)
Seasons: Best from mid-June through Oct
Trail surface: Dirt trail
Other trail users: Equestrians and hunters (in season)
Canine compatibility: Dogs must be under control
Fees and permits: None. Group size limit: No more than 15 people per group with a maximum combination of 25 people and pack or saddle animals in any one group. Camping and campfires are prohibited within 100 feet of all streams and trails.
Maps: USGS Gore Mountain, Tyler Mountain, and Green Ridge; Nat Geo Trails Illustrated 119 Yampa/Gore Pass
Trail contacts: Medicine Bow-Routt National Forest, Yampa Ranger District, Yampa; (970) 638-4516; www.fs.usda.gov/mbr/
Other: FR 100 is closed by winter snow about 14 miles from the trailhead. The trail is neither maintained nor marked for winter use.

Finding the trailhead: *With shuttle:* These directions assume you would like to hike mostly downhill. From Yampa, drive 8 miles north on CO 131 to Routt CR 14. Turn right onto RCR 14 and drive about 3.5 miles to RCR 16. Turn right onto RCR 16, following the LYNX PASS signs. Drive 1.6 miles, then turn left by some condo buildings to stay on RCR 16. In 1.3 miles, turn right, and continue on RCR 16 for another 5.4 miles. The trailhead is past mile marker 8, on the left side. There is parking on the left by the trailhead. Leave one car here. Continue south about 13.5 miles on RCR 16, which becomes FR 270, to Gore Pass Road (CO 134). Turn left onto CO 134 and drive 3.1 miles east to FR 250. Turn left onto FR 250. At the first fork, stay left. At all junctions, stay on FR 250, driving for 11.1 miles to Red Dirt Road (FR 100). The last mile of FR 250 is a little rough, and low-clearance vehicles should go very slowly. Turn left onto Red Dirt Road (FR 100). Drive 5 miles north. The trailhead is on the left side of the road, past mile marker 11. You can camp near the east trailhead—remember to stay at least 100 feet from streams, trails, and the road. There are no facilities at either trailhead. **GPS:** N40 11.87' / W106 36.36'

Without shuttle: These directions assume you would like to hike mostly downhill. From Kremmling, drive west and north on US 40 about 6 miles to CO 134/Gore Pass Road. Turn left onto Gore Pass Road and drive about 4.2 miles west to Red Dirt Road (FR 100). At the first two forks, stay right. At the third fork at FR 101 (also Grand CR 191), around mile 4.8, stay left. In another 1.7 miles, reach FR 250 and stay right. Follow the signs for Buffalo Park. The trailhead is on the left side of the road, about 11.6 miles from Gore Pass Road.

The Hike

Silver Creek Trail traverses the southern part of the Sarvis Creek Wilderness, designated by Congress in 1993. This wilderness is unique because it is not composed of "rocks and ice" like so many other national forest wilderness areas in Colorado. Although heavily forested, its pristine and primitive nature qualified it for wilderness status.

The Sarvis Timber Company harvested trees in the Service Creek area in the mid-1910s using portable mills. Old-timers insist the area's original name was Sarvis. Some mapmaker, however, decided that "sarvis" was a common mispronunciation of the word "service" and placed the name "Service Creek" on the map. The wilderness area designation tried to right the incorrect spelling by using Sarvis.

The Civilian Conservation Corps (CCC) built much of the Silver Creek Trail. After the 1929 stock market crash and subsequent depression, 13.6 million Americans were unemployed by 1933. That year Congress passed the Emergency Conservation Work Act, creating what became known as the CCC. Young, unemployed, unmarried men between the ages of eighteen and twenty-five were eligible to join. Conservation of natural resources—reforestation, forest fire fighting, erosion control, trail building and maintenance, development of state parks, and other public works—became the CCC's mission. The US Army built camps, the government furnished food and clothing, and the Departments of the Interior and Agriculture provided work projects and leadership. Each man earned $30 per month, of which $25 was sent home to his family.

The CCC is credited with building 46,854 bridges, 3,116 fire lookout towers, and 318,076 dams to help with erosion control, plus numerous buildings and trails. By 1937 the CCC employed more than 500,000 young men, working on projects all over the United States. The army operated more than 2,500 camps to house all the workers.

The men of the CCC performed excellent work. According to Forest Service personnel, the CCC workers who built the Silver Creek Trail created one that is easy to maintain. It has great drainage, rolling dips, and cribbed walls. Moss now covers the rock walls, making them difficult to see.

From the east trailhead, the hike follows several old logging roads, now closed to motorized travel. The trail gradually gains elevation to the wilderness boundary, which is nearly the highest point of the trail. From here you drop into the Silver Creek drainage, with marshy meadows hidden behind trees to the south. The granite rocks along the trail take on some interesting shapes. After crossing a marshy section, the remains of a log cabin rest on the left. The former occupants are unknown, but the notched logs still show careful work by the cabin's builder. "Shiprock" sticks up its prow to the right a little farther down the trail. Colorful aspens frame the boulders in the fall.

As you round a ridge, check out the view down the drainage. The various lumps and cliffs of rock are composed of Precambrian granite (quartz monzonite). Precambrian

Bend in Silver Creek

rocks formed over 600 million years ago when molten magma oozed up into other rocks, cooled slowly, and became the granite you see today. Granite tends to erode like an onion peels, hence some of the rounded shapes. The red trees, or ghost trees, were killed by mountain pine beetles in the 1990s and early 2000s. Although these tiny insects are part of the natural forest cycle, they reproduced in epidemic proportions due to drought, which weakened trees, making them more susceptible to the beetles. Very cold winters kill many beetles, but winters have been relatively mild. Treating the acres of trees involved became impossible. Be aware that these dead trees can fall at any time, particularly in high winds. Park your car and place your tent away from them. Be careful while hiking too, and keep your dog with you on the trail here.

Sometimes Silver Creek runs swiftly down a tiny canyon, leaping over little cascades. Other times it broadens and sparkles in the sun. Deep pools attract fish—sit and watch for a while. Some good campsites can be found up on low ridges to the north of the trail—an appropriate 200-plus feet from the trail and creek, but close enough to fetch water easily. While you hike and camp, remember to use your Leave No Trace skills!

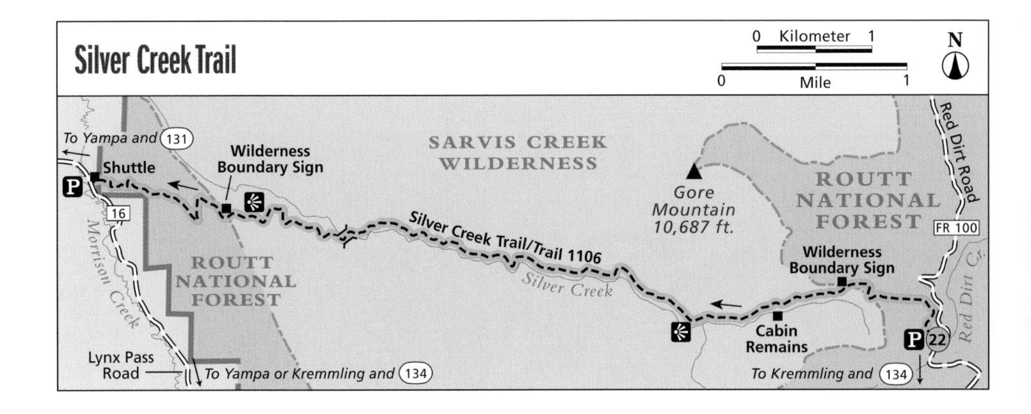

About two-thirds of the way into the hike, the trail crosses Silver Creek at a wide spot. The trail then swings away from the creek and eventually traverses a steep slope, leaving the creek far below. After topping the ridge, you drop down on south- and west-facing slopes. The vegetation changes here, adapting to the dryness and heat. Ponderosa pines, Gambel oaks, sagebrush, and grasses replace the lodgepole and spruce-fir forest.

This area is very popular during hunting season. Bow and black powder hunters are plentiful during September. Be considerate and wear some blaze-orange clothing and tie a bright orange bandanna around your dog's neck.

Miles and Directions

- 0.0 Start at the east Silver Creek (Trail 1106) Trailhead, by the bulletin board. Elevation: 9,730 feet. Walk back to the road, turn left, and walk up the road, over the creek to the trail.
- 0.1 Silver Creek Trail starts to the left of the road at the big mounds of dirt used to close the old logging road to motorized vehicles. Hike up the dirt mound onto the doubletrack Silver Creek Trail.
- 1.5 The trail forks; turn left and walk up the old logging road.
- 1.6 Reach the wilderness boundary sign. Elevation: 9,840 feet. GPS: N40 12.37' / W106 37.47'
- 2.5 The cabin remains are on the left. GPS: N40 12.19' / W106 38.37'
- 3.6 Round a ridge with a good view down the Silver Creek drainage.
- 8.0 Cross Silver Creek. Elevation: 8,900 feet. GPS: N40 12.86' / W106 43.48'. (***Note:*** Be careful in early summer when the creek runs high. The current may be swift.)
- 10.2 Reach the wilderness boundary sign. GPS: N40 13.02' / W106 45.08'
- 11.5 Top a ridge and begin the final descent to the west trailhead.

11.6 The trail forks; stay to the left (actually go straight downhill as there's a viewpoint off to the right).

12.3 Reach the Silver Creek west trailhead bulletin board. If you're coming up from this direction, please stop to read up-to-date area information. (***Note:*** From here to the trailhead parking, you'll be on private property. The Forest Service has permission for the trail to cross here. Please respect the private property!)

12.4 Arrive at the west Silver Creek Trailhead. Elevation: 7,960 feet. GPS: N40 13.33' / W106 46.73'

◀ *Rocks that look like Legos*

23 Kelly Lake

Beautiful Kelly Lake sits snuggled in a glacial basin between a high ridge to the west and the craggy Medicine Bow Mountains to the east. Overnight backpacking is the best way to explore this pleasant area, but don't rule out a long day hike to visit this little jewel. The trail starts out on logging roads through meadows, crosses two forks of the Canadian River, and passes through old timber cuts. The middle section of the hike travels on logging roads and singletrack trail. The final section is singletrack, gaining elevation to a scenic high alpine valley full of wildflowers.

Start: From the trailhead at the end of Jackson CR 41
Distance: 13.6 miles out and back
Approximate hiking time: 7 to 9 hours
Difficulty: Most difficult due to length
Elevation gain/loss: 2,545-foot gain/400-foot loss
Seasons: Best from July through Sept
Trail surface: Dirt trail, rocky in a few areas
Other trail users: Equestrians and mountain bikers, snowmobiles in winter
Canine compatibility: Dogs must be on leash
Fees and permits: Daily entrance fee or annual parks pass required
Maps: USGS Gould, Johnny Moore Mountain, and Rawah Lakes; Nat Geo Trails Illustrated 114 Walden/Gould and 112 Poudre River/Cameron Pass
Trail contacts: State Forest State Park, 56750 Highway 14, Walden; (970) 723-8366; http://parks.state.co.us/Parks/StateForest
Other: Campfires are prohibited in the backcountry, so bring a stove. If you're backpacking, please sign the trailhead register. Remember to treat any water from streams and lakes before drinking.

Finding the trailhead: From Walden, drive 19.2 miles east on CO 14 to the KOA Campground and entrance to State Forest State Park. Turn left onto Jackson CR 41, drive 0.2 mile to the entrance station, and pay the fee. Continue driving on JCR 41 for 8.4 miles, past several turnoffs (4WD roads, campgrounds, and picnic areas). Watch for cattle and moose along the road. Arrive at the loop at the end of JCR 41. Parking is on the west side, along with a vault toilet. The trail starts at the northeast end of the loop. Bring your own water as none is available at the trailhead. **GPS:** N40 36.87' / W106 01.30'

The Hike

Kelly Creek and Kelly Lake are named after an Irishman who lived in the area in the late 1800s. Not much is known about Crazy Kelly, but the story goes that he was very religious and would tell people he lived in heaven. He made his home in a cabin along Kelly Creek, and reportedly the local pack rats were his friends. Human friends found his body in the cabin on April 17, 1898, mostly consumed by pack rats. They burned his cabin, so the cabin remains you see along the trail did not belong to this interesting character.

◀ *Kelly Lake*

State Forest State Park has an unusual history. When Colorado became a state on August 1, 1876, the federal government granted about 3 million acres of land and 4 million acres of mineral rights to the state to help fund public education. Sections 16 and 36 in every township became state school lands. The Colorado State Board of Land Commissioners (SLB) manages these areas. In 1938 a land exchange between the SLB and the USDA Forest Service occurred. Sections 16 and 36 in various national forests in Colorado were exchanged for national forest land near Gould, creating 70,980 contiguous acres. In 1953 the Colorado legislature passed legislation establishing the Colorado State Forest (CSF). Grazing, forestry, and recreation continued as it had before the designation.

Between about 1940 and 1970, lumber camps harvested timber in CSF, earning money for state schools. Today's Bockman Campground was the site of Bockman Lumber Camp, the largest in Colorado, supporting over one hundred men and their families. By 1955 several camps harvested close to 10 million board feet of lumber. Citizens complained about the timber operations, and by 1975 the lumber camps had closed.

CSF became a state park in 1970, and two years later the SLB leased the land to what has become Colorado State Parks for recreation management. The forest resource management contract was awarded to the Colorado State Forest Service. The state forest service was created by the Colorado legislature in 1955 as a division of what is now Colorado State University in Fort Collins. The state forest service provides protection and management of the state's forests (versus the national forests) and educates private landowners in forested areas about fire prevention and protection.

Today the state forest service uses adaptive management strategies to maintain a healthy forest. Some techniques include timber harvesting, researching and monitoring harvest results, wildlife monitoring (signs of healthy habitat) in conjunction with the Colorado Division of Wildlife, water quality monitoring (in particular for sediment loads), and livestock grazing from July through September to stimulate healthy range and forest.

State Forest State Park offers a wealth of recreation opportunities year-round. Four campgrounds with 158 developed campsites, over sixty dispersed campsites, and six cabins are available for your getaway. Never Summer Nordic, Inc. operates eight yurts (round Mongolian tents on wooden platforms) and two huts, available year-round.

Boating is allowed on North Michigan Reservoir, and fishing is popular on lakes and streams. Motorized trails provide hours of exploring. Hikers, mountain bikers, equestrians, cross-country skiers, and snowshoers enjoy many trails leading to high alpine lakes. Several geocache sites have been created throughout the park, and geocachers can rent GPS units at the Moose Visitor Center.

Moose were reintroduced to North Park in 1978 and 1979. These huge ungulates can grow to 6 feet tall at the shoulder, weigh up to 1,000 pounds, and reach 9.5 feet long. Their long spindly legs give them a top-heavy appearance. They typically live in forested areas near lakes and marshes. They graze on grasses, bushes, and underwater

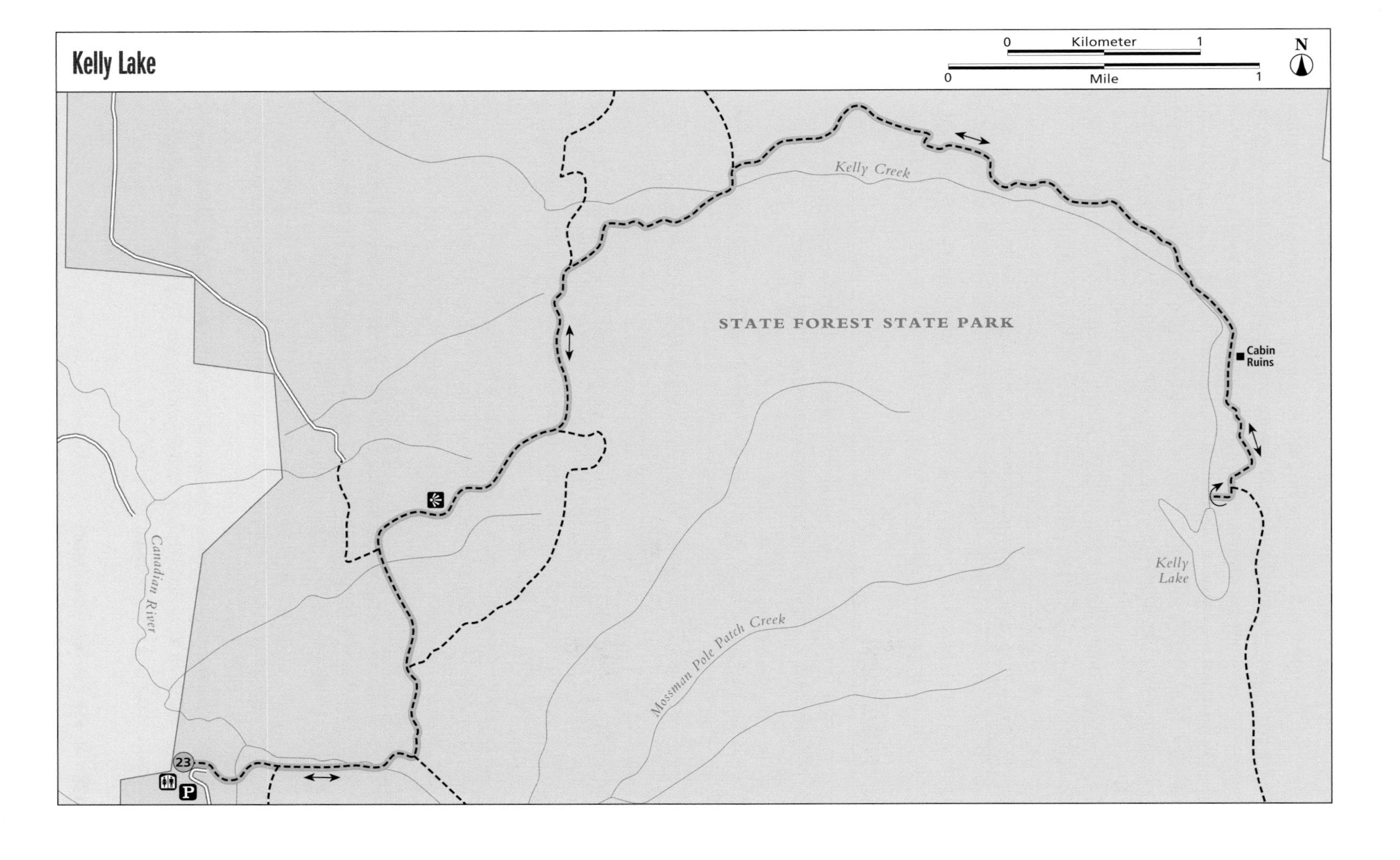
Kelly Lake
0
Kilometer
1
0
Mile
1
N
STATE FOREST STATE PARK
Kelly Creek
Cabin
Ruins
Kelly
Lake
Mossman Pole Patch Creek
Canadian River
23
P

vegetation in summer, and on willows in winter. Being huge creatures, they have few predators and seldom show fear of humans. Extremely protective of their young and their private space, they will chase humans and dogs—and they are fast. Keep an eye out for these magnificent creatures while you're hiking, and give them plenty of space.

The hike starts by descending a ridge to the South Fork of the Canadian River through a lodgepole pine forest. The red dead trees have been killed by the mountain pine beetle. After crossing several meadows the trail meanders through an aspen forest with colorful flowers. At about mile 4.3 the trail winds along the base of a boulder field, then climbs steeply uphill. Purple monkshood and larkspur line the path. By mile 6, you're in a beautiful alpine valley with Engelmann spruce, subalpine fir, marshy areas, and gorgeous wildflowers. Kelly Creek sparkles in the sun. The trail climbs steeply up a ridge, passing a little waterfall. Suddenly Kelly Lake appears down in its bowl, craggy peaks bordering its east side. If you're camping, please remember to camp at least 100 feet (and hopefully 200 feet) away from streams and lakes and 0.25 mile from trails. Enjoy this special nook in State Forest State Park!

Miles and Directions

0.0 Start at the trailhead at the end of JCR 41. Elevation: 8,660 feet. The low point of this hike, near the South Fork of the Canadian River, is at 8,540 feet.

0.75 An unmarked trail goes left. Continue hiking up the road.

0.8 Reach the junction with a trail to the North Fork Canadian yurt. Continue to the left up the road.

1.2 Reach the junction with the doubletrack trail to Kelly Lake and Clear Lake. Turn left. GPS: N40 37.15' / W106 00.49'. (***Option:*** You can continue walking up the road. Skip ahead to mile 3.0.)

1.6 Reach the junction with the trail to Clear Lake. Continue straight ahead and uphill.

1.8 Reach a point with a nice view to the northwest of the Mount Zirkel Wilderness and North Park. GPS: N40 37.60' / W 106 00.49'

2.4 Arrive at the junction with a closed road. Walk a few more feet uphill to another road and turn left onto that road, heading north.

3.0 Reach the junction with the Kelly Lake Trail. Turn right onto the singletrack trail. GPS: N40 38.29' / W105 59.90'

4.7 Reach the top of a steep section. You're entering a narrow valley. The trail crosses Kelly Creek several times in the next 1.3 miles. The trail can be wet and muddy in this section.

6.1 Look for cabin ruins to your left. GPS: N40 38.03' / W105 57.45'. After a few more creek crossings, the trail climbs steeply for the last 0.6 mile. You'll drop about 70 feet from a ridge (10,875 feet) to the lake.

6.8 Arrive at Kelly Lake. Elevation: 10,805 feet. GPS: N40 37.64' / W105 57.54'. Enjoy lunch and the beautiful scenery or set up your campsite. Return the way you came.

13.6 Arrive back at the trailhead.

24 Seven Lakes

The Seven Lakes Trail (Trail 1125) to Seven Lakes starts on the gentle Red Elephant Nature Trail, passing through lodgepole, spruce, and fir forest. Turning west, it climbs gently to the Mount Zirkel Wilderness boundary near Big Creek Falls. The trail wanders along Big Creek, then climbs a very steep section with many switchbacks. Excellent views of Big Creek Lakes can be seen from several viewpoints. The next section goes through old-growth forest and into flower-filled meadows just below Seven Lakes. The lakes are in a high, open area with views of Red Elephant Mountain and the Continental Divide. The lakes are a peaceful backpacking destination.

Start: From the Seven Lakes Trailhead near Big Creek Lakes Campground
Distance: 12.2 miles out and back
Approximate hiking time: 5 to 9 hours (recommended 2- to 3-day backpack)
Difficulty: Difficult due to length and one steep section
Elevation gain/loss: 1,773-foot gain/60-foot loss
Seasons: Best from mid-June to mid-Oct
Trail surface: Dirt trail with some flat sections, occasional rocks and mud, and one section of many steep switchbacks
Other trail users: Equestrians, anglers, mountain bikers (not within the wilderness), hunters (in season)
Canine compatibility: Dogs must be on leash on the Red Elephant Nature Trail (about the first mile), then under control on the rest of the trail
Fees and permits: Day-use fee payable at the trailhead parking lot; America the Beautiful pass accepted (display in vehicle window). Group size limit: No more than 15 people per group with a maximum combination of 25 people and pack or saddle animals in any group.
Maps: USGS Pearl and Davis Peak; Nat Geo Trails Illustrated 116 Hahns Peak/Steamboat Lake
Trail contacts: Medicine Bow–Routt National Forest, Parks Ranger District, Walden; (970) 723-2700; www.fs.usda.gov/mbr
Other: The access road is closed about 13 miles from the trailhead in winter. Snowmobile or cross-country ski on the road; the trail is neither maintained nor marked for winter use.

Finding the trailhead: From Walden, drive north a little more than 9 miles on CO 125 to Cowdrey. Turn left onto Jackson CR 6W. The road becomes gravel in about 5 miles. Drive a total of 18.8 miles from Cowdrey to FR 600/JCR 6A. Turn left. The road narrows as it enters the national forest. Be careful of oncoming vehicles as the road is not wide enough for two cars. Drive 5 miles to the junction with FR 689. Turn left, staying on FR 600. In 0.7 mile, enter the Big Creek Lakes Campground—go straight ahead at the campground entrance. Follow the hiker signs. There's a bulletin board with the campground fee station and rules 0.5 mile from the entrance. Continue another 0.2 mile and turn left into the Seven Lakes Trailhead. Water is available at the campground. A vault toilet is located in the center of the parking circle. A day-use self-service pay station is located by the trailhead bulletin boards. Please sign the trail register. **GPS:** N40 55.88' / W106 37.15'

Seven Lakes Trail

The Hike

The Mount Zirkel Wilderness was one of the original five Colorado wilderness areas designated by Congress in the Wilderness Act of 1964. This area around Big Creek Falls and Seven Lakes was added in 1993.

In 1867 Congress authorized a geological and natural resource survey along the fortieth parallel. Clarence King, just five years out of the Sheffield Scientific School at Yale, was appointed Geologist in Charge of the Geological Exploration of the Fortieth Parallel. King hired two assistant geologists, three topographic aides, two collectors, a photographer, and support men. He chose well-educated scientists who had studied at Yale or Harvard, and the geologists had even completed advanced studies in German universities. One geologist was Ferdinand Zirkel, who developed a common classification system for American and European rocks. For his contribution to science, a peak in the Park Range was named after him in 1874.

The Park Range forms the backbone of the Mount Zirkel Wilderness area. As the range stretches north toward Wyoming, it becomes known as the Sierra Madre. Part of the Sierra Madre near Seven Lakes produces the Encampment River, which flows north into the North Platte River. On the other side of the Continental Divide, the Elk River drains many of the high valleys, feeding its water into the Yampa River and eventually into the Colorado. The Park Range is composed mainly of Precambrian metamorphic rocks like gneiss and schist, with some granite interspersed. These rocks are around 1.7 billion years old. Glaciers covered the area at various times, and Seven Lakes are probably one result.

This area escaped the miners' shovels and road building. The land has not been altered or changed by humans as much as in other parts of Colorado. The Continental Divide by Seven Lakes appears to be a gentle ridge. The area hosts a spectacular display of July wildflowers, including paintbrushes, red elephants, pussytoes, penstemons, blue gentians, and varieties of yellow composites. Red Elephant Mountain (11,569 feet) raises its head and watches over the entire trail to Seven Lakes. This peak apparently reminded someone a long time ago of an elephant head and trunk. Can you see it?

The first part of the trail follows the Red Elephant Nature Trail. Pick up a nature guide at the trailhead. A forest fire swept through this area in the 1920s and the resulting lodgepole forest had little deadfall compared to the older, moister spruce-fir forest. Fire is important to the natural health of the forest, creating different vegetation pockets that support various plants and animals. However, by 2005 the mountain pine beetle invaded the lodgepole forest, killing many of the trees. The USDA Forest Service has removed many dead lodgepole, which pose a danger to hikers and could generate a hot fire. In several places, nice plank bridges cross wet areas. A lily pad–covered pond lies nestled in a cradle of trees.

After the trail turns west to follow Big Creek, an open area provides good views of Upper Big Creek Lake. A prominent cliff face towers above the wilderness boundary. Just beyond, down a little trail to the left, is Big Creek Falls. Not overly huge, the falls is still impressive. Take a break and enjoy the cool creek and falls before heading on. Beetle-kill trees are not removed in the wilderness area, so be aware of possible falling trees, especially on high-wind days.

The trail stays close to Big Creek for a while, then gradually climbs up a flower-filled section of trail with numerous seeps. Cow parsnip, pearly everlasting, and alder line the trail. After crossing an unnamed creek, take a quick break since the trail climbs steeply from here. More than fifteen switchbacks take you up 750 feet in 0.5 mile. The trail then levels out and rolls gently through a nice old-growth forest past some beautiful meadows. A final climb threads through flower-filled meadows and on to Seven Lakes.

Follow the faint trail to the left of the first lake to reach the biggest lake, which is stocked yearly with native trout. There is a nice campsite above the largest lake, at an appropriate distance from the water. The Forest Service requests that all camps be located at least 100 feet away from lakes, other water sources, and trails, and that no new campfire rings be built. Use existing fire rings, make a mound fire, or preferably use a stove. Be aware of lightning danger in open areas.

While visiting Seven Lakes, take time to explore the open spaces up to the Continental Divide to the south, or maybe take a side trip up Davis Peak to the north.

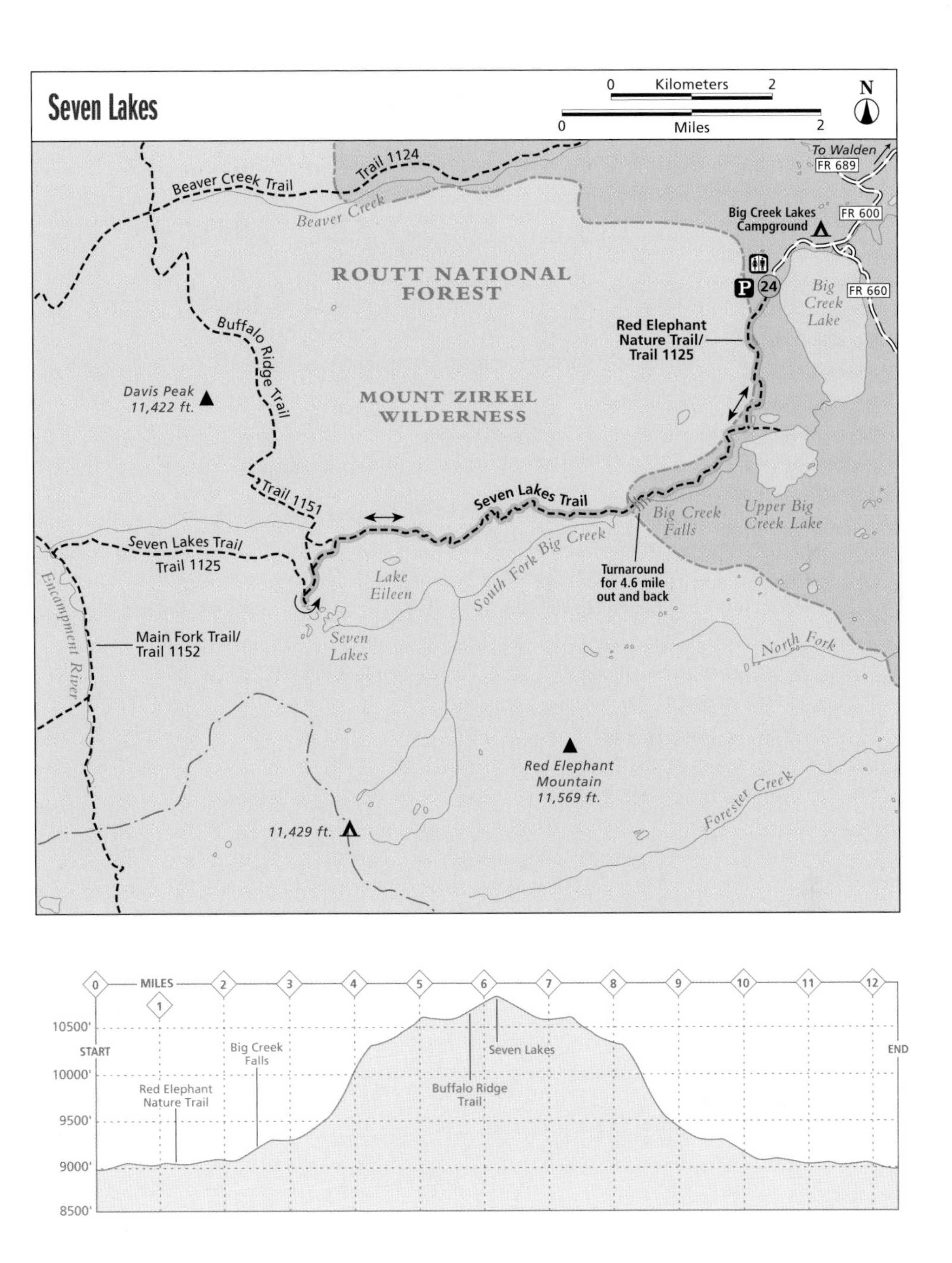

Big Creek Falls

Miles and Directions

0.0 Start at Seven Lakes Trailhead near Big Creek Lakes Campground. Elevation: 9,020 feet. Head up Seven Lakes Trail (Trail 1125). The Red Elephant Nature Trail shares the trail. (Pick up a nature guide at the trailhead.)

1.25 The Red Elephant Nature Trail breaks left. Stay right, continuing on Seven Lakes Trail.

2.3 Reach the wilderness boundary sign. Big Creek Falls is off to the left. Elevation: 9,200 feet. GPS: N40 54.55' / W106 38.17'. (***Option:*** For a shorter hike, turn around and return the way you came for a moderate 4.6-mile out and back.)

3.4 Come to a creek crossing.

4.3 Reach the top of a steep climb with switchbacks.

5.1 Come to a nice meadow on the left, followed by an old-growth spruce forest.

5.7 Reach a trail junction with the Buffalo Ridge Trail (Trail 1151). Stay to the left and head uphill.

6.0 Come to a trail junction with Seven Lakes Trail and the trail to Seven Lakes. Stay to the left (more straight ahead) and hike to the lakes.

6.1 Reach the first of the Seven Lakes. (***Side trip:*** Hike an additional 0.25 mile to view the biggest of the Seven Lakes. Elevation: 10,733 feet. GPS: N40 53.78' / W106 40.98'.) Otherwise, return the way you came.

12.2 Arrive back at the trailhead.

NORTHWEST

Lying where the Rocky Mountains meet the Colorado Plateau, the northwest section of Colorado is a mixture of mountains, plains, plateaus, and canyons. Dinosaurs roamed the western edge where several trails (such as the Trail Through Time on the Colorado-Utah border) and museums in Grand Junction and Fruita show the ancient beasts both in the ground and assembled. Although not in Colorado, be sure to visit Dinosaur National Monument's Quarry Visitor Center and Exhibit Hall, located about 7 miles north of Jensen, Utah (21 miles west of Dinosaur, Colorado), where bones still lie in the tilted rock, forming one wall of the quarry building.

John Wesley Powell floated through this region on his way to the Grand Canyon, losing a boat on the wild Green River after passing through the Gates of Lodore. Both the Yampa and Green Rivers have accomplished the seemingly impossible—they have down-cut through mountains, creating steep and beautiful canyons. Early human inhabitants also left their marks, with petroglyphs carved in rock walls in Dinosaur National Monument and at Canyon Pintado south of Rangely. Later inhabitants included outlaws such as Butch Cassidy, the Sundance Kid, and Matt Rush, who hid out in Browns Park. For a little high-wire excitement, drive over the one-lane swinging bridge across the Green River on Moffat CR 83.

25 Storm King Fourteen Memorial Trail

This trail, built by volunteers, is a memorial to fourteen firefighters who lost their lives on Storm King Mountain in July 1994. Interpretive signs explain wildland firefighting and this unfortunate disaster. You can stop at the observation point to look across to the ridge where the firefighters died, or hike farther to the memorial sites. The trail is a journey into a burned land, now recovering. The steep trails give you a brief insight into and feeling for the work of those who fight wildland fires.

Start: From the Storm King Fourteen Memorial Trailhead
Distance: 4.4-miles out and back
Approximate hiking time: 3.5 to 4.5 hours
Difficulty: Moderate to the observation point; most difficult to the memorial sites due to steepness
Elevation gain/loss: 1,280-foot gain/440-foot loss
Seasons: Best from Apr through Nov
Trail surface: Dirt trail mainly on south- and southwest-facing slopes, fairly steep in spots, slippery when wet, open ridge near observation point
Other trail users: Hunters (in season)
Canine compatibility: Dogs must be on leash
Fees and permits: None
Maps: USGS Storm King Mountain; Nat Geo Trails Illustrated 123 Flat Tops SE/Glenwood Canyon
Trail contacts: Bureau of Land Management, Colorado River Valley Field Office, Silt; (970) 876-9000; www.blm.gov/co/st/en/fo/crvfo.html
Other: No water is available on the trail.

Finding the trailhead: From Glenwood Springs, take I-70 west to exit 109/Canyon Creek. Turn right, then immediately right again onto the frontage road. Head back east past Canyon Creek Estates for 1 mile to a dead end with a parking lot. The trail starts by several interpretive signs at the east end of the lot. There is a portable toilet but no water at the trailhead. **GPS:** N39 34.43' / W107 26.02'

The Hike

On July 2, 1994, a very natural event occurred. A lightning strike started a small fire in a piñon-juniper-Gambel oak forest on Storm King Mountain (8,793 feet). Several large wildland fires were already burning across Colorado, strapping firefighting resources. The small fire received low priority. By July 5 the fire covered five acres and crews arrived to build fire lines. But Mother Nature had other plans. By mid-afternoon on July 6, a dry cold front passed through the region, causing very strong winds that fanned the fire into a roaring inferno traveling much faster than any human could run, especially uphill. The fire soon consumed over 2,100 acres. Fourteen firefighters could not escape the 100-foot-high flames racing toward them. Thirty-five

Clothes memorial on a ghost tree

Memorial sites

others escaped either by hunkering down in their fire shelters or by slipping down an eastern gully to the highway.

Although forest fire is a natural and important process, the fire on Storm King Mountain endangered homes and businesses in West Glenwood to the east and Canyon Creek Estates to the west. The trees on Storm King also provided essential erosion control. Storm King and surrounding mountains are a combination of red sandstone and shale, called the Maroon Formation, deposited over eons by inland seas. When shale gets wet, mudslides often result.

Volunteers built this trail in 1995 to honor wildland firefighters nationwide and to provide an insight into their experiences. The trail begins with several interpretive signs about the July 1994 fire. They invite you to imagine being a firefighter, hiking up steep slopes and carrying thirty to sixty pounds of equipment.

The trail climbs steeply along the south side of a ridge, through rabbitbrush, wild roses, Mormon tea, and cheatgrass, with numerous log steps to hike up. Where the trail turns to follow the west side of a ridge, a small sign relates the camaraderie of firefighters and gives you a chance to take a few deep breaths. The Colorado River roars below, as does I-70. The trail continues to climb through piñon-juniper forest. The steepness of the trail is tiring even with a light pack. About 0.25 mile up a sign announces entry into Bureau of Land Management (BLM) lands. Switchbacks take you steadily uphill. A bench provides a handy place to check out the western view and catch your breath. Down valley, I-70 twists like a serpent, following the river's contours. The Grand Hogback and Coal Ridge form the horizon to the south.

At 0.6 mile the trail reaches a ridge at 6,280 feet. Storm King Mountain, with scorched sticks and green Gambel oak, comes into view. You can see how the fire raced up gullies to different ridges. The trees to the right of the trail are snags of their former selves. To the left, most trees are green and alive. Narrow-leaved penstemon

MORE ABOUT STORM KING

Two Rivers Park in Glenwood Springs contains a memorial to the fourteen firefighters who died on Storm King Mountain. A bronze sculpture depicting three wildland firefighters is surrounded by a garden, pictures, and information about each of the lost firefighters.

To reach Two Rivers Park from the Storm King Fourteen Memorial Trail, take I-70 eastbound. Exit at West Glenwood and turn left under the highway, then turn right onto US 6 eastbound. Go 1.8 miles to Devereux Drive and turn right. Drive 0.3 mile, crossing over I-70, and look for the park on the left. Turn left into the park. The memorial garden is straight ahead.

The story of the Storm King Mountain Fire (mistakenly reported as being in South Canyon) is captured in the book *Fire on the Mountain* by John N. McLean, published in 1999. The History Channel produced a video, *Fire on the Mountain,* in 2002; www.historychannel.com. Many interesting articles, including the report of the investigation team, can be found via the Internet.

and blue flax flowers grow among the ghostly trunks. Across the gully Gambel oak once again covers the slopes, although junipers and piñon pines may take forty to one hundred years to reestablish themselves.

The trail follows a mostly flat ridge for 0.4 mile to the observation point. Three large interpretive signs explain the events of that fateful July day. With a pair of binoculars, you can see the slope that twelve firefighters scrambled up trying to reach safety. Look closely for the pair of crossed skis marking one memorial site. You can turn around here or continue to the memorial sites.

To reach the memorial sites on the next ridge, continue on the trail left of the interpretive signs. If you hike this trail, be aware that several sections are very steep with loose footing. Once on that ridge a trail to the left leads to where two helitack crewmembers died, across a steep little gully by a rock outcropping. The trail to the right leads to the slope where nine members of the Prineville, Oregon, Hotshots crew and three smokejumpers died. To reach the twelve sites, walk about 0.1 mile to a trail that switchbacks down the west slope. Memorial sites are noted with the firefighters' names.

The BLM and families request that you stay on the trail and do not walk straight down between the crosses—however, the trail is hidden by bushes and hard to find. The area between crosses is extremely steep and prone to erosion. Look around, see and feel the steepness of the slope. Imagine what it would be like to have a fire chasing you up that hill. Read the poem at trail's end below the memorial sites and reflect for a moment on people who are willing to give their lives to protect the lives and property of others.

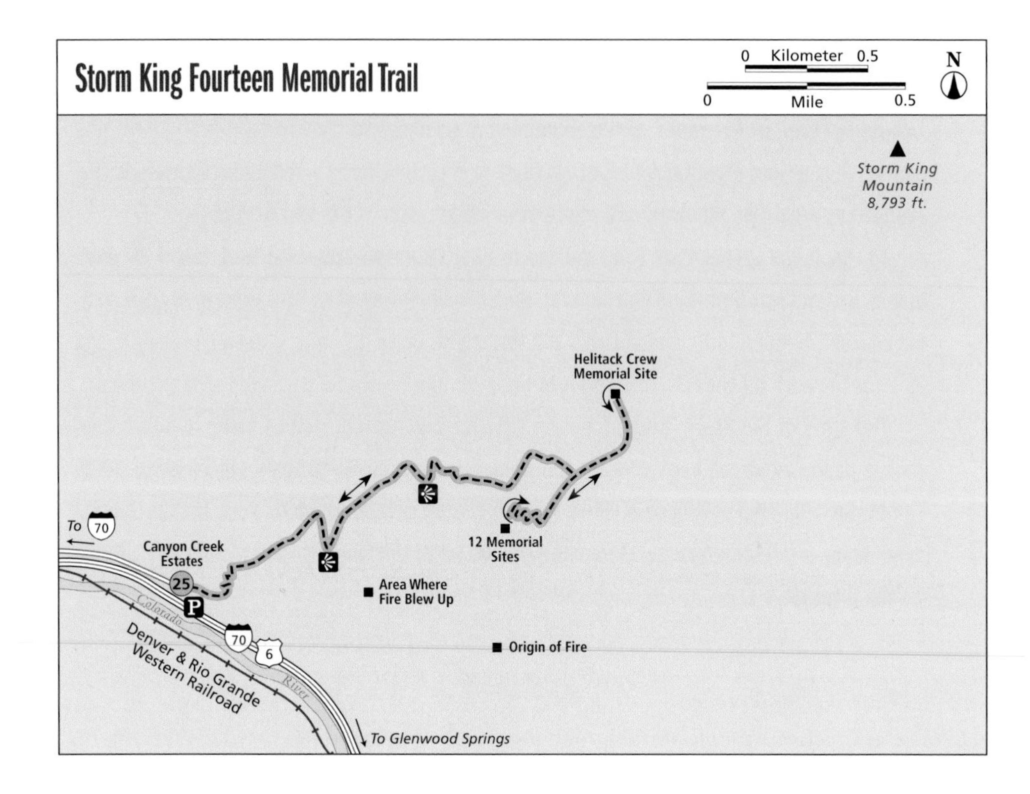

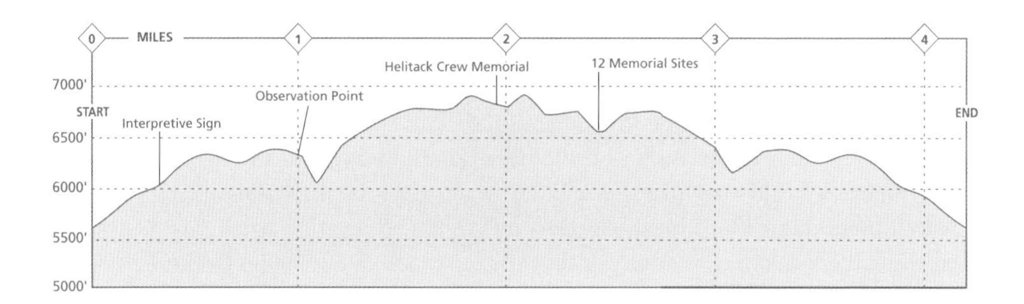

Miles and Directions

0.0 Start at the trailhead east of Canyon Creek Estates. Elevation: 5,680 feet. Take a few minutes to read the interpretive signs. (***Note:*** The first part of the trail crosses private property, which the BLM has permission to use for this trail. Please respect the owners' property rights.)

0.25 Reach the BLM boundary sign.

0.3 Reach a bench and interpretive sign on the right side of the trail. This is a good place to catch your breath and enjoy the view down the Colorado River.

0.6 Gain a ridge with views of Storm King Mountain and the burned area.

1.0 Arrive at the observation point with interpretive signs. Elevation: 6,360 feet. GPS: N39 34.68' / W107 25.35'. (***Option:*** You can turn around here for a shorter, moderate hike.)

1.2 Reach the bottom of the first gully, contour around into the second gully, and start climbing up to the next ridge.

1.7 The trail comes to a T intersection. Elevation: 6,680 feet. GPS: N39 34.66' / W107 24.95'. Take the left trail to the helitack crew memorial site.

2.0 Arrive at the helitack crew memorial site. Look across the deep little gully near a rock outcropping to see the crosses. Head back toward the T intersection.

2.3 Arrive back at the T intersection. Proceed ahead to the other twelve memorial sites.

2.4 The trail switchbacks downhill past the memorial sites that are marked with signs along the trail. (***Note:*** Please remember to stay on the trail that switchbacks [versus the trail that goes straight downhill]. When you see the Scott Blecha sign, the trail turns right into the bushes. If you walk to Blecha's stone, you'll end up walking straight down an extremely steep slope between the crosses. The area between crosses is prone to erosion.)

2.5 The trail ends below the twelve memorial sites. GPS: N39 34.59' / W107 25.08'. Walk to the end to read the poem. Return the way you came.

2.7 Arrive back at the T intersection. Turn left to head downhill and return to the observation point.

4.4 Arrive back at the trailhead.

26 Coyote and Squirrel Trails

Coyote Trail winds past limestone caves, through a lush riparian and forested area, then climbs above for a bird's-eye view of Rifle Falls. Kids of all ages will love exploring the caves. Bring a flashlight for the largest one. Squirrel Trail crosses East Rifle Creek and winds through Gambel oak forest to the base of a red sandstone cliff. The trail continues along the Grass Valley Canal, which takes water to Harvey Gap Reservoir. Hiked together, the trails make a lopsided figure eight through a naturally and historically interesting area along East Rifle Creek.

Start: From the Rifle Falls State Park picnic ground
Distance: 1.8-mile double loop
Approximate hiking time: 1 to 2 hours
Difficulty: Mostly easy with some steep sections
Elevation gain: 140 feet (two at 70 feet each)
Seasons: Year-round except after snowstorms
Trail surface: Paved road, dirt road, dirt trail
Other trail users: Wheelchair users (on first part of Coyote Trail), anglers, mountain bikers
Canine compatibility: Dogs must be on leash
Fees and permits: Daily entrance fee or annual parks pass required
Maps: USGS Rifle Falls; Nat Geo Trails Illustrated 125 Flat Tops SW/Rifle Gap
Trail contacts: Rifle Falls State Park, Rifle; (970) 625-1607; parks.state.co.us/parks/riflefalls

Finding the trailhead: From I-70 exit 90 for Rifle, head north on CO 13 through town. In about 4 miles, turn right onto CO 325 and drive another 4 miles to Rifle Gap Reservoir. Stay on CO 325, which turns right and goes over the dam. Drive another 5.6 miles to the Rifle Falls State Park entrance. Pay the fee here or at the self-serve kiosk. Turn left and drive 0.2 mile through the campground to the picnic area. Park here. A vault toilet and water are available. **GPS:** N39 40.58' / W107 41.92'

The Hike

Lined with red sandstone and limestone cliffs, Rifle Falls State Park is a showplace with a 60-foot triple waterfall, lush riparian and forested areas, wildlife habitat, and a nice picnic area and campground. Two trails, named after local inhabitants, wander through the park for a complete tour. Interpretive signs along Coyote Trail explain the natural and social history of the area.

The original configuration of Rifle Falls consisted of one wide sheet of water, with some early pictures showing multiple ribbons of water. In 1908 the Rifle Light, Heat, and Power Company was incorporated to provide electricity to the town of Rifle. This group built the first hydroelectric plant in Colorado by diverting part of East Rifle Creek through a pipe descending the cliff at Rifle Falls. As a result, Rifle Falls became two ribbons of water plus the pipeline. Thirteen miles of transmission

◀ *Rifle Falls from overlook*

Trail along Grass Valley Canal

cable linked Rifle with the power plant. In town, 8 miles of wires, twenty-five streetlights, and wiring for most buildings were installed. Rifle received its first electricity from the power plant on December 31, 1909. The company merged with Public Service Company in 1926. Public Service sold the property to the Colorado Game and Fish Department in 1959, at which time the plant was closed. The stone power plant was torn down in 1971. With the removal of the pipe, the falls have reverted to three streams of water.

The cliffs that create the falls are made of calcium carbonate from creeks flowing underground in limestone deposits upstream. Thousands of years ago the creek ran over some obstacle, which geologists believe was a giant beaver dam. The water left deposits that developed into today's cliffs. You can approach the falls from various sides, getting sprayed no matter which way you choose. To the right of the falls, Coyote Trail winds past limestone caves, created by water eroding the cliff from the inside out. Some are shallow, while one is large enough (90 feet) to need a flashlight to explore. Bats live in these caves, so be respectful if they are hanging out. The caves contain interesting formations such as flowstone, popcorn stone, and stalactites hanging from the ceiling. Watch your head as you hike from cave to cave. One place in particular has very low clearance.

Outside the caves, cottonwoods, box elders, chokecherry trees, hawthorns (emphasis on thorns), coyote willows, and a little stream line the trail. Blue Steller's jays squawk overhead. The trail curves around and up until you are on top of the cliff. The Bobcat Trail to the Rifle Fish Hatchery branches to the north just before the falls. (The hatchery was completed in 1954 as the largest trout hatchery in the state.) Old metal pipes and wooden water diversions still remain from the hydroelectric plant days. The quickly flowing water disappears over the cliff in a white froth as it takes the plunge. Observation decks hang beyond the cliff for a bird's-eye view and a potential adrenaline rush. The trail down is steep, but stairs make the trek a little easier. The riparian area around the falls creates wildlife-watching opportunities.

Various stories exist about how Rifle Creek was named. Most stories develop the theme of someone leaving or finding a rifle leaning against a tree along the creek. Another legend refers to a custom of cowboys firing their rifles at a roundup ground near the confluence of the three creeks.

After arriving back at the picnic area, walk through the main campground past the fee kiosk to Squirrel Trail. This trail takes you to the Grass Valley Canal, built between 1891 and 1894. At the same time, a dam was being built about 5 miles away (as the crow flies), across a gap in the Grand Hogback. This tilted ridge is the western Colorado version of the Dakota Hogback west of Denver. The canal brings water from East Rifle Creek to Harvey Gap Reservoir, which stores irrigation water for farms and ranches. The reservoir is in Harvey Gap State Park.

Squirrel Trail follows the creek through the walk-in campground, then crosses it on a swinging bridge. Gambel oaks on the other side create a thick forest, a cool treat on a hot day. The trail twists and climbs up the side of the canyon to the base of the cliff. A T intersection appears after one steep stretch. Turn left and head uphill to where the trail meets the canal before it enters the tunnel. The water is clear and deep. The dirt road along the canal takes you back to the picnic ground by going downhill at the left-hand curve.

Rifle Falls has attracted visitors since the 1880s. Many people consider this area the Hawaii or Costa Rica of Colorado. The swank Zerbe Resort housed tourists for a number of years, starting around 1903 until, unfortunately, it burned down in 1922.

Miles and Directions

0.0 Start at the picnic ground at the closed pipe gate on the paved road. Elevation: 6,500 feet. Head north toward Rifle Falls on the Coyote Trail.

0.1 View the Rifle Falls area and interpretive signs. (***Note:*** You might get sprayed by the falling water mist.)

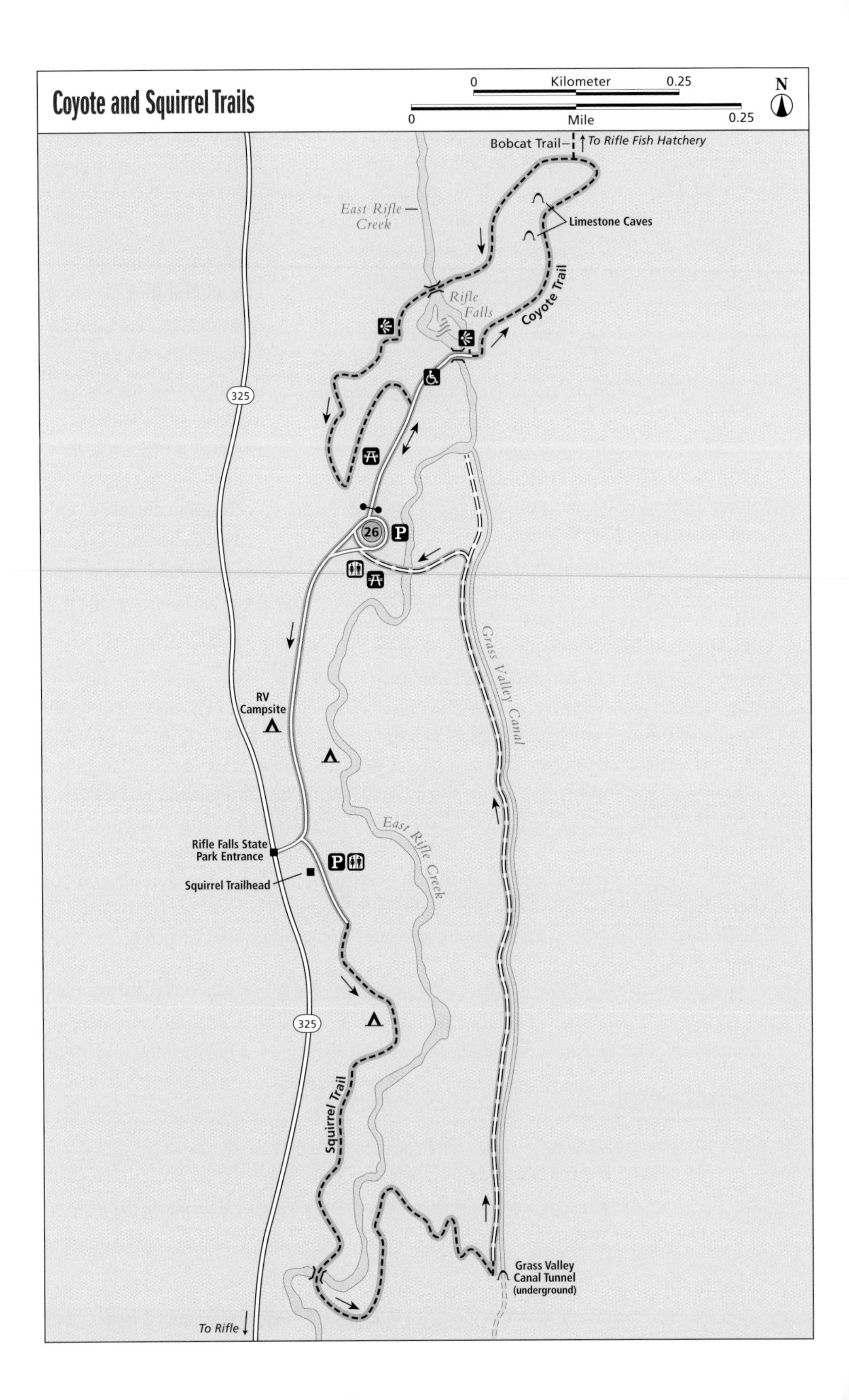
Coyote and Squirrel Trails
0
Kilometer
0.25
0
Mile
0.25
N
Bobcat Trail
To Rifle Fish Hatchery
East Rifle Creek
Limestone Caves
Rifle Falls
Coyote Trail
325
26
P
Grass Valley Canal
RV Campsite
East Rifle Creek
Rifle Falls State Park Entrance
Squirrel Trailhead
P
325
Squirrel Trail
Grass Valley Canal Tunnel (underground)
To Rifle

0.2 Reach the start of the limestone caves.

0.3 Come to the intersection with Bobcat Trail to the fish hatchery. Go straight ahead to the falls overlook. Elevation: 6,600 feet.

0.5 Turn left onto the observation deck for a great view of the falls. Just beyond, the trail drops downhill, sometimes steeply down concrete steps, back to the picnic area.

0.6 Arrive back at the dirt road in the picnic area. Turn right and walk on the road back to the parking lot then through the campground toward the entrance station.

0.8 Reach the Squirrel Trailhead to the left of the entrance station. GPS: N39 40.40' / W107 41.93'

1.1 Stay to the right at campsite 20, drop down, and cross East Rifle Creek on a swinging bridge.

1.35 Squirrel Trail climbs steeply and comes to a T intersection. Turn left and continue uphill on the trail.

1.4 The trail joins the dirt road along the canal at the water tunnel.

1.7 Come to a fork and go left down the road.

1.8 Arrive back at the picnic ground.

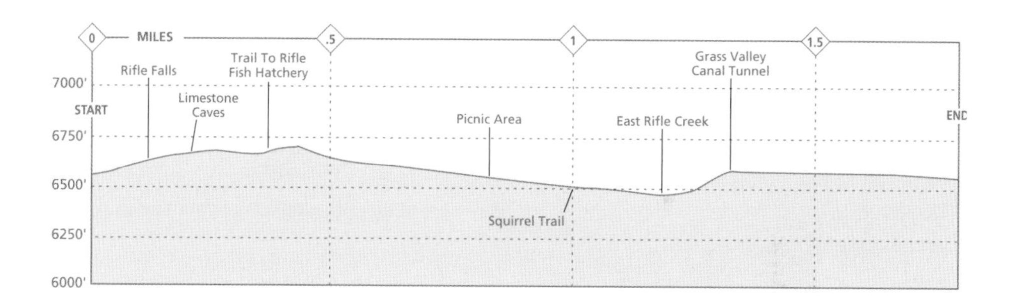

27 Marvine Loop

This hike takes you to the top of the White River Plateau in the Flat Tops Wilderness via East Marvine Trail and loops back to the same trailhead via Marvine Trail for a multiday backpacking trip. The public resource and wilderness preservation history in this area is significant. Part of the hike travels through dense spruce-fir forest conveying a primeval feeling. Once on the plateau, the land rolls along through subalpine meadows and alpine tundra punctuated by clumps of trees and short peaks. Small lakes and ponds abound. Take time to climb Big Marvine Peak or explore the various lakes on your own. Camping is available below the plateau and on top.

Start: From the East Marvine (Trail 1822) Trailhead
Distance: 23.2-mile loop backpack.
Approximate hiking time: 3 days minimum to explore the Flat Tops
Difficulty: Most difficult due to length, elevation gain, and steep sections
Elevation gain/loss: 3,120-foot gain/290-foot loss
Seasons: Best from late June to mid-Oct
Trail surface: Dirt trail with some muddy sections and several bridgeless creek crossings
Other trail users: Equestrians, anglers, hunters (in season)
Canine compatibility: Dogs must be under control
Fees and permits: None. Group size limit: No more than 15 people per group with a maximum combination of 25 people and pack or saddle animals in any one group.
Maps: USGS Big Marvine Peak, Lost Park, Oyster Lake, and Ripple Creek Pass; Nat Geo Trails Illustrated 122 Flat Tops NE/Trappers Lake
Trail contacts: White River National Forest, Blanco Ranger District, Meeker; (970) 878-4039; www.fs.usda.gov/whiteriver
Other: The access road to the trailhead opens from mid- to late May and remains open through the end of the hunting seasons in Nov. Trails are neither maintained nor marked for winter use.

Finding the trailhead: From Meeker, drive east on CO 13 to where it curves north, and turn right onto Rio Blanco CR 8. Follow the FLAT TOPS TRAIL SCENIC BYWAY sign. In about 28.5 miles (past mile marker 28), turn right onto a dirt road by the MARVINE CREEK sign. In 0.2 mile, turn left by Fritzlans Guest House onto RBCR 12, which later becomes FR 12. Trailhead parking is 5.1 miles down FR 12 on the left. Park away from the corrals reserved for outfitters. There is no water or toilet at the trailhead. Both are available at the two nearby campgrounds (fee areas). **GPS:** N40 00.55' / W107 25.47'

The Hike

While hiking up the trail, notice the pockmarked rocks. The White River Plateau is capped with dark basalt from volcanic eruptions that started around 25 million years ago. These eruptions lasted about 17 million years. After cooling off for another 7 million years, an ice age took hold. An ice cap formed over the plateau between 18,000 and 12,000 years ago. Melting glaciers left numerous little lakes and ponds below and on top of the plateau.

Big Marvine Peak and top of plateau

Many years later Ute Indians, also called the People of the Shining Mountains, camped in the Flat Tops on the northern end of the White River Plateau during the summer. Deer, elk, bison, and rabbits provided meat. Berries, wild onions, and the root of the yampa rounded out their diet.

As white settlers moved into the area, grazing and timber harvesting ran rampant and forest fires raged. Concerned citizens lobbied to protect western public resources. In 1891 President Benjamin Harrison set aside the White River Timber Land Reserve. White River is the second-oldest national forest in the United States. The Flat Tops area earned another special place in history in 1919. The USDA Forest Service sent landscape architect Arthur Carhart to Trappers Lake, at the base of the Flat Tops, to survey the area for summer cabins. Instead, Carhart recommended that this beautiful area be set aside and protected from development. He noted: "There are a number of places with scenic values of such great worth that they are rightfully property of all people. They should be preserved for all time for the people of the Nation and the world. Trappers Lake is unquestionably a candidate for that classification."

Carhart later joined Aldo Leopold and began the movement that created the Wilderness Preservation System. The Flat Tops Primitive Area was established in 1932 with special protections. After many years of negotiation, President Lyndon B. Johnson signed the Wilderness Act of 1964. Congress elevated the primitive area to the Flat Tops Wilderness in 1975. The second-largest wilderness area in Colorado is home to the largest elk herd in the state. Keep an eye open for deer and elk while you're hiking. Other wildlife you might encounter includes black bears, bobcats, pine martens, foxes, coyotes, marmots, and pikas.

When meeting horses on the trail, step off on the downhill side until the horses pass, keeping your dog under control, preferably on leash next to you. If a horse wants more room, it will move off the trail away from you. It is safer for both the horse and rider if the horse heads uphill. If the trail is narrow, ask the rider for instructions.

The trail follows East Marvine Creek through aspen, Gambel oak, and lodgepole pine forests. Occasional grassy meadows provide views of the Flat Tops escarpment and Little Marvine Peaks. Follow along a small stream, then past the 2-mile mark, where ponds and small lakes start to appear. The trail climbs steadily up through aspen, Engelmann spruce, and subalpine fir. Numerous creeks intersect the trail, and some can be tricky to cross depending on water level. Most creeks have muddy edges and no log bridges, so you'll have to rock hop.

After contouring around a ridge, Rainbow Lake lies to the left. A few campsites can be found on the ridge above it. Beyond Rainbow Lake the trail levels off and loses some elevation as it runs across meadows and tiny creeks. It finally rejoins East Marvine Creek and passes an energetic cascade before climbing steeply up the side of the Flat Tops. The spruce-fir forest is thick and dark here. Bark beetles infested the forest in the 1940s, and many dead snags make the forest appear ancient. Wood decays slowly in the high, dry Colorado climate. How large animals like elk can maneuver through the tangled dark forest almost defies the imagination.

Two long switchbacks lead to the base of the escarpment. When you find a flat spot, take a breather and enjoy the view. Scan the surrounding cliff bands for silver ribbon waterfalls. Six short switchbacks take you even higher, and two final switchbacks bring you close to the edge of the plateau. The climb is still not quite over, but becomes gentler now. You have gained about 1,000 feet in the last mile.

A large cairn holding up a tree trunk greets you at the top edge. A small lake is just beyond, then another and another. Little Marvine Peaks rise to the north, with Big Marvine Peak dominating the southwest view. The subalpine meadows roll along with patches of spruce-fir. After the third little lake, the trail splits. The left branch heads for Twin Lakes and Oyster Lake Trail, while the right branch (an unofficial trail) leads to a good fishing lake and toward Big Marvine Peak. From here you can explore and camp many places. Take a couple of days to enjoy the open high country of the Flat Tops. Then head south on the Oyster Lake Trail to Marvine Trail to make a loop back to the trailhead parking area where you started.

Rainbow Lake

Please remember to camp at least 100 feet (about thirty-five adult steps) away from streams, lakes, and trails. Using a lightweight cookstove instead of a fire will avoid leaving permanent scars on the land. By practicing Leave No Trace techniques, hikers can enjoy a pristine experience and find solitude in the Flat Tops Wilderness for many years.

Miles and Directions

0.0 Start at the East Marvine Trailhead (Trail 1822). Elevation: 8,091 feet.

0.1 Cross the sturdy bridge over East Marvine Creek. At the T intersection, turn right onto the trail and head uphill with the creek on your right.

1.4 The trail leaves East Marvine Creek to follow a small stream.

1.7 The trail splits; stay to the right. (***Note:*** The trail can get very muddy in this stretch.)

2.7 Johnson Lake is on the right. GPS: N40 00.27' / W107 23.30'

3.25 Come to the junction with Wild Cow Park Trail (Trail 2244). Stay to the right on East Marvine Trail.

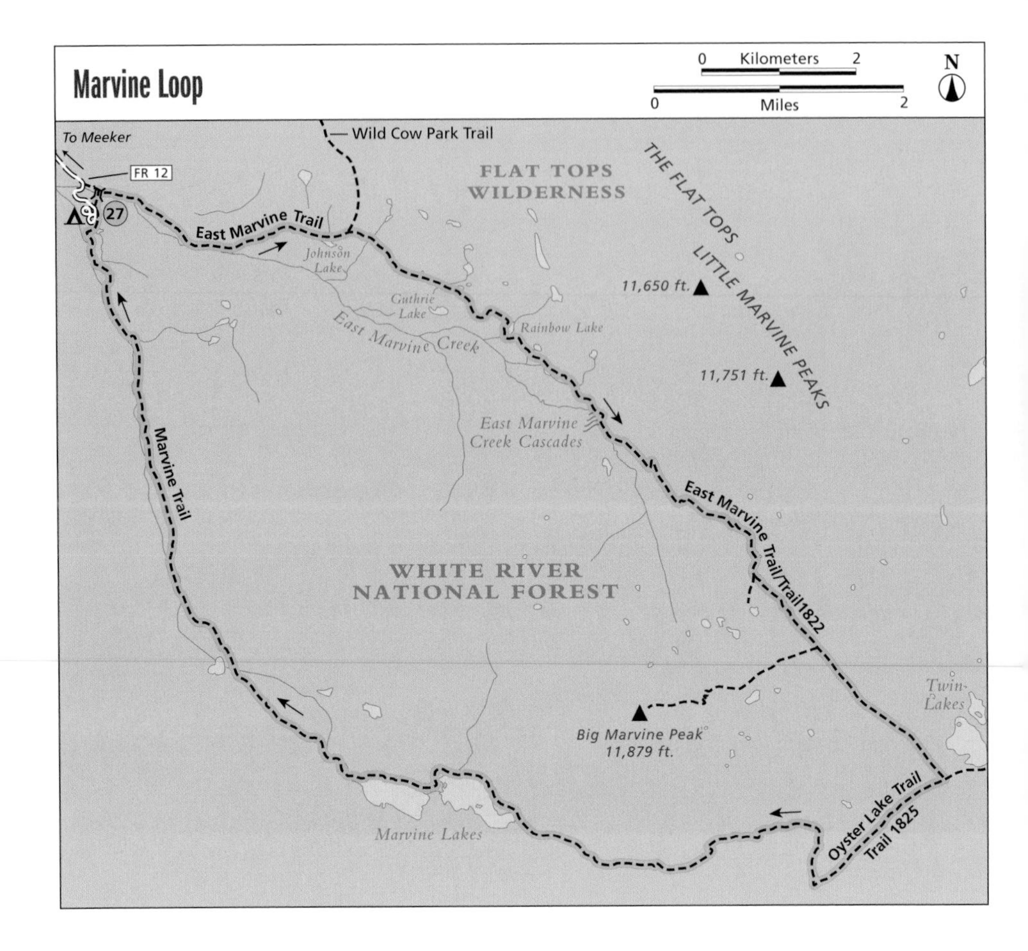

5.0	Reach Rainbow Lake.
7.3	The trail splits. The right spur (nonsystem trail) goes to Ned Wilson Lake. The high point is just past here at about 11,180 feet.
8.5	Reach the junction with the trail to Big Marvine Peak. Continue on the East Marvine Trail.
10.75	Reach the junction with the Oyster Lake Trail (Trail 1825). Elevation: 10,989 feet. GPS: N39 56.52' / W107 17.75'. Turn right onto Oyster Lake Trail.
12.2	Turn right onto the Marvine Trail (Trail 1823) and drop down the escarpment. GPS: N39 55.83' / W107 18.90'
17.4	Reach Marvine Lakes.
19.2	Reach Slide Lake. Ford Marvine Creek near the lake, being very careful, especially if the creek is high.
23.2	Arrive at the Marvine Trailhead, at the same parking area where you started. GPS: N40 00.53' / W107 25.46'

A LITTLE UTE INDIAN HISTORY

Ute territory once covered about 150,000 square miles of mountainous Colorado, Utah, and southern Wyoming. The Utes were divided into seven bands, each with its own hunting territory. The White River band called a large area of northwest Colorado their home, including the Flat Tops. For hundreds of years they roamed the huge territory, following game with the seasons. The southern bands had early contact with the Spanish and obtained horses. Accomplished horsemen, their battle skills were feared by whites and other Native American tribes alike.

The Utes tried to live in peace with the new white settlers. Chief Ouray of the Tabeguache band realized that fighting would result in disaster. Although the Utes lived in different bands, Ouray was recognized as the spokesman for all Utes by the US government. He crafted treaties very favorable to his people. The treaties, however, were either broken or modified by the government as the pressure for gold and homesteading increased. The treaty of 1868 stipulated that no white man could enter Ute territory, covering the western third of Colorado, without Ute permission.

The government created Indian agencies to provide supplies for the Utes and hopefully keep the peace. One agency was located near present-day Meeker on the White River. Nathan Meeker became agent in 1878. The next year Meeker decided that the Utes should farm a grassy pasture being used for their prized horses. Farming was not part of the Ute way of life, and a disagreement ensued. Meeker requested reinforcements. Led by Major Thornburgh, troops crossed into Ute territory without permission. Who fired the first shot is unknown, but the resulting battle ended in the death of Meeker, as well as many soldiers and Utes. Angry whites banished all Utes to reservations in 1880, with the White River band going to the Uintah Reservation in Utah.

28 Black Mountain (West Summit) Trail

This hike climbs to the west summit of Black Mountain, a volcanic plateau in the Elkhead Mountains. The trail first winds through an aspen forest with vegetation so thick at times that you might feel the need for a machete. The trail then proceeds into drier lodgepole and spruce-fir forests. Once up on the plateau, a spur trail takes you to a raptor viewing area complete with an interpretive poster and views west toward Dinosaur National Monument and Utah.

Start: From the Cottonwood Trailhead at the east side of Freeman Reservoir
Distance: 7.4 miles out and back
Approximate hiking time: 3.5 to 5 hours
Difficulty: Difficult due to elevation gain and some rough trail sections
Elevation gain: 2,055 feet
Seasons: Best from mid-June to mid-Oct
Trail surface: Dirt trail with wet areas and some rocky sections
Other trail users: Equestrians, mountain bikers, hunters (in season)
Canine compatibility: Dogs must be on leash at the trailhead, in the parking lot, and in the campground and under control elsewhere.
Fees and permits: Day-use fee required for Freeman Recreation Area; America the Beautiful pass accepted
Map: USGS Freeman Reservoir
Trail contacts: Medicine Bow-Routt National Forest, Hahns Peak/Bears Ears Ranger District, Steamboat Springs; (970) 870-2299; www.fs.usda.gov/mbr
Other: The access road is closed by snow about 7.2 miles from the trailhead in winter. The road is used by snowmobiles. The trail is neither maintained nor marked for winter use. Water is sparse on the trail.

Finding the trailhead: From the intersection of US 40 and CO 13 in Craig, head north 13.4 miles on CO 13 to just past mile marker 103. Turn right onto Moffat CR 11 (which becomes FR 112) and drive 9.2 miles to Freeman Recreation Area. Pay the day-use fee at the self-service station. Continue another 0.4 mile to the east end of the reservoir, turn left, and go another 0.1 mile to the parking area at the trailhead near the campground. The hike description starts at the east trailhead. Water and vault toilets are at the campground (fee area). **GPS:** N40 45.83' / W 107 25.37'

The Hike

In the Elkhead Mountains of northwestern Colorado, Black Mountain forms a 1.75-mile-long plateau that rises north of Craig. From a distance it does indeed look black. The Elkheads were formed by the same volcanic eruptions that shaped the Flat Tops and White River Plateau between 25 million and 17 million years ago. At the eastern edge of a desert zone, the Elkheads capture enough moisture to feed the Elkhead, Little Snake, and Yampa Rivers. Ute Indians lived and hunted here. Although very popular in fall with hunters because of large elk, deer, and pronghorn antelope herds, summer finds the area less used than the wilderness areas to the east and south. Aspens flourish in the Freeman Reservoir area and on the lower part of Black Mountain, making this trail a colorful fall hike.

Black Mountain Trail through aspen

Aspens and willows growing along Little Cottonwood Creek border the first part of the trail. The lush aspen forest provides a home to many animals and plants. Colorado columbine, the state flower, grows in aspen forests. Pink Wood's rose, white geranium, yellow heartleaf arnica (named for its heart-shaped leaves), pinkish-purple fireweed, dandelion, blue harebells, various paintbrushes, pussytoes, white Mariposa lily, and wild strawberries cover the ground. Larkspur, pearly everlasting, and white to pinkish yarrow are common. In moister areas, tall cow parsnip, with its teeny flowers forming a lacy doily, and deep purple monkshood grow in profusion. Cow parsnip is often confused with Queen Anne's lace. Monkshood is aptly named, with its monk's cowl flowers. Listen for the *chick-a-dee-dee-dee* of the mountain chickadee, a small gray and black bird that lives here year-round. Elk and deer find ample food in aspen forests, including grasses and bushes such as serviceberry, snowberry, twinberry, and chokecherry, along with Rocky Mountain maple.

The aspen tree is an interesting plant. Started from seed, expansion of a stand occurs when lateral roots sprout new shoots, forming a clone. Various sets of aspen change color at different times or exhibit different hues—the look-alike bunch is the same plant. Aspens sprout quickly after fire, mining, logging, or other disturbances

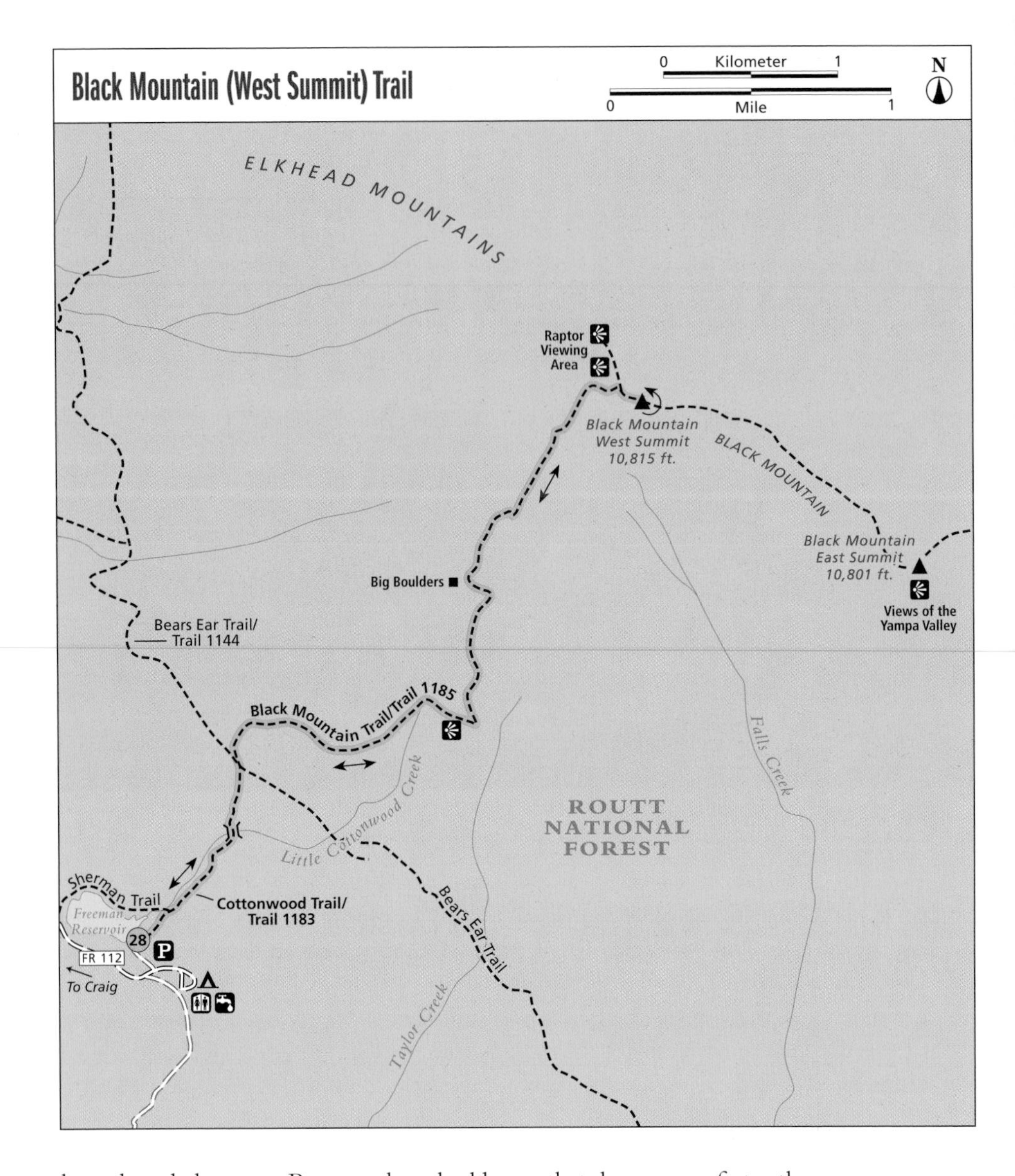

have denuded an area. Because they shed leaves that decompose faster than evergreen needles, aspens return nutrients to the soil more rapidly than other trees. The soil is richer, fostering an environment for other plants, which in turn contribute nutrients to the soil. Aspens, however, are susceptible to about twenty different diseases, making one wonder how they survive so well.

Elk depend on aspen trees, especially during harsh winters when they cannot uncover buried grasses. Scraping bark off with their lower teeth, they feast on the cambium layer just under the bark. Watch for elk teeth marks as you hike. Black bears enjoy many fruits of the aspen forest, from aspen buds and catkins in spring to berries produced by the numerous shrubs. They sometimes climb aspens, leaving claw marks as testimony to their exploits. Avoid surprising bears that are trying to fatten up before winter.

The hike starts along the east shore of Freeman Reservoir, then heads up the Little Cottonwood Creek drainage. The trail can be very muddy after heavy rains. Farther on, one section is very rocky as it climbs to the Bears Ears Trail (Trail 1144). When you reach Black Mountain Trail (Trail 1185), head north to a big aspen stand. Thick forest undergrowth sometimes obscures the trail. Watch your footing as aspen forests are notorious for hidden roots and fallen trees waiting to twist an ankle. Some large boulders lend a rock-garden atmosphere along trail sections. A few clearings present views to the south and west, including of Freeman Reservoir about 1,000 feet below.

The trail curves up a ridge and enters spruce-fir forest. It climbs steadily to a flat spot below the plateau with views to the north. The big boulders make a nice rest spot. The trail then drops about 60 feet into an open area where a large boulder field on the right lines a thumb of the plateau. After a few tight switchbacks, the trail continues to climb to a saddle on the plateau. After hiking around a boulder field, you'll come to another open area. A spur trail heads north to the raptor viewing area, where an interpretive sign explains why golden and bald eagles enjoy soaring and playing above the edge of Black Mountain. The west summit is a little farther to the northeast. A sign denotes the summit, barely discernible on the fairly flat plateau top. The trail beyond the west summit continues another 1.5 miles to the east summit (10,801 feet), with views of the Yampa Valley.

Miles and Directions

0.0 Start at the Cottonwood Trailhead at the east end of Freeman Reservoir. Elevation: 8,760 feet. Follow Cottonwood Trail (Trail 1183).

0.2 Pass the junction with the Sherman Trail (Trail 1010) coming in from the left. Keep hiking straight on Cottonwood Trail.

0.6 Cross Little Cottonwood Creek on a bridge.

0.8 Reach the trail junction of Cottonwood and Bears Ears Trails. Turn left and head uphill on the Bears Ears Trail (Trail 1144).

0.9 Reach the trail junction of Bears Ears Trail and Black Mountain Trail (Trail 1185). Turn right up Black Mountain Trail. GPS: N40 46.41' / W107 24.97'

1.8 Enjoy the views to the south and east as you leave the aspen forest.

2.6 Come to a right switchback and a flat area near big boulders. (***Note:*** This is a good rest stop.)

3.3 The trail reaches the edge of a plateau.

3.6 The spur trail to the raptor viewing area. Stay right to go to the summit. (***Side trip:*** Taking the out-and-back spur to the raptor viewing area will add a total of 0.5 mile to your hike. Raptors enjoy the thermals in this area. The viewpoint has an interpretive sign explaining the soaring birds of prey you might be lucky enough to see.

Freeman Reservoir from Black Mountain Trail

GPS: N40 47.65' / W107 23.50'. On a clear day you can see west to Dinosaur National Monument and the Uinta Mountains in Utah.)

3.7 Reach the west summit of Black Mountain (10,815 feet). GPS: N40 47.45' / W107 23.30'. Turn around and retrace your tracks back to the start.

7.3 Reach the junction with a trail from the left, but with no sign. Keep going straight ahead or you'll end up back at the campground.

7.4 Arrive back at the trailhead.

29 Devils Canyon

This hike takes you into an easily accessible canyon in the Black Ridge Canyons Wilderness area. The trail first crosses open high-desert country of rabbitbrush, junipers, and other thorny plants. It then makes a loop in Devils Canyon, below huge walls of Wingate sandstone and interesting rock formations. Part of the loop follows the creek bottom and should be avoided during thunderstorms. Hiking beneath immense sandstone cliffs and past amphitheaters in a colorful canyon is a real treat! Keep an eye out for desert bighorn sheep and rattlesnakes.

Start: From the Devils Canyon Trailhead
Distance: 6.9-mile double lollipop
Approximate hiking time: 3 to 5 hours
Difficulty: Moderate due to length and terrain
Elevation gain: 620 feet, plus lots of undulations over gullies and drainages
Seasons: Year-round; avoid hot summer days
Trail surface: Dirt roads (nonmotorized) and trails
Other trail users: Equestrians and hunters (in season)
Canine compatibility: Dogs must be under control.
Fees and permits: None
Maps: USGS Mack and Battleship Rock; Nat Geo Trails Illustrated 502 Grand Junction/Fruita; Latitude 40° Fruita, Grand Junction
Trail contacts: Bureau of Land Management, Grand Junction; (970) 244-3000; www.co.blm.gov/co/st/en/fo/gjfo.html
Other: This area may be closed between Jan 15 and May 15 to protect bighorn sheep lambing areas. There is little to no water on the trail. Bring plenty of water (one gallon per person or dog per day), especially if it's hot.

Finding the trailhead: From I-70, take exit 19 for Fruita. Drive south on CO 340 about 1.3 miles to Kingsview Road. Turn right and drive another 1.2 miles to the turnoff to Devils Canyon. Turn left and drive to the big parking lot 0.2 mile down this dirt road to the left. There are vault toilets at the trailhead. **GPS:** N39 08.39' / W108 45.36'

The Hike

The Black Ridge Canyons Wilderness area was designated by Congress on October 5, 2000, and signed into law by President Bill Clinton on October 24, 2000. The wilderness shares its eastern border with Colorado National Monument. The Black Ridge Canyons area includes the second-largest collection of arches in the country outside of Arches National Park. Access to the arches is via a long trail or a rough 4WD road, then a hike. The grandeur of this area can also be seen on an easier hike into Devils Canyon. If you ask how the canyon got its name, locals will simply state: "It's hotter than Hell!"

Devils Canyon lies on the northeastern edge of the Uncompahgre Plateau. Uncompahgre roughly means "rocks that make the water red" in the Ute language. About 300 million years ago, forces pushed ancient (over 1.7 billion years old) "basement" rock upward to form Uncompahgria, the forerunner of today's Uncompahgre Plateau. About 65 million years later, Uncompahgria had eroded to a plain barely

above the level of an inland sea. A delta or floodplain collected red sand on the coastal plain. As the climate changed, the sea receded and windblown sand filled the area. Visualize tall buff and salmon-colored dunes, like those in Great Sand Dunes National Park and Preserve.

Then the climate changed again, becoming moister, and streams began to flow across the area. Conglomerate comprised of mud and pebbles formed, as did other sand deposits. Over the millennia other seas and dunes covered these sediments, and under great pressure the dunes and conglomerate became rock. The Kayenta Formation of sandstone and conglomerate forms a caprock, or hard-to-erode sandstone, that protects the old dunes, now known as Wingate sandstone. The red floodplain sand changed into the Chinle Formation. Cliffs of Wingate sandstone tower 100 to 200 feet into the sky in Devils Canyon. Look around at the cliffs and try to find the elephant's tail, the coke bottles or ovens, and the tiki head formations eroded by the elements.

This area is harsh and wild. Temperatures soar in the summer, creating an oven effect. In winter, temperatures can drop below freezing. Desert bighorn sheep and mountain lions live here. An interpretive sign near the trailhead explains ways to watch wildlife without disturbing them. Bighorn sheep are especially affected by humans and pets during lambing season, from February through May. Please watch and enjoy from a distance and keep your dog next to you! The cliffs shelter peregrine falcons—watch for these beautiful birds of prey.

Another area resident that is very fragile is the crypto, a black lumpy growth on the sand. This interesting combination of green algae, bacteria, fungi, lichens, mosses, and cyanobacteria holds the sandy soil together so other plants may grow.

The hike starts out on a road closed to public motorized vehicles. The first part is relatively flat, with sparse vegetation of rabbitbrush, sagebrush, some thorny plants, and a few hardy junipers. After traveling along several roads, the hike turns onto a singletrack trail. A few places require careful observation to find the cairns that mark the route. The cliffs of the canyon loom ahead. Drop into a creekbed and follow it for a little while among cottonwood and ash trees and some tamarisk. Do not hike here if there are thunderstorms anywhere in the area in case of flash floods.

At the start of the long loop, the trail climbs steeply to the right out of the creek bottom. As you hike along, look back down into the canyon bottom to your left to see black rock walls with shiny mica and lots of lichen. These rocks are the "basement" rocks of Uncompahgria. On the right, sandstone cliffs are a colorful parfait of yellow and pink (think ice cream). Continue climbing through black rocks, mica, and white quartz. The trail traverses the Chinle Formation at the base of the cliffs, undulating across many little creek gullies. Look to the right into each little amphitheater for alcoves or other interesting rock features. The buzz of cicadas and lyrical song of the canyon wren may fill the air.

◀ *Former sheepherder's cabin in Devils Canyon*

Domesticated sheep once grazed in Devils Canyon. At the south end of the loop, an old sheepherder's cabin still stands. The cabin provides a little shade and a great place for lunch. To finish the loop the trail drops, crosses the creek, then climbs to the bench above. Again the trail undulates across many little dry creek gullies. Near the close of the loop is a great view of the Grand Valley and the Book Cliffs to the north. A little farther downstream, continue along the creekbed to add variety to your hike and another mini-loop back to the trailhead.

Miles and Directions

0.0 Start at the Devils Canyon Trailhead kiosk with bulletin boards. Elevation: 4,580 feet.

0.15 Come to a trail junction. Turn left and continue down the dirt road (Trail D1), which is closed to public motorized vehicles.

0.2 Stop and read the bulletin board, containing interesting area information.

0.4 Come to the trail junction with Trail D5. Turn left onto Trail D1 and follow the dirt road, passing any singletrack trails.

0.5 Reach a junction with multiple trails. Turn right here onto Trail D1 and follow the dirt road. You'll return via the left road. GPS: N39 08.14' / W108 45.54'

0.8 Come to a trail junction. Turn left here onto Trail D4. When you reach a wash, look carefully for rocks and cairns and cross the wash.

1.1 Look carefully for cairns as the trail drops about 60 feet into the canyon to the left. GPS: N39 07.77' / W108 45.84'. When you reach the creekbed, cross the creek, turn right onto Trail D3, and travel upstream. (***Note:*** During thunderstorms, do not enter in case of flash flood!)

1.2 Reach the wilderness boundary sign, which is off to your right.

1.4 Reach the start of the loop. Turn right onto Trail D3. Cross the creek and head steeply uphill. The trail meanders past various amphitheaters and cliffs, and up and down little gullies.

3.7 Reach the south end of the loop at the old sheepherder's cabin. Elevation: 5,200 feet. GPS: N39 06.21' / W108 45.93'. This is a great lunch spot. Find the trail on the north side of the cabin to finish the loop. The trail drops into Devils Creek, then follows the bank on the east side.

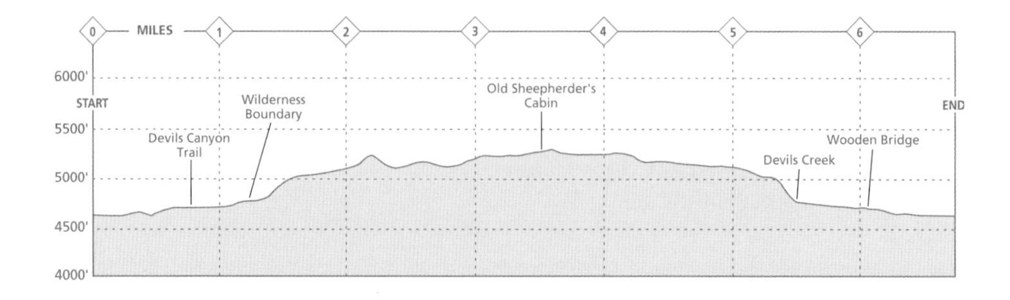

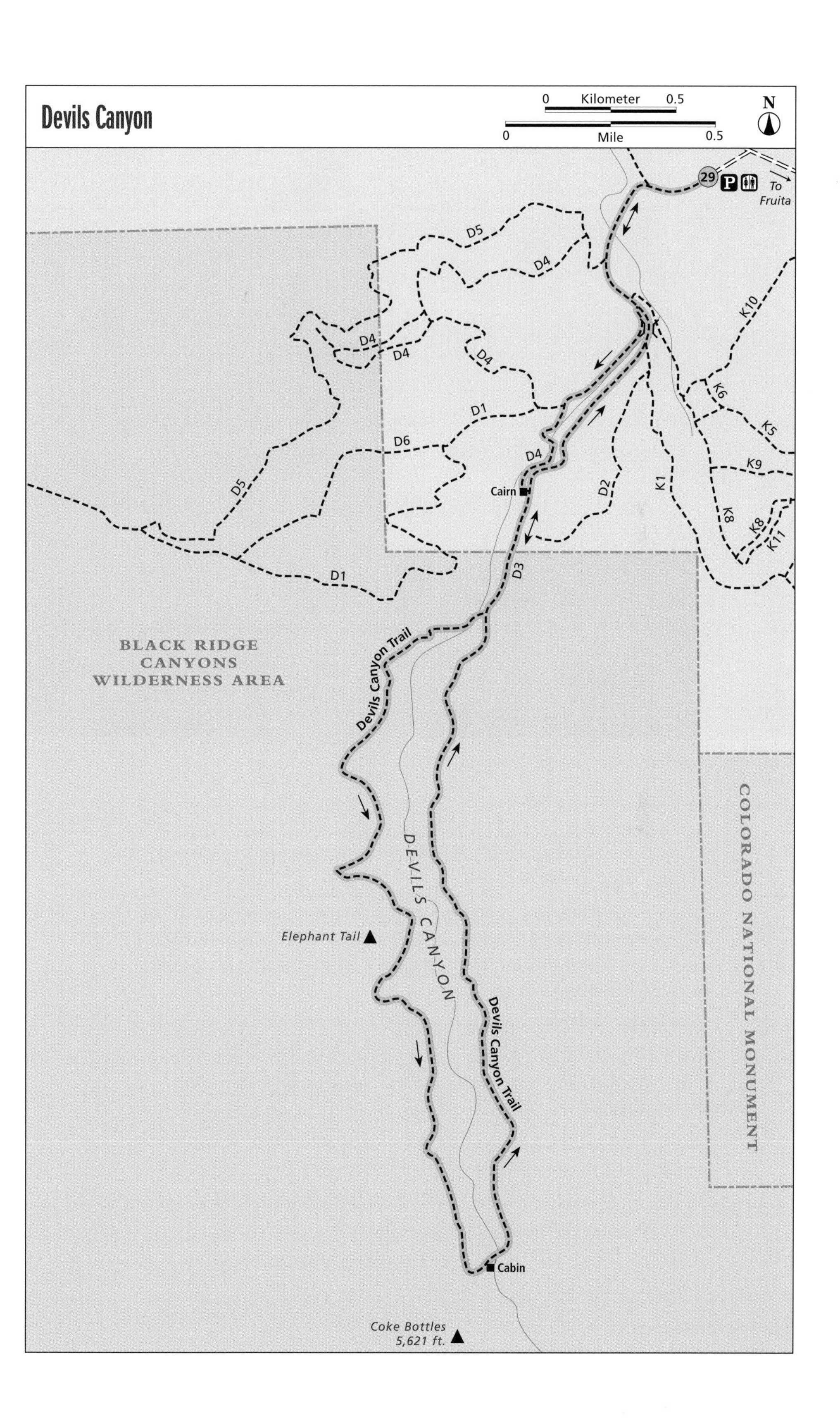

Devils Canyon
0 Kilometer 0.5
0 Mile 0.5
N
29
To Fruita
D5
D4
D4
D4
D4
D1
D6
D4
D5
Cairn
D2
K1
K10
K6
K5
K9
K8
K8
K11
D3
D1
BLACK RIDGE CANYONS WILDERNESS AREA
Devils Canyon Trail
DEVILS CANYON
Elephant Tail
Devils Canyon Trail
COLORADO NATIONAL MONUMENT
Cabin
Coke Bottles 5,621 ft.

View at mile 1.5 of cliffs in Devils Canyon

5.5 The trail drops back down into Devils Creek and starts to retrace the route on which you came (same as mile 1.4).

5.8 Come to a trail junction (same as mile 1.1). You came into the canyon via the left trail. For more variety on the return trip, stay to the right in the creekbed on Trail D3 (unless there's danger of flash flood) and make another mini-loop back to the trail junction at mile 0.5 above.

6.2 Arrive at a trail junction. Take the left trail, still D3, which climbs out of the creekbed on a slickrock ledge to avoid a tight spot, then drops back down to the creek.

6.3 At a trail junction with a road, turn left and walk down the road across a little wooden bridge.

6.4 Come to a trail junction (same as 0.5 mile). Go straight on Trail D1 to return to the trailhead. Trail D1 to the left is the way you walked into the canyon. Return on either trail.

6.9 Arrive back at the trailhead.

SOUTHEAST MOUNTAINS

The geological feature called the Front Range ends at Cheyenne Mountain near Colorado Springs. But to keep things reasonably equal north and south, Colorado Springs and the area immediately west is included in this section.

Colorado Springs, at the base of Pikes Peak (14,115 feet), contains an interesting assortment of businesses and attractions. The US Air Force Academy is located to the north, and the Olympic Training Center is in town. El Paso County has developed a system of trails, and the Pike National Forest offers many hiking opportunities as well. By no means the highest of the fourteeners, Pikes Peak holds the honor of rising the farthest above its base, giving it a formidable profile. Inspired by the view from the top of Pikes Peak in 1893, Katherine Lee Bates wrote the lyrics for "America the Beautiful," which read: "Oh beautiful for spacious skies, for amber waves of grain, for purple mountains majesty, above the fruited plain . . ."

To the west of "the Springs," Florissant Fossil Beds National Monument holds a treasure trove of petrified giant redwood trees and a world-famous source of fossilized insects. Mueller State Park and Dome Rock State Wildlife Area offer both a refuge for elk and bighorn sheep, and a multitude of hiking trails through this former ranching area.

30 Susan G. Bretag/Palmer Loop

This excellent loop hike, following four different trails, offers spectacular views of the Garden of the Gods and Pikes Peak from rocky ridges and wooded valleys. Your dog will have lots of smells to sniff at the various trail forks, as horses and mountain bikers are known to travel the various trails.

Start: From the trailhead on the north side of the main Garden of the Gods parking lot
Distance: 2.6-mile loop
Approximate hiking time: 1 hour
Difficulty: Moderate
Elevation gain: 200 feet
Seasons: Year-round
Trail surface: Singletrack dirt path and doubletrack paved trail
Other trail users: Mountain bikers and equestrians on parts of the trail
Canine compatibility: Dogs must be on leash
Fees and permits: None
Map: USGS Cascade
Trail contacts: Colorado Springs Parks, Recreation, and Cultural Services, 1401 Recreation Way, Colorado Springs, CO 80905-1975; (719) 385-5940; www.springsgov.com
Other: Colorado Springs city park rules apply

Finding the trailhead: From I-25, take exit 146 and drive west on Garden of the Gods Road until it dead-ends at 30th Street against the mountain front. Turn left (south) onto 30th Street and drive south to Gateway Road, opposite the Garden of the Gods Visitor and Nature Center. Turn right (west) onto Gateway Road and follow it until it merges with Juniper Way Loop, a one-way loop road that encircles the main Garden of the Gods zone. Turn right (north) onto the one-way road and follow it to a large parking lot on the left. The trailhead is at the north side of the parking lot at a crosswalk. **GPS:** N38 53.00' / W104 52.63'

Alternatively, approach from I-25 and downtown Colorado Springs by driving west on Cimarron Street/US 24 from I-25 to Ridge Road, 0.5 mile past 31st Street. Exit right and follow Ridge Road north to a stop sign at Colorado Avenue. Cross Colorado Avenue (the road may be busy) and drive up a steep hill on Ridge Road to the Garden of the Gods. At Juniper Way Loop, go right and drive to the main parking lot on the north side of the park.

The Hike

This wonderful hike follows parts of four different trails around the main red-rock zone of the Garden of the Gods. The first section, following Palmer Trail, climbs onto ridges west of North and South Gateway Rocks before dipping down to Scotsman Picnic Area. The next segment follows Scotsman Trail back to the central Garden zone, where it picks up the paved Perkins Central Garden Trail. The last part follows the Susan G. Bretag Trail north up a broad valley east of the rock formations.

The trails are singletrack except for a wide concrete sidewalk section. Expect great views and a close-up, intimate experience with the unique rock formations and the transitional ecosystems found here. Most of the trail is quiet, with few other hikers, although the section through the main Garden zone is busy. The trail also crosses the park roads four times. Be sure to use the crosswalks.

Start the hike at the trailhead on the north side of the main parking lot off Juniper Way Loop. Walk north across the road to a trail junction. Go left on the Palmer Trail. The trail coming in from the right, the Susan G. Bretag Trail, is the return trail. The first trail segment on the Palmer Trail, named for General William Jackson Palmer, the founder of Colorado Springs, runs 1.2 miles from the junction to the Scotsman Picnic Area, southwest of the central Garden zone.

Paralleling the road, the Palmer Trail goes northwest through copses of scrub oak before arcing south. It slowly gains elevation and after 0.3 mile reaches a scenic overlook. Walk 75 feet southeast off the trail for the best view and photo opportunity. All the main rock formations—North Gateway Rock, South Gateway Rock, Gray Rock, Keyhole Rock, Montezuma Ruins, and the Three Graces—tower to the south, their ragged outlines etched against the sky.

Past the overlook the trail turns west and contours through a shallow canyon before climbing onto east-facing slopes opposite North Gateway Rock, the park's highest formation. The trail continues climbing through a piñon pine and juniper woodland until it reaches a high point and then descends to a shoulder. This is another great viewpoint. Note the Kissing Camels, a small arch perched atop North Gateway Rock on the left, and the Weeping Indian, the white rock profile of an Indian face on South Gateway Rock. Continue south down the trail and reach a junction 0.8 mile from the trailhead. From here a short trail heads left to the central Garden zone. Stay straight on the Palmer Trail, ignoring another side trail that jogs over to the road 100 feet farther down.

The Palmer Trail passes beneath the west face of the Giant Footprints, a couple of tilted slabs composed of 220-million-year-old Fountain Formation sandstone, then descends southwest parallel to the park road through scrub oak for 0.4 mile. When the trail reaches the edge of the road at 1.2 miles, you're opposite the Scotsman Picnic Area. Cross the road to a parking lot and cross a bridge. A restroom, open in summer only, is to your left. Go right on the Scotsman Trail.

Follow the Scotsman Trail northeast for 0.36 mile. The sandy trail, often used by horses, slowly climbs. At an obvious junction, keep left and hike to the Juniper Way Loop road. Cross the road just north of a parking area and follow a trail into the central Garden zone.

The next 0.5 mile of trail follows the paved Perkins Central Garden Trail, the Garden's most popular trail. Hike north and then east on the paved path, passing north of the Three Graces and Montezuma Tower, both slender spires popular with rock climbers. At an obvious T junction, go left (north) and hike to the Gateway, the huge gap between North and South Gateway Rocks. At the trail junction here below the dedication plaque, turn right onto a paved trail and walk 0.15 mile east to Juniper Way Loop.

The last trail segment follows the Susan G. Bretag Trail for 0.5 mile back to the trailhead and parking lot. Cross the road at a crosswalk and turn left onto the marked trail. Follow the wide trail north in a valley between rock formations on the west and

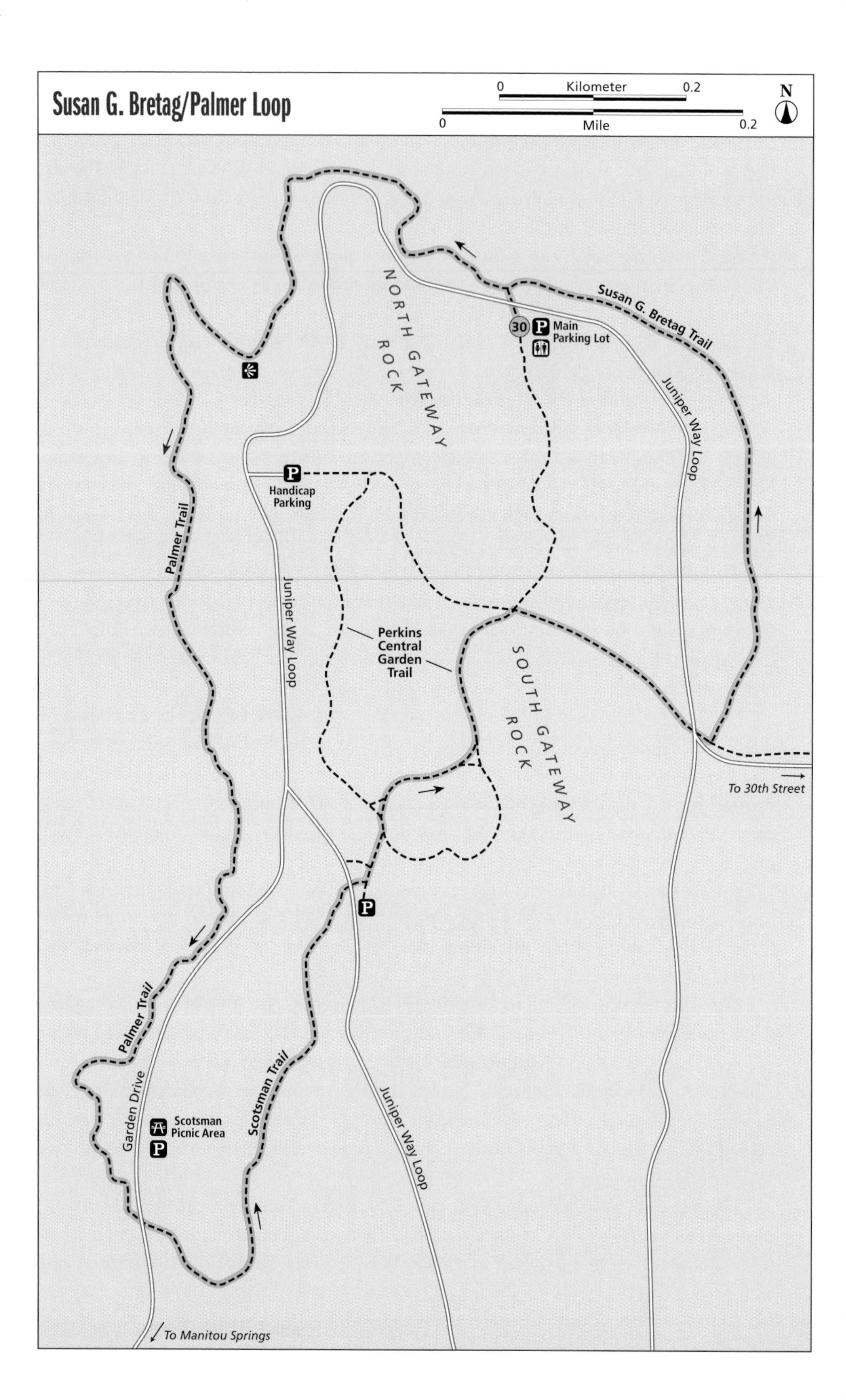
Susan G. Bretag/Palmer Loop
0
Kilometer
0.2
0
Mile
0.2
N
NORTH GATEWAY ROCK
SOUTH GATEWAY ROCK
Susan G. Bretag Trail
30
Main Parking Lot
Juniper Way Loop
Handicap Parking
Palmer Trail
Perkins Central Garden Trail
To 30th Street
Scotsman Trail
Scotsman Picnic Area
Garden Drive
To Manitou Springs

a hogback to the east. The trail crosses a meadow covered with grass and yucca. After 0.3 mile it reaches a Y junction with the Dakota Trail. Keep left and follow the Susan G. Bretag Trail, which bends northwest. End your hike at the start of the Palmer Trail. Cross the road back to the trailhead. If you're thirsty or need the facilities, a water fountain and restrooms are located on the southeast side of the parking lot.

Miles and Directions

0.0 Start at the trailhead on the north side of the main Garden parking lot. Cross the road to a T junction and turn left (west) onto the Palmer Trail.

0.3 Come to a scenic overlook on the left.

0.8 Reach a junction with a short trail to the Garden zone on the left. Go straight.

1.2 Reach a road opposite the Scotsman Picnic Area. Cross the road to the left and then cross a bridge to reach Scotsman Trail. Go right.

1.6 End the Scotsman Trail at Juniper Way Loop. Cross the road to the central Garden zone. Follow the trail straight to the paved Perkins Central Garden Trail.

2.1 End the Perkins Central Garden Trail at the Juniper Way Loop on the east side of the park. Cross the street and turn left (north) onto the Susan G. Bretag Trail.

2.6 End the Susan G. Bretag Trail at the junction with the Palmer Trail. Go left across the road to return to the trailhead and parking lot.

31 Thompson Mountain

This interesting hike makes a rolling loop through part of the Deer Haven Ranch, managed by the Bureau of Land Management to preserve its natural values and provide recreational opportunities. The trail winds through ponderosa pines, Douglas firs, and meadows. Open areas, including a side trip to Thompson Point, provide nice views of Pikes Peak, the Wet Mountains, and the Sangre de Cristo Range.

Start: From the Wilson Creek (Trail 5827A) Trailhead
Distance: 7.6-mile lollipop
Approximate hiking time: 3.5 to 5.5 hours
Difficulty: Difficult due to elevation gain
Elevation gain/loss: 1,420-foot gain/420-foot loss
Seasons: Year-round except after big snowstorms
Trail surface: Single- and doubletrack dirt trail
Other trail users: Equestrians, mountain bikers, hunters (in season)
Canine compatibility: Dogs must be under control
Fees and permits: None
Maps: USGS Gribble Mountain and Rice Mountain; Nat Geo Trails Illustrated 137, Pikes Peak/Cañon City
Trail contacts: Bureau of Land Management, Royal Gorge Field Office, Cañon City; (719) 269-8500; www.blm.gov/co/st/en/fo/rgfo.html
Other: No facilities at the trailhead. Minimal water is found along the trail; bring your own.

Finding the trailhead: From the intersection of CO 115 and US 50 in Cañon City, drive west on US 50 about 9.5 miles, past the Royal Gorge turnoff (restaurants and motels here), to CO 9. Turn right onto CO 9 and head north approximately 8.7 miles to Fremont CR 11. Turn right onto FCR 11, watching for deer along this twisty paved road. (You're on the Gold Belt Scenic Byway.) Drive 5.3 miles to the DEER HAVEN RANCH sign, just past mile marker 5, and turn right onto FCR 69, a well-graded narrow dirt road. Drive slowly to avoid collisions with oncoming traffic or cattle because this area is open range. Drive 3.3 miles to the WILSON CREEK TRAIL (Trail 5827A) sign and turn right. Park immediately in the meadow. **GPS:** N38 36.62' / W105 20.98'. (***Note:*** Drive the extra 0.2 mile to the trailhead bulletin board *only* if the road is dry and you have high clearance. The road can be extremely wet and muddy, and driving through the mud only makes the muddy area larger. Even the BLM has been known to get stuck on this road.)

The Hike

Charlie and Lee Switzer first started cattle ranching in the Thompson Mountain area back in the 1870s. Their 640 acres covered open range, rolling hills, and fields of bunchgrass. During the Cripple Creek–Victor gold rush, they supplied beef to the miners. Around 1900 Toll Witcher bought the ranch from the Switzers, then sold it to Lon Gribble in 1914 or 1915. During World War I the price of cattle rose. With his profit Gribble built a new house in 1917. While digging the basement, he struck solid rock in one corner. After digging 4 feet into the rock, he struck water. Gribble constructed a water tank of sorts and built the kitchen right above it. The two-story house had two bedrooms downstairs and four upstairs, a big fireplace, and a full

Pikes Peak from stem part of trail

basement. Lumber for the house was hauled from Cañon City with a four-horse team. The house cost $12,000 to build, a substantial sum in those days. You passed the historic house (still a private residence) on the way to the trailhead.

Gribble also established a sawmill, with a Case tractor to run it. He hired a worker to run the mill and others to cut the timber. He sold the lumber to the coal mines south of Cañon City for mine props. By 1932 cattle prices had fallen and a hard winter took its toll on Gribble's ability to pay his loans, resulting in foreclosure on Gribble's ranch.

According to a story titled "Last Wilson Creek Roundup," in the June–July 1976 *Frontier Times,* Dud Van Buskirk, who was Lon Gribble's brother-in-law, bet Gribble that Fred Short could hold a cow by the tail for five minutes. Short walked into the herd of cattle and grabbed the tail of a two-year-old heifer. The heifer ran as fast as she could, out of the herd and up along the fence. Fred was hanging on. After about 100 feet, the heifer decided to head back to the herd, "stopped right quick and turned back down the fence. Fred, however, just kept going—about 10 feet to a step—till he fell and lit on his face."

In 1940 Floyd Murphy bought the old Switzer Ranch and actually made it profitable. He grazed a string of relay horses and was one of the best relay riders in America. He also grazed cattle. He sold the ranch about ten years later at $10 per acre.

After several other owners, the Richard King Mellon Foundation and the Conservation Fund of Arlington, Virginia, bought the land, then donated it to the Bureau of Land Management in 1992 to "provide significant wildlife habitat, riparian, and wetland habitat, recreation opportunities, protect scenic quality and to improve stewardship and access to adjoining public land." The donation amounted to 4,900 acres. On National Trails Day in 1993, a groundbreaking ceremony was held to initiate the current trail. The Rocky Mountain Back Country Horsemen and the Medicine Wheel Bicycle Club have steadily worked on the trail.

The hike starts up a drainage, then turns up another drainage at a check dam. The first part climbs steadily through the forest, then up a ridge. As you gain elevation, keep an eye open to the right for views of Pikes Peak. In a beautiful ponderosa pine forest, the trail is marked with brown carsonite signs. Mica flecks sparkle in the trail.

Pass through a gate at 2.2 miles, then descend through a flower-filled meadow to a pond where the loop part of the trail begins. Take the left fork first. The trail follows occasional trail markers. It heads down another drainage to a metal cattle trough. From the descending trail you can see the rocky knob of Thompson Point. After the cattle trough the trail heads up a broad drainage to a saddle. A spur trail, Trail 5827B, heads to the left to Thompson Point. Wilson Creek Trail (Trail 5827A) turns right here and eventually climbs, descends, and climbs again to an open area with views of Cap Rock. Turn right here and follow the two-track trail that winds through forest and meadow and back to a gully. Turn right at the gully and walk back to the first pond and dam to end the loop. Head back to your vehicle the way you came.

Thompson Mountain covers a large area, its gentle ridges surrounding drainages and meadows. It's definitely not the typical Colorado pointy-topped mountain.

Miles and Directions

0.0 Start in the meadow near the WILSON CREEK TRAIL (Trail 5827A) sign. Elevation: 7,620 feet. Hike up the dirt road.

0.2 Reach the bulletin board for the trail. Please stop and read the area information and regulations.

0.4 Look for an old rock fence to your right.

0.6 Curve left at the directional sign.

0.7 Reach the remains of an old one-room house with corrugated siding.

1.2 The trail reaches a saddle and turns right up the ridge. (***Note:*** During the next 0.4 mile, look to the right for views of Pikes Peak through the trees.)

2.2 Reach a fence and gate. Elevation: 8,250 feet. GPS: N38 36.28' / W105 22.51'. Use the metal gate to the left—remember to close the gate behind you. The trail descends the meadow to a trail junction sign. (***Note:*** Nice views to the southwest of the Wet Mountains and the Sangre de Cristo Range.)

2.4 Reach the junction of Water Tank Trail and Thompson Mountain Trail. The loop trail is really across the gully to the west. You can turn left onto Water Tank Trail and follow the trail through the trees, turning right to cross the little dam. However, willows are

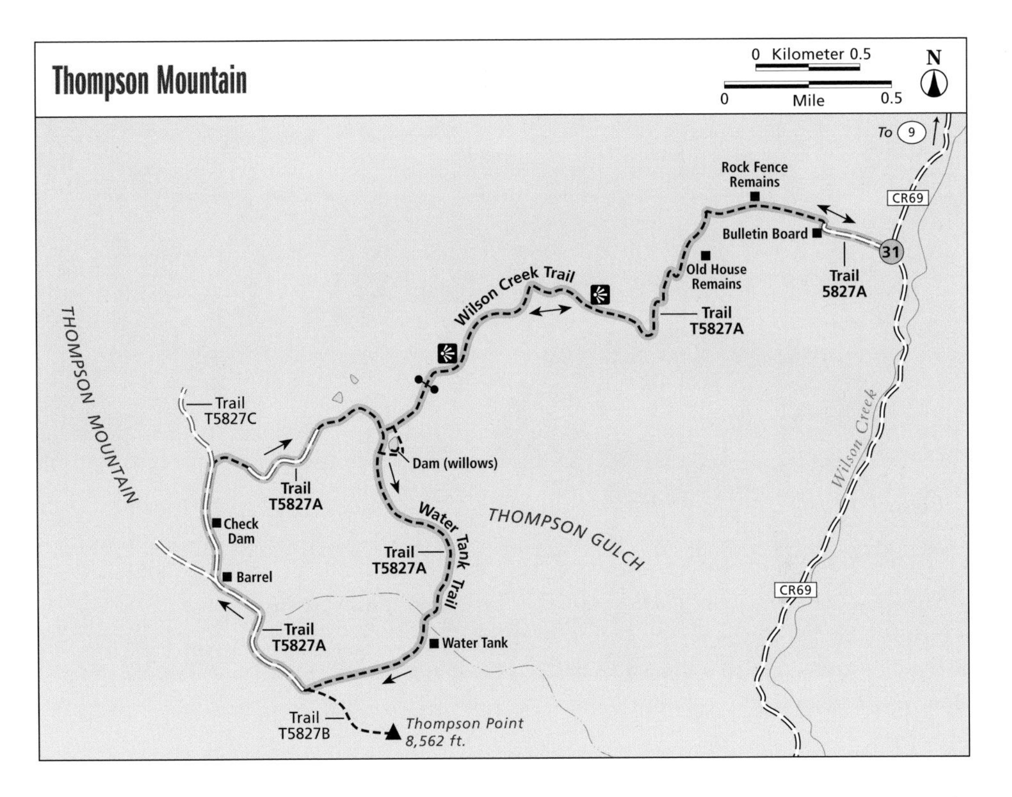

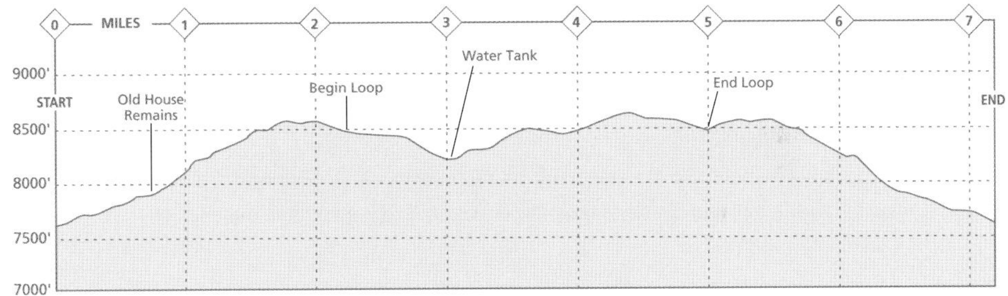

overtaking the top of the dam. Instead, head toward the gully to the west on the north side of the pond and make your way to the other side. The trail comes to a T intersection. The loop in the trail starts here. Turn left and follow the trail through the forest, then descend toward a creek.

3.0 Enter a meadow. Look downhill as you hike and you'll see a circular water tank, a narrow water trough, and a creek. Head to the water tank.

3.1 Drop down past the metal water tank and cross the creek. GPS: N38 35.67' / W105 22.56'. You'll find the trail on the other side, which takes you up and around into a grassy open meadow and drainage. Head uphill toward a saddle.

Water trough along trail

3.6	Reach the saddle and a trail junction. Turn right and follow the two-track Trail 5827A uphill. (***Note:*** Look to your left for some interesting rock formations.) (***Side trip:*** If you'd like to hike up to Thompson Point, turn left onto Trail 5827B. Out-and-back distance to Thompson Point is about 1 mile, to a point beyond the rocky outcropping.)
3.8	Follow the trail downhill to the right. As you approach a gully, the road turns left and starts heading uphill again.
4.1	Enter an open area with a rusted barrel stuck in the ground to your right. Continue uphill on the trail to a check dam at mile 4. Continue along the trail to the left of the dam.
4.4	Enter an open, flat area with three trail posts. Elevation: 8,580 feet. GPS: N38 36.08' / W105 23.27'. Trail 5827A turns right while Trail 5827C goes straight ahead and starts heading slightly downhill. Turn right here and follow Trail 5827A as it curves toward some ponderosas. (***Note:*** There are great views of various hills ahead, with Thompson Point and the Sangre de Cristo and Wet Mountains behind you.)
4.9	Arrive in an open meadow. A big rock outcropping is on your left. Continue across the meadow toward ponderosas. The trail curves a little to the left, then the right. You'll come to a gully, then turn right and follow the trail back to the start of the loop.
5.2	Reach the trail junction sign for Water Tank Trail and Thompson Mountain Trail. Head uphill and return the way you came.
7.4	Arrive back at the trailhead bulletin board.
7.6	Arrive back at the parking area in the meadow.

32 Mount Cutler Trail

Climb through a pine and fir forest in North Cheyenne Cañon Park to the summit of 7,164-foot Mount Cutler, which offers panoramic views of Colorado Springs. With its easy terrain and small elevation gain, this is a good hike to start on when introducing your dog to the world of hiking.

Start: From the Mount Cutler Trailhead
Distance: 1.9 miles out and back
Approximate hiking time: 1 to 2 hours
Difficulty: Easy
Elevation gain: 367 feet
Seasons: Year-round; icy in winter
Trail surface: Singletrack dirt trail
Other trail users: Runners
Canine compatibility: Dogs must be on leash
Fees and permits: None
Map: USGS Manitou Springs
Trail contacts: Colorado Springs Parks, Recreation, and Cultural Services, 1401 Recreation Way, Colorado Springs, CO 80905-1975; (719) 385-5940; www.springsgov.com

Finding the trailhead: From I-25, take the Nevada Avenue/CO 115 exit (exit 140 B). Drive south on South Nevada Avenue/CO 115 for about a mile and turn right (west) onto Cheyenne Road. Follow Cheyenne Road for 2.6 miles to its end at Cheyenne Boulevard. (If you approach via Cheyenne Boulevard, stay right on Cheyenne Boulevard at this intersection.) Go left (west) on Cheyenne Boulevard for 0.1 mile to a Y intersection. Turn right, through an open gate, into North Cheyenne Cañon Park. Drive 1.4 miles up the park road to the Mount Cutler Trailhead on the left.
GPS: N38 47.50' / W104 53.23'

The Hike

Serene, peaceful, and seemingly remote, North Cheyenne Cañon is a gem tucked away on the southwest side of Colorado Springs. Just beyond charming residential districts, a winding road climbs west into this spectacular canyon, which is also one of the city's oldest parks.

The hike up Mount Cutler is the easiest and most accessible summit climb in the Pikes Peak region. Expect great views across North and South Cheyenne Cañons, an easy grade, peaceful pine and fir woods, and airy exposure on the last section. Be careful, and watch your children and dog as you hike along the exposed trail above South Cheyenne Cañon, especially if you make the short hike out to the east summit, which perches above dangerous and vertical cliffs. Some of the footing is on loose, slippery gravel scattered atop the granite bedrock.

Mount Cutler offers stunning panoramic views from its rounded summit of dark forests spilling down steep mountainsides, the North and South Cheyenne Creek drainages, towering granite formations, and tumbling Seven Falls, as well as vistas of Colorado Springs and the high plains to the east. The wide trail climbs steadily but is an easy climb, with a thrilling touch of exposure as you traverse across the west- and south-facing shoulders of the mountain.

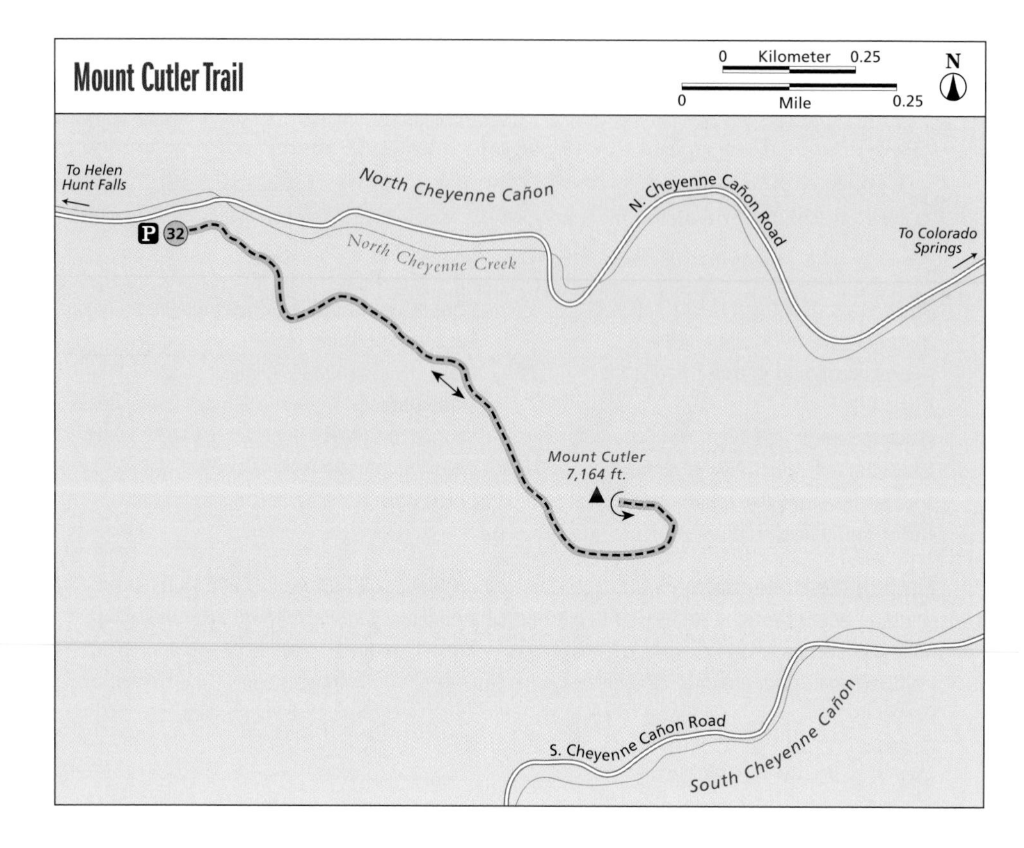

From the parking lot and trailhead at 6,797 feet in North Cheyenne Cañon, hike up the broad, well-used path through a dense evergreen forest that provides welcome shade in summer. The trail gently climbs and at 0.26 mile reaches an overlook with views of distant downtown Colorado Springs. The trail continues climbing, crossing steep slopes littered with fallen trees. The trail flattens out briefly beneath a squat rock tower, then bends through a gully and climbs again, reaching an outlook at 0.4 mile. An excellent view opens across the cliff-lined canyon to the sprawl of Colorado Springs.

At 0.5 mile is a saddle that separates North and South Cheyenne Cañons. The Mount Muscoco Trail heads right here. Keep straight ahead on the well-trod path for Mount Cutler. The trail traverses onto the dry southwest side of the mountain. Below, sparse pines cling to rocky soil. The narrow trail edges across an exposed slope, with steep cliffs and drop-offs to your right. Keep your children and your dog in check here. As you hike, look down to the right from the trail and you'll glimpse Seven Falls cascading far below.

The trail continues spiraling upward onto the south slope, passing a trail marker at a switchback at 0.75 mile. Keep left and scramble up the final steep trail section to

7,164-foot Mount Cutler's broad rounded summit at 0.95 mile. The summit offers 360-degree views, with the city and vast plains spreading east to the distant horizon and the monumental peaks of the Front Range looming to the west.

To return to the trailhead from Mount Cutler's summit, follow the trail in reverse. It's all downhill—and the views are just as good as on the way up.

Option

Go left (east) from the main trail on one of two trails. A short distance east of the main path, these two join together. Follow the trail another 0.25 mile east to Cutler's lower summit. This lofty perch, surrounded by airy cliffs, yields superb views of Colorado Springs and the Broadmoor Hotel area below.

Miles and Directions

0.0 Begin at the Mount Cutler Trailhead.

0.4 Arrive at an overlook.

0.5 Reach the saddle separating North and South Cheyenne Cañons.

0.95 Arrive at the summit of Mount Cutler. Retrace your steps toward the trailhead.

1.9 Arrive back at the trailhead.

33 Newlin Creek Trail

Newlin Creek Trail wanders up a narrow canyon following the remains of an old logging road. Due to floods and deterioration, it's tough to tell that this trail was once a road. Rocky cliffs loom over the trail in spots, while little waterfalls and cascades dance down the creek. After crossing one wooden bridge, the trail crosses the creek numerous times on logs and rocks. The most interesting features of this hike lie in the destination meadow. An old steam boiler, flywheel, and chimney are all that remain of a sawmill operation.

Start: From the Newlin Creek (Trail 1335) Trailhead near Florence Mountain Park
Distance: 5.0 miles out and back
Approximate hiking time: 2.25 to 4 hours
Difficulty: Difficult due to elevation gain
Elevation gain: 1,400 feet, plus lots of little undulations at creek crossings
Seasons: Best from mid-May to early Nov
Trail surface: Dirt trail with numerous creek crossings, rocky in places
Other trail users: Equestrians and hunters (in season)
Canine compatibility: Dogs must be under control
Fees and permits: None
Map: USGS Rockvale
Trail contacts: San Isabel National Forest, San Carlos Ranger District, Cañon City; (719) 269-8500; www.fs.usda.gov/psicc
Other: No facilities at the trailhead. Bring water in case the creek is low. Treat water obtained from Newlin Creek.

Finding the trailhead: From the intersection of CO 115 and CO 67 in the middle of Florence, drive south on CO 67 for 4.3 miles to Fremont CR 15. The intersection is marked as NATIONAL FOREST ACCESS and for the Newlin Creek Trailhead. Turn right onto FCR 15. The road forks in 2.7 miles; stay on FCR 15 by driving on the right fork. The road turns to dirt in another 0.9 mile. The road forks in another 0.8 mile; stay right, following the sign to Florence Mountain Park. The entrance to the mountain park is designated by two big log posts on either side of the road in another 1.2 miles. At the junction in another 0.1 mile, marked AMPHITHEATER, go straight. In another 0.2 mile there's an intersection where you continue straight, then pass the caretaker's house on the left. Follow the signs to Newlin Creek Trailhead. In 0.5 mile, pass the national forest boundary sign; the road narrows. It's another 0.1 mile to the trailhead. The trailhead is about 10.8 miles from the middle of Florence. **GPS:** N38 16.00' / W105 11.30'

The Hike

Newlin Creek is nestled in the northeastern end of the Wet Mountains. Early explorers, such as the Gunnison Expedition of 1853–54, perceived that rain constantly fell on this mountain range and named it accordingly. Streams ran high in late winter and early spring, and summer thunderstorms flooded creekbeds. Newlin Creek was probably named after a local by the same name who lived in Locke Park to the west.

Oil was discovered near the town of Florence in 1881, and some wells are still producing oil today. Coal mining also became a big industry in the late 1800s. Coal

Boiler and flywheel

Creek lies just north of Newlin Creek. The discovery of silver on the west side of the Wet Mountains created booming mining towns such as Silver Cliff and Westcliffe. Coal and silver mines needed much timber for shoring up mine shafts and for residential and commercial buildings. The forests of the Wet Mountains provided an opportunity for an entrepreneur to supply lumber to industries on both sides of the range.

Nathaniel F. Herrick, originally from Canada, lived in Galena near Locke Park, southwest of Cañon City and a few miles west of Newlin Creek, with his wife and children. He grabbed at the opportunity to own a lumber mill and built a road and sawmill up Newlin Creek. The hand-built road measured about 5 feet in width and in places was supported with rock walls. Herrick hauled a huge steam boiler and flywheel to a nice meadow where he also built a cabin, complete with stone chimney. The boiler used water from Newlin Creek to run the flywheel and power a saw to cut lumber.

On November 28, 1887, Herrick signed a chattel mortgage with W. D. McGee and W. F. Hasidy for $900. The "chattel" involved the sawmill, including the engine, boiler fixtures, and tools; five horses and one mule with their harnesses; and two log wagons and a Studebaker wagon along with the log chains. According to the mortgage record, the sawmill was "situated on Newland Creek in said County of Fremont,

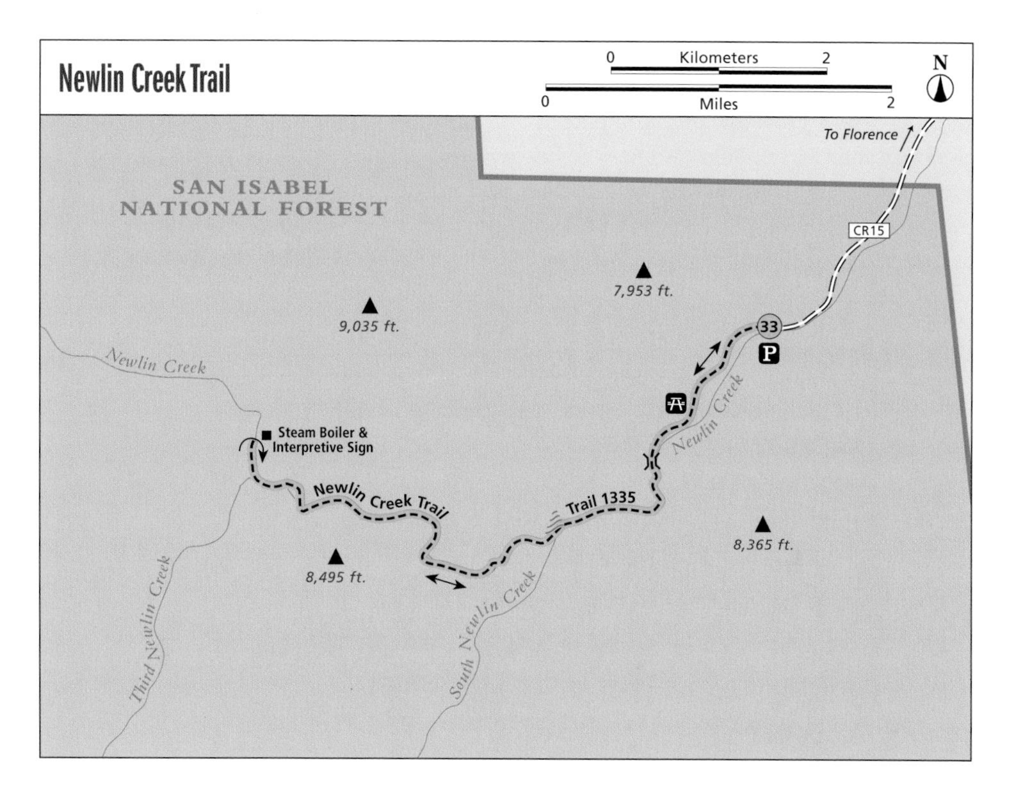

23 or 24 miles from Cañon City." Unfortunately, after Herrick had all the equipment set up and mortgaged, he died the very next month at the age of sixty-one. The lumber mill was apparently abandoned soon thereafter. The road was destroyed by floods and rockslides and the equipment remained in place.

Today the steam boiler lies rusting amid aspen trees next to Newlin Creek. Some bricks lie near its base. Pipes point in different directions, and the flywheel sits forlorn and disconnected. Exactly how much time it took to haul this equipment from Cañon City or Florence is unknown, but it must have been quite an effort. Look carefully at the boiler for an interesting gargoyle-type face and other inscriptions.

The hike follows Newlin Creek up to the steam boiler meadow. Between rockslides and floods, it's hard to tell today that any type of wagon road existed along the creek. The trail twists through forests of Douglas fir, ponderosa pine, and Gambel oak. A picnic table sits just before the trail slips between steep canyon walls. Enjoy the fancy wooden bridge that crosses Newlin Creek, since you'll be using rocks and logs to cross creeks numerous times over the duration of the hike. Watch the creek for mini-waterfalls and cascades. Look up occasionally for interesting pointy cliffs and rocks. Farther up the canyon you'll hike along an open slope with Gambel oak above,

◀ *Little waterfall near mile 1.5*

then head back into the trees, where the undergrowth is dotted with red columbine, heart-leafed arnica, Wood's rose, strawberries, pussytoes, and some nice aspen.

A few creek crossings later, you enter a little meadow on the left (west) side of the creek. An interpretive sign outlines the history of the equipment beyond, along with a location diagram. The old boiler and other equipment lie among the trees. Remember the equipment is protected as historical items under the Antiquities Act. Please do not climb on or disrupt the remains. The meadow is a wonderful picnic spot. Enjoy and return the way you came.

Miles and Directions

0.0 Start at the trailhead parking area for Newlin Creek Trail (Trail 1335). Elevation: 7,000 feet. Please sign the trail register.

0.5 Come to a picnic table.

0.6 The trail crosses Newlin Creek on a wooden bridge with handrails.

0.9 The trail goes through an area of big boulders with rocks in the trail.

1.0 Come to the first of many creek crossings without a bridge.

1.5 Reach a nice 4-foot-high waterfall off to the right of a creek crossing.

1.7 There's a tricky creek crossing on slopey rock (like slickrock).

2.5 Arrive in a little meadow. A nice interpretive poster explaining the history of the boiler and location of artifacts is to your right. Elevation: 8,400 feet. GPS: N38 15.71' / W105 13.00'. Return the way you came.

5.0 Arrive back at the trailhead.

34 The Crags Trail

After a short climb, this excellent hike leads through serene meadows below granite cliffs and boulder-strewn hillsides, with excellent views of Pikes Peak's northern shoulders. While this is a relatively easy trail for your dog, be sure to bring the proper items—water, waste bags, snacks—for your furry friend because this can be a longer trail to complete.

Start: From The Crags Trailhead by the restrooms at Crags Campground
Distance: 4.0 miles out and back
Approximate hiking time: 2 to 3 hours
Difficulty: Easy
Elevation gain: 700 feet
Seasons: Best from Apr through Oct; snowy in winter
Trail surface: Singletrack dirt trail
Other trail users: Mountain bikers
Canine compatibility: Dogs must be on leash
Fees and permits: None
Maps: USGS Pikes Peak and Woodland Park
Trail contacts: Pike National Forest, Pikes Peak Ranger District, 601 S. Weber St., Colorado Springs, CO 80903; (719) 636-1602; www.fs.usda.gov
Other: Skis or snowshoes required in winter

Finding the trailhead: Take the Cimarron Street/US 24 exit (exit 141) from I-25. Follow US 24 west for about 24 miles up Ute Pass and through Woodland Park to the town of Divide. Turn left (south) onto CO 67 and drive 4.3 miles south to a left (east) turn onto Teller CR 62, marked with a CRAGS CAMPGROUND sign. Follow the rough dirt road through the Rocky Mountain Mennonite Camp for 3.2 miles to Crags Campground on the left. Park on the right in a parking lot surrounded by a split-rail fence. The trailhead is across the road, next to the restrooms. Alternatively, hike up the road through the campground to The Crags Trailhead at its east end. **GPS:** N38 87.13' / W105 11.96'

The Hike

With its gentle grades and unsurpassed mountain beauty, The Crags Trail (Trail 664), may be the perfect day hike in the Pikes Peak region. The trail slowly climbs up a subalpine valley below high summits, offering all the exposure and views of a full-fledged mountain ascent, but your thighs and lungs won't feel the burn like they would if you climbed neighboring 14,115-foot Pikes Peak. The valley the trail winds up is beautiful in summer, with wildflower-strewn meadows, warm temperatures, and plentiful wildlife.

Take your time on this hike. Although the trail is relatively easy, its starting elevation is 10,040 feet and it ends at 10,800 feet. If you're coming from sea level, watch for altitude sickness, including headache and nausea. On summer afternoons, watch for severe thunderstorms with lightning moving across The Crags. Carry a raincoat and retreat to your car if you see incoming bad weather. Drinking water is available at the campground.

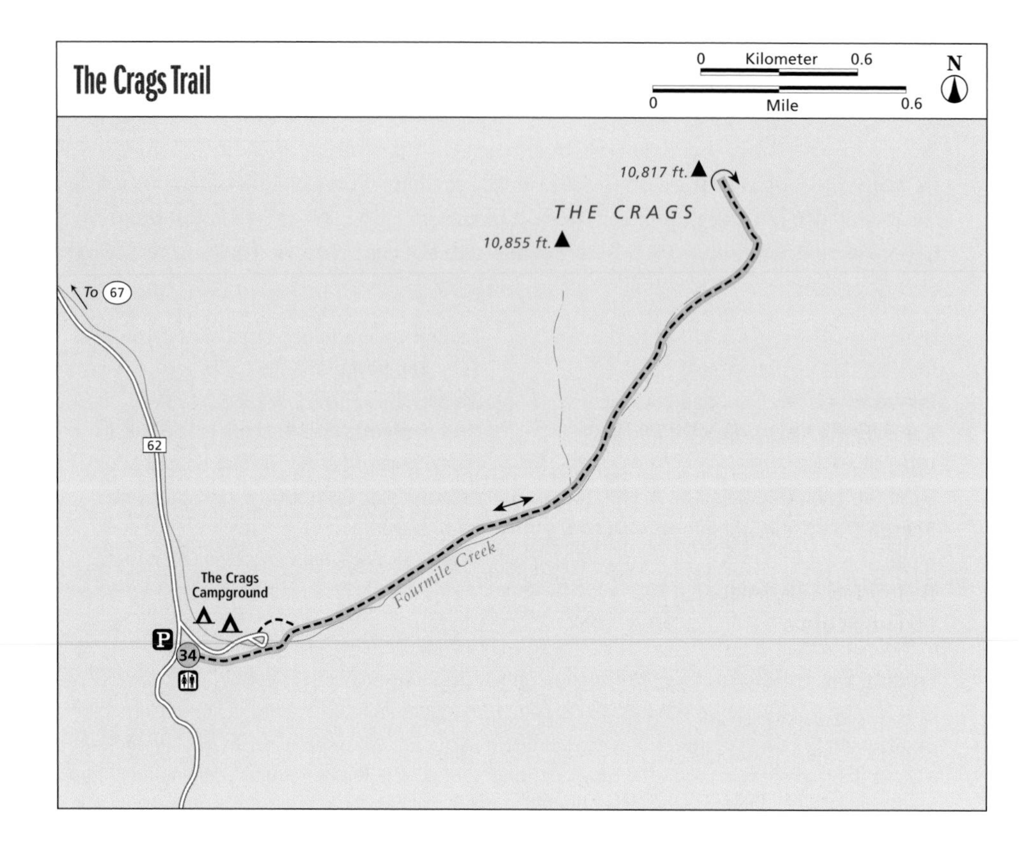

From the trailhead by the restrooms, the trail crosses Fourmile Creek, and the most difficult part of the hike begins. The trail switchbacks up a steep hillside, quickly gaining elevation before leveling off above Crags Campground. Curve around a hillside and drop back down to a trail junction. Stay to the left, minding the trail marker for The Crags and paralleling the tumbling creek.

The trail passes through a jumbled boulder field before opening into a broad, grassy expanse. The trail heads east up the narrowing valley before reaching a broader meadow. Here the creek makes wide meanders across the valley floor, its banks densely lined with willows. Outcroppings of granite line the hillside to the left. Aspen trees and tall Engelmann spruce and subalpine fir trees stand sentinel-like along the edge of the meadow. Ahead rises Pangborn's Pinnacle, a mighty stone dome that towers above the valley.

The Crags Trail briefly jogs to the left, climbing higher before dropping back into the meadow. Approaching a large granite dome on the north, the trail splits. Keep to the right track, with the cliff to the left. The trail then tracks through a swampy marshland before climbing back onto solid ground.

The bare northwest shoulder of Pikes Peak looms to the right, and other cliffs and crags fill steep slopes above the narrowing valley. When the valley crimps down, the trail passes a cliff to the right at 1.2 miles. This is an excellent place to rest on its bedrock slabs, enjoying the trickle of the creek and taking in the valley you just hiked up. This is also a good turnaround point, since the next 0.5-mile trail segment gains lots of elevation and is heavily wooded.

Continue hiking up a narrow canyon on the rustic trail and then climb an abrupt, steep gully. Watch the trail—it can be easy to lose as it switches back and forth over tree roots and lumpy boulders. Eventually you'll reach a high saddle at 1.7 miles. The trail goes left here and climbs to a small summit with a big view and the trail's end point at 2 miles. This is a great place to sit down and enjoy breathtaking, expansive views. To the east is a huge granite buttress called Old Ironsides; farther east are the Pikes Peak Highway, a couple of reservoirs, and the flat top of the Rampart Range. On a clear day you can even see the distant prairie horizon. Also check out the ancient weathered limber pines that inhabit this windswept ridge.

To return, retrace the trail. Take care to remain on the trail as you descend the wooded gully below the saddle.

Miles and Directions

0.0 Start at the The Crags Trailhead next to the campground restrooms.

1.2 The trail passes a cliff to the right. (***Option:*** Turn around here to avoid the trail's steepest section.)

1.7 Reach the saddle and follow the trail to the left.

2.0 The trail ends with summit views. Retrace your steps.

4.0 Arrive back at the trailhead.

35 Spanish Peaks Traverse

This hike wanders past several volcanic dikes on the south side of West Spanish Peak. The dikes are fascinating and the views into New Mexico go forever on a clear day. The trail winds through forests of bristlecone, limber, and lodgepole pine, aspen, spruce, subalpine fir, and white fir, with some Gambel oak for good measure. An unmarked overlook by a little dike provides a good view of East Spanish Peak—a good turnaround point for the out-and-back hiker. Beyond the overlook the hike continues descending to the Trujillo cabin, then climbs to the saddle between the two peaks. It descends a final time along the north side of West Spanish Peak to the north trailhead at the upper end of FR 442, then descends to Huerfano CR 360.

Start: From the Apishapa (a-PISH-a-pa) Trailhead
Distance: 12.9 miles point to point
Approximate hiking time: 6.5 to 8.5 hours
Difficulty: Most difficult due to length and elevation gain and loss
Elevation gain/loss: 2,540-foot gain/3,860-foot loss
Seasons: Best from June to mid-Oct
Trail surface: Dirt trail with some rocky sections across talus fields, rough dirt road
Other trail users: Equestrians
Canine compatibility: Dogs must be under control
Fees and permits: None. Group size limit: No more than 15 people per group with a maximum combination of 25 people and pack or saddle animals in any one group.
Maps: USGS Spanish Peaks and Herlick Canyon
Trail contacts: Pike/San Isabel National Forest, San Carlos Ranger District, Cañon City; (719) 269-8500; www.fs.usda.gov/psicc
Other: No facilities at the trailhead. There is little to no water on the trail; bring your own. FR 46 is closed by snow 9.3 miles from the trailhead in winter. The trail crosses several avalanche paths on the south side of West Spanish Peak and is neither maintained nor marked for winter use from either trailhead.

Finding the trailhead: *For shuttle:* Drive to the south end of La Veta on CO 12 to Cuchara Street, next to La Veta Medical Clinic. Turn left onto Cuchara Street. In about 0.3 mile Cuchara Street ends but the road curves right and becomes Huerfano CR 36. Continue on HCR 36. In 1 mile, turn left at the HUAJATOLLA VALLEY sign (HCR 360). In 0.5 mile, turn right where the road lazy Ts onto HCR 360. The road straight ahead is a dead end. In 4.1 miles the road Ys—go right on HCR 360. Drive another mile on this somewhat twisty but maintained dirt road to the WAHATOYA TRAIL (TRAIL 1304), FR 442 sign. **GPS:** N37 25.34' / W104 58.65'. There's a good place to park in about 0.1 mile down the hill. Set up your car shuttle here. With a high-clearance vehicle, you can drive 2 miles up FR 442 to the north Wahatoya Trailhead.

To get to the southern trailhead, where the hike starts, return to La Veta the way you came. Drive south on CO 12 about 17 miles to the top of Cucharas Pass. Turn left onto Cordova Pass Road (FR 46) and drive another 10.8 miles, keeping left at two intersections that are well marked. Pass through the Apishapa Arch, which was cut through a dike by the Civilian Conservation Corps. A little farther down the road, the Apishapa Trailhead will be on your left. **GPS:** N37 20.63' / W104 59.45'

◀ *Apishapa Arch on way to trailhead*

The Hike

Seeing rain clouds gather over what are today known as the Spanish Peaks, Indians named them Wahatoya, "Breasts of the World." Rain provided drinking water and helped crops grow—both essential to life. You might also see spellings of Huajatolla or Guajatolla. Over the years the peaks have been named Twin Peaks, the Mexican Mountains, and Dos Hermanos (Two Brothers).

The first documented sighting of these peaks came in 1706, when Juan de Ulibarri explored this area for Spain. The peaks, long a landmark for Native Americans, trappers, and explorers, were a welcome sight for travelers on the Mountain Branch of the Santa Fe Trail, indicating an end to the dry, open plains.

The peaks are also important in the world of geology. About 100 million years ago, an inland sea covered much of North America. Sediments were deposited as the sea rose and subsided, then turned into rock over millennia. About 35 million years ago, after the present Rockies had risen, and while volcanic eruptions were creating the San Juan Mountains to the west, molten magma pushed its way up into the sedimentary rocks, which cracked and buckled from the pressure. The magma oozed into vertical cracks still below the earth's surface, then cooled and hardened. When the entire region was uplifted about 5,000 feet some 5 million years ago, these volcanic intrusions rose also. Erosion washed away the softer sedimentary rocks, leaving behind two peaks and many dikes. Geologists have identified more than 400 dikes around the Spanish Peaks. Looking like huge stone fences, they have been given colorful names like Devils Stairsteps. This hike between the Spanish Peaks and through the dikes is a trip through geologic time.

Circumnavigating the peaks is the Scenic Highway of Legends, commemorating the many legends that surround the peaks. One legend tells of a tribe of giants who once lived around Wahatoya. They quarreled among themselves and built rock walls about chest high for protection. They hurled huge boulders at each other. The gods of Wahatoya, angered by the wars, stopped the rains. The giants stopped fighting and left in search of water. One warrior remained behind to guard the valley, but the others never returned. The guard grew tired and sat to rest. The gods turned him to stone for his dedication. The rock is now known as Goemmer's Butte, a volcanic plug south of La Veta.

In pre-Spanish days a saga told of gold being used as offerings to the Aztec deities. One of the Aztec rulers established a dazzling court and "the gods of the Mountain Huajatolla became envious of the magnificence of his court and they placed demons on the double mountain and forbade all men further approach." Years later, in the mid-1500s, when Coronado returned to Mexico after abandoning his search for the fabled cities of gold, three monks remained behind to convert the natives. Legend has it that two were killed, while the third monk, Juan de la Cruz, found the gold mines. He forced Native Americans to extract the precious metal from the mines. Ready to return to Mexico, he killed the tribesmen and left with the gold carried by pack animals. The demons became angry, and the priest and his treasure disappeared.

Dike and Sangre de Cristo Mountains

According to some versions, a settler found gold nuggets years later. In any case, the tales of lost treasure drew people to the area in search of the lost gold and mines.

The area (not including FR 442) was designated the Spanish Peaks Wilderness area in November 2000. Volunteers for Outdoor Colorado helped the USDA Forest Service build a new 4-mile section of trail higher on the south slope of West Spanish Peak to connect the Wahatoya and Apishapa Trails and avoid private property. Many different types of trees line the trail, including ancient bristlecone pines. You can see west to the Sangre de Cristos, south to the mesas near Trinidad, and farther yet to the volcanoes in northeastern New Mexico. The most interesting parts are the little passages through the volcanic dikes.

The featured hike is a roller-coaster ride, climbing about 1,160 feet in elevation, then losing about 1,920 feet, only to climb another 1,380 feet to the saddle between the two peaks. Finally the trail traverses the north flank of West Spanish Peak, descending 480 feet to the north trailhead at the wilderness boundary, then descending another 1,460 feet to HCR 360. The longer hike between the two peaks gives you an intimate view of the Spanish Peaks Wilderness, but those looking to

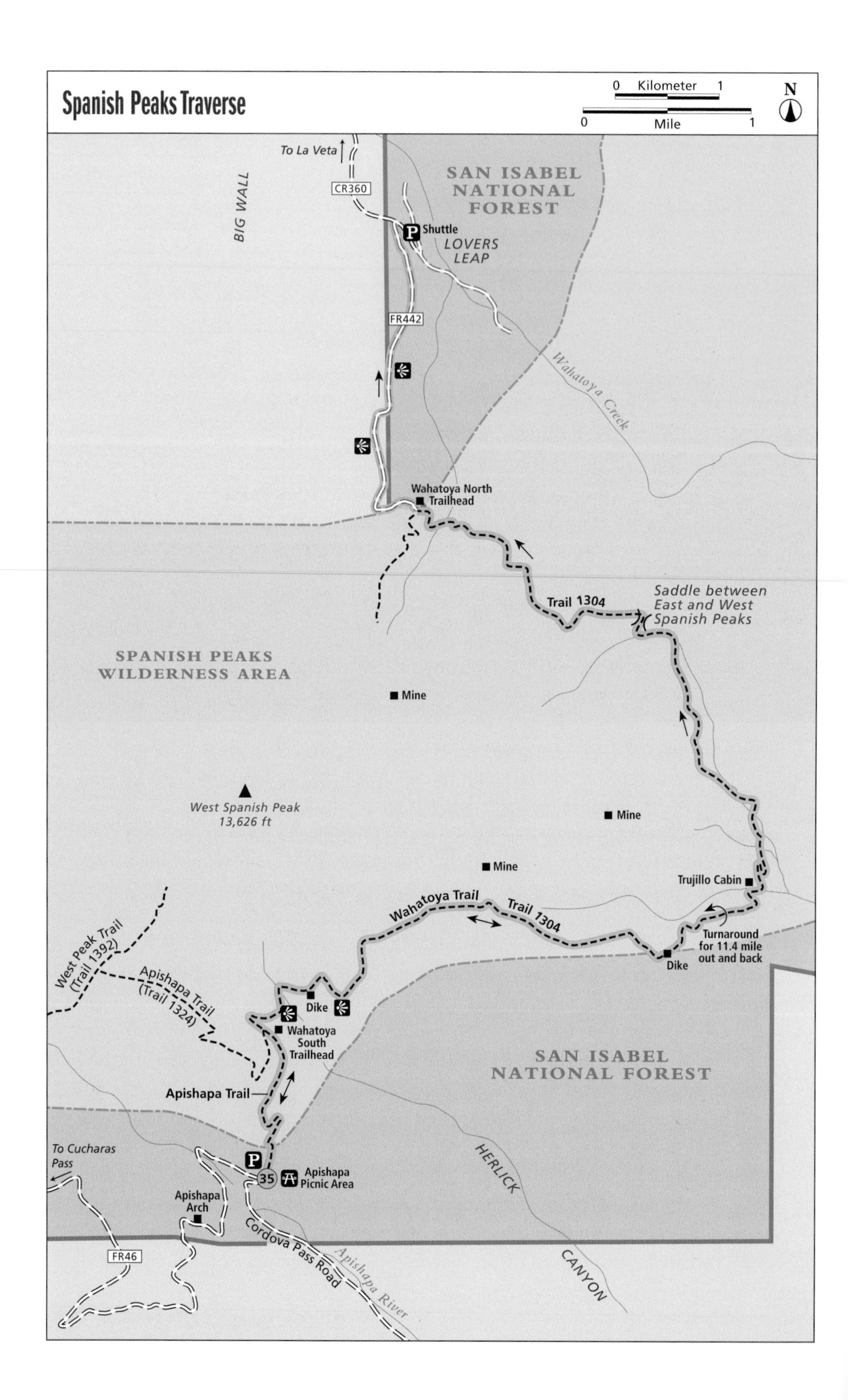

Spanish Peaks Traverse
0 Kilometer 1
0 Mile 1
N
To La Veta
CR360
BIG WALL
SAN ISABEL NATIONAL FOREST
Shuttle
LOVERS LEAP
FR442
Wahatoya Creek
Wahatoya North Trailhead
Trail 1304
Saddle between East and West Spanish Peaks
SPANISH PEAKS WILDERNESS AREA
Mine
West Spanish Peak 13,626 ft
Mine
Mine
Trujillo Cabin
Wahatoya Trail
Trail 1304
Turnaround for 11.4 mile out and back
Dike
West Peak Trail (Trail 1392)
Apishapa Trail (Trail 1324)
Dike
Wahatoya South Trailhead
SAN ISABEL NATIONAL FOREST
Apishapa Trail
To Cucharas Pass
35
Apishapa Picnic Area
Apishapa Arch
HERLICK
CANYON
FR46
Cordova Pass Road
Apishapa River

make an equally enjoyable out-and-back hike can turn around at a little dike with a viewpoint of East Spanish Peak, after dropping only 1,430 feet. The shorter hike allows you to experience the large variety of trees and the area's geology without the roller-coaster effect.

Miles and Directions

0.0 Start at the Apishapa Trailhead, following the Apishapa Trail. Elevation: 9,720 feet.

1.5 Turn right onto the Wahatoya Trail (Trail 1304) GPS: N37 21.42' / W104 59.53'. (***Note:*** The Apishapa Trail continues to the left and intersects with West Peak Trail [Trail 1392], which in turn heads up West Spanish Peak.)

2.1 Pass through a little dike.

5.3 Cross through a passageway (gap) in a large dike.

5.7 Reach an unmarked overlook at a dike. The trail curves right here and continues downhill. Walk ahead and uphill about 90 feet to a good view of East Spanish Peak. Elevation: 9,450 feet. GPS: N37 21.88' / W104 55.67'. Continue on the trail as it heads downhill. (***Option:*** This is an excellent turnaround point for an 11.4-mile out-and-back hike. Simply return the way you came. Approximate hiking time: 6 to 7.5 hours.)

6.3 Reach the Trujillo cabin. Continue on the trail downstream about 0.1 mile to the crossing of South Fork Trujillo Creek.

8.9 Reach the saddle between East Spanish and West Spanish Peaks and the Huerfano and Las Animas county line. Elevation: 10,340 feet. GPS: N37 23.40' / W104 57.05'

10.9 Arrive at the Spanish Peaks Wilderness boundary, the Wahatoya Trailhead, and the upper end of FR 442. GPS: 37 23.91' / W104 58.45'. From here, hike down FR 442 (not in wilderness), which is open to motorized use.

11.6 There's a great view of a big dike to the west from an imbedded dike to the left of the trail.

12.9 Arrive at the trailhead at HCR 360. Elevation: 8,400 feet.

36 Horsethief Falls

A steady climb leads to Horsethief Park, a high mountain meadow, and ends at a cascading waterfall on the western slope of Pikes Peak.

Start: From the parking area near the old Little Ike Tunnel
Distance: 2.2 miles out and back
Approximate hiking time: 1 to 2 hours
Difficulty: Moderate due to technical terrain
Elevation gain: 460 feet
Seasons: Best from May through Oct; snowy in winter
Trail surface: Dirt path
Other trail users: Mountain bikers and equestrians
Canine compatibility: Dogs must be on leash
Fees and permits: None
Maps: USGS Pikes Peak and Cripple Creek North
Trail contacts: Pike National Forest, Pikes Peak Ranger District, 601 S. Weber St., Colorado Springs, CO 80903; (719) 636-1602; www.fs.usda.gov
Other: Snowshoes required in winter

Finding the trailhead: From I-25, take the Cimarron Street/US 24 exit (exit 141) and head west. Drive up US 24 through Ute Pass and Woodland Park to the town of Divide. Go left in Divide onto CO 67. Drive 9.2 miles south on CO 67, pass a closed-off tunnel on the left, and go around a curve. The gravel parking area and trailhead is on the left at the other end of the old Little Ike Tunnel. **GPS:** N38 50.06' / W105 08.24'

The Hike

Located off CO 67, an oft-traveled route between Divide and the historic mining town of Cripple Creek, the Horsethief Falls Trail (Trail 704B) offers the solitude and beauty of the Rocky Mountains without straying far from the beaten path. The singletrack dirt trail ends at the crystalline falls, which spills over a jumble of granite boulders. The waterfall is most dramatic in early summer, when it's swollen with snowmelt from Sentinel Point, a spur of Pikes Peak. Although steep at the beginning, the trail is perfect for families, kids, and dogs. It's also a great winter hike on snowshoes.

Most of the elevation is gained during the first 0.5 mile of the hike. Departing from the right corner of the parking lot at 9,740 feet, the trail climbs briskly above the road and rounds a wide switchback. The path traverses above a blocked-off area above the old tunnel, then zigzags back right and enters forested north-facing slopes in a deep valley.

The sound of the highway traffic fades as the wide track steadily ascends, traversing a shelf across a steep slope. Small moss-covered granite boulders are strewn about the hillside beneath a dark evergreen forest, offering plenty of shade, and the distant sound of rushing water drifts up from the valley below.

After scrambling over a short rocky section, the trail finally levels out at 0.6 mile and edges alongside a gently rushing creek in lovely Horsethief Park to a trail

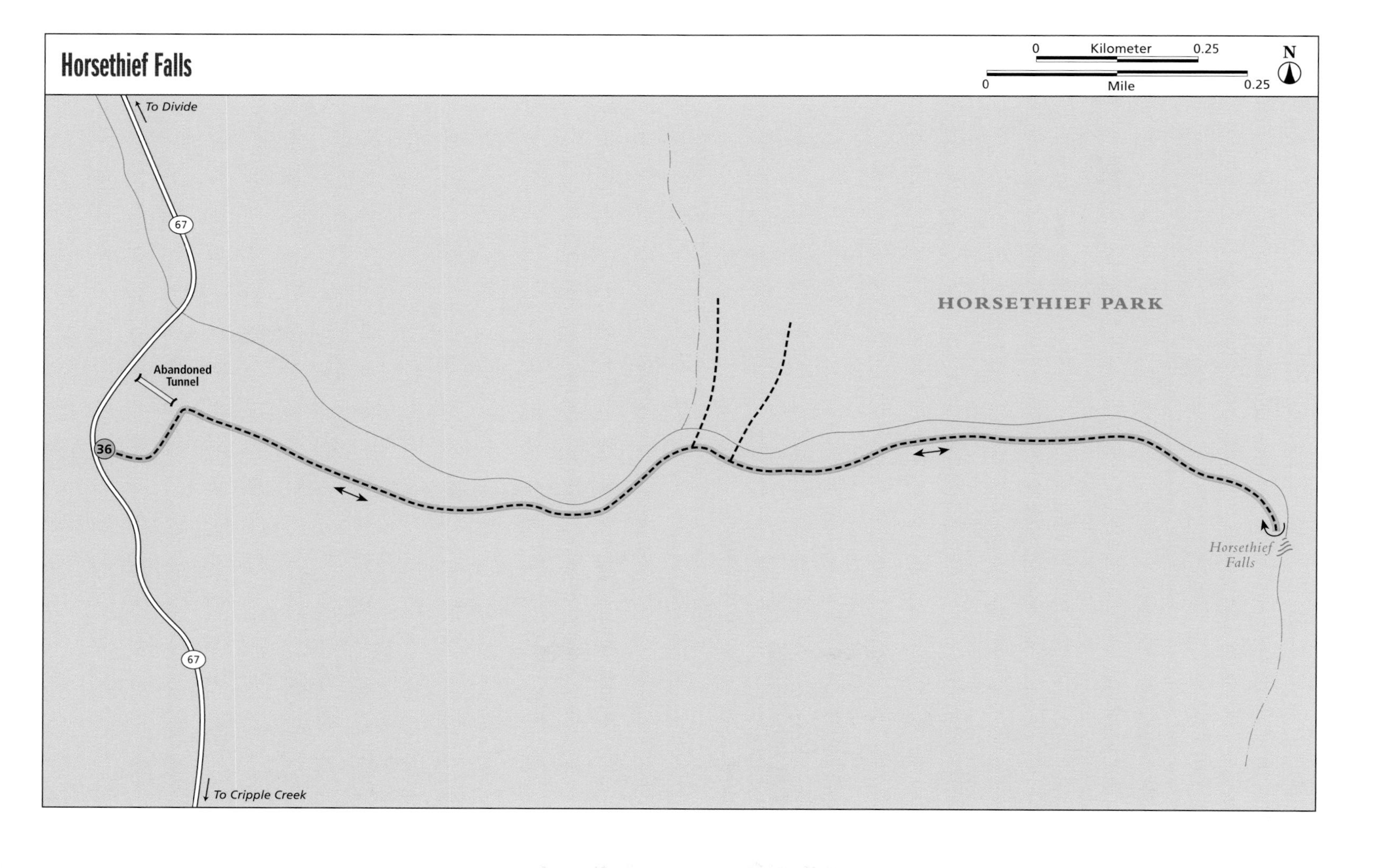
Horsethief Falls
0
Kilometer
0.25
0
Mile
0.25
N
To Divide
67
Abandoned
Tunnel
36
HORSETHIEF PARK
Horsethief
Falls
67
To Cripple Creek

junction with the Ring the Peak Trail system. Go straight on the main trail; pass beside placid ponds created by beaver dams and head east along the edge of a broad meadow. Across the valley, stands of young aspen, gleaming gold in September, cling to hills that rise from the grassy basin. The trail, slowly climbing up Horsethief Park, is a scenic delight. Also look for cabin ruins, perhaps used by the horse thieves for which the park is named.

Sentinel Point, a prominent pointed summit on the west side of Pikes Peak, looms directly ahead. At 0.7 mile the trail jogs back into the woods at a marked junction with the Pancake Rocks Trail. Go straight and rejoin the willow-lined stream.

After meandering through a forest of tall spruce and fir trees, the trail terminates at the base of Horsethief Falls at 1 mile. The cold mountain stream rushes over the center of an eroded boulder and cascades down a section of granite bedrock. Cross logs over the stream to rest on rocks on the north side, or climb the hillside for 0.1 mile to a perch above the falls at 10,200 feet. Either choice is perfect for a quiet picnic or nap in the sun. In dry years, little water tumbles down the falls.

After exploring Horsethief Falls, return as you came—it's a quick 1.1-mile hike downhill from the falls to your car.

Miles and Directions

0.0 Start at the trailhead on CO 67.

0.6 The steep climb ends and the trail reaches Horsethief Park. Go straight at the junction with Ring the Peak Trail.

0.7 Go straight at the junction with Pancake Rocks Trail.

1.0 Arrive at the base of Horsethief Falls.

1.1 Reach the top of Horsethief Falls. Retrace your path downhill to the trailhead.

2.2 Arrive back at the trailhead.

37 Reilly and Levsa Canyons

This hike first follows the Levsa Canyon Nature Trail and then about 2.6 miles of the Reilly Canyon Trail. Winding through piñon pine and juniper forest gives you an idea of the land through which early settlers traveled, especially on the Mountain Branch of the Santa Fe Trail (where I-25 now exists). The suggested turnaround point is a bench where the trail approaches Trinidad Lake and has a good view of the dam. Look for deer in some of the meadows. While hiking you can catch views of Fishers Peak, as well as the old coal mines and town sites on or below the south shore.

Start: From the Trinidad Lake State Park campground
Distance: 6.4 miles out and back with a loop
Approximate hiking time: 2.5 to 4.5 hours
Difficulty: Moderate due to length and a few steep sections
Elevation gain/loss: 390-foot gain/360-foot loss
Seasons: Year-round except after big snowstorms
Trail surface: Dirt trail with a few steep sections
Other trail users: Mountain bikers
Canine compatibility: Dogs must be on leash
Fees and permits: Daily entrance fee or annual parks pass required
Map: USGS Trinidad West
Trail contacts: Trinidad Lake State Park, Trinidad; (719) 846-6951; http://parks.state.co.us/parks/trinidadlake

Finding the trailhead: From Trinidad, drive 3.9 miles southwest on CO 12 from its intersection with I-25 to the Trinidad Lake State Park entrance. CO 12 is the Scenic Highway of Legends, so follow the scenic byway signs. Turn left onto the park road. The entrance station is about 0.5 mile on the left. Stop and pay the entrance fee. Drive less than 0.1 mile and turn right at the campground entrance. At the fork in the road, turn left and drive to the restrooms, where parking and water are available (take water with you). The trailhead is across from the restrooms. **GPS:** N37 08.65' / W104 34.18'

The Hike

The Mountain Branch of the Santa Fe Trail passed nearby what is today Trinidad Lake State Park. I-25 basically follows the old trail over Raton Pass, just south of the city of Trinidad. These lands were home to many Native American tribes: Comanche, Kiowa, Cheyenne, Arapaho, Jicarilla Apache, and Ute. They traveled over the plains, hunting bison, elk, antelope, and deer and creating trails that laid the foundation for the Santa Fe Trail.

What we now know as New Mexico belonged to Mexico and the Spanish in the early 1800s. Spain prohibited trade between the United States and Santa Fe. In 1821 the Mexican people revolted against Spanish rule and gained their independence.

One American entrepreneur, William Becknell, left Franklin, Missouri, in August 1821 and headed to Santa Fe with trade goods on pack animals. He traveled over Raton Pass, taking two days to roll boulders out of the way so his pack animals could

View of Trinidad Lake from interpretive post 11

pass. This route later became the Mountain Branch of the Santa Fe Trail. Becknell reached Santa Fe in mid-December and quickly sold his goods. In exchange for manufactured goods and supplies, the Mexicans traded gold, silver, fur, and mules. Becknell returned to Missouri by an overland route that avoided Raton Pass, arriving home in January 1822. Later that year Becknell traveled back to Santa Fe with more trade goods, using wagons on the 780-mile overland route, which became known as the Cimarron Cutoff. The round-trip between Missouri and Santa Fe took two to three months.

For the next twenty-five years, the Cimarron Cutoff was the preferred route to Santa Fe, being 100 miles shorter than the Mountain Branch, with rolling plains and no mountain obstacles. Two disadvantages were a lack of water along one 60-mile stretch and travel through the hunting grounds of unpredictable Comanche, Kiowa, and Apache tribes. In 1846 two events caused the Mountain Branch over Raton Pass to become the preferred route. First, a bad drought occurred in 1846, drying out the few springs and streams along the Cimarron Cutoff. The Mountain Branch followed the Arkansas River, which always had some water, even if one had to dig in

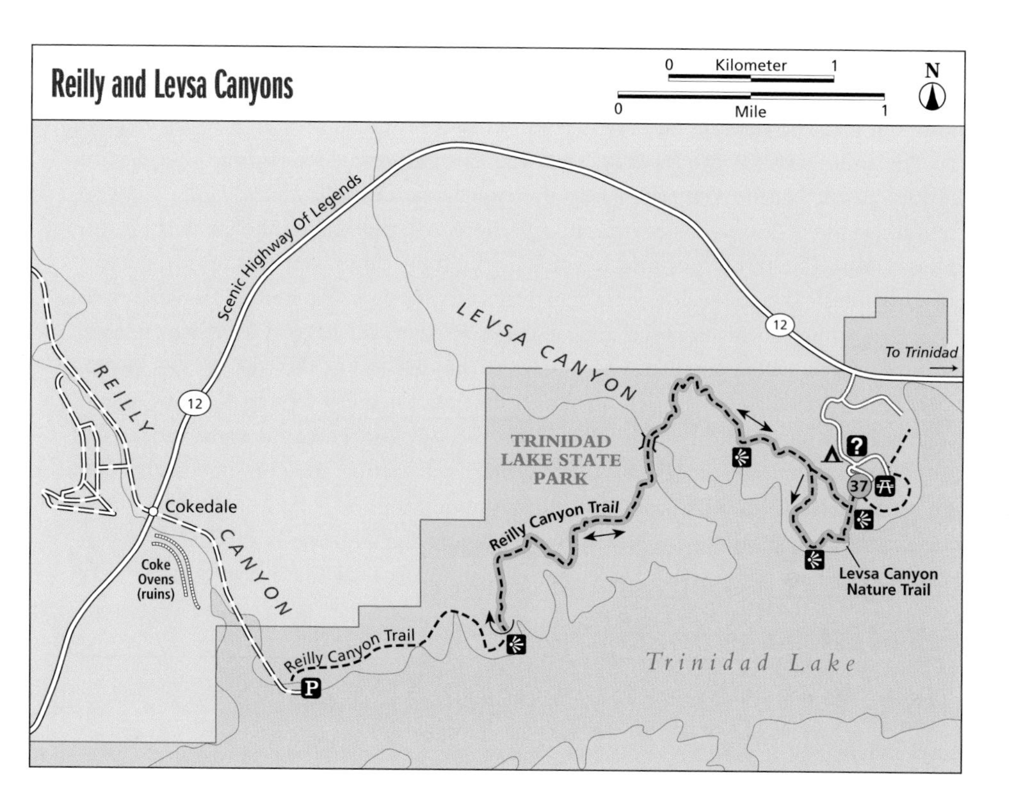

the streambed to find it. Second, Bent's Fort was also located on this route. General Stephen Kearney moved his army along the Mountain Branch to run military excursions into Mexico. Kearney also drove his wagon supply trains over Raton Pass after improving the trail. The Mexican-American War started in 1846 and resulted in New Mexico becoming part of the United States in 1848.

Raton Pass provided many challenges to early trail users. Before crossing the pass, people camped along the Purgatoire River on the east side, a welcome relief after the endless dry prairies. The town of Trinidad was founded here around 1862. From a travel account written in 1846, progress could be as little as 600 to 800 yards a day as men hauled wagons by hand over the great rocks. It took five days to cross the pass, a distance of about 30 miles. One place was so narrow that one little slip sent mules, wagons, and people to a certain death.

In 1865 the legislatures of Colorado and New Mexico granted "Uncle Dick" Wooton a charter to build a toll road over Raton Pass. Wooton blasted away the rocks and widened the road. Tolls ranged from five cents per head of cattle to $1.50 per wagon. In one fifteen-month period, the collected tolls totaled $9,193! The completion of a railroad line from Trinidad to Santa Fe in 1880 eliminated the need for the Santa Fe Trail.

As you hike the Reilly Canyon Trail, imagine driving a horse-drawn wagon through the area. Some of the trail appears fairly negotiable while other sections, dropping into the canyons and ravines, would be a bit dicey.

The route starts at the trailhead near the campground. Hike up the first part of Levsa Canyon Nature Trail, then take the right fork and follow the Reilly Canyon Trail for about 2.2 more miles (the mileage noted on the bulletin board starts at this intersection). The trail drops into Levsa Canyon, then climbs out and wanders across a high stretch. Dropping down another little canyon to a flat stretch, the trail then climbs to a big slab of slickrock and descends to Trinidad Lake. A bench to rest on awaits you. From here you can see the dam at the east end of the lake.

If you want to add some mileage, hike another 1.4 miles west to Reilly Canyon itself, for a 9-mile round-trip. Either way, on the way back, take the right fork at the Levsa Canyon Nature Trail/Reilly Canyon Trail intersection and continue back along the nature trail. It drops, climbs, and drops, providing good views of the area across the lake where coal mines and towns resided before the dam was built, plus of Fishers Peak (9,655 feet) to the south. Watch for blue piñon jays and deer as you hike.

Miles and Directions

0.0	Start at the trailhead near the campground restrooms. Elevation: 6,340 feet.
0.05	At the fork, go right to follow the Levsa Canyon Nature Trail.
0.1	At the fork, take the right branch of the Levsa Canyon Nature Trail and head uphill.
0.3	Arrive at the intersection of the Reilly Canyon Trail and Levsa Canyon Nature Trail. Turn right onto Reilly Canyon Trail.
1.5	Cross the bridge in Levsa Canyon.
2.6	There's a mound of slickrock on the right.
2.9	Reach a bench and a view of the dam. This is the turnaround point. Elevation: 6,370 feet. GPS: N37 08.18' / W104 35.59'
5.6	Come to the trail intersection of Reilly Canyon Trail and Levsa Canyon Nature Trail. Turn right (more like straight) onto Levsa Canyon Nature Trail.
5.9	Reach a bench at sign #11 for the nature trail with a nice view of Trinidad Lake.
6.3	Reach the other end of the Levsa Canyon Nature Trail loop. Take the trail on the right. At the next intersection, turn left.
6.4	Arrive back at the trailhead.

38 Lower Barr Trail

Barr Trail climbs 13 miles to the summit of Pikes Peak, but this great day hike follows the trail's first 3 miles up Mount Manitou to wonderful views of the surrounding mountains.

Start: From the Barr Trailhead on Hydro Street
Distance: 6.4 miles out and back
Approximate hiking time: 3 to 5 hours
Difficulty: Moderate
Elevation gain: 1,600 feet
Seasons: Year-round; cold and icy in winter
Trail surface: Wide singletrack dirt path
Other trail users: Runners
Canine compatibility: Dogs must be on leash
Fees and permits: None
Map: USGS Manitou Springs
Trail contacts: Pike National Forest, Pikes Peak Ranger District, 601 S. Weber St., Colorado Springs, CO 80903; (719) 636-1602; www.fs.usda.go

Finding the trailhead: To reach the Barr Trailhead from I-25, take the Cimarron Street/US 24 exit and drive west on US 24 for 5.4 miles to the first Manitou Springs exit. The exit ramp circles onto Manitou Avenue. Turn right and drive west on Manitou Avenue for 1.4 miles (following signs for the cog railroad) to a roundabout at its intersection with Ruxton Avenue. Turn left (southwest) at the roundabout onto Ruxton and travel 0.8 mile, past the cog railroad depot to Hydro Street. Turn right (northwest) onto Hydro Street and drive uphill 0.1 mile to the parking area and trailhead. (***Note:*** The parking lot is usually full, especially in the morning. If it is, park on Ruxton Avenue below the cog railroad depot. Do not park in the cog railroad parking lots.) **GPS:** N38 51.34' / W104 56.04'

The Hike

Pikes Peak, looming 8,000 feet above Colorado Springs, is one of America's most famous mountains. The summit of the 14,115-foot peak is reached by auto road, cog railroad, and the Barr Trail, which climbs 12.6 miles from Manitou Springs to the summit. Barr Trail is a difficult hike up Colorado's thirty-first-highest peak, not an easy day hike. Instead, do this shorter, 6.4-mile round-trip hike up the trail's lower section and sample some of its best terrain and views.

This hike, switchbacking up the eastern face of 9,250-foot Rocky Mountain, a spur of Mount Manitou, features easy grades on the wide trail, fabulous views, and moderate hiking. Take your time and plenty of rest breaks, especially if you aren't accustomed to the altitude, and you will be fine. Wear sturdy shoes, maintain a steady pace, and carry water and energy drinks in summer. At the top you'll be rewarded for your efforts.

Begin the hike at the trailhead at a parking area on Hydro Street. Hike up switchbacks on the trail, which traverses back and forth across the mountain's east face above Englemann Canyon to the south. After 0.3 mile you reach a trail junction. Bend sharply right on Barr Trail. As you slowly climb through scrub oak, ponderosa pine,

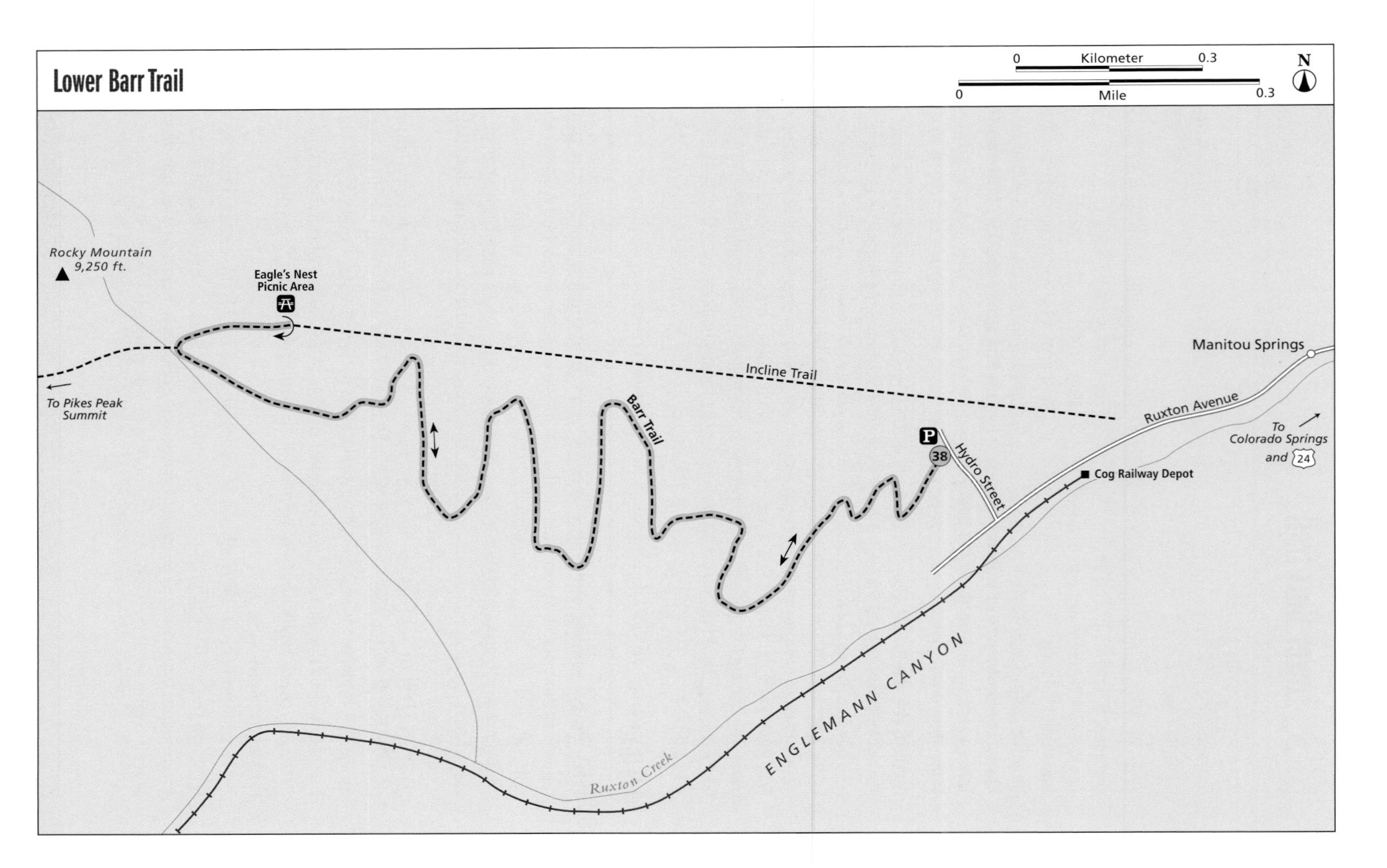
Lower Barr Trail
0
Kilometer
0.3
0
Mile
0.3
N
Rocky Mountain
9,250 ft.
Eagle's Nest
Picnic Area
To Pikes Peak
Summit
Incline Trail
Barr Trail
38
Hydro Street
Manitou Springs
Ruxton Avenue
To
Colorado Springs
and 24
Cog Railway Depot
ENGLEMANN CANYON
Ruxton Creek

and Douglas fir, great views unfold of Manitou Springs below, the red rocks of Garden of the Gods to the northeast, and sprawling Colorado Springs beyond. Hiking up Barr Trail from Manitou Springs to the summit is like taking a telescoped journey from Mexico to the Arctic, passing through almost all the major ecological life zones.

A trail marker at 1 mile designates your elevation as 7,200 feet. Past here, large granite boulders line the trail. You pass a lofty rock outcrop at 1.8 miles that offers spectacular views of Englemann Canyon to the south. This is a good picnic spot and, if you're tired, a turnaround point.

Barr Trail continues west, alternately traversing steep slopes and climbing switchbacks up the south-facing side of Rocky Mountain. Rocky slopes spill into the canyon, and if you look closely you'll spot the tracks of the cog railroad below. Farther along, the trail ducks through a tunnel of boulders that have fallen against one another like giant dominos and passes a small concrete tunnel on the right. At 2.6 miles you reach a trail junction at No Name Creek. To finish the hike, turn right onto Incline Trail. (Barr Trail continues straight west from the junction, toward Barr Camp and the Pikes Peak summit.)

Follow the flat, wide Incline Trail east past a granite cliff to a trail fork. Go left (east) on the upper trail, which heads slightly downhill to the EAGLE'S NEST TRAIL sign at 3 miles. Keep right (east) on the descending trail to a stunning overlook and the hike's turnaround point at Eagle's Nest Picnic Area. From this lofty perch you'll enjoy an eagle's view of the city below, spreading east to the tawny prairie and the distant horizon.

Catch your breath, take a drink of water, and rest your feet for a few minutes. Now tighten your boot laces and head back the way you came. The return trip, all of it downhill, goes fast. Remember the trail junctions on the way down. Stick to the well-beaten trail and you'll be fine.

Miles and Directions

0.0 Start at the Barr Trailhead at the parking area on Hydro Street.

0.3 At the junction, go right on the main trail.

1.0 Pass the 7,200-foot elevation marker.

1.8 Rest at the overlook rocks. (***Option:*** Turn around here for a 3.6-mile round-trip hike.)

2.6 Reach the Incline Trail intersection. Turn right onto the Incline Trail.

3.2 Come to the Eagle's Nest Picnic Area, the hike's turnaround point. Retrace your steps.

6.4 Arrive back at the trailhead.

39 Red Rock Canyon Trail

A classic hike flanked by towering sandstone walls follows an old road in the heart of Red Rock Canyon Open Space.

Start: From the trailhead at the east side of the park's main parking lot
Distance: 2.2 miles out and back
Approximate hiking time: 1 to 2 hours
Difficulty: Easy
Elevation gain: 150 feet
Seasons: Year-round
Trail surface: Doubletrack dirt path
Other trail users: Runners, mountain bikers, equestrians
Canine compatibility: Dogs must be on leash
Fees and permits: None
Maps: USGS Manitou Springs; trail map available at park website (below)
Trail contacts: Colorado Springs Parks, Recreation, and Cultural Services, 1401 Recreation Way, Colorado Springs, CO 80905-1975; (719) 385-5940; www.springsgov.com

Finding the trailhead: Red Rock Canyon Open Space is directly south of Garden of the Gods and US 24. To access the area from downtown Colorado Springs and I-25, take the Cimarron Street/US 24 exit (exit 141) and drive west about 3.5 miles toward the mountains. Access the parking areas and trailheads by turning left (south) onto Ridge Road from US 24, which is the only left turn between 31st Street and the first Manitou Springs exit. Use extreme caution turning on and off the busy highway. Drive south on Ridge Road for 0.1 mile and turn left into the park. Drive through a roundabout and go left. Park at the first parking area. (***Note:*** Portable toilets and a map are located at the trailhead at the east end of the lot. Additional parking is available at a lot at the end of the park road to the southeast.) **GPS:** N38 51.08' / W104 52.71'

The Hike

The Red Rock Canyon Trail explores Red Rock Canyon, the centerpiece of Red Rock Canyon Open Space. The city of Colorado Springs purchased the park's 787 acres in 2003. Red Rock Canyon itself is a milelong canyon lined with ruddy sandstone cliffs and floored by scrub oak, cottonwood trees, and grassy meadows. The canyon also harbors archaeological and historical sites, including a quarry that operated from 1886 until 1915.

Begin the hike from the trailhead at the east side of the main parking lot, located on the north side of the park opposite US 24. Portable toilets and a trail map are at the trailhead. An alternative parking area is located past the first parking area at the end of the park road below Red Rock Canyon. If you park here, knock 0.4 mile off your hike.

The first trail segment runs east and then south for 0.35 mile before joining an old road. Just east of the trailhead is a junction with the Mesa and Greenlee Trails, which head south up a closed road. Continue straight and pass the left side of a biking area. Past here the wide trail bends south. Follow the trail between the south parking area and a sandstone cliff that was quarried in the nineteenth century. The trail slowly climbs and then bends east to join the old Red Rock Canyon road. (If you started from the south parking area, it's 0.15 mile to this point.)

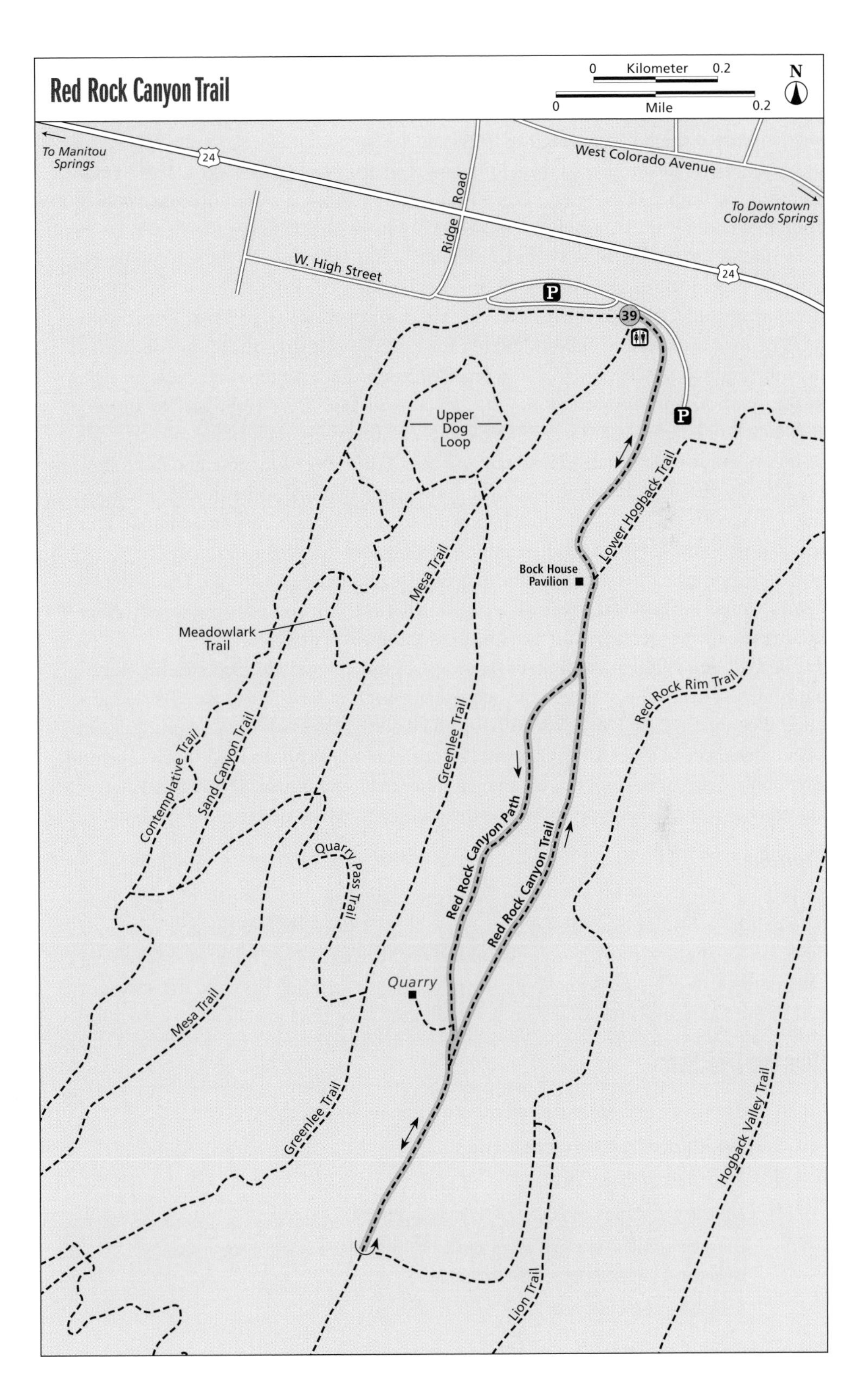

Red Rock Canyon Trail
0 Kilometer 0.2
0 Mile 0.2
N
To Manitou Springs
24
West Colorado Avenue
To Downtown Colorado Springs
Ridge Road
W. High Street
24
P
39
P
Upper Dog Loop
Lower Hogback Trail
Mesa Trail
Bock House Pavilion
Meadowlark Trail
Red Rock Rim Trail
Greenlee Trail
Contemplative Trail
Sand Canyon Trail
Red Rock Canyon Path
Red Rock Canyon Trail
Quarry Pass Trail
Quarry
Mesa Trail
Greenlee Trail
Hogback Valley Trail
Lion Trail

Hike up the road 0.1 mile, passing a locked gate, to the site of the old Bock house, now a picnic and rest pavilion. Red Rock Canyon once belonged to John George Bock, who assembled the house during the 1920s and 1930s.

After Bock's death his two sons, John and Richard, wanted to build a World Trade Center here with golf courses, luxury homes and condos, a shopping center, office buildings, a sports arena, and thirteen lakes. They were unable to get the area rezoned, so in the 1970s it was turned into a landfill and gravel pit. In the 1990s another developer attempted to resurrect the Bock plan but was denied annexation by both Manitou Springs and Colorado Springs, leaving the door open for its purchase as parkland.

The next trail section follows the old road on the east side of the canyon for 0.4 mile to its junction with Quarry Pass Trail. (***Sidetrip:*** For an alternative hike, go right at the pavilion and descend stone steps to a small lake. Bear right and follow the singletrack 0.5-mile Red Rock Canyon Path, a hiker-only trail, along the west side of the canyon to the Quarry Pass Trail junction. For a diversion, go right and follow the Quarry Pass Trail 0.1 mile up to the nineteenth-century stone quarry, a historic site. The sandstone blocks quarried here were loaded on train cars on a railroad spur that ran into the canyon and then shipped to Denver, Kansas, and Texas. The stone, however, didn't weather well, and the canyon's quarries closed by 1915. This side trail climbs to the quarry. Make sure you climb the stone staircase into the quarry. After visiting the quarry, retrace your steps back to the main trail.)

The last trail segment continues south for 0.25 mile on the old road, steadily climbing a hill to a major junction and the hike's turnaround point at 6,400 feet. Take a minute and enjoy the view. Directly west across the wooded canyon is the Wiggins Wall and a deep defile called Black Bear Canyon. This and the other cliffs in Red Rock Canyon are popular with rock climbers, who enjoy more than one hundred established climbing routes. From this high point, retrace the trail north to the parking lot.

Options

Several excellent loop hikes fan out from the end of the Red Rock Canyon Trail. The best hike continues south up the canyon for 0.15 mile before turning west up a deep canyon. Follow the 1.3-mile Roundup Trail up and out of the canyon, then dip across the heads of a couple shallow canyons before descending north to the southern end of the Contemplative Trail. This 3.5-mile loop hike is an excellent easy day hike.

Miles and Directions

0.0 Begin at the trailhead at the east end of the park's main parking lot.

0.35 Reach a junction with a closed dirt road.

0.45 Reach the pavilion and lake.

0.85 Arrive at the junction with Quarry Pass Trail. Go straight.

1.1 End the first half of your hike at the top of a hill at a three-way trail junction. Turn around and hike back toward the trailhead.

2.2 Arrive back at the trailhead.

SOUTH-CENTRAL MOUNTAINS

The great rift valley of the Rio Grande cuts right through the heart of the South-Central Mountains region. To the west, the San Juan Mountains contain some of the most rugged country in Colorado. The last grizzly in Colorado was supposedly killed here, and some may still hang out undercover. Farther north the Collegiate Peaks are 14,000-foot summits named after Ivy League universities. To the east the jagged crest of the Sangre de Cristo Range rises above the sand dunes it helps create. Centered around an unusual geological feature, the Great Sand Dunes National Park and Preserve encompasses a 30-square-mile area in the San Luis Valley with 700-foot-high sand dunes. From Native American tribes to Spanish explorers to settlers and miners all searching for their own riches, the South-Central Mountains region has a rich and diverse history.

The Spanish first journeyed into the San Luis Valley in the late 1500s. Their legacy remains in the town of San Luis, the oldest permanent settlement in the state (established in 1851), and Our Lady of Guadalupe in Conejos, the oldest parish in Colorado. The state's Spanish history is also reflected in many place names, such as Del Norte, Costilla County, and Antonito. Most streams flowing into the San Luis Valley, one of the highest alpine valleys in the world, sink into its sandy and gravelly floor. The Alamosa, Monte Vista, and Baca National Wildlife Refuges, San Luis Lakes State Park, and Blanca Wetlands provide welcome resting spots for migrating waterfowl and shorebirds. Surprisingly, potatoes are the main farm crop in the San Luis Valley. Even more surprising, an unusual farm and tourist attraction north of Alamosa called Colorado Gators harbors alligators and raises tilapia (a tropical freshwater fish) in 87°F water flowing from a 2,000-foot-deep geothermal well.

One of Colorado's historic narrow gauge railroads still carries visitors back in time to the late 1800s, when trains transported silver and gold. Leaving from Antonito, the Cumbres-Toltec Scenic Railroad heads west and south through beautiful country, a spectacular fall trip when the aspens turn gold. Crossing the Colorado–New Mexico border eleven times, the trip ends in Chama, New Mexico. The Rio Grande Scenic Railroad connects La Veta to Alamosa, Antonito, and Monte Vista, offering entertainment at an outdoor amphitheater along the way.

40 Middle Frisco Trail

Middle Frisco Trail follows sparkling, gurgling Middle San Francisco Creek and its tributaries up to San Francisco Lakes. Starting among stands of ponderosa pine and Douglas fir, the trail slowly gains elevation, eventually switchbacking up to a nice spruce-fir forest and subalpine meadows. Wildflowers are abundant along the trail in July. Keep an eye open for elk and cattle. Near the upper lake, there is an ancient bristlecone pine forest. The lower part of the trail is fantastic when the aspen are golden yellow and orange. The lakes are snuggled in high basins between Bennett Peak and Pintada Mountain.

Start: From the Middle Frisco (Trail 801) Trailhead
Distance: 12.9 miles out and back
Approximate hiking time: 6 to 8.5 hours
Difficulty: Most difficult due to length and elevation gain
Elevation gain: 2,520 feet
Seasons: Best from mid-June to mid-Oct
Trail surface: Dirt trail
Other trail users: Equestrians, mountain bikers, hunters (in season)
Canine compatibility: Dogs must be under control
Fees and permits: None
Maps: USGS Jasper and Horseshoe Mountain; Nat Geo Trails Illustrated 142 South San Juan Wilderness/Del Norte (Middle Frisco Creek is on this map, but the trail isn't.)
Trail contacts: Rio Grande National Forest, Divide Ranger District, Del Norte; (719) 657-3321; www.fs.usda.gov/riogrande
Other: Bring your own water or a water treatment system with you.

Finding the trailhead: In Del Norte, head toward the east end of town to find French Street (Rio Grand CR 13). There's a big green-and-white sign stating NATIONAL FOREST ACCESS SAN FRANCISCO CREEK. Turn south onto French Street. In about 1.8 miles the pavement ends and CR 13 becomes a good gravel road. Stop and read the bulletin board on the right side of the road in another 1.9 miles. The trailhead is another 6.1 miles down the dirt road (9.8 miles total from Del Norte). The trail starts on the left after passing the cattle guard/fence where FR 320 starts. There's a large parking area with no facilities. Cattle graze in the area. **GPS:** N37 33.40' / W106 23.75'

The Hike

Locals and several signs call these trails, creeks, and lakes by the nickname "Frisco." The official name on topo maps is "San Francisco." So, you're in the correct spot at the Middle Frisco trailhead. A little farther down the road is West Frisco Trail, open to all-terrain vehicles (ATVs) and dirt bikes.

San Francisco Creek is a tributary of the mighty Rio Grande del Norte (Great River of the North), named by Spanish explorers. On the western edge of the San Luis Valley, the town of Del Norte took its name from the river. Early native peoples of the Folsom culture lived in the valley more than 10,000 years ago. Starting around 1300 the Moache and Tabeguache bands of Utes called this area home. Juan Bautista de Anza headed north from Santa Fe in 1779 to quiet the Comanches who were causing trouble for the Spanish. He commanded an army of 700 men from Santa Fe and 200 Ute-Apaches. They camped about 5 miles downstream from Del Norte.

The Spanish divided parts of southern Colorado into land grants. These huge tracts were normally given to individuals or small groups. The Guadalupe Land Grant on the west side of the Rio Grande was designated for one hundred families and their descendants. In 1859 Juan Bautista Silva led fourteen families 200 miles, from New Mexico to the fertile pastures along San Francisco Creek, to settle part of this land grant. It took one month to travel that distance! The newcomers named their town La Loma de San Jose, planted crops, and raised livestock.

In 1870 gold was discovered in the San Juan Mountains southwest of La Loma, and Summitville became the major gold camp. Del Norte, founded in 1871, developed into a major mining supply center for Lake City, Silverton, Summitville, and others. Del Norte was so prosperous that one rich mine owner proposed a separate state called San Juan with Del Norte as its capital.

In the 1880s cattlemen and sheepherders disputed over ranges, but actually agreed to boundaries. Sheep grazed between the Rio Grande and San Francisco Creek, while cattle ruled the grasses from San Francisco Creek south to Rock Creek. Today cattle graze near Frisco Lakes.

The trail heads off through aspen groves and meadows and is soon surrounded by forests of limber pine, ponderosa pine, and Douglas fir. Middle Frisco Creek is tiny and lively, a pleasant hiking companion. Aspen becomes the dominant tree species, occasionally alternating with conifers. The trail breaks out of the woods into a meadow area with Pintada Mountain (12,840 feet) to the left, a large ridge delineating the drainage's east side. A few bristlecone pines have stood guard here for centuries. A series of twelve switchbacks soon take you even higher. Colorful wildflowers like cinquefoil, death camas, Indian paintbrush, stonecrop, and columbine brighten the climb. As you hike up the ridge, the cliffs above the upper lake resemble the edge of a volcanic crater. The mountains here are part of one of the ancient volcanic calderas that formed the San Juan Mountains. Glaciers carved the upper cirques. A stand of ancient bristlecone pines grows west of the trail.

If you want to hike up the peak above the cliffs, walk back to the junction with the Middle Frisco Cut-off Trail, turn left onto it, and hike about 0.7 mile to the West Frisco Trail. Turn left and head to the summit.

According to records in Del Norte, in 1932 during the Depression, calves sold for three cents per pound, and two dozen eggs cost fifteen cents.

To either overlook the lower lake or hike down to it, cross the creek below the upper lake, wander through a field of old-man-of-the-mountain (alpine sunflowers), then descend a little. There are some good campsites along the hike in and near the lakes. Remember to camp at least 100 feet away from streams, lakes, and trails. The area around the lakes is high subalpine, and trees take years to grow. Wildlife and birds depend on the trees and dead branches.

Lower Frisco Lake

If you camp up high, bring a stove and candles and forgo the campfire to protect the fragile ecosystem.

A little bird you may notice flying overhead near the lakes is the white-crowned sparrow. It indeed looks like a sparrow, but has white around its eyes and a black cap. Watch for a while if you catch sight of one. They pick insects off dead branches. These little sparrows winter as far south as Mexico. When spring arrives, they fly north to mate and nest in the tundra. Their nests are hidden beneath willows, which provide both shelter and the proper temperature to hatch their tiny eggs.

Middle Frisco Trail is an enjoyable hike in a pretty area. The Trail Wise Back Country Horsemen help maintain the trail. The area shows little sign of human use, so please practice Leave No Trace skills.

Miles and Directions

0.0 Start at the Middle Frisco (Trail 801) Trailhead. Elevation: 9,500 feet. Head toward the creek on Middle Frisco Trail. Reach a brown carsonite post shortly after the

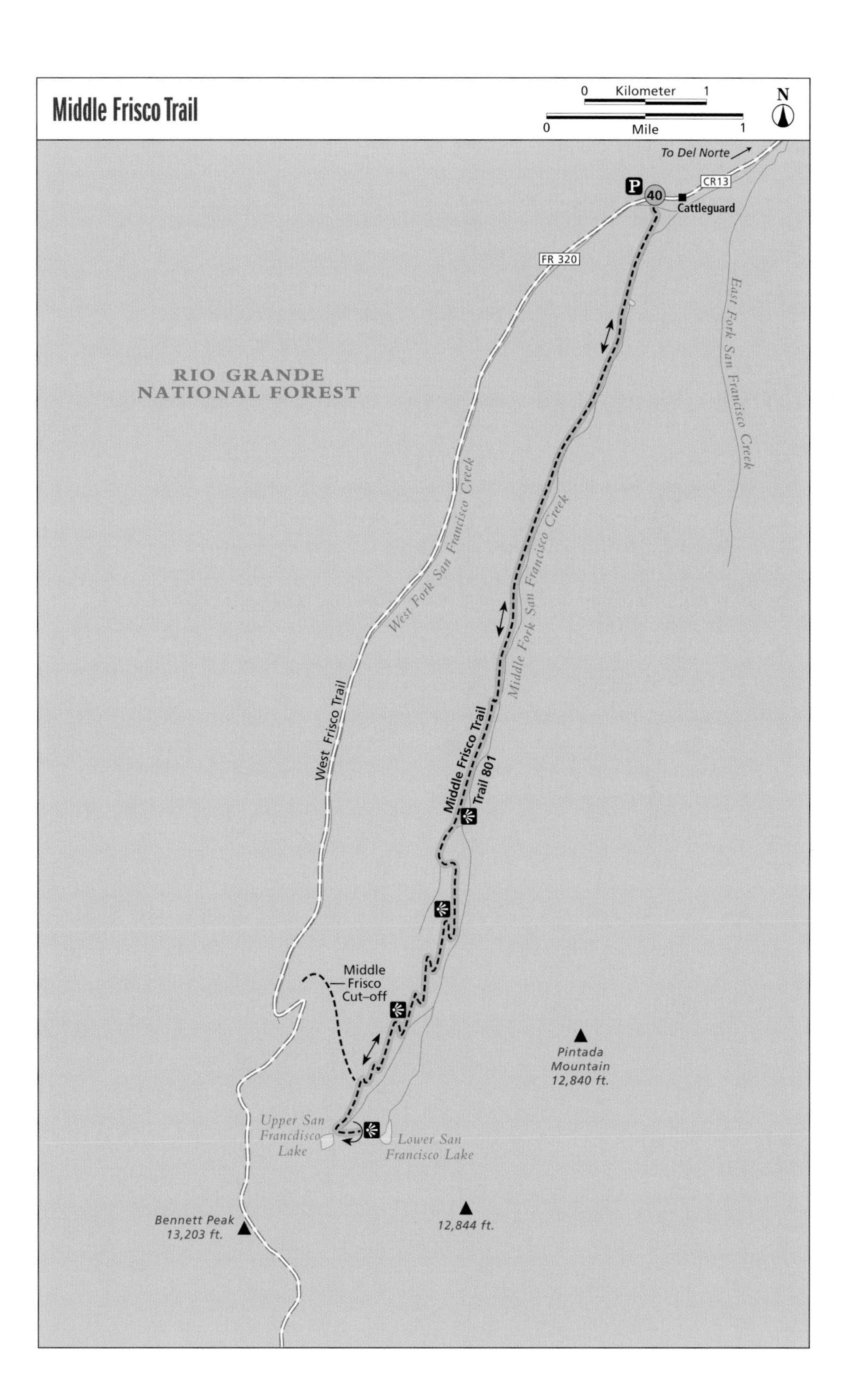

Middle Frisco Trail
0 Kilometer 1
0 Mile 1
N
To Del Norte
CR13
40
Cattleguard
FR 320
RIO GRANDE
NATIONAL FOREST
East Fork San Francisco Creek
West Fork San Francisco Creek
Middle Fork San Francisco Creek
West Frisco Trail
Middle Frisco Trail
Trail 801
Middle
Frisco
Cut–off
Pintada
Mountain
12,840 ft.
Upper San
Francdisco
Lake
Lower San
Francisco Lake
Bennett Peak
13,203 ft.
12,844 ft.

trailhead. Go past this post to the left. At the creek's edge, look right. You'll see a little bridge that looks like a flat ladder. Walk across the bridge to find the trail on the other side, which climbs up through aspen and into a meadow. The trail is easy to follow from here.

3.4 The trail enters a large meadow area with a view of Pintada Mountain to the left. GPS: N37 30.77' / W106 24.82'. (***Note:*** Look for some bristlecone pines here.)

3.6 The trail makes a big U curve. Follow the curve and not a spur trail.

4.1 The trail starts a series of switchbacks. Occasionally a spur trail leads off a switchback, but stick to the main trail unless you're looking for a campsite. (***Note:*** Look north occasionally for good views of the San Luis Valley and the Sangre de Cristo Range.)

5.1 The trail crosses a flatter area with a nice view of the cliffs above upper San Francisco Lake. More switchbacks to come!

5.8 The switchbacks are finished, and the trail follows a little creek down to the left. There are many cattle trails in this area. Stay on the trail heading toward the cliffs.

6.1 The Middle Frisco Cut-off Trail (nonmotorized) goes to the right and connects to the West Frisco Trail (Trail 850/motorized). (***Side trip:*** You can climb Bennett Peak from the West Frisco Trail [watch out for lightning]. Turn right onto the cut-off trail and hike 0.7 mile to West Frisco Trail, turn left, and follow the ridge about 1.3 miles to the peak.)

6.3 Arrive at the outlet to upper San Francisco Lake. Elevation: 12,000 feet. GPS: N37 29.40' / W106 25.52'. Continue left across the outlet toward the lower lake.

6.45 Enjoy a nice overlook of the lower lake. GPS: N37 29.37' / W106 25.37'. Return the way you came. (***Note:*** This area makes a good lunch spot if you don't want to hike down and back up again. Watch for white-crowned sparrows nearby and elk in the high meadows to the east and south.)

12.9 Arrive back at the trailhead.

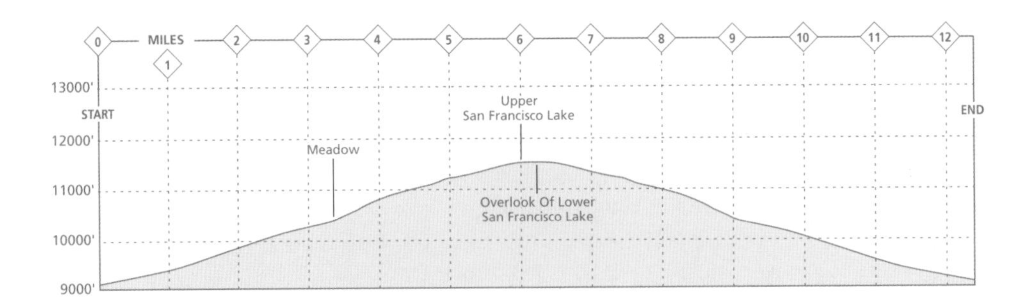

41 Alberta Peak: Continental Divide National Scenic Trail

This hike follows the Continental Divide National Scenic Trail south from Wolf Creek Pass to Alberta Peak. It climbs through a pleasant spruce-fir forest and passes near a ski lift at Wolf Creek Ski Area. Beyond the ski lift the trail winds through the forest, then out onto the edge of a ridge with great views to the south and west. Passing through willows, the trail ascends above tree line with views in all directions and beautiful alpine wildflowers. A short scramble takes you to the top of Alberta Peak (11,870 feet), with its resident pikas.

Start: From the top of Wolf Creek Pass, on the south side by the interpretive signs
Distance: 6.0 miles out and back
Approximate hiking time: 2.5 to 4 hours
Difficulty: Moderate due to mostly gentle trail and distance
Elevation gain: 1,013 feet, plus about 80 feet in undulations
Seasons: Best from July to Oct
Trail surface: Dirt trail
Other trail users: Equestrians, mountain bikers, hunters (in season)
Canine compatibility: Dogs must be under control
Fees and permits: None
Maps: USGS Wolf Creek Pass; Nat Geo Trails Illustrated 140 Weminuche Wilderness
Trail contacts: Rio Grande National Forest, Divide Ranger District, Del Norte; (719) 657-3321; www.fs.usda.gov/riogrande
Other: No water on the trail; bring your own. Do not hike along the ridge if a thunderstorm and lightning are in the vicinity!

Finding the trailhead: From South Fork, drive west on US 160 for 19.4 miles to the top of Wolf Creek Pass. Park on the south side by the interpretive signs. There are no facilities here. The last part of this trail is above tree line. **GPS:** N37 28.98' / W106 48.09'

The Hike

In 1978 Congress designated a National Scenic Trail along the Continental Divide, snaking from the Canadian border across Montana, Wyoming, Colorado, and New Mexico to the Mexican border. Because some ridges on the actual divide might be difficult or dangerous, a 50-mile-wide corridor on either side could be used for the trail. Approximately 1,900 miles of trails and seldom-used roads shaped the initial configuration of the 3,100-mile trail. Ultimately designated the Continental Divide National Scenic Trail (CDNST), most of the trail is closed to motor vehicles.

Benton Mackaye, founder of the Appalachian Trail, first proposed the idea for the CDNST in 1966. Congress authorized a study of his idea under the National Trails System Act of 1968. The study reported that trail users would access great scenery, various ecosystems and life zones, and historical areas while crossing twenty-five national forests and three national parks (Glacier, Yellowstone, and Rocky Mountain). In 1971 Baltimore attorney Jim Wolf finished hiking the Appalachian Trail and looked for another such adventure. He started hiking the Divide Trail from the Canadian border and became a strong proponent for the CDNST.

Trail and view northwest from summit

The CDNST legislation gave the USDA Forest Service responsibility for coordinating the completion of the trail. Congress, however, did not appropriate funding to finish it. The corridor crosses National Park Service and Bureau of Land Management lands, and even though existing trails would be used in places, many miles needed maintenance or improvement. Proposed routes also crossed private property in some areas, requiring negotiations with landowners for either purchase or access of the trail corridor.

Two organizations formed to aid the CDNST. First, Jim Wolf founded the Continental Divide Trail Society (CDTS) in 1978. Today the CDTS continues with its mission: "[Dedicated to] the planning, development, and maintenance of the [Continental Divide Trail] as a silent trail." CDTS's efforts focus on the selection and development of the best possible route and on providing reliable information to trail users. Check out www.cdtsociety.org for more information.

The second organization, the Continental Divide Trail Alliance (CDTA), was founded by Bruce and Paula Ward in 1995. CDTA assists federal land managers to complete, manage, and protect the trail. They organize volunteer efforts to build and maintain new and old sections of trail, coordinate an Adopt-a-Trail program, and work with legislators to appropriate funding. Find more information at www.cdtrail.org.

By 2010 about 71 percent of the CDNST had been completed. However, many miles of existing trail are in need of repair or need to be rerouted from motorized routes or environmentally sensitive areas.

The trail to Alberta Peak travels across a meadow to the south of Wolf Creek Pass. After you cross the bridge and enter the trees, the trail splits in several directions. Turn left to follow the official trail, which then curves right and up. The trail climbs gently along the west side of the ridge. The Wolf Creek Ski Area's ski runs are on the east side. People from the San Luis Valley have skied on Wolf Creek Pass since the 1930s. In 1937 they formed the Wolf Creek Association and in 1938 installed rope tows on the north side of the highway. In 1956 another corporation formed and built a poma lift at the existing site. In 1976 the Pitcher family purchased Wolf Creek Ski Area and continues to own and manage it today. You can get a firsthand view of what a ski area looks like without snow at about 1.5 miles, where the top of a ski lift stands silently, waiting for snow to give it life again.

After another patch of forest, you'll arrive at an expansive view of Treasure Mountain (11,910 feet) and points to the southwest. Treasure Mountain earned its name from several legends about a chest full of gold that was buried in the area. Unfortunately, no one has ever found the gold. The trail follows the edge of the ridge, which drops steeply to the west. Curving left, it sneaks between willow bushes and emerges above tree line. The lake to the east is Alberta Park Reservoir. The snowshed to the northeast protects US 160 from frequent avalanches. Wolf Creek Pass typically receives the most snowfall in Colorado, averaging 460 inches of snow annually. Colorful alpine wildflowers bloom along the trail.

From this section, Alberta Peak, the hike's destination, rises meekly to the southeast. It's an easy scramble up the boulder field and grassy slopes to the top. The 360-degree view is worth the extra effort. Resident pikas sun themselves between hasty trips collecting grass and flowers for their winter hay piles. Continue farther along the CDNST if you wish. Watch out for lightning!

Miles and Directions

0.0 Start at the trailhead at the top of Wolf Creek Pass, on the south side. The Continental Divide National Scenic Trail (CDNST) continues south from the left side of the interpretive signs. Elevation: 10,857 feet.

0.1 Cross a bridge and turn left at the T intersection.

0.4 The trail comes to a lazy T intersection. Turn right and continue uphill. (The branch straight ahead takes you to a ski run.)

1.1 The trail makes several switchbacks, with great views to the west and northwest.

1.5 The trail passes near a chairlift to the left and a boulder field to the right. Stay to the right above the boulder field and you'll see the trail. GPS: N37 28.16' / W106 48.34'

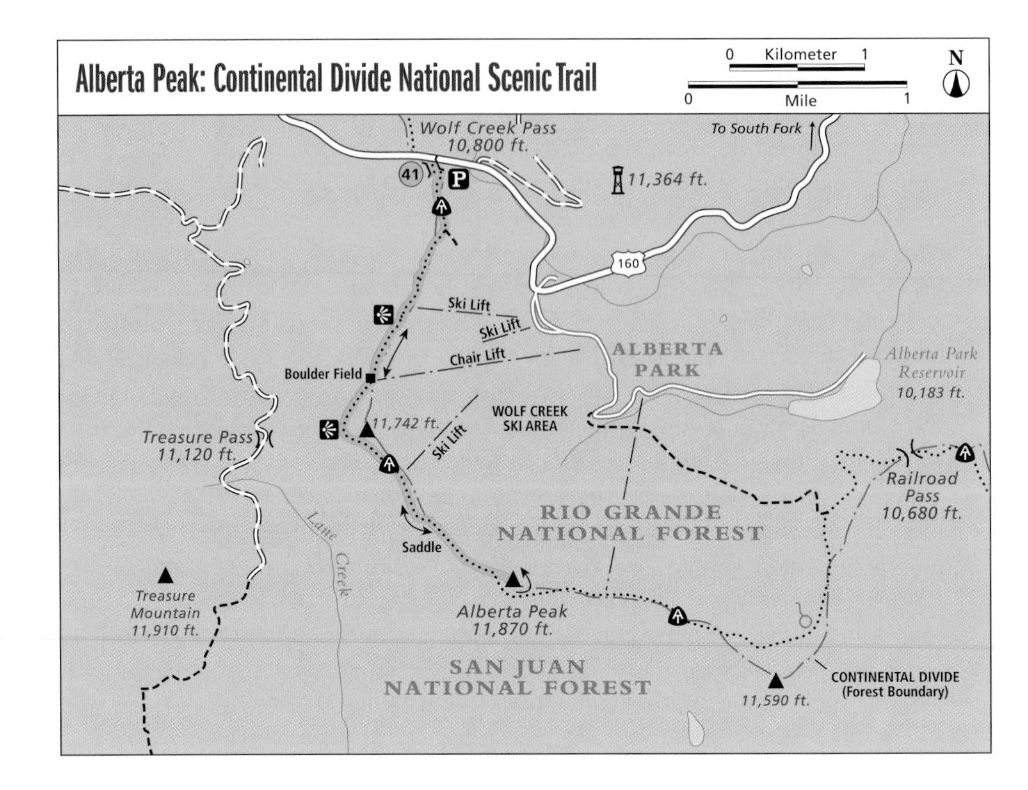

1.9 The trail opens up to the right with a view of Treasure Mountain.

2.2 The trail travels the edge of a ridge with a steep drop-off.

2.6 The trail drops slightly to a saddle with good views in most directions. You can readily see Alberta Peak from here. GPS: N37 27.52' / W106 48.00'

2.9 The CDNST continues along the steep south side of Alberta Peak. You can continue on from here for as long as you like. (***Note:*** Be aware of any lightning danger!) Turn left by the post and scramble up the gentle northwest side of Alberta Peak.

3.0 Reach the top of Alberta Peak, with wonderful panoramic views. Elevation: 11,870 feet. GPS: N37 27.35' / W106 47.65'. Return the way you came.

6.0 Arrive back at the trailhead.

42 Williams Creek Trail

The Williams Creek Trail (Trail 587) in the Weminuche Wilderness reaches the Continental Divide in 10.1 miles. This hike description guides you to the first crossing of Williams Creek. Traveling above the creek, you'll see various volcanic rock shapes from eroded fins to fluted cliffs. The trail progresses through forests of Douglas and white fir, limber pine, Gambel oak, aspen, and some beautiful wildflowers. Watch for deer. At the creek crossing, a little area to the right makes a great lunch stop. You can continue on the trail for a long day hike or a multiday backpack. Crossing Williams Creek can be challenging or unsafe during spring runoff.

Start: From the Williams Creek (Trail 587) Trailhead
Distance: 6.0 miles out and back
Approximate hiking time: 2.5 to 4 hours
Difficulty: Moderate due to mostly gentle terrain
Elevation gain: 720 feet, plus 340 feet of undulations
Seasons: Best from mid-June to mid-Oct
Trail surface: Dirt trail, sometimes rocky
Other trail users: Equestrians and hunters (in season)
Canine compatibility: Dogs must be under control
Fees and permits: None. Group size limit: No more than 15 people per group with a maximum combination of 25 people and pack or saddle animals in any one group.
Maps: USGS Cimarrona Peak; Nat Geo Trails Illustrated 140 Weminuche Wilderness
Trail contacts: San Juan National Forest, Pagosa Ranger District, Pagosa Springs; (970) 264-2268; www.fs.usda.gov/sanjuan
Other: There is a vault toilet at the trailhead. The Palisades Horse Camp across the parking lot has water, if the pump by the vault toilet doesn't work. The access road is typically closed in the winter beyond the boat ramp at Williams Creek Reservoir, about 3 miles from the trailhead. The trail is neither maintained nor marked for winter use.
Special Considerations: Check with the USDA Forest Service for up-to-date camping restrictions around certain lakes and hot springs, and fire restrictions in certain drainages. Also check on the latest information about bears and protecting food if you're backpacking.

Finding the trailhead: The Williams Creek Trailhead is just past Cimarrona Campground, about 27 miles from Pagosa Springs. The road intersections are well marked. Starting on the west side of Pagosa Springs, turn north onto Piedra Road (Archuleta CR 600) from US 160. In about 6.4 miles the road becomes dirt (FR 631). At about 13 miles the road forks; stay to the left on FR 631 (the right fork is FR 633). The road crosses Piedra Bridge at about 16.1 miles; continue straight ahead on FR 631. The road forks again at about 17.8 miles; take the left fork (right fork is FR 636). At about mile 22 the road forks yet again; this time take the right fork onto FR 640 (Williams Lake Road). In a little over 1 mile, Williams Creek Reservoir is on the right. When the road forks again at about mile 25.6, take the right fork (the left fork goes to Poison Park). Drive about another 1.4 miles to the Williams Creek (Trail 587) Trailhead. **GPS:** N37 32.49' / W107 11.84'

The Hike

The Williams Creek Trail is one of many gateways into the Weminuche Wilderness. Multiday loop trips can be designed starting at the Williams Creek Trailhead and returning via Indian Creek Trail or Cimarrona Creek Trail. Hikers can also traverse the wilderness and exit in the Rio Grande Valley to the north.

The Weminuche Wilderness is the largest designated wilderness in Colorado. The process started back in 1927, when the concept of preserving land in its natural state started to become popular. In 1932 the Forest Service established the San Juan Primitive Area, which covered the southern slopes of the San Juans. The Rio Grande Primitive Area was also created on the northern San Juan slopes. In 1964 Congress passed the Wilderness Act; however, the Weminuche was not one of the initial wilderness areas. This area was considered for wilderness status starting in 1968, causing both alarm and enthusiasm among locals. Sheep and cattle had grazed in the area for many years. Ranchers feared they might lose their grazing permits and the predator population would increase. Mining interests in the western part of the San Juans became a hot topic, too. Existing mining claims were not immediately impacted by the Wilderness Act, nor were grazing permits.

According to *Walking in Wildness: A Guide to the Weminuche Wilderness* by B. J. Boucher, during the early efforts for wilderness designation in the 1960s, Ian M. Thompson, then editor of *The Durango Herald,* was an avid wilderness advocate. Thompson wrote in a special wilderness supplement to the newspaper: "The 'Wilderness' effort we are engaged in at this time is, in one respect, a pitifully futile struggle. Earth's total atmosphere is man-changed beyond redemption. Earth's waters would not be recognizable to the Pilgrims. Earth's creatures will never again know what it is to be truly 'wild.' The sonic thunder of man's aircraft will increasingly descend in destructive shock waves upon any 'wilderness area' no matter how remote or how large. We are attempting to save the battered remnants of the original work of a Creator. To engage in this effort is the last hope of religious men."

A proposal to create the Weminuche Wilderness by combining the San Juan and Rio Grande Primitive Areas and adding some additional land was submitted to Congress in 1971. Recreational opportunities were emphasized, as were water quality and quantity. Water is the liquid gold of Colorado, and disputes over water rights and control are a never-ending battle in the state. For three years the proposal suffered through political haggling and boundary adjustments. Finally, in 1975 Colorado senators Peter H. Dominick and Floyd K. Haskell sponsored the bill that created the 405,031-acre Weminuche Wilderness. The name came from the Weeminuche band of Utes, who once thrived here.

Congress expanded the Weminuche in 1980 and again in 1993. Today the total area stands at approximately 488,210 acres in both the San Juan National Forest (Pacific drainage) and the Rio Grande National Forest (Atlantic drainage). A wilderness team

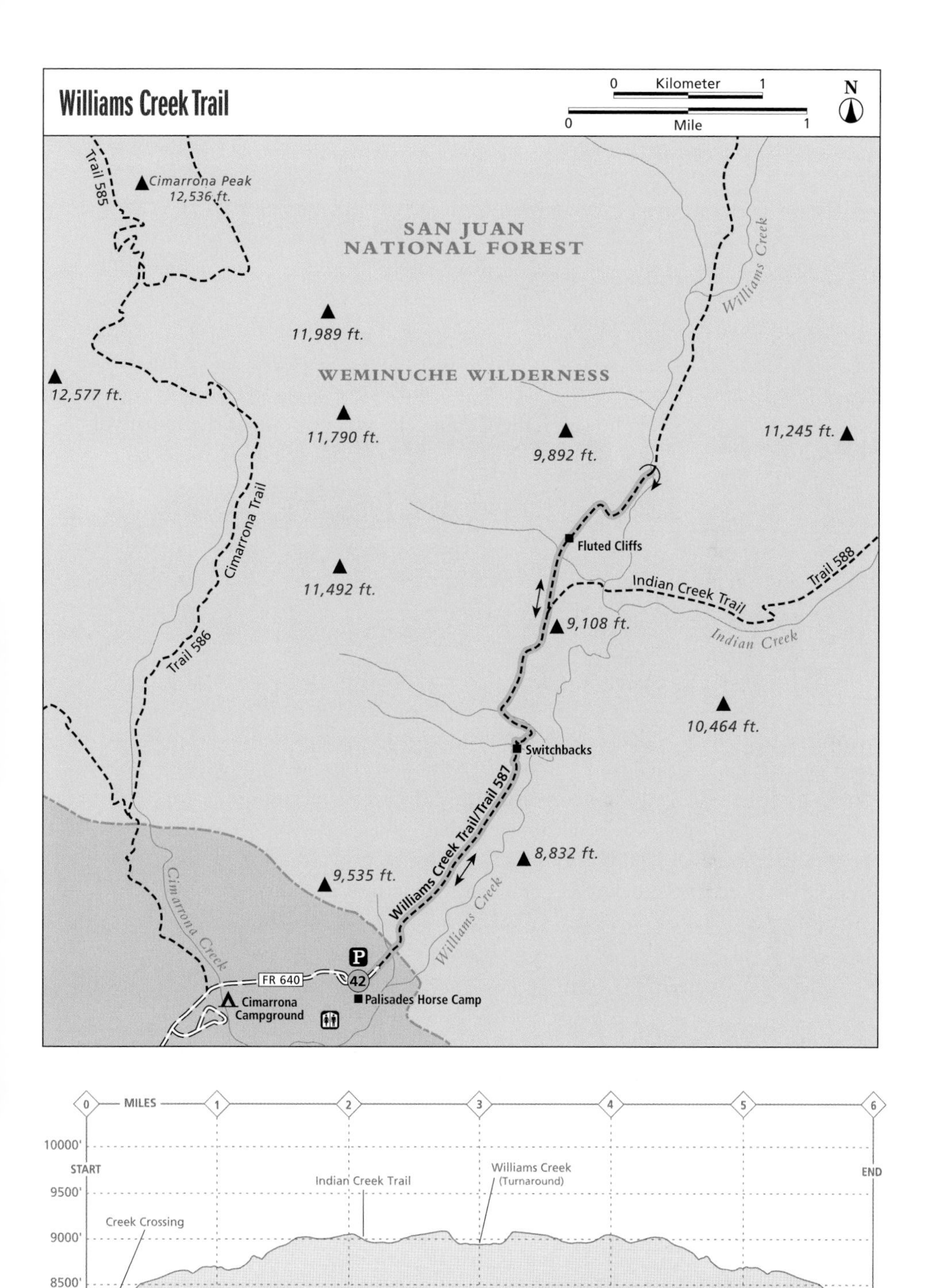
Williams Creek Trail
0 Kilometer 1
0 Mile 1
N
Trail 585
Cimarrona Peak
12,536 ft.
SAN JUAN
NATIONAL FOREST
Williams Creek
11,989 ft.
WEMINUCHE WILDERNESS
12,577 ft.
11,790 ft.
9,892 ft.
11,245 ft.
Cimarrona Trail
Fluted Cliffs
Trail 588
Indian Creek Trail
11,492 ft.
9,108 ft.
Indian Creek
Trail 586
10,464 ft.
Switchbacks
Williams Creek Trail/Trail 587
8,832 ft.
9,535 ft.
Cimarrona Creek
Williams Creek
P
FR 640
42
Cimarrona
Campground
Palisades Horse Camp
MILES
0
1
2
3
4
5
6
10000'
9500'
9000'
8500'
8000'
START
END
Creek Crossing
Indian Creek Trail
Williams Creek
(Turnaround)

comprising land managers from both forests provides consistent management for the Weminuche Wilderness.

The hike starts along a doubletrack that quickly becomes a trail. After crossing a boulder-filled waterway, which is often dry, you'll enter the Weminuche Wilderness. The trail gradually ascends. The large pinecones on the ground belong to the limber pine. Limber pines have five needles to a packet on very flexible branches, which give the species its moniker. As the trail becomes steeper, it narrows considerably, so watch for oncoming horse traffic and ask what to do if you meet equestrians. Usually the hiker steps off the trail on the downhill side, but this could prove difficult in one stretch. Along with the first view of Williams Creek, you'll notice an interesting area with eroded volcanic rock to your right.

The trail winds up and down around little creek drainages while slowly gaining elevation. The undergrowth thickens in several places with ferns, geraniums, subalpine larkspur, Wood's rose, and aspen trees. In some areas subalpine larkspur and cow parsnip stand about 5 feet tall. The Spanish called Williams Creek *huerto,* meaning "gardenlike" or "orchard." About 2.5 miles in, you cross a nice meadow with cliffs to the left that appear fluted. Cross over a ridge and drop to the Williams Creek crossing for lunch.

If you are backpacking, please remember to camp at least 100 feet away from streams, lakes, and trails per Forest Service regulations for this area. By practicing Leave No Trace techniques, the Weminuche will remain pristine for your next visit and for future generations.

Miles and Directions

0.0 Start at the Williams Creek (Trail 587) Trailhead. Elevation: 8,360 feet. Please remember to sign the trail register.

0.2 Enter the Weminuche Wilderness area.

1.2 The trail switchbacks above eroded features in the cliff along Williams Creek.

2.1 Reach the junction with Indian Creek Trail. GPS: N37 33.84' / W107 10.98'. Stay left on Williams Creek Trail.

2.6 Enter a large meadow with fluted cliffs to the left.

2.8 Cross a ridge and drop down to Williams Creek.

3.0 Arrive at the creek crossing. Elevation: 8,960 feet. GPS: N37 34.34' / W107 10.51'. (***Note:*** There's a nice lunch spot to the right along the creek.) Return the way you came.

6.0 Arrive back at the trailhead.

◀ *Fluted cliffs*

43 Devils Creek and Lake

The hike to Devils Lake is a great warm-up or practice hike for anyone wanting to climb the 14,000-foot peaks near Lake City. The elevation gain is similar, but at lower altitude. For those wishing a shorter hike, the old cow camp at mile 2.6 is a good turnaround point. The Devils Creek Trail into the Powderhorn Wilderness was constructed in 1994. The relatively undisturbed Cannibal and Calf Creek Plateaus contain one of the largest, relatively flat alpine tundra areas in the lower United States. The Cannibal Plateau is named after the area's famous cannibal, Alferd Packer.

Start: From the Devils Creek Trailhead
Distance: 13.6 miles out and back
Approximate hiking time: 7 to 12 hours (recommended 2- to 3-day backpack)
Difficulty: Strenuous due to elevation gain and altitude
Elevation gain: 3,600 feet
Seasons: Best from mid-June to mid-Oct; closed Apr to mid-June to protect elk calving areas
Trail surface: Dirt trail and old nonmotorized ranch road, steep in places, through alpine tundra
Other trail users: Equestrians and hunters (in season)
Canine compatibility: Dogs must be under control
Fees and permits: None, except for commercial guides or outfitters
Maps: USGS Alpine Plateau, Cannibal Plateau, and Powderhorn Lakes; Nat Geo Trails Illustrated 141 Telluride/Silverton/Ouray/Lake City and 139 La Garita Wilderness/Cochetopa Hills; Latitude 40° Southwest Colorado (shows part of the trail)
Trail contacts: Bureau of Land Management, Gunnison Field Office, Gunnison; (970) 641-0471; www.blm.gov/co/st/en/fo/gfo.html. Gunnison National Forest, Gunnison Ranger District, Lake City; (970) 641-0471 or (970) 944-2500; www.fs.usda.gov/gmug
Other: The road along the creek is mostly one vehicle wide, so be very careful. The bridge over the Lake Fork Gunnison River is closed until June 15 each year to protect elk calving areas. The area is closed Apr to mid-June. The access road may be closed by snow in winter. The trail is neither maintained nor marked for winter use. There are no facilities at the trailhead, and camping is not allowed. Bring your own water.

Finding the trailhead: From Lake City, drive north on CO 149 for about 7 miles, from the post office to a dirt road heading northeast. The turn is about 0.5 mile north of mile marker 79. Turn right onto the next road, which drops steeply to the river, and follow it 0.5 mile across the Lake Fork Gunnison River and up a hill to a dirt road signed TRAILHEADS. Turn left onto this road and continue about 0.4 mile to the Devils Creek Trailhead. With slow, careful driving, most 2WD cars should be able to reach the trailhead. **GPS:** N38 08.04' / W107 17.07'

The Hike

High peaks and high plateaus surround Lake City. The plateaus were formed by both lava and ash flows, estimated to be as thick as 5,000 feet. More recently, ice age glaciers scraped and molded the land, leaving U-shaped valleys, moraines, lakes, and tarns (ponds).

Cow camp

Volcanic activity also deposited gold, silver, and other precious metals in cracks and crevices. In 1871 J. K. Mullen and Henry Henson found the Ute-Ulay veins west of Lake City. This treasure, however, lay in Ute territory guaranteed by the Treaty of 1868.

In the fall of 1873 Alferd Packer was serving a jail sentence in Salt Lake City, Utah Territory, for counterfeiting. Hearing of gold discoveries in Colorado Territory, Packer bragged of his knowledge of the area. A group from Provo heard his boasts, paid his fine, and hired him to guide them to the Breckenridge area. The group of twenty-one men left Provo in November 1873. By mid-January they arrived at the winter camp of Chief Ouray, the Ute's spokesman. Chief Ouray warned them against proceeding, especially with the unusually severe winter. But gold blinds wisdom, and five men plus Packer left Ouray's camp in early February. They headed toward Los Pinos Indian Agency, southeast of Gunnison, via a shortcut across the mountains.

Alferd Packer arrived alone at the agency on April 16, 1874. Apparently healthy, his first request was for a drink of whiskey. He also started spending money on drinks and games in nearby Saguache, although he was known to have had little money when he left Utah. Packer's various stories conflicted, and local Utes reported finding strips of human flesh along his trail. At one point Packer agreed to lead a party to the bodies, but then became disoriented and refused to go farther. Artist J. A. Randolph found five skeletons near Lake City during the summer and sketched the gruesome site. Another story credits Captain C. H. Graham, a prospector, with the discovery. All five men had been shot, and one body was headless. Packer was jailed in August 1874, but soon escaped. He was recaptured in 1883.

Packer was found guilty of premeditated murder and sentenced to execution on May 19, 1883, in Lake City. The execution was overturned because the murders occurred in Ute territory. Packer was tried again in Gunnison in 1886, found guilty of five counts of murder, and sentenced to forty years in the state penitentiary at Cañon City. In 1900 the owners of the *Denver Post* requested parole for Packer as part of a publicity maneuver for the paper. After several interesting incidents, Governor Charles S. Thomas paroled Packer in 1901. Packer died in 1907 and is buried in a Littleton cemetery. Just south of Lake City, local citizens established a memorial to Packer's victims.

From Devils Lake, hike northeast on the North Calf Creek Trail (Trail 460), then north to the top of Calf Creek Plateau for an overlook into beautiful Powderhorn Lakes.

The Devils Creek Trail was completed in 1994 as a western access to the Powderhorn Wilderness. The area sees relatively little use (more during hunting season), so take care to keep it pristine. The trail climbs steadily and fairly steeply through forests of ponderosa pine, Douglas fir, juniper, aspen, and sage to an old cow camp. The trail also crosses a large meadow. Be careful during thunderstorms—this section is very exposed to lightning. The historic cow camp is protected as an antiquity, so please be respectful and leave it untouched. No camping is allowed inside or within 50 feet of the cabins. For a shorter 5.2-mile out-and-back hike, return the way you came from here. To reach Devils Lake in another 4.2 miles, continue hiking up the trail.

The trail winds more gently up along Devils Creek, through aspen groves and into thick spruce-fir forest, finally traveling along the creek at times. Switchbacking away from the creek, the trail enters another open meadow where a forest fire raged more than thirty years ago. Several steep switchbacks through thick forest bring you to a beautiful subalpine meadow, full of colorful wildflowers in July. Cairns mark the trail. Enter a final patch of forest where you need to look closely to find the path. After another flower-filled meadow, the trail reaches tree line at about 12,000 feet. Follow the cairns while climbing through open alpine tundra and rocks. The trail then flattens, crossing more alpine tundra and rocks that reflect the area's volcanic history. Head south across the tundra to Devils Lake.

If you are backpacking, please camp below tree line during thunderstorm season for your own safety. Water is usually available in Devils Creek—be sure to treat it—to about the meadow (created when a forest fire killed the trees) . If you camp near the lake, please follow BLM regulations and camp at least 150 feet away, out of sight of other visitors, and use only camp stoves, to protect the fragile tundra. Several grassy bluffs above the lake provide excellent camping spots and are more resistant to damage than the alpine tundra near the lake.

As you hike, think of the volcanic flows and seas of ice that have been replaced with fragile alpine tundra plants. Imagine Alferd Packer's party, trudging through snow and meeting its gruesome death.

Uncompaghre Peak from Devils Creek Trail

Miles and Directions

0.0 Start at the Devils Creek Trailhead. Elevation: 8,480 feet. Remember to sign the trail register.

0.6 The trail makes a left "L" by a big rock thumb.

0.8 The trail comes to a T intersection with an old road. GPS: N38 07.90' / W107 16.65'. Turn left and continue uphill on the road.

1.0 The road enters a long sagebrush meadow and continues in the open for 0.5 mile. (***Note:*** Be careful of lightning.)

1.5 The road curves left above the aspen grove.

1.8 Reach the wilderness boundary sign. GPS: N38 08.22' / W107 15.95'

2.0 The trail turns right and leaves the road. Follow the trail and do not return to the road as the trail crosses it a few more times. (***Note:*** The BLM requests visitors stay on the trail when it departs from the old road to avoid creating areas where erosion will occur.)

2.6 The old cow camp appears on the left side of the trail. GPS: N38 08.39' / W107 15.27'. (***Note:*** There's a big flat rock that's ideal for a break.) (***Option:*** For a day hike [three to five hours], return the way you came, arriving back at the trailhead at 5.2 miles.)

3.1 Pass some huge Douglas firs. (***Note:*** In an open spot, look back to the west for a view of Uncompahgre Peak, which at 14,309 feet is Colorado's sixth-highest peak. The Cannibal Plateau is above on your right.)

3.4 The trail is finally next to the creek, and you can see it!

4.4 The trees thin as you enter an old burned area. The trail follows a little ridge. (***Note:*** Be careful of lightning.)

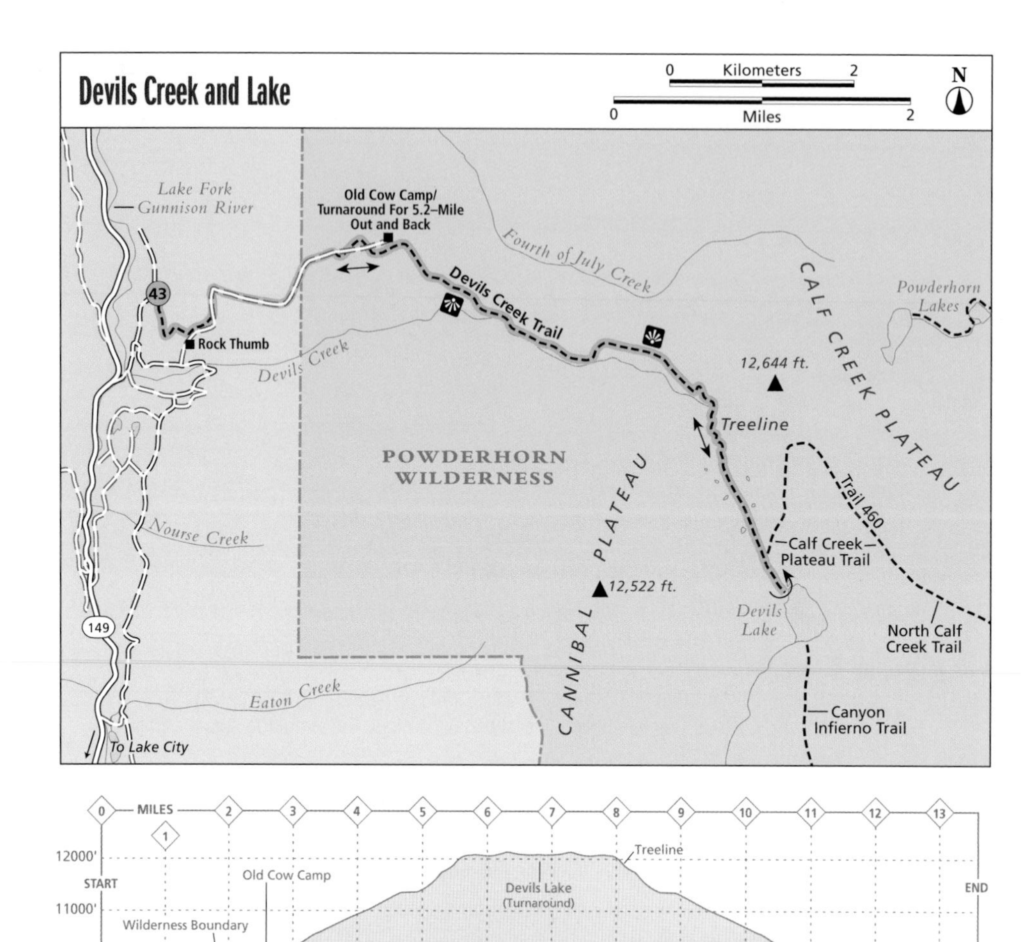

5.3 The trail leaves the forest and enters a colorful meadow. Follow the cairns along the right side of the meadow until you see some crossing the meadow. Cross and enter another patch of trees (the trail is faint here), cross another meadow, and then follow more cairns.

5.5 The trail is now above tree line. GPS: N38 07.20' / W107 12.78'. Follow the cairns across the alpine tundra and rocks. When cairns no longer exist, keep heading south and downhill to Devils Lake.

6.8 Reach Devils Lake. Elevation: 11,980 feet. GPS: N38 06.33' / W107 12.28'. Return the way you came. (***Option:*** You can make a longer trip by connecting with other trails in the area.)

13.6 Arrive back at the trailhead.

44 Washington Gulch Trail

Washington Gulch Trail offers several options. The main goal is the ridge at about 11,400 feet, with spectacular views of the Maroon Bells–Snowmass Wilderness and the Raggeds Wilderness. The flowers are sensational during July. The hike starts at the Gothic-side trailhead, climbing through fields of wildflowers and spruce-fir forest to the ridge. The out-and-back option returns from here. The point-to-point option descends to the Washington Gulch side, passing an old mine with relics. A high-clearance vehicle is required to reach the west-side trailhead. Be mindful of mountain bikers the entire way.

Start: From the Washington Gulch (Trail 403) Trailhead near Gothic Campground
Distance: 3.9 miles point to point
Approximate hiking time: 1.5 to 2.5 hours
Difficulty: Difficult due to elevation gain
Elevation gain/loss: 1,940-foot gain/410-foot loss
Seasons: Best from mid-June through Sept
Trail surface: Dirt trail with some steep sections
Other trail users: Equestrians, mountain bikers, hunters (in season)
Canine compatibility: Dogs must be on leash. This is a popular mountain bike trail, so keep dogs leashed for their safety as well as bikers' safety.
Fees and permits: None
Maps: USGS Oh-Be-Joyful; Nat Geo Trails Illustrated 133 Kebler Pass/Paonia Reservoir; Latitude 40° Crested Butte, Taylor Park
Trail contacts: Gunnison National Forest, Gunnison; (970) 641-0471; www.fs.usda.gov/gmug
Other: Gothic Campground is about 0.1 mile south of the Gothic-side trailhead. No facilities at either trailhead.

Finding the trailhead: *With shuttle* (requires high-clearance vehicle): Drive north and east on Gothic Road from the Crested Butte Chamber of Commerce (located in the old train station at the corner of Elk Avenue and Gothic Road in Crested Butte) toward the town of Mount Crested Butte. Turn left at Washington Gulch Road (GCR 811/FR 811) in about 1.7 miles. From this intersection, drive about 8 miles up Washington Gulch. The trailhead is on the right side of the road, just up the hill beyond a very sharp and steep left switchback and above the cabins at Elkton by the Painter Boy Mine. Drop one vehicle off here and return to Gothic Road. **GPS:** N38 58.05' / W107 02.53'

To reach the Gothic-side trailhead for the start of the hike, turn right at the intersection of Gothic Road and Washington Gulch Road, continuing north on Gothic Road (GCR 317). The pavement ends at mile 3.7. Drive down the dirt road, which becomes FR 317 just past Gothic and the Rocky Mountain Biological Laboratory. The Washington Gulch Trailhead is located on the left side of the road about 10 miles from Crested Butte, or 6.4 miles from where the pavement ends. **GPS:** N38 58.93' / W107 00.40'

The Hike

Gothic Mountain (12,625 feet), south of the Washington Gulch Trail, received its name from the interesting rock formations on its east side that resemble Gothic cathedral spires. In May 1879 John and David Jennings discovered silver at the head of

Ruby Range and Raggeds

Copper Creek east of Gothic Mountain and named their discovery the Sylvanite. The deposit of silver in wire form was so rich that it often brought in over $15,000 per ton. From 1880 to 1910 the Sylvanite Mine produced over $1 million worth of silver.

Hopeful miners arrived in droves, searching the surrounding hills and valleys for ore, praying to strike it rich. A few months after the deposit was discovered, the town of Gothic was laid out at the confluence of East River and Copper Creek. In one week's time, one hundred tents and cabins reportedly sprang up. Two sawmills were set up and had a hard time keeping up with the demand for lumber. By the end of 1879, more than 200 buildings had been constructed and over 500 people lived in the area. The next summer the town boasted five law firms, four grocery stores, three restaurants, two general mercantile stores, a bank, three doctors, two hotels, and the usual assortment of saloons, gambling halls, and dance halls. A nightly bonfire on Main Street allowed the locals to tell stories and smoke their tobacco. Gothic became the supply center for the area's various small camps and mines.

Transporting ore out of, and goods into, town was a challenge. The East River Toll Road was the main route in 1879. Eventually another road was built around the

An amazing toll road was built over Schofield Pass, connecting the towns of Marble and Aspen with Gothic and Crested Butte. The road was only 7 to 8 feet wide in places, instead of the usual 10 feet. Freight traffic normally negotiated an 8 percent grade, with 12 percent being the maximum. Schofield Pass, near the Devil's Punchbowl, however, is a steep 27 percent grade!

west side of Crested Butte (12,162 feet), saving several miles. Gothic even supplied Aspen via a road up Copper Creek, over East Maroon Pass, and down Maroon Creek. Gothic eventually boasted a population of 8,000 people, until the Silver Panic of 1893 signaled the end of the "City of Silver Wires."

In 1928 the Rocky Mountain Biological Laboratory (RMBL) moved into the remaining buildings at Gothic, tearing down some and remodeling others. RMBL was the dream of Dr. John C. Johnson, a biology professor at Western State College at Gunnison. Johnson purchased land and old buildings to create a research and training facility for field biologists. Scientists use the surrounding national forest, wilderness, and Gothic Research Natural Area to hone their investigative and research skills.

The hike starts at the Gothic side of Washington Gulch Trail, as it is more accessible and easier to find. The trail starts by climbing up switchbacks through a field of cornhusk lilies and tall larkspurs. As the trail winds higher, the Elk Mountains expand into view to the east. Columbine, Indian paintbrush, and varieties of sunflowers add color along the trail. Rock Creek rumbles downhill to the left. At times the vegetation is so tall and hanging over the trail that you might feel a machete would be useful. In about 1 mile a cirque on Gothic Mountain comes into view. The mountain will dominate the southern view for most of the hike. Keep an eye out for deer. The trail enters a relatively flat meadow with a red mountain looming just beyond. This is Mount Baldy (12,805 feet).

After crossing Rock Creek the trail meanders a long way through spruce-fir forest and meadows before making a final steep zigzag climb to a fantastic scenic overlook. There's even a "scenic pullout" to the right of the main trail, a great place for lunch. Looking east you can see into the Maroon Bells–Snowmass Wilderness, including the top of one of the Bells. Notice how the rock is folded on one ridge of Avery Peak, across Gothic Road. Tremendous uplifting forces created these mountains. Walk west across the trail to a field of beautiful flowers. Looking west to the Raggeds Wilderness and Ruby Range, you can see Daisy Pass (11,600 feet) snaking upward to the ridge. Washington Gulch lies below.

The overlook area is the turnaround point for the optional out-and-back hike. To continue into Washington Gulch, the trail gently descends about 1 mile to Washington Gulch Road near the Painter Boy Mine, another great ore producer in its day. Remember, old mines can be extremely dangerous—stay out!

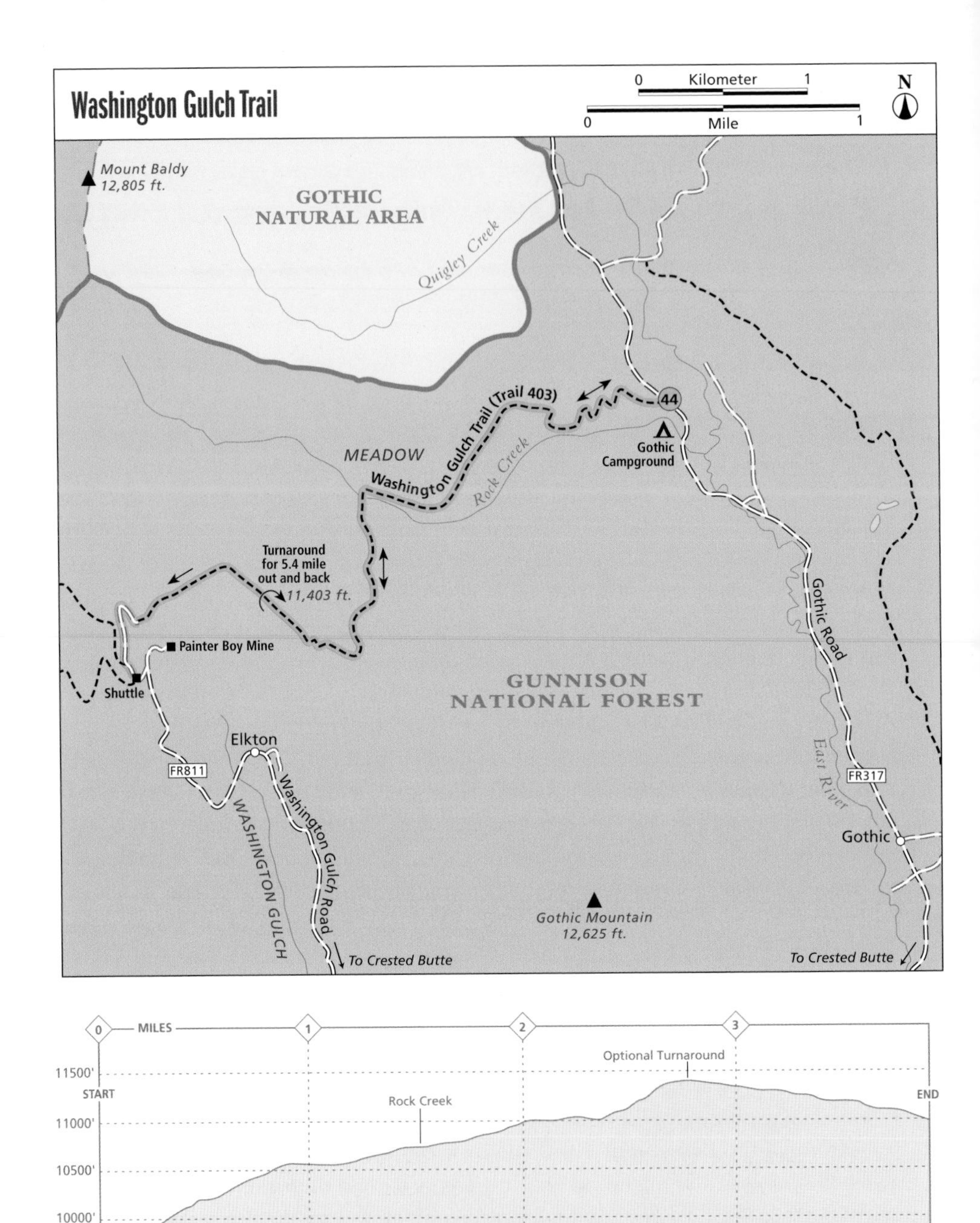

As you hike along, enjoying the fabulous views and fantastic wildflower show, visualize miners streaming through the area, searching for the strike that would make them rich.

View near the east trailhead

Miles and Directions

0.0 Start at Washington Gulch (Trail 403) Trailhead north of Gothic. Elevation: 9,460 feet.

1.3 Reach a meadow with a view of Mount Baldy.

1.5 Cross Rock Creek.

1.7 Encounter steep switchbacks.

2.1 Reach a marshy meadow with a view of Gothic Mountain.

2.5 Encounter more steep switchbacks. Views of the Ruby Range are to the left and Elk Mountains to the right.

2.7 Reach a scenic overlook. Elevation: 11,380 feet. GPS: N38 58.22' / W107 01.87'. Great place for lunch! Make sure to check out the spectacular views both east and west, then continue down the trail toward Washington Gulch. (***Option:*** For a 5.4-mile out-and-back without a shuttle, turn around here and return the way you came. Approximate hiking time: 2.5 to 3.5 hours.)

3.7 Reach an old mine and relics. GPS: N38 58.18' / W107 02.57'

3.9 Arrive at the Washington Gulch–side trailhead. Elevation: 10,990 feet. (***Note:*** This trailhead is an optional starting point. It can also be the turnaround point for a 7.8-mile out-and-back hike.)

45 Ptarmigan Lake

The hike to Ptarmigan Lake winds through spruce-fir forest, gently climbing into an area of beautiful subalpine meadows dotted with tarns and little lakes. For flower aficionados, the meadows show off beautiful wildflowers in July. After a little climb up the side of a cirque, you arrive at crystal-clear Ptarmigan Lake. Another 0.3 mile leads to a saddle with a view down into South Cottonwood Creek. This hike travels above tree line, so if the weather is threatening a thunderstorm, stay at the lower lakes.

Start: From the Ptarmigan Lake Trailhead off the Cottonwood Pass road
Distance: 6.6 miles out and back
Approximate hiking time: 3 to 4 hours
Difficulty: Difficult due to elevation gain and altitude
Elevation gain: 1,490 feet to the lake
Seasons: Best from July through Sept
Trail surface: Dirt trail with some boulders and rocks
Other trail users: Equestrians, anglers, mountain bikers, hunters (in season)
Canine compatibility: Dogs must be under control
Fees and permits: None
Maps: USGS Mount Yale and Tincup; Nat Geo Trails Illustrated 129 Buena Vista/Collegiate Peaks
Trail contacts: San Isabel National Forest, Salida Ranger District, Salida; (719) 539-3591; www.fs.usda.gov/psicc
Other: Vault toilet at the trailhead, but no water. The Cottonwood Pass road is closed by snow from late Nov to May about 4 miles before the trailhead. The trail is neither maintained nor marked for winter use.

Finding the trailhead: From Buena Vista, drive about 14.5 miles west on Chaffee CR 306, which later becomes FR 306, heading to Cottonwood Pass. The trailhead is on the south (left) side of the road about 0.1 mile in. **GPS:** N38 48.22' / W106 22.45'

The Hike

Cottonwood Pass was originally a toll road from Buena Vista, connecting with other roads leading to Crested Butte, Gothic, and eventually Aspen in the 1870s. Harvard City, which you pass on the way from Buena Vista to the trailhead, boomed for a couple of years as placer claims were located along Cottonwood Creek. Lode mines were discovered and developed in 1874. Freighters also stopped at Harvard City to repack their loads for the long and difficult climb over the Continental Divide. Times changed, and the road connecting Aspen and Leadville over Independence Pass, opened in 1881, drew traffic away from Cottonwood Pass. The mines in the area couldn't match new mines farther west, and the miners moved on.

Cottonwood Pass, named after the many trees lining the creek alongside the road, fell into disrepair. The USDA Forest Service repaired and improved the road for automobile travel in the late 1950s. Several trailheads and good fishing are all accessible via the road today. The pass is closed during the winter, but is open to various winter sports.

Several lakes in Colorado bear the name Ptarmigan. The white-tailed ptarmigan, *Lagopus leucurus,* is a member of the grouse family that lives year-round above tree line and in the krummholz just below. Krummholz refers to the stunted, twisted tree hedges growing at the edge of tree line. It's usually made up of subalpine fir, Engelmann spruce, or limber pine. Ptarmigans are masters of disguise: During winter they wear snow-white feathers, which turn mottled brown and white in the summer. It's easy to almost step on one because they blend in so well with the rocks. As you hike, look for these birds. Little chicks follow after mom in the summer. If approached, the mother pretends to have a broken wing to draw predators away from her chicks. Please do not harass ptarmigans to see if they'll pretend an injury, and do not let your dog chase them.

Winter finds the male ptarmigan still above tree line, sometimes in the shelter of the krummholz and sometimes in willow thickets hidden below the snow. Females winter in willows below tree line. The ptarmigan is one animal that may gain or maintain weight during harsh Colorado mountain winters by eating the energy-rich buds of willow bushes. To save energy in the spring, willows set their leaf buds during the prior autumn.

White-tailed ptarmigan appear to be monogamous, although after the chicks hatch, the female raises them alone. Mating time in the spring, like molting, is triggered by lengthening daylight and other changes in climate.

If you head around the lake on the trail to the little saddle, look up to the left and notice the streams of rocks heading down toward the lake. Freezing and thawing, which occurs most of the year, can force rocks buried underground up to the surface. On steep slopes the unearthed rocks roll into depressions. If one rock stops, others may roll into it or along a small water depression, causing a streamlike appearance. In more level places the rocks may form polygons or garlands. This "patterned ground" is common in Colorado's alpine tundra.

The hike starts in thick spruce-fir forest, opening occasionally as two boulder fields flow over the trail. Watch for raspberry bushes among the boulders. Although you can hear Ptarmigan Creek in the distance, the trail keeps a good distance until you are almost to the lake. The hike continues through spruce-fir forest without much of a view. At about mile 1.2, cross a dirt road (FR 346—4WD access to the trail). Go straight and don't turn onto the road. The trail continues to wind and switchback gently through the forest.

About 2.4 miles in, the trees are less dense and more flowers appear. Some possible campsites come into view away from the trail. (Camp at least 200 feet from the trail, lakes, and streams.) Then the world opens,.with Jones Mountain on the right and Gladstone Ridge on the left. You can see the edge of the cirque that contains Ptarmigan Lake. Flower-filled meadows dotted with little ponds and a lake line the trail.

Continue hiking through the meadows, jump across Ptarmigan Creek, and two switchbacks later arrive at the lake. Mount Yale (14,196 feet) looms large to the northeast. Two other high peaks rise above other ridges. Those high points are Mount

Ptarmigan Lake from saddle

Harvard (14,420 feet) and Mount Columbia (14,073 feet). The pointy peak between you and the fourteeners is Turner Peak (13,233 feet).

If the weather is good, continue another 0.3 mile to the saddle for views down Grassy Gulch and South Cottonwood Creek. The views to the east and northeast of the Collegiate Peaks are worth the short climb.

Miles and Directions

0.0 Start at the Ptarmigan Lake (Trail 1444) Trailhead. Elevation: 10,650 feet. In 350 feet, cross a bridge over Middle Cottonwood Creek. The trail register is on the other side—please sign in.

0.2 Reach the first boulder field.

0.7 Reach the second boulder field.

1.2 Cross a dirt forest road. GPS: N38 47.53' / W106 22.15'. Go straight on the clearly marked trail. (FR 346 provides access to the trail, but only by 4WD vehicle.)

2.5 Reach the first little kettle pond on the right, and a lake down to the left.

2.9 Cross Ptarmigan Creek.

3.2 Arrive at Ptarmigan Lake. Elevation: 12,132 feet. GPS: N38 46.68' / W106 02.93'. Hike another 0.1 mile to the other side of lake.

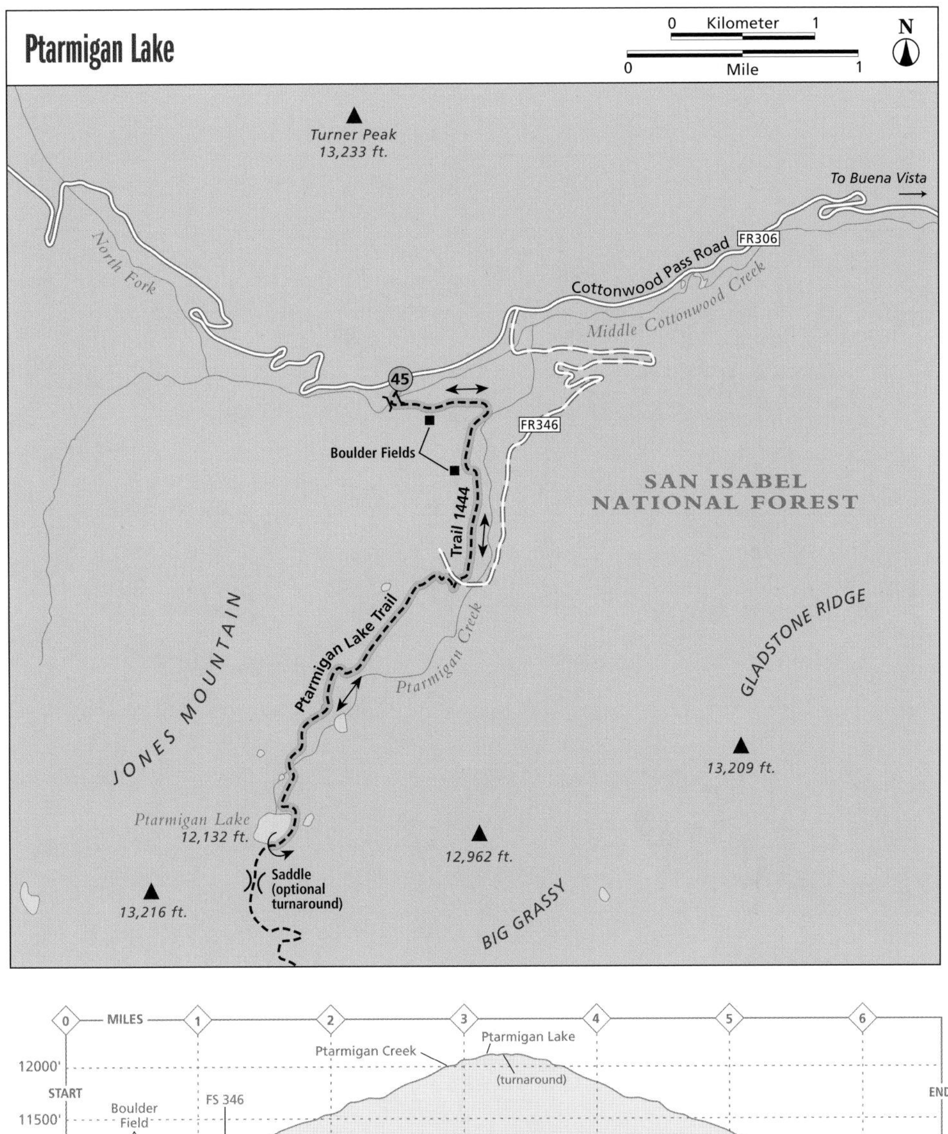

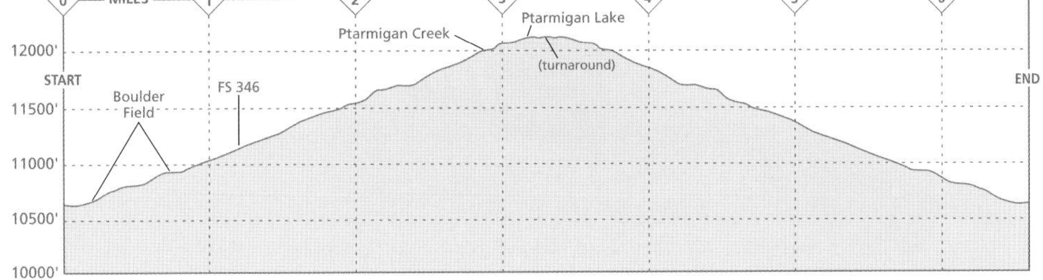

3.3 Reach the south side of the lake. Return the way you came. (***Side trip:*** Continue another 0.3 mile to the saddle between the Middle Cottonwood and South Cottonwood drainages. This side trip will add 0.6 mile and about 20 minutes to the hike.)

6.6 Arrive back at the trailhead.

SOUTHWEST

Land of the Ute and the Ancestral Puebloans (formerly called Anasazi), the Four Corners area and San Juan Mountains are rich in culture, history, and beauty. Hiking opportunities abound in both canyons and on rugged mountain trails. Thirteen of Colorado's fifty-four peaks over 14,000 feet are located in this region.

Ouray has long been known as the Little Switzerland of America and also boasts about its hot springs for those weary bones and muscles. Telluride is just 10 miles away from Ouray as the crow flies, about 18 miles on 4WD roads, or 49 miles by twisty highway. The feats of miners and road builders from Ouray to Durango and Telluride to Lake City take on a new meaning after touring and hiking the steep, rough terrain of this region. The San Juan Mountains, born of explosive volcanoes and later carved into sharp pinnacles and cirques by several glacial periods, provide years of exploring for any hiker. The Million Dollar Highway, connecting Ouray and Silverton, is another accomplishment of stubborn humans who had to get from Point A to Point B through horrendously rugged country. Avalanches still claim lives today on this highway.

To the west lies the Uncompahgre Plateau, an interesting geological uplift between mountains and canyons. To its east and west, rivers have carved canyons through its back and along its edges. Dominguez Canyon Wilderness and National Conservation Area, on the east edge of the Uncompahgre Plateau, contains petroglyphs, an old mine, and a seasonal waterfall, plus desert bighorn sheep. Farther east, the Gunnison River has carved its skinny canyon through ancient Precambrian bedrock, now preserved by the Black Canyon of the Gunnison National Park and the Gunnison Gorge National Conservation Area.

Bridge across Gunnison River

46 Big Dominguez Canyon

The Big Dominguez Canyon Trail wanders up a beautiful canyon cut in the side of the Uncompahgre Plateau. Desert bighorn sheep were reintroduced here in 1983 and 1985—watch rocky areas and cliff tops for them. Ancient people have traveled through the canyon for at least 1,500 years. Keep your eyes open for (but hands off) petroglyphs pecked in boulders along the trail. Remains of an old mine straddle the trail 6 miles from the parking lot. This red sandstone canyon is part of the Dominguez Canyon Wilderness, designated by Congress in March 2009.

Start: From the Bridgeport Trailhead
Distance: 13.0 miles out and back (turn around sooner for shorter hikes)
Approximate hiking time: 5.5 to 8.5 hours
Difficulty: Difficult due to distance; shorter, moderate hikes available
Elevation gain: 680 feet, plus some small undulations
Seasons: Best in spring and fall; summer can be very hot
Trail surface: Dirt trail, rocky in a few areas
Other trail users: Equestrians
Canine compatibility: Dogs must be under control
Fees and permits: None
Map: USGS Triangle Mesa
Trail contacts: Bureau of Land Management, Dominguez-Escalante National Conservation Area, 2465 S. Townsend Ave., Montrose; (970) 240-5367; www.blm.gov/co/st/en/nca/denca.html
Other: Plans have been in the works to reroute the trail from its current location along the railroad tracks to a safer alternative. Check the website or call the BLM office to check current status. Be sure to read the visitor information at the trailhead and follow all safety recommendations regarding hiking near the railroad tracks. (***Note for backpackers:*** If you camp along the Gunnison River, please camp in designated campsites. The first part of Big Dominguez Canyon [to about 4 miles from the parking lot] and Little Dominguez Canyon [to the south end of the Rambo property] are day-use only and closed to camping. Please use Leave No Trace techniques and camp at least 100 feet away from small streams. Big Dominguez Creek is dry part of the year, the creek is not always near the trail, and the water, when available, must be treated. Bring your own water—one gallon per person per day is recommended, plus a gallon per day for your dog.)

Finding the trailhead: *From the junction of CO 92 and US 50 in Delta,* drive 19.2 miles north on US 50 to Bridgeport Road. Turn left onto Bridgeport Road and drive 3.3 miles to the dead end, where there's a parking lot but no facilities. The trailhead is on the left (south) side of the parking lot.

From Grand Junction, drive south on US 50 to Bridgeport Road, near mile marker 52. Turn right onto Bridgeport Road; drive 3.3 miles to the parking lot at the dead end. No facilities. **GPS:** N38 50.95' / W108 22.30'

The Hike

On March 30, 2009, President Barack Obama signed legislation designating the Dominguez-Escalante National Conservation Area (NCA) and the Dominguez Canyon Wilderness area. Encompassing 209,610 acres of beautiful canyon country carved out of the eastern edge of the Uncompahgre Plateau, the NCA designation will

Rock art panel

conserve and protect these lands for wildlife, flora, and future human generations. Public meetings and discussions held over three years set the stage for the legislation. The lands are managed by the Bureau of Land Management, and the agency is tasked with creating a resource management plan to provide for the long-term protection and management of the NCA and wilderness. A citizen's advisory committee has been established to aid in the process. The lands are withdrawn from mining and mineral leasing, but grazing, access to inholdings, control of invasive species, fire prevention, and existing water rights protection are still allowed. The Dominguez Canyon Wilderness consists of 66,280 acres within the NCA.

Long before the Spanish and white settlers arrived, Native Americans wandered these western canyons hunting game and collecting plants, successfully living in the arid climate. These Archaic peoples arrived perhaps as far back as 6500 BC. Over time, people living around the Uncompahgre Plateau in western Colorado borrowed ideas from their neighbors, the Fremont and the Ancestral Pueblo (Anasazi), and incorporated them into their culture while maintaining a unique way of living. Archaeologists describe their lifestyle as the Uncompahgre Complex or Gateway Tradition. The petroglyph panel by the BLM's ARCHAEOLOGICAL SITE sign, located along the trail, is categorized as Uncompahgre style, which existed for about 2,000 years between 1000 BC and AD 1000. The figures on the rock were pecked or carved into it, typically with a bone or an antler. The Uncompahgre style differs from the Fremont style found farther north in Colorado and Utah. Fremont rock art typically uses huge-bodied figures to depict heroes or supernatural beings. The figures in Big Dominguez Canyon tend to be smaller and more humanlike. Bears are common in the Uncompahgre style, and one is apparent on the panel you'll see. Bighorn sheep figures are plentiful. Unfortunately, a few modern folks have defaced parts of the rock art panels in the area—notably with words and a spaceship. Please respect this ancient art and do not touch. Oils from our hands promote deterioration. Human-like figures riding horses and other shapes were pecked into another rock by the Utes, who later roamed these canyons.

Petroglyph panels throughout western Colorado indicate that bighorn sheep were hunted by these early peoples. Over time, with westward expansion in the 1800s and early 1900s, bighorn were extirpated from this area. The Colorado Division of Wildlife reintroduced the desert bighorn (*Ovis canadensis nelsoni*) to the Big Dominguez area in 1983 and 1985. Slightly smaller and lighter in color than their cousins, the Rocky Mountain bighorn, they live in small groups in arid canyons, using the rocks and cliffs for protection from predators. Ewes (females) and lambs stay together while the rams create their own herds. They eat sparse desert vegetation, from which they gather water, and drink at water holes or creeks every few days. They even eat cacti, using hooves and horns to remove the spines. During summer's hot days they find shady shelter. At other times they eat during the day and rest at night. Rams grow spiral horns with a new ring emerging each year. Horns can reach 30 inches long with a base circumference of 15 inches. Ewes' horns are 12- to 17-inch spikes. Weighing up to 200 pounds, the rams win mating privileges through head-butting contests with each other. Mating season typically occurs in late fall, with lambs born in April and May.

Watch for bighorn sheep on the canyon rims. If they are down in the canyon, be sure to keep your dog under control. Bighorn sheep have been adversely affected by human activities, from loss of habitat to overhunting to contracting diseases from domestic sheep and cattle.

The trail up Big Dominguez Canyon sometimes looks like a road—it was. Miners built the road to access the uranium mine at mile 6.1. Not much else is known about this mine, although it was probably active during the region's uranium boom between 1940 and the 1960s.

This hike takes you to the junction with the Cactus Park Trail, but turn around sooner if you'd like. The canyon contains many beautiful features, from red rock cliffs with interesting formations to various desert plants to old mining remains. Enjoy your visit to this wonderful canyon.

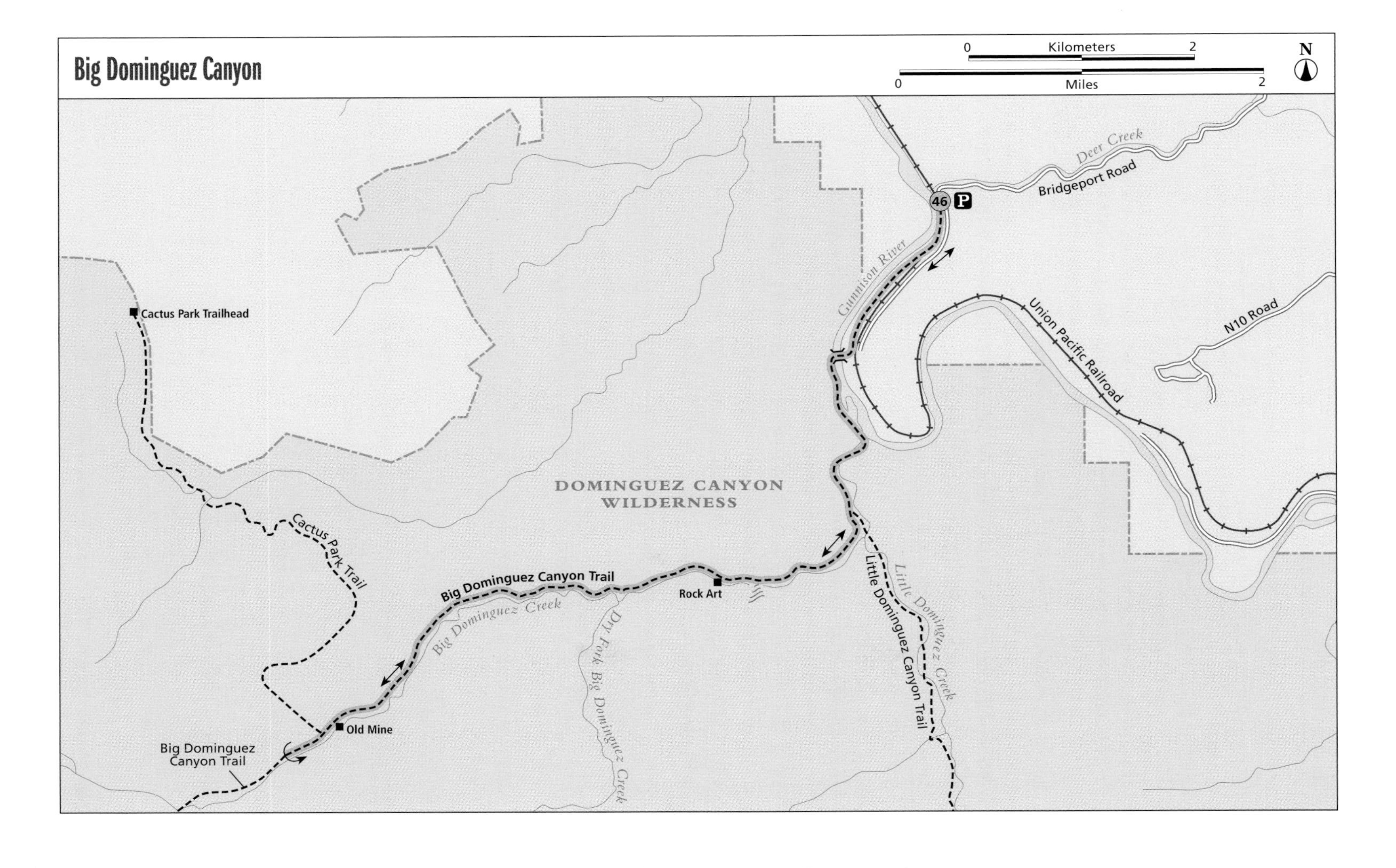
Big Dominguez Canyon
0
Kilometers
2
0
Miles
2
N
46
P
Bridgeport Road
Deer Creek
Gunnison River
Union Pacific Railroad
N10 Road
Cactus Park Trailhead
Cactus Park Trail
DOMINGUEZ CANYON
WILDERNESS
Big Dominguez Canyon Trail
Big Dominguez Creek
Rock Art
Dry Fork Big Dominguez Creek
Little Dominguez Canyon Trail
Little Dominguez Creek
Old Mine
Big Dominguez
Canyon Trail

Miles and Directions

0.0 Start at the trailhead to the left (south) of the parking lot. Elevation: 4,720 feet. The first 0.3 mile travels along the railroad tracks. If a train is present, wait until it passes. If the train is stopped, wait until the train moves before crossing at the one designated crossing. Delays can be up to 1 hour.

0.3 Cross the tracks at the designated railroad crossing.

1.0 Walk past the trail to the first bridge on the right. This bridge is private. Continue straight ahead, then turn right on the trail to the interpretive signs and the second bridge. N38 50.19' / W108 22.81'. Cross the Gunnison River and turn left.

1.7 Arrive at the trailhead bulletin board near the wilderness boundary.

2.3 Arrive at a trail junction. Turn right to hike up Big Dominguez Canyon. The two-track trail to the left goes up Little Dominguez Canyon. GPS: N38 49.34' / W108 22.75'

3.1 A side trail marked by cairns heads to the left to a big waterfall (when Big Dominguez Creek has water in it).

3.25 Reach an archaeological site. Please take only pictures–touching, defacing, or tracing any rock art is prohibited. Please leave the petroglyphs intact for others to enjoy. These sites are sacred to Native Americans. (***Option:*** For a shorter, moderate hike, turn around here and return the way you came.)

3.7 The trail curves left over rocks–follow the cairns. In another 0.1 mile the trail passes through a tunnel created by two huge rocks leaning against each other.

4.0 Reach the approximate end of the day-use area.

4.6 The trail climbs up black lava rock.

6.1 The trail passes by the remains of a mine. Remember to leave all artifacts for others to enjoy.

6.5 Arrive at the Cactus Park Trail junction. Elevation: 5,400 feet. GPS: N38 48.13' / W108 26.12'. Turn around and return the way you came. Just before this junction is a flat area to the south that is a great lunch spot.

13.0 Arrive back at the parking lot.

47 Upper Roubideau Area Loop

This hike explores the upper section of the Roubideau Area, a special part of the Uncompahgre Plateau. First descend on Old Roubideau Trail (Trail 105) from (Gray) Cow Camp to Pool Creek. Aspen trees abound for a beautiful fall hike. After reaching Pool Creek Trail (Trail 113), the trail ascends along tiny Pool Creek through forests of aspen and spruce-fir. The point-to-point hike ends at Pool Creek Trailhead, or you can loop back to Old Roubideau Trailhead via the Parallel Trail (Trail 139). The trail disappears in numerous places so only attempt this hike if you like route-finding challenges.

Start: From the Old Roubideau (Trail 105) Trailhead
Distance: 8.6-mile loop
Approximate hiking time: 3.5 to 5.5 hours
Difficulty: Difficult due to elevation gain on the return and route-finding challenges
Elevation gain/loss: 1,510-foot gain/1,510-foot loss
Seasons: Best from June through Oct
Trail surface: Dirt trail
Other trail users: Equestrians and hunters (in season)
Canine compatibility: Dogs must be under control. Elk bed and graze along this trail. Cattle also graze in this area. Best to keep dogs leashed to avoid conflicts with wildlife and cattle.
Fees and permits: None. Group size limit: No more than 15 people per group with a maximum combination of 25 people and pack or saddle animals in any one group.
Map: USGS Antone Spring
Trail contacts: Uncompahgre National Forest, Ouray Ranger District, Montrose; (970) 240-5300; www.fs.usda.gov/gmug
Other: No facilities at the trailhead. The cow camp is an active operation and cattle graze in the area. Please respect the range permittee's rights. The access road closes in winter 23.5 miles from the trailhead. The road is used by snowmobiles. The trail is neither maintained nor marked for winter use. Bring your own water or water purification system.

Finding the trailhead: From Montrose, head west on CO 90 from its intersection with US 550. In 2 miles CO 90 turns left. In 1 more mile CO 90 turns right. At Oak Grove Elementary, another 0.9 mile, CO 90 turns left. In another 4.5 miles, stay to the left on CO 90 heading to Nucla, by a sign that reads No Winter Maintenance. You are now on CR 90, an all-weather gravel road, but it might be full of washboards. The Uncompahgre National Forest boundary is in another 12 miles, where CR 90 becomes FR 540. There's a T intersection (FR 402) 2.8 miles farther. Go straight ahead, staying on FR 540/FR 402 toward Columbine Pass. At the next fork, 0.7 mile farther up the road, take the right branch (FR 402/Divide Road). (Do *not* go to Nucla.) Continue on FR 402, past several roads coming in from either the right or left, for 7 miles. Turn right onto FR 546 (East Bull). Go right at the fork with FR 547 at mile 0.75. In another 0.25 mile, arrive at the cow camp. Park off the dirt road. **GPS:** N38 22.21' / W108 14.34'

The Hike

The Uncompahgre Plateau extends about 100 miles, running north-south from the San Miguel River to the Colorado River. Rising like a submarine west of Montrose,

the plateau is quite rugged. It's a land of multiple uses: hiking trails, 4WD roads, and a long mountain bike route—the Tabeguache Trail. Ute Indians hunted this area, as local names attest. Tabeguache means "place where the snow melts first." As noted in a journal kept by the 1776 Dominquez-Escalante expedition, the Utes called the river to the east the Ancapagari (which, according to our interpreter, means Red Lake), because they say that near its source there is a spring of red-colored water, hot and ill-tasting.

The Roubideau *(roo-bi-doe)* Area was created by the 1993 Colorado Wilderness Bill. Because the headwaters of its creeks start outside its designated boundaries, Congress denied it full wilderness protection. Water rights in Colorado create many hotly contested arguments and lawsuits. To avoid potential conflicts, the "Roubideau Area" is managed as wilderness, except its water. Some people call it a baby wilderness. The area is closed to motorized and mechanized use, logging, and mining.

Antoine Robidoux headed to Santa Fe from St. Louis in 1824. His family, long involved in the fur trade, wanted to take advantage of trading with newly independent Mexico. Robidoux and an old family friend explored regions northwest of Santa Fe in what became western Colorado and eastern Utah. Beaver were plentiful, and Ute Indians were eager to trade pelts for European tools. Antoine became a Mexican citizen, and by 1828 had obtained from the Mexican government an exclusive hunting and trading license to the area he had explored a few years earlier.

Rough terrain made for difficult travel on trading routes in those days. Instead of using the established Old Spanish (California) Trail through southwestern Colorado, then traveling north into his territory, Robidoux headed north to the San Luis Valley. Turning west he followed an old American Indian trail over Cochetopa Pass into the Gunnison Valley, then into the Uncompahgre Valley. Just below the confluence of the Gunnison and Uncompahgre Rivers, he built his first trading post, Fort Uncompahgre. For years the Utes had wintered nearby at the Ute Council Tree, a huge old cottonwood that still stands. They brought pelts from their lands in exchange for modern conveniences.

Historical documents indicate some of the inventory sold at Fort Uncompahgre included silk and cotton bandanas, scarves, trousers, shirts, jackets, combs, mirrors, linen thread, needles, blanketing material, scissors, cotton material, steel knives, fire steels, copper cooking pots, tea, coffee, sugar, and leaf tobacco. Food staples also filled the shelves. Modern implements made life easier for the Utes. But as life improved in this tough country, the winds of change started blowing. The Oregon Trail farther north became the preferred trading route, and more white people settled in Ute territory, creating unrest. The United States won the area during the Mexican-American War. By 1844 Robidoux's trade kingdom crumbled. Angered by a Mexican attack on a Ute village with no reparation from the Mexican government, the Utes went on a

◀ *Old Roubideau Trail through aspen forest*

Near the junction of Old Roubideau and Pool Creek Trails

rampage in 1844, even attacking Fort Uncompahgre and killing most of the Mexican workers. Two years later Fort Uncompahgre was in ruins.

Over the years Fort Uncompahgre's exact location was lost. Perhaps the flooding Gunnison wiped out its traces. Local citizens built a replica of the fort closer to Delta and opened it to visitors on June 30, 1990.

This hike lets you wander in the cool highlands of the Uncompahgre Plateau, away from the bustle of Delta and Montrose. The Old Roubideau Trail switchbacks down to the Goddard Creek drainage, crosses the creek, then climbs up to wander through gently sloping aspen forest. Elk bed and graze in the lush grasses. Some aspens bear scars of carved names and dates—this practice exposes aspen to various diseases. Approaching the Pool Creek drainage, the trail drops with views down into Roubideau Creek. Cattle enjoy the plentiful grasses in this section and their trails go every which way. Upon reaching Pool Creek, a 0.4-mile jaunt downhill (left) on the Pool Creek Trail brings you to Roubideau Creek, a pleasant place for lunch.

The hike up Pool Creek Trail gains 1,271 feet in 2.7 miles. The trail is overgrown in some areas, but it stays on the north side of the creek. Notice the difference in

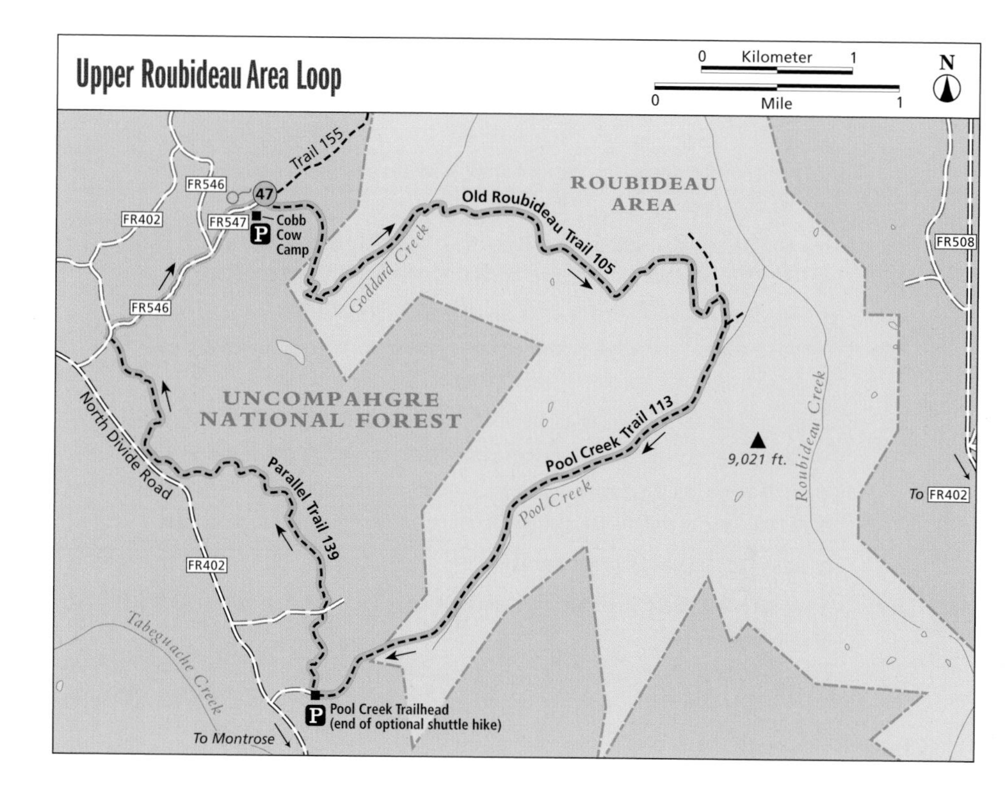

vegetation. The south side of the creek is sunny and grassy, while the north-facing side is steep, cool, and moist with dark spruce-fir forest dominating. At Pool Creek Trailhead, return to Old Roubideau Trailhead via the Parallel Trail (Trail 139), which you intersect at the Pool Creek Trailhead. Or meet your shuttle vehicle, if you've chosen the point-to-point option; see below.

Miles and Directions

0.0 Start at the cow camp where the dirt road Ys. Elevation: 9,440 feet. Walk straight ahead on the road to the right of the old buildings. (The right fork dead-ends.) About 260 feet down the road, look to your right for the brown carsonite post that indicates the trail is open to hikers and equestrians. The Old Roubideau Trail (Trail 105) starts at this post, which is easy to miss, so be observant.

0.5 Reach the Roubideau Special Area boundary. The trail switchbacks down into Goddard Creek.

1.25 Cross Goddard Creek.

1.9 Cross another drainage. The trail contours along a hill through pleasant aspen forest.

2.3 The trail curves left but isn't obvious. Look for blazes on trees to the right to find the faint trail. GPS: N38 21.91' / W108 12.76'

2.8 The trail splits. Turn left and drop to the southeast. It curves to the south, then turns east. Arrive at a tall clump of Gambel oak. GPS: N38 21.88' / W108 12.35'. The trail heads uphill slightly to the left, then disappears. Head east cross-country until you intersect a trail. Turn right. Cross the flatter bench area; with some luck find a trail and continue downhill to the right. If you lose this trail, find the easiest way to walk down to Pool Creek.

3.3 Reach a T intersection with the Pool Creek Trail (Trail 113). GPS: N38 21.78' / W108 12.30'. (***Option:*** Turn left here for an 0.8-mile out-and-back spur to Roubideau Creek.) Turn right here to head uphill toward the Pool Creek Trailhead.

3.9 The trail crosses a gooey gully, which can be a little tricky. You might need to walk down the dry creek a few feet to find an easy place to walk across.

5.3 Cross a little water seep coming from under a boulder to the right side of the trail.

5.6 Arrive at the Pool Creek Trailhead. GPS: N38 20.57' / W108 14.07'. Turn right and walk a few steps to the access road, where you go straight ahead onto Parallal Trail (Trail 139), also called the Tabeguache Trail on the sign. This trail is multiple use.

6.0 Cross a road and head straight ahead.

7.75 Arrive at FR 546 (East Bull). Turn right and walk down this road. Turn right when the road forks at FR 547.

8.6 Arrive back at your vehicle and the trailhead near the cow camp.

Option

For a shorter point-to-point hike with your dog—5.6 miles, leave a shuttle vehicle at the Pool Creek Trailhead. Turn right off FR 402 at the 5.4-mile mark, where the sign reads POOL CREEK TRAILHEAD. Do not turn right at 3.6 miles at Pool Creek FR 548. The trailhead and shuttle drop-off is 0.2 mile in. GPS: N38 20.58' / W108 14.07'. Park one car here and drive the second back to FR 402 and turn right, resuming with the directions to the Old Roubideau Trailhead at the cow camp, above. Approximate hiking time: 2.5 to 4 hours.

48 Jud Wiebe Memorial Trail

The Jud Wiebe Trail climbs up and across the hill north of Telluride between Butcher and Cornet Creeks. Although short, it has its steep moments, as very precipitous mountains surround Telluride. This trail is a good early season south-facing hike and a great warm-up for longer, more difficult trails in the area. From various points, Bridal Veil and Ingram Falls, the ski area, spectacular craggy peaks, and the town below come into view. The trail was completed in 1987 in memory of Jud Wiebe, a Forest Service employee who designed the trail.

Start: From the trailhead at the top of Aspen Street
Distance: 2.7-mile loop
Approximate hiking time: 1.5 to 2.5 hours
Difficulty: Difficult due to some steeper sections
Elevation gain: 1,150 feet
Seasons: Best from June to mid-Oct
Trail surface: Dirt road and dirt trail
Other trail users: Equestrians (some trail sections), mountain bikers, hunters (in season)
Canine compatibility: Dogs must be on leash
Fees and permits: None
Maps: USGS Telluride; Nat Geo Trails Illustrated 141 Telluride/Silverton/ Ouray/Lake City; Latitude 40° Telluride, Silverton, Ouray
Trail contacts: Uncompahgre National Forest, Norwood Ranger District, Norwood; (970) 327-4261; www.fs.usda.gov/gmug

Finding the trailhead: Find a parking place in Telluride or park in the free parking area across from the visitor center and take the Galloping Goose shuttle into downtown. Walk to Aspen Street (0.4 mile east of the visitor center) and uphill to the top of the street. The west end of the trail starts here. **GPS:** N37 56.45' / W107 48.71'

The other option is to walk to Oak Street and head uphill to the top of the street to the east end of the trail. **GPS:** N37 56.42' / W107 48.66'. Walk along Tomboy Road to the pipe gate and bulletin board and turn left. The hike description starts at the Aspen Street trailhead.

The Hike

Telluride, an old mining town snuggled at the mouth of a box canyon, is experiencing a second wave of success. The first came with the mining frenzy in the 1870s, as miners swarmed over the rugged San Juan Mountains looking for gold, silver, and other precious metals. Today the spectacular mountain scenery has attracted writers and artisans, and the ski area (opened in 1972) has created a new building frenzy.

The San Juan Mountains were born of volcanic fire and ash and sculpted by the scraping of glaciers. Eruptions started about 35 million years ago and lasted more than 13 million years. During one phase the volcanoes were so explosive that they often collapsed into themselves, forming calderas. Hot mineralized water oozed up through cracks and faults underground and around the calderas, leaving behind gold, silver, zinc, copper, and lead. Within the last 2 million years, various glaciers covered the area. The

Ballard and Wasatch Mountains

San Miguel glacier carved the U-shaped valley floor in which Telluride sits. Spectacular Bridal Veil Falls, at the head of the box canyon, drops 365 feet from a hanging valley.

In 1875 John Fallon discovered ore rich in zinc, lead, copper, iron, silver, and gold. Nearby, the Union Mine also started recovering rich ore. J. B. Ingram discovered that Fallon's claim and the Union were bigger than the legal limit by about 500 feet. He laid claim to the area in between, calling it the Smuggler. The Smuggler's ore contained 800 ounces of silver and 18 ounces of gold per ton. The Union and Smuggler merged and became one of the major producers in Telluride. The Tomboy Mine, about 5 miles up Tomboy Road, started operations in 1880 and continued until 1928. In 1897 it sold for $2 million!

The mountains around Telluride contain over 350 miles of tunnels (think San Francisco to Los Angeles), some going all the way through the mountains to the Million Dollar Highway between Ouray and Silverton. The town itself was established as Columbia in 1878, when 80 acres were laid out and incorporated. It became the county seat of newly established San Miguel County in 1883. The post office, however, had a problem getting mail to Columbia, Colorado, often sending it to Columbia, California, instead. A name change was inevitable. Telluride, the name of a gold-bearing tellurium compound, was chosen for the new moniker in the 1880s.

The rich ore-bearing peaks surrounding Telluride hold a lurking danger—the white death. Three hundred inches of annual snowfall combined with steep terrain result in fairly regular avalanches. In 1902 an avalanche demolished part of the Liberty

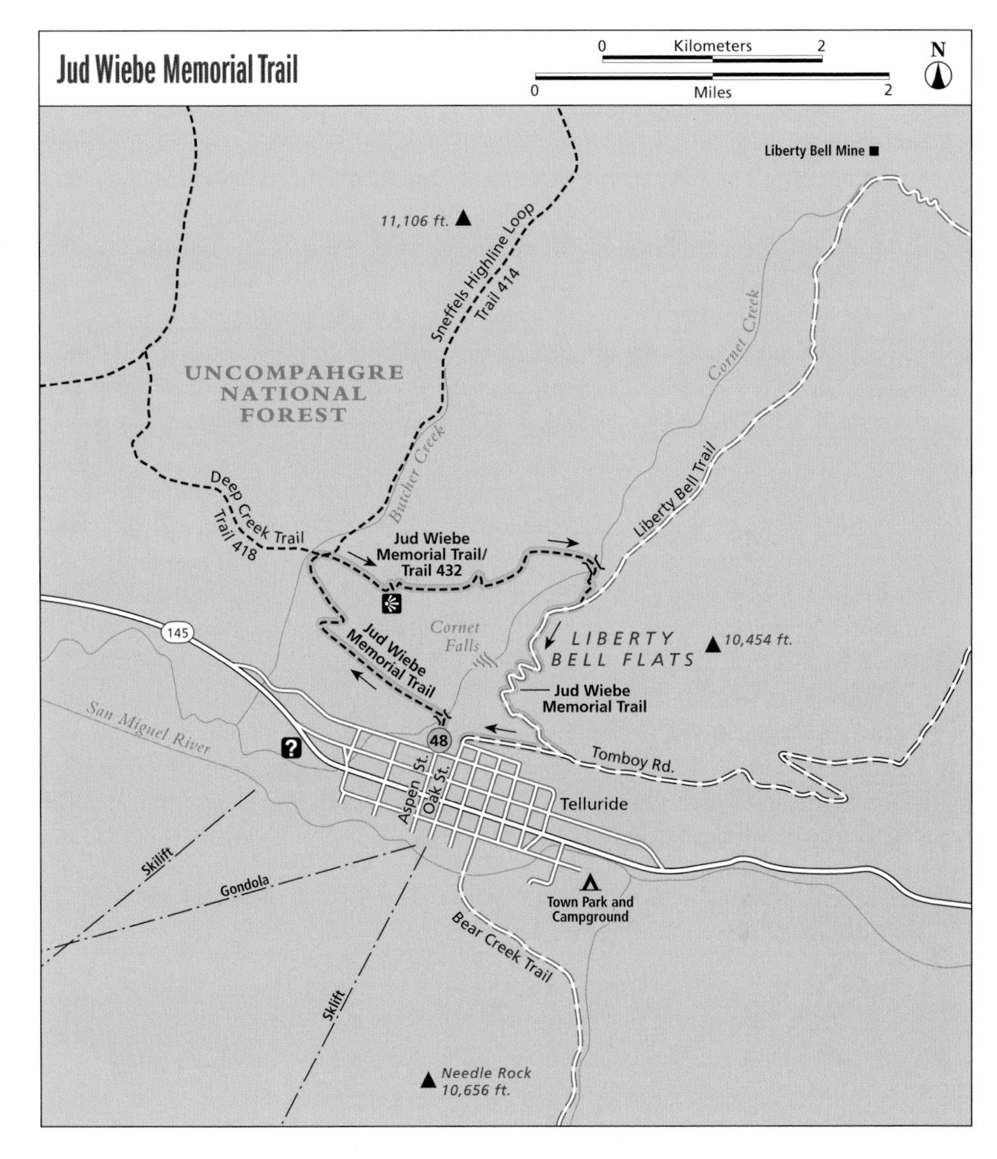
Jud Wiebe Memorial Trail
Kilometers
0
2
Miles
0
2
N
Liberty Bell Mine
11,106 ft.
Sneffels Highline Loop
Trail 414
Cornet Creek
UNCOMPAHGRE
NATIONAL
FOREST
Butcher Creek
Liberty Bell Trail
Deep Creek Trail
Trail 418
Jud Wiebe
Memorial Trail/
Trail 432
145
Cornet
Falls
Jud Wiebe
Memorial Trail
LIBERTY
BELL FLATS
10,454 ft.
Jud Wiebe
Memorial Trail
San Miguel River
48
Tomboy Rd.
Aspen St.
Oak St.
Telluride
Skilift
Gondola
Town Park and
Campground
Bear Creek Trail
Skilift
Needle Rock
10,656 ft.

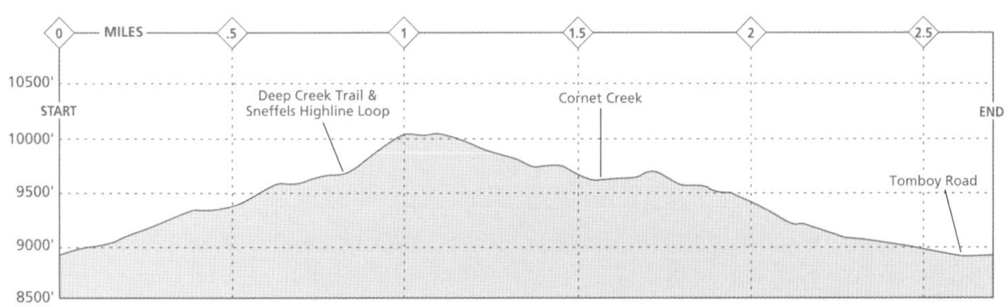
0
MILES
.5
1
1.5
2
2.5
10500'
10000'
9500'
9000'
8500'
START
END
Deep Creek Trail &
Sneffels Highline Loop
Cornet Creek
Tomboy Road

Bell Mine (farther up the road you'll hike down), killing seven men and injuring several others. While the rescue party was recovering the bodies, a second avalanche swept through. The rescuers escaped without additional injuries or deaths. However, as they made their way back to Telluride a third avalanche roared down, killing three and injuring five. In one winter (1905–06) with unusually heavy snows, one hundred people died in avalanches in the area. Snow isn't the only thing to go sliding around Telluride. In 1914 Cornet Creek overflowed, sending 8 feet of mud down Colorado Avenue, Telluride's main street.

The Jud Wiebe Trail (Trail 432) starts at the bulletin board at the top of Aspen Street. Continue uphill to the bridge over Cornet Creek and turn left. The trail climbs steadily and after a couple of switchbacks comes to a junction with the Deep Creek Trail (Trail 418). The Jud Wiebe Trail takes off to the right and continues climbing.

You soon arrive at a viewpoint, locally called Breakfast Rock, with views of Telluride and the surrounding lofty peaks. A few more switchbacks lead to an open area with more fantastic views. To the west is the San Miguel River, heading downstream along a glacial moraine. You might even catch a glimpse of the La Sal Mountains near Moab, Utah. The San Miguel Mountains, home to three 14,000-foot peaks, line up along the horizon. To the south and east, peaks rise dramatically and the gondola climbs the hill from town along ski runs. Ingram and Bridal Veil Falls tumble from cliffs to the east.

The trail meanders down through a lush aspen forest and crosses a bridge over Cornet Creek. Climbing further, the trail then intersects the nonmotorized road to Liberty Bell Mine. This flat area once served as the local playing field for baseball games between miners and town residents. Turn right and follow the steep road down past the town water tank to Tomboy Road. Turn right and walk down the road to the top of Oak Street and back to town.

Miles and Directions

0.0 Start at the trailhead bulletin board at the top of Aspen Street. Elevation: 8,880 feet. In a few feet, turn left and walk across the bridge that crosses Cornet Creek.

0.7 Reach a junction with Deep Creek Trail (Trail 418) and Sneffels Highline Loop (Trail 414). Turn right to continue on the Jud Wiebe Trail (Trail 432).

1.1 Come to an open meadow and slope with fantastic views.

1.6 Cross the bridge over Cornet Creek.

1.7 Reach the junction of Jud Wiebe Trail and a nonmotorized road, which leads to Liberty Bell Mine. GPS: N37 56.70' / W107 48.36'. Turn right and walk down the road.

2.2 The town water tank is on the right.

2.6 Reach the junction of Jud Wiebe Trail and Tomboy Road, which leads to Tomboy Mine. At a pipe gate and bulletin board, turn right and walk down Tomboy Road.

2.7 Arrive at the Oak Street trailhead. Elevation: 8,920 feet. Return to wherever you parked your vehicle.

49 Cascade and Portland Loop

This pleasant hike loops along Cascade Falls Trail and Portland Trail in Ouray's Amphitheater area. The trail offers nice views of surrounding mountains, jagged cliffs, and mining operations. The hike includes the trail to Upper Cascade Falls. This spur trail switchbacks its way past cliffs for great views of the surrounding mountains. After enjoying the falls, you can walk to the Chief Ouray Mine's bunkhouse.

Start: From the trailhead at the top of the Amphitheater Campground
Distance: 6.8-mile lollipop (with a moderate 3.6-mile loop option)
Approximate hiking time: 2.5 to 6 hours
Difficulty: Most difficult due to the steep trail to the upper falls and bunkhouse
Elevation gain: 1,920-foot gain (including undulations)
Seasons: Best from May through Oct
Trail surface: Dirt trail, steep and narrow to Upper Cascade Falls
Other trail users: Equestrians, mountain bikers, hunters (in season) on lower parts of the loop
Canine compatibility: Dogs must be under control on the trail and on leash in the parking lot and campground. Dogs are not recommended on the upper section of the Cascade Falls Trail due to narrowness.
Fees and permits: None
Maps: USGS Ouray; Nat Geo Trails Illustrated 141 Telluride/Silverton/Ouray/Lake City; Latitude 40° Telluride, Silverton, Ouray
Trail contacts: Uncompahgre National Forest, Ouray Ranger District, Montrose; (970) 240-5300; www.fs.usda.gov/gmug
Other: There is an outhouse in the campground. Bring your own water.

Finding the trailhead: From Ouray, drive south out of town on US 550 to the entrance road to the Amphitheater Campground. Turn left onto the campground road and drive 1.1 miles on the paved road to the trailhead at the top of the campground. **GPS:** N38 01.31' / W107 39.59'

The Hike

The Ouray area is a jumble of geologic history, from ancient bedrock to glacially carved features. Leadville limestone formed in a sea over 325 million years ago. Reddish rock remains from the erosion of Uncompahgria, part of the Ancestral Rockies. Another sea helped form Dakota sandstone. Then the explosions of the San Juan volcanoes started, leaving deep deposits of ash and breccia (broken rocks) called San Juan tuff, of which the Amphitheater seen from the Portland Trail is a good example. Hot mineralized water deposited gold, silver, and other metals in the Leadville limestone during the volcanic era. Ice age glaciers carved craggy peaks and scoured the valley north from Ouray, leaving the moraine by Ridgway.

This combination of geologic events produced a gold and silver bonanza for prospectors. On a hunting and fishing expedition in summer 1875, A. J. Staley and Logan Whitlock meandered up the Uncompahgre River to the headwall by the current site of Ouray and discovered veins of ore, which were subsequently named the Trout and

Amphitheater

the Fisherman lodes. In August of that same year, A. W. Begole and Jack Eckles found the Cedar and Clipper lodes where the hot springs pool is today. As hopeful miners arrived in town, Captain Cline and Judge Long laid out a town site that they called Uncompahgre City.

The next spring Chief Ouray and his wife, Chipeta, arrived in town to talk with the townspeople. Ouray was chief of the Tabeguache band of Utes, who lived in the Ouray-Montrose area. Half-Ute and half-Apache, Ouray rose to power as a skilled negotiator. He was friendly to the white man, realizing that fighting could decimate his people. He hoped that through negotiations, his people would survive and perhaps keep some of the land they had called home for hundreds of years. The latter did not happen. The Utes were organized into seven different bands, each with its own leader. Because of his oratorical skill, the US government regarded Ouray as spokesman for all Utes, a status not always acknowledged by other Ute chiefs. Over time Chief Ouray gained much respect among white people. Uncompahgre City was renamed to Ouray in his honor.

Ouray continued to grow, its mines producing mainly silver. The transportation of ore and supplies was a struggle for many years. In 1887 the Denver and Rio Grande Railroad finally reached Ouray, adding to its prosperity. The Silver Crash of 1893, which killed many other mining towns, proved a mere burp to Ouray. A gold discovery on Gold Hill northeast of town saved the day.

Being surrounded by steep mountains posed occasional problems for Ouray. In July 1909 a downpour filled creek channels with tons of water and debris. Portland Creek, above which part of this hiking loop travels, roared into town, covering the first floor of the Elks Building with mud. It continued into J. J. Mayer's furniture store, carrying carpet rolls and furniture down Main Street.

In wintertime the drive south via Red Mountain Pass is very prone to avalanches, as is witnessed by a marker at one switchback. It commemorates a minister, his two daughters, and three snowplow drivers who met their untimely demise in the "white death."

On the way to the trailhead, stop at the first switchback just south of town. Look to the northeast and you can see the Chief Ouray Mine buildings perched on a shelf in the cliffs. Believe it or not, the trail to Upper Cascade Falls takes you there without the need for ropes.

The hike starts by contouring around a ridge, then above a drainage. The intersection of Upper Cascade Falls Trail (Trail 213) and Portland Trail (Trail 238) is reached in about 0.8 mile. The spur trail to Upper Cascade Falls and the Chief Ouray Mine climbs steeply from the junction, zigzagging its way up a precipitous mountainside. The trail is good, although narrow in a few spots. When you reach a ledge, the walking becomes easier, but can be dangerous in bad weather. Take time to enjoy the fantastic views. The trail rounds a ridge near some interesting rock outcroppings and drops slightly to Upper Cascade Falls. You can cross Cascade Creek (***Note:*** This crossing can be tricky in high water with the falls just downstream) and continue 0.1 mile to explore the old mine bunkhouse and see Ouray far below. The trail past the bunkhouse is not maintained and can be treacherous.

Return to the junction of Upper Cascade Falls and the Portland Trail and turn left to continue the loop. When crossing the big gully, you can imagine the force of water that races down the steep cliffs. The hike continues through spruce-fir forest and climbs a little ridge to intersect with the Portland Cutoff Trail (Trail 238.1A) to the Portland Mine. Stay to the right on Portland Trail, enjoy the views into Portland Creek, and continue switchbacking down through a nice forest with aspens. At the next intersection, turn right onto Upper Cascade Falls Trail. After crossing the big gully again, the trail climbs back up to complete the loop and return to the trailhead.

Miles and Directions

0.0 Start at the trailhead at the top of Amphitheater Campground. Elevation: 8,520 feet.

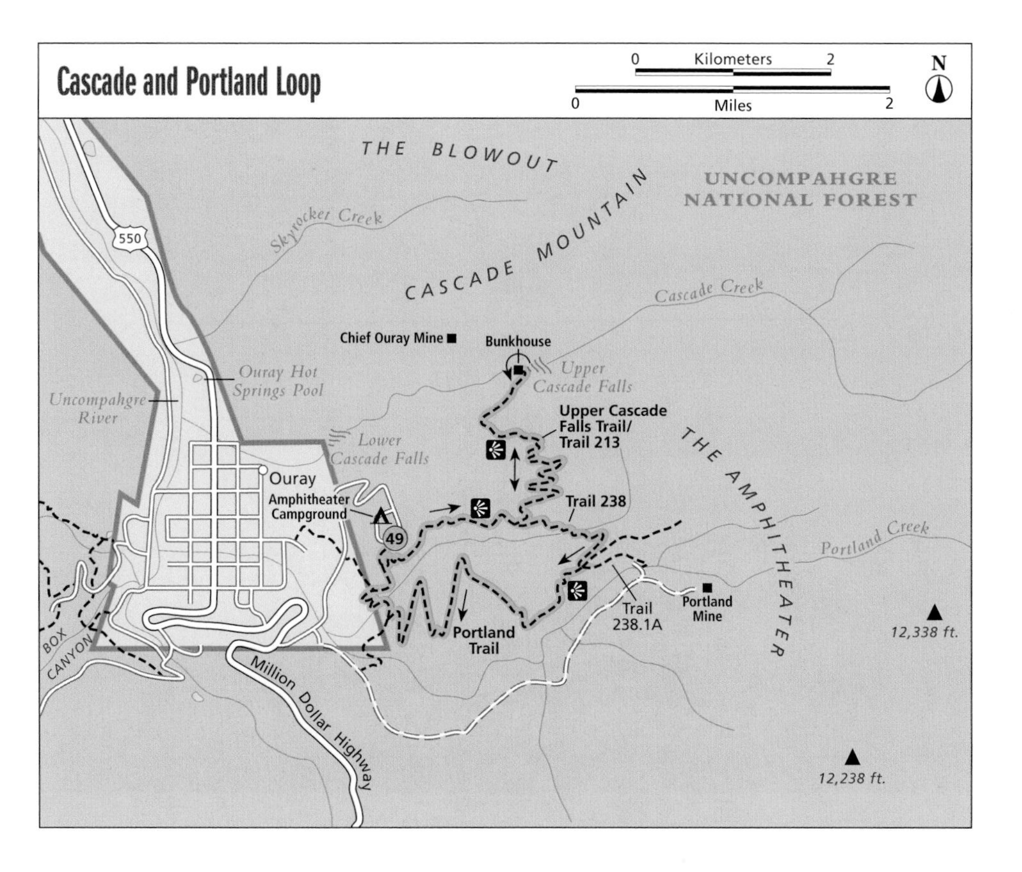

0.2 Reach a trail junction and trail register. Turn left and head uphill. (You'll return to this junction later.)

0.5 The Lower Cascade Falls Trail (Trail 255) comes in from the left. Continue straight ahead and uphill.

0.8 Reach the junction of the Upper Cascade Falls Trail (Trail 213) and the Portland Trail (Trail 238). GPS: N38 01.35' / W107 39.26'. Turn left onto the Upper Cascade Falls Trail, heading for Upper Cascade Falls and the Chief Ouray Mine bunkhouse. (***Option:*** For a shorter, easier hike turn right and follow the Portland Trail. This option will make for a 3.6-mile loop.)

2.0 Round a ridge by some interesting rock formations.

2.2 Reach Upper Cascade Falls. Elevation: 10,000 feet. GPS: N38 01.76' / W107 39.15'

2.4 Arrive at the bunkhouse for the Chief Ouray Mine. Take a look inside, then return the way you came. (***Note:*** The trail beyond is not maintained and can be treacherous.)

◀ *Chief Ouray Mine bunkhouse*

Creek crossing below Upper Cascade Falls

2.6	Return to Upper Cascade Falls.
4.0	Arrive back at the junction of the Upper Cascade Falls Trail and the Portland Trail. Turn left onto the Portland Trail to complete the loop.
4.3	Cross a large gully that shows the power of water.
4.6	Reach the junction of the Portland Trail and the Portland Cutoff Trail (Trail 238.1A). GPS: N38 01.24' / W107 38.94'. Turn right to stay on the Portland Trail.
4.7	Enjoy the scenic view.
6.2	Reach a trail junction. The Portland Trail curves right here. The trail to the left goes to the Portland Trailhead. Recross the large gully that you crossed higher up.
6.5	Reach a trail junction. Turn right onto the Upper Cascade Falls Trail to return to the trailhead. The trail climbs here.
6.6	Reach the trail junction with the trail register. This junction completes the loop. Turn left; the trailhead is just around the ridge.
6.8	Arrive back at the trailhead.

50 Pass and Coal Creek Loop

This hike makes a loop above Coal Bank Pass via Pass Creek Trail (Trail 500) to the foot of impressive Engineer Mountain, then north on the Engineer Mountain Trail (Trail 508) to return on Coal Creek Trail (Trail 677). The wildflowers are spectacular on many sections of this hike during July and early August. Several places offer great views of the West Needle Mountains in the Weminuche Wilderness to the east and north to the mountains between Silverton and Telluride. The final 1.3 miles of the hike are along US 550 and can be avoided with a car shuttle.

Start: From the Pass Creek (Trail 500) Trailhead near the top of Coal Bank Pass
Distance: 7.8-mile loop
Approximate hiking time: 3 to 5 hours
Difficulty: Difficult due to elevation gain
Elevation gain: 1,700 feet (including undulations)
Seasons: Best from mid-June through Oct
Trail surface: Dirt trail with some grassy areas, steep in spots
Other trail users: Equestrians, mountain bikers, hunters (in season)
Canine compatibility: Dogs must be under control
Fees and permits: None
Maps: USGS Engineer Mountain; Nat Geo Trails Illustrated 141 Telluride/Silverton/Ouray/Lake City; Latitude 40° Durango and Southwest Colorado
Trail contacts: San Juan National Forest, Columbine Ranger District, Bayfield; (970) 884-2512; www.fs.usda.gov/sanjuan
Other: Bring your own water as not much is easily accessible.

Finding the trailhead: From Silverton, drive south about 13.6 miles on US 550. Turn right just before the top of Coal Bank Pass to enter a gravel parking area where you can access the Pass Creek Trailhead. There is a vault toilet on the east side of the highway at Coal Bank Pass. **GPS:** N37 41.95' / W107 46.71'

The Hike

While driving from Silverton to the trailhead, compare the numerous craggy peaks to the south and east with the more rolling terrain and scattered peaks to the west. Engineer Mountain (12,968 feet) and the area of the hike are readily visible from just south of Molas Pass. Engineer Mountain itself is comprised of sandstone and shale that eroded from part of the Ancestral Rockies called Uncompahgria. These sediments add red color to the peak. The lower slopes are limestone formed from marine sediments in an ancient sea. The rolling hills were lava and ash flows, signs of the volcanic origins of the San Juan Mountains. Glaciers placed the final touches on this area. Engineer Mountain rose above an immense ice cap during more recent ice ages, the last of which only ended about 11,000 years ago.

Across the highway, craggy Twilight Peak is often seen while hiking down the Coal Creek Trail. Although some geologists say coal doesn't exist near Coal Bank

Engineer Mountain and trail sign

Pass, records in Silverton indicate that people found some type of inefficient coal near here and used it for fuel until the coal mines near Durango were discovered.

Engineer Mountain looms large above the surrounding rolling hills. How the mountain was named is not certain, but historians believe the Hayden Survey (1870–79) coined the name. "Engineer" most likely commemorates a survey engineer versus a railroad engineer. The San Juan region contains two Engineer Mountains, the other located on the Alpine Loop Scenic Byway (4WD) between Ouray and Lake City.

The Pass Creek Trail starts in a field of cornhusk lily, cow parsnip, subalpine larkspur, Indian paintbrush, death camas, geraniums, and columbines. Cornhusk lily (false hellebore) is the large, white-flowered plant with big green leaves resembling cornhusks. Another common name for this member of the lily family is skunk cabbage. The other large plant with clusters of white flowers is cow parsnip, which some people mistakenly call Queen Anne's lace. Both grow in moist areas such as this meadow and are often found with another moisture-loving plant, subalpine larkspur. These three can grow taller than most hikers, forming green walls along the trail. The larkspur is a member of the buttercup family, sporting purple petals with a long spur.

Without a close look it can be mistaken for monkshood, which also loves moist areas. Death camas has six joined petals with a yellow band and red stamens. Both death camas and cornhusk lily are poisonous to humans.

The amount and type of flowers change with forest and meadow as you hike along. The trail enters a spruce-fir forest and wanders around little ridges. A little pond surrounded by elephant heads lies in an open meadow at about 1.2 miles. Elephant head, also called little red elephant, is an appropriate name for these pink-to-purple flowers that love boggy areas. The elephant trunk sticks out from the ears as if trumpeting sunny days. Other boggy area plants can be seen along various sections of trail. Globeflowers with their overlapping cream-colored petals, marsh marigolds with their more separated white petals, king's crowns (ruby flowers), occasional queen's crowns (pink flowers), and Parry's primroses with magenta-to-purple flowers line the trail in wetter areas. After about 2 miles the hills are covered with yellow, rosy, or magenta paintbrush flowers in a profusion of color. As the trees thin, Colorado blue columbine, the state flower, makes a showy appearance. Engineer Mountain towers above the seas of tiny wildflowers like a castle surrounded by its moat.

When you reach the intersection with Engineer Mountain Trail (Trail 508), turn right and follow Engineer Mountain Trail across the open alpine fields. Willows grow here, along with varieties of paintbrush, king's crown, American bistort, Parry's primrose, columbine, elephant head, and alpine avens—all commingled as if a higher power had emptied packages of mixed wildflower seeds.

The trail proceeds north, crossing the head of Coal Creek. Turn right at the marked junction and follow the trail across a little ridge. Just beyond is a trail junction. Turn right, follow the trail through willows, then head down to a saddle. At the saddle the trail disappears in the grasses but is marked by cairns. Turn right and drop down into the Coal Creek drainage, where the trail reappears near a wooden post in the meadow. The flowers aren't as spectacular along Coal Creek, but the occasional views of Twilight Peak are. The trail drops, sometimes steeply, above Coal Creek, then makes several switchbacks down to US 550. If you haven't set up a car shuttle, follow US 550 back to the trailhead. Be sure to put your four-footed friend back on leash.

Miles and Directions

0.0 Start at the Pass Creek (Trail 500) Trailhead. Elevation: 10,680 feet.

1.2 A little pond is on the left.

1.5 The trail makes a big right switchback.

2.3 Engineer Mountain comes into view, followed by fantastic fields of wildflowers.

2.5 Reach the trail junction with Engineer Mountain Trail (Trail 508). Elevation: 11,660 feet. GPS: N37 42.22' / W107 47.87'. Turn right and follow Engineer Mountain Trail, heading north. (***Note:*** A left turn will take you to US 550, south of Coal Bank Pass, in about 4 miles.)

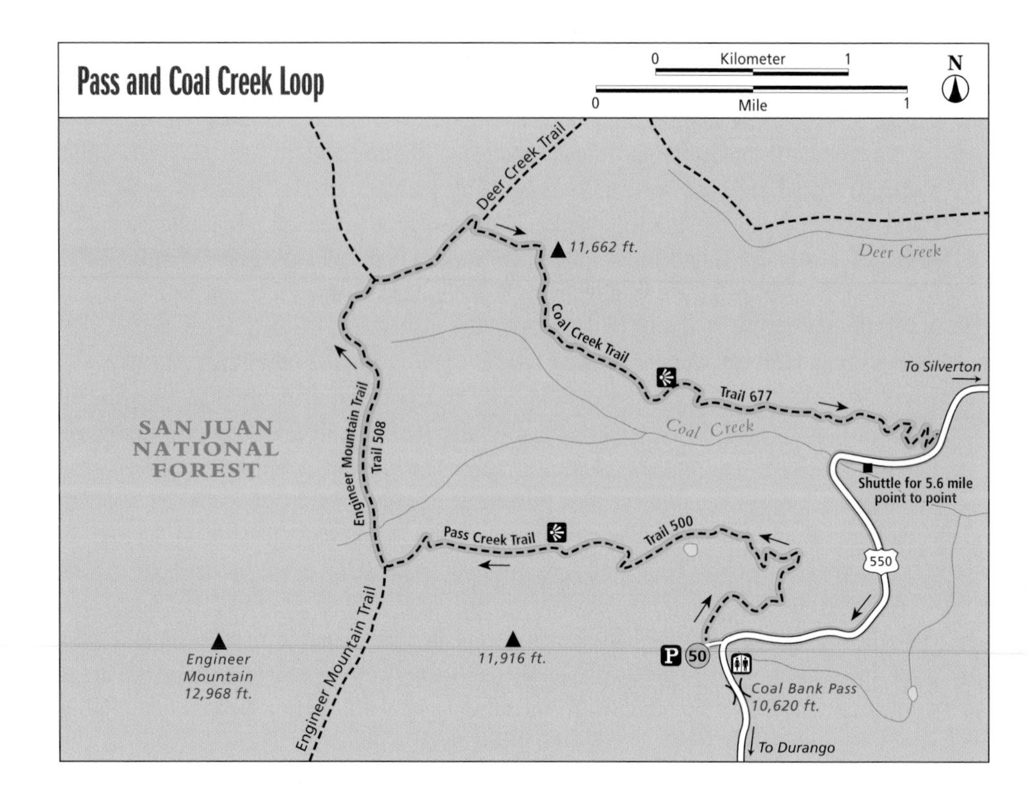

3.3 Reach the top of the Coal Creek drainage. (***Note:*** There's a little saddle to the left for a view to the west. Good lunch spot.)

3.5 The trail forks. Turn right onto Coal Creek Trail (Trail 677) (***Note:*** You can also go farther north on Engineer Mountain Trail to intersect with the Colorado Trail.)

4.0 The trail rounds a ridge. Just past the top there's a sign on a tree that points to Coal Creek Trail. Just past there is a big cairn. Turn right at the cairn, then go a little downhill and look carefully to the left for the trail through a willow patch. GPS: N37 43.16' / W107 47.53'

4.3 The trail disappears at a saddle in the ridge, but is marked by cairns. Turn right and head downhill in the meadow. Stay to the left along a little gully. Look for a log post in the meadow below. GPS: N37 43.01' / W107 47.29'. If you don't see the trail, stay close to the little gully and you'll come upon the path in about 0.1 mile. Turn left onto the trail, which soon curves to the left.

5.1 Enjoy the view of craggy peaks to the east, including Twilight Peak, the closest.

6.5 Reach Coal Creek Trailhead along US 550. Elevation: 10,280 feet. GPS: N37 42.51' / W107 46.06'. To complete the entire loop hike, continue walking along the road, being mindful of oncoming traffic.

Flowers and Engineer Mountain

7.7 Cross the highway and turn right onto the dirt road to the Pass Creek Trailhead.

7.8 Arrive back at the trailhead.

Option

If you have two vehicles, you can make this a point-to-point hike of 6.5 miles. From Silverton, drive south about 12.4 miles on US 550. At mile marker 58, leave one car at the dirt parking area on the left side of the road just before a large left switchback. GPS: N37 42.51' / W107 46.06'. Then proceed to the Pass Creek Trailhead for the start of the hike. There is a vault toilet on the east side of the highway at Coal Bank Pass. Turn right just before the top of Coal Bank Pass to enter a gravel parking area where you can access this trailhead. Follow the Miles and Directions to mile 6.5. Turn right, cross the road, and walk about 0.1 mile along the left side up to the parking area, and your shuttle vehicle, back at mile marker 58.

HASPELS

51 First Fork and Red Creek Loop

The First Fork Trail follows a sparkling little creek up to Missionary Ridge northeast of Durango. Although parts of this forest burned in 2002, the vegetation is lush and trees are growing again. The trail travels through a forest of Douglas fir, ponderosa pine, Gambel oak, and aspen. After joining the Missionary Ridge Trail, head northeast through mixed conifer and aspen forests and several beautiful meadows, with occasional views north to the craggy San Juan Mountains. Return via Red Creek Trail, which drops down several steep switchbacks, then past huge aspens. The trail intersects the road about 0.3 mile above the First Fork Trailhead. A beautiful hike when aspens are golden!

Start: From the First Fork Trailhead
Distance: 10.0-mile loop
Approximate hiking time: 4.5 to 7 hours
Difficulty: Difficult due to distance and some steep spots
Elevation gain: 2,150 feet (including undulations)
Seasons: Best from May through Oct
Trail surface: Dirt trail, sometimes steep
Other trail users: Equestrians, mountain bikers, hunters (in season)
Canine compatibility: Dogs must be under control
Fees and permits: None
Maps: USGS Durango East, Hermosa, Lemon Reservoir, and Rules Hill (these maps are ancient and the trail is not shown on them); Nat Geo Trails Illustrated 145 Pagosa Springs/Bayfield; Latitude 40˚ Southwest Colorado
Trail contacts: San Juan National Forest, Columbine Ranger District, Bayfield; (970) 884-2512; www.fs.usda.gov/sanjuan
Other: No facilities at the trailhead. Although water may be available in First Fork and Red Creek, cattle graze in this area, so be sure to purify any creek water before drinking, or bring your own water. Because of the Missionary Ridge fire of 2002, some portions of the access road may be subject to mudslides. The road is closed by snow 0.9 mile from the trailhead. The trail is neither maintained nor marked for winter use.

Finding the trailhead: From the intersection of US 550 and College Drive in Durango (near the train station), drive 0.2 mile into downtown on College Drive to East 3rd Avenue, turn left on East 3rd, and drive 0.7 mile to the intersection of East 3rd and 15th Street and Florida Road. Turn sort of right onto Florida Road/La Plata CR 240 and drive 9.4 miles northeast to the sign COLVIG SILVER CAMPS. Turn left here onto dirt LPCR 246 and drive 1 mile past the camps. The road gets rougher and bumpier. In another 0.3 mile there is a gate, which you may have to open and close. You can park here, off the road. The road beyond is best negotiated with a high-clearance vehicle (4WD not necessary). A parking area is available about 0.25 mile beyond the gate. Park here if the road is getting too rough for your vehicle. The trailhead and a small parking area are another 0.35 mile from this point. The trailhead is marked by a TRAIL sign on the left side of the road. Vehicles are not allowed beyond this point. **GPS:** N37 21.31' / W107 44.50'

Carving of firefighter near Vallecito Reservoir

The Hike

Many early settlers to the Animas Valley were Civil War veterans. Legend has it that one morning, fog cloaked a ridge northeast of Durango. The veterans noticed a similarity with Missionary Ridge, site of a famous Civil War battle near Chattanooga, Tennessee. The ridge has since been known as Missionary Ridge.

On June 9, 2002, a small fire started along the Missionary Ridge Road, allegedly by a discarded cigarette. Little moisture had fallen during winter, and spring continued to be very dry and hot. Reservoirs were lower than usual and the land was parched. The extremely dry trees quickly became torches, and the fire burned 6,500 acres the first day. Helicopters dropped buckets of water on the fire, slurry bombers covered trees with fire retardant, and ground crews created fire breaks and put out spot fires. The fire continued to spread in the dry forest, fanned by typical afternoon winds. Because of dry vegetation the fire even burned downhill, an unusual event. By July 17 officials declared the fire was contained after burning eighty-three buildings and 73,391 acres of forest, and causing some 2,100 people to flee at times. The fire actually continued to burn in small patches until winter snows finally extinguished the stubborn flames.

One firefighter died, his life snuffed out by a falling tree. A tour of tree carvings depicting firefighters and other emergency responders in action can be seen around Vallecito Lake, just east of this hike. The carvings were created in dead ponderosa pine trees. One tree and nearby plaque commemorates the fallen firefighter.

From the smoke and media reports, people envisioned the entire area from Missionary Ridge to Lemon Reservoir to Vallecito Lake as being burned to a crisp. Forest fires typically jump around, and this one was no exception. Burned homes were surrounded by unburned forest, while blackened forest encircled unburned homes. This hop-skip-jump phenomenon is readily observed throughout this hike.

In early August a few rainstorms passed over the burned area. In places where trees and ground cover had been destroyed, roots no longer held the soil together. As rain moistened the charred earth, mudslides flowed downhill across roads, into homes and businesses, making a mess of everything in their way. One slide closed the access road to First Fork Trail. Geologists studied one newly created arroyo and discovered that fires and resulting debris flows have occurred in the Vallecito Valley about every 350 years for the last 3,500 years!

By early October 2002, little Gambel oak shoots started to poke through the burned ground. Crop dusters dropped pounds of plant and grass seeds, which sprouted the next spring, along with seeds already in the ground. Within two years grasses, aspen sprouts, and flowers grew knee-high. While you can still see the effects of the fire, nature continues to heal the burned scars.

Starting up First Fork Trail, you'll first cross Red Creek then come upon a gate. Please close the gate behind you, as cattle graze in this area. The trail follows little First

Scorched ponderosa pine and aspen 

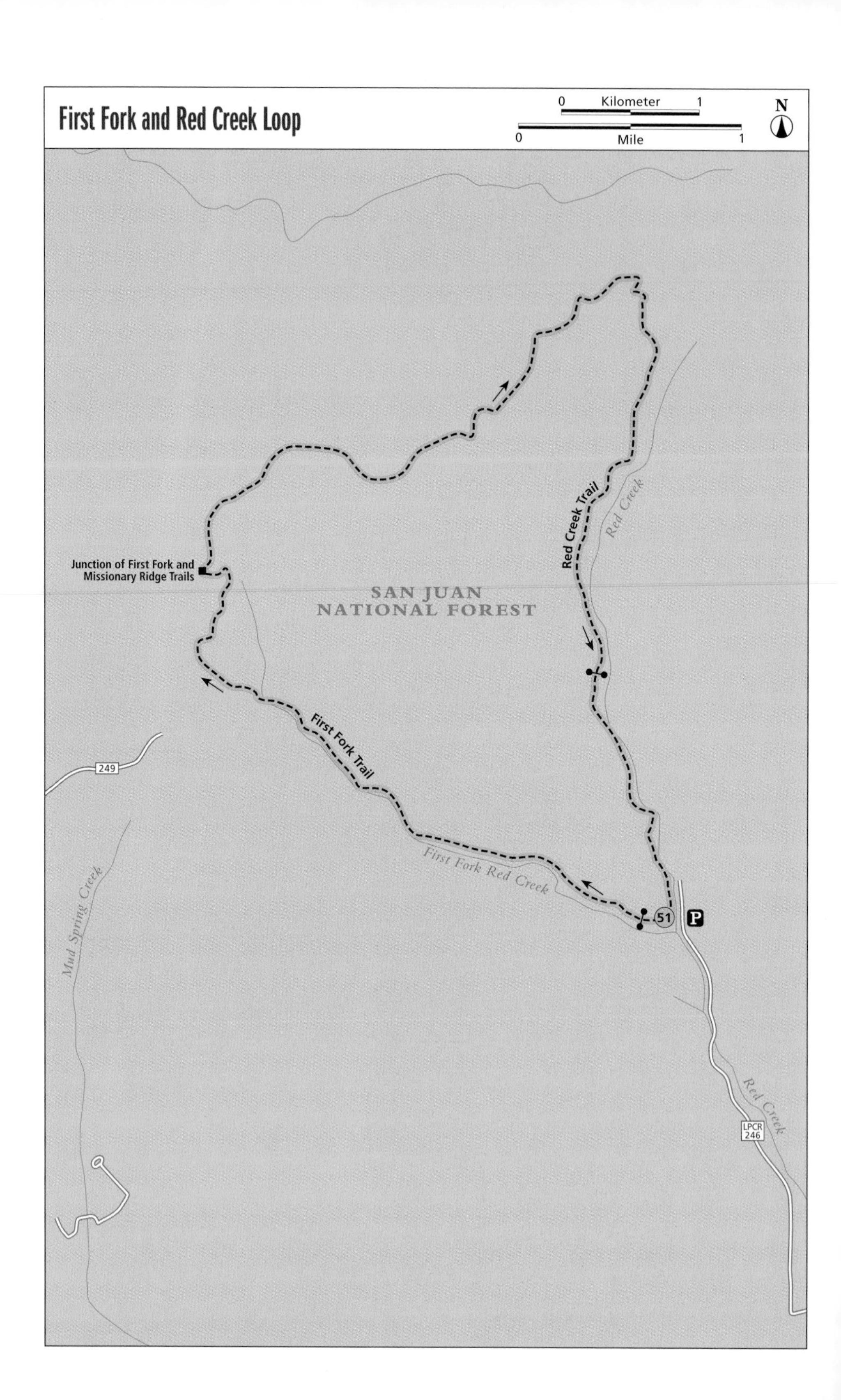

First Fork and Red Creek Loop
0 Kilometer 1
0 Mile 1
N
Junction of First Fork and
Missionary Ridge Trails
SAN JUAN
NATIONAL FOREST
Red Creek Trail
Red Creek
First Fork Trail
First Fork Red Creek
249
51
P
Mud Spring Creek
Red Creek
LPCR
246

Fork, where flowers sometimes grow waist high. You'll hike in and out of areas that were burned in the fire. In one place the general area has been burned except for one tree. In a large open area, the trail climbs steeply, drops, and climbs again.

When you come to a Y intersection, know that you are not at Missionary Ridge. Turn left and continue up to a T intersection with the Missionary Ridge Trail, passing through a burned area. The fire scorched many parts of the ridge, but aspen are once again growing and the vegetation is quite thick among the ghost trees. One advantage of the fire: The view to the north of the craggy San Juan Mountains and the Hermosa Cliffs has improved.

Continue hiking along the ridge, over one saddle to a second saddle. Here the Red Creek Trail drops off the ridge to the right. After switchbacking steeply off Missionary Ridge, Red Creek Trail then wanders through a huge, beautiful aspen forest (making an excellent fall hike) and shoulder-high cow parsnip that sometimes hides the trail. Watch for elk and deer. When you come to a road, turn right to return to your vehicle.

Miles and Directions

0.0 Start at the First Fork Trailhead. Elevation: 7,880 feet. Immediately cross Red Creek and soon arrive at a gate. Remember to close the gate behind you.

2.7 Arrive at an open area filled with bushes. A cliff looms ahead of you. The trail climbs steeply, then drops down and climbs up again.

3.3 The trail arrives at a Y intersection. Turn left here to continue climbing to Missionary Ridge Trail.

3.4 Reach the junction with Missionary Ridge Trail. GPS: N37 22.62' / W107 46.83'. Turn right and proceed north, then east along the ridge.

4.8 Arrive at a large meadow ringed with little aspen and some conifers.

5.2 The trail starts descending, sometimes steeply.

5.5 Pass by an old stile. Before the fire the trail crossed a fence on the stile.

6.0 After dropping and switchbacking down, arrive at a saddle. The trail appears to fork. Take the trail to the left that goes around the hill in front of you. Lots of bushes and flowers grow along the contouring trail.

6.5 Reach the junction with the Red Creek Trail. Elevation: 9,840 feet. GPS: N37 23.74' / W107 44.68'. Turn right, drop down, and follow the steep switchbacks. The trail sign faces east, so look carefully for it.

6.8 The trail mellows out and meanders through a thick aspen forest with lush vegetation.

8.5 Come to a gate. Make sure to close it behind you. Cross the creek to the left. The trail crosses the creek a number of times as you continue down. There are some nice red cliffs along the trail also.

9.7 Arrive at a dirt road (closed to motorized traffic). GPS: N37 21.51' / W107 44.50'. Turn right and walk down the road back to your vehicle.

10.0 Arrive back at the First Fork Trailhead.

Appendix A: Hiking Gear

Day Hike Gear

Certain items are necessary, and desirable, to make your day hikes with your dog safer and more enjoyable. The following list describes gear options that can increase your safety and that of your dog and enhance your hiking experience. Many of the day hike equipment items are also essential building blocks to a successful backpacking excursion.

Collars and Harnesses

Either a collar or harness is suitable, but a colorful harness makes your dog more visible and identifies him as domestic. For dogs of intimidating size or appearance, a colorful harness emphasizes their pet status. It is easier to restrain a dog by a harness than a collar when necessary. In addition, a harness is a safer restraint (a collar could slip off or choke the animal) if your dog were ever in a predicament requiring you to pull him out of water or hoist him up a hillside. Harnesses are safer than collars off leash because they reduce the risk of neck injury or suffocation from a snag or tangle in brush or with a branch. With an adult dog who insists on pulling you along, the harness will give you more control and prevent damage to his neck and throat.

Fabric: Although leather is the most durable, nylon collars and harnesses are available in vibrant colors, are usually adjustable, and dry more quickly and without

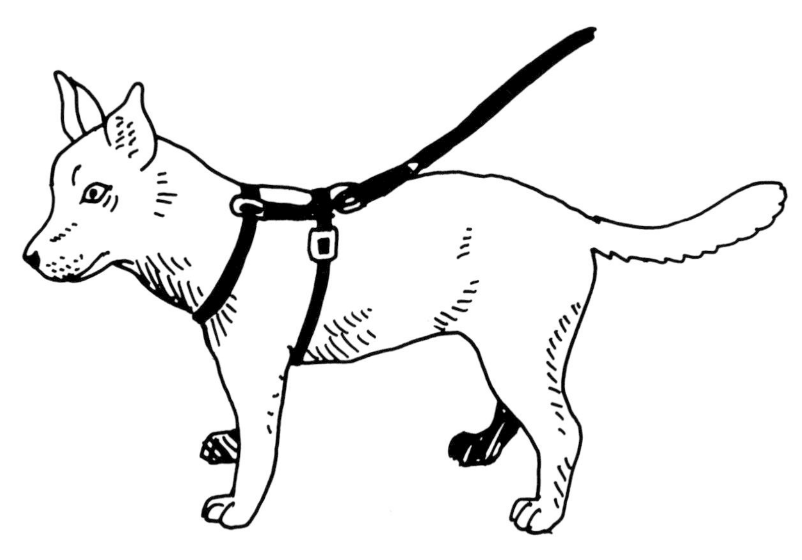

Harness

shrinkage. Your dog is less likely to lose a collar or harness with a plastic snap-in clasp than a metal buckle when he's running, swimming, and jostling about.

Fit: You should be able to easily slip your flat hand under the collar and rotate it; however, the collar should not be so loose that it can slip over your dog's head. A puppy will need to be fitted with a new collar a few times as he grows. Harnesses need to fit loosely enough to allow full expansion of the chest and a free stride.

Many trainers now consider choke collars an inhumane training tool, and a choke collar as a permanent collar can be deadly. To mention a few real-life scenarios: a dog strangled when another dog's jaw got twisted in the choke collar during rambunctious play; a dog snagged his choke collar on a low branch while running through the brush; and a dog slipped and fell off a boulder, hanging himself at the end of a leash and choke collar.

Identification Tags

The sight, smell, or sound of another animal could lure your dog away, and thunder or gunshots could startle your dog and cause her to run off. Whatever the reason for the separation, you want to facilitate a reunion. On the trail a tag is the most obvious way to reunite a lost dog and its owner. The information should at least include the dog's name (first and last name), home telephone number with area code, cell phone number, and street address (not a PO box). If another person gets close enough to your dog to see the tag, the first thing he or she will look for is a name. Calling the dog by its name will establish some communication and trust. The telephone number allows the finder to leave a message with someone in your household or on your answering machine.

Temporary identification: In addition to her permanent tag, your dog needs a temporary identification tag when you are hiking out of town. The tag should have the dates and telephone number telling when and where you are staying in the area, (campground, friend's house, or hotel) and your cell phone number. If you are on a day hike, write the name of the trail, your destination, and the trailhead where you are parked.

An identification tag is a must.

Securing the tag: Loop rings are more secure than S rings for attaching tags. Small plastic luggage tags on a loop ring make inexpensive and reusable temporary tags.

Leashes

A leash that will suffer the abuse of the trail (streams, rain, snow, and rocks) must be durable. On the one hand, a colored nylon webbing leash is light, dries quickly, and is easy to spot when you lay it down. You can design your own leash inexpensively by buying nylon webbing by the foot at a mountaineering store and the clasp at a hardware store.

On the other hand, leather leashes stay the cleanest and last forever. Place a piece of colored tape or tie a strand of colored fabric to the handle to make finding the leash easier when it is on the ground. Leather leashes are often required in obedience classes.

If you are hiking in a strictly on-leash environment, expandable leashes blend control and freedom. The leashes come in varied lengths and strengths based on dog weight. An expandable leash can also convert into a tie-out line.

Bandannas

A colorful bandanna around a dog's neck sends two important messages. It can say "cute," which helps make big dogs look less intimidating to those hikers who may be fearful of them. In the forest a bright bandanna also says "domestic," which helps distinguish dogs from game during hunting season. For extra visibility, tie the bandanna on a colorful harness.

Reflective Vest

If you are going to hike during hunting season, your dog should wear a bright, lightweight reflective vest, specially designed for sporting dogs. This will help distinguish your dog from wildlife.

Booties

If your dog is only an occasional hiker that spends most of his time sauntering across the lawn at home, his pads may get tender after just a couple of miles. Booties can give relief to your dog's sore paws until his pads toughen, as well as prevent cuts from crusty or icy trail conditions. Your dog should practice wearing booties at home before using them on the trail.

Where to buy booties: Booties come in different sizes and materials and are available through pet supply stores, mail-order and online outlets, and mountaineering stores, and are also advertised in dogsledding magazines.

Booties help protect tender paws.

Dog Packs

Although it is a good idea to introduce young dogs to the idea of packs, loaded packs should be used only on fit, medium-to-large adult dogs (thirty-five pounds or more). Most packs are designed to lie on the dog's back like a saddle with a pouch on each side. The pack weight should not exceed one-quarter to one-third of your dog's weight. (For example, a forty-pound dog should not carry more than ten to thirteen pounds of evenly distributed weight.)

Packs are more appropriate for overnight trips than day hikes. There's significantly more gear when you go overnight, and it's a good use of dog power to train a medium- or large-size dog to assist by carrying her booties, first-aid kit, food and treats, and other accessories related to her needs. (See the introduction for pack training information.)

Choosing packs: Packs are sold in pet supply stores, outdoor recreation stores, and mail-order and online outlets. They come in different sizes with adjustable straps. Look for the design that best conforms to your dog's body. The pack should feature breathable material, rounded corners, and padding for additional comfort.

Pack fitting: Your dog's comfort depends on a proper fit. The pack should sit on his shoulders between the base of the neck and just short of the hips. There should be one strap that clips on the front of his chest and one or two belly straps to stabilize the pack. Straps should be tight enough to keep the pack in place but loose enough to allow full stride without chafing and comfortable expansion of the chest for breathing.

Loading the pack: Stuff the pack with crumpled newspaper first. Then, once your dog is accustomed to the pack and his endurance has built up, gradually increase the load from 10 percent of his weight not to exceed one-quarter to one-third of his weight. If you use a pack only occasionally, keep the weight on the lighter side. The weight should be equal and evenly distributed to avoid interfering with your dog's balance.

Pack safety: Keep your dog on leash when he is wearing his pack. Packs can make balance awkward when negotiating narrow mountainside trails or crossing fast streams. Give him a break every hour or so by removing the pack so he can enjoy the freedom you both came for by playing, swimming, and rolling around without risking injury to himself and damage to his pack and cargo.

Life Vest

A life vest is important to have if you are going to hike near rivers and lakes or if you have to cross high water, especially with dogs who are drawn to water. An elderly or tired dog is more at risk in the water during a hike than she would be at the beach for the day.

Flashlight and Extra Batteries

You will be thankful for a flashlight—especially one that fits in a day pack—if you are still hiking after sunset.

Matches and Cigarette Lighter

Temperatures can drop quickly after the sun goes down. If you are lost or injured, a fire can help keep you warm until daylight or help arrives. Put matches and a strike strip in a pill bottle to protect them from the elements. Gas clicker lighters are lightweight and can be easier to use in inclement weather.

Lightweight Nylon Tarp

In an emergency, a tarp makes a lightweight shelter from sun, wind, and rain. Purchase a lightweight one at a local hardware or outdoor store.

Flyers for a Lost Dog

Carry a few photocopied flyers with your dog's photo, name, and a contact phone number. If the unthinkable happens, you can fill in a description of the area where your dog was lost and post flyers at the trailhead, campground, and ranger station and carry one to show to other hikers along the way.

Food

Dogs require a balanced diet made up of five essential nutrients: protein, fat, carbohydrates, minerals, and vitamins.

Types of Food

Human food (cooked poultry, meat, and rice) is tasty and freshest but requires more preparation and planning. Commercial dog food comes moist (canned), semimoist (sealed pouches), and dry.

Dry kibble is convenient but should be supplemented with a dab of healthy, nutritious, and tasty human food or quality canned dog food.

Read the ingredients and choose a premium brand from the supermarket or pet supply store, avoiding brands with animal by-products and corn fillers. Choose a formula that matches your dog's age group and activity level, such as puppy growth, adult maintenance, high performance, or senior for less active dogs.

Dogs with restricted diets due to medical conditions or allergies are often fed "prescription" brands obtained from a veterinarian. The breeder and your veterinarian can help guide you in choosing appropriate foods for your dog.

FOOD/EXERCISE RISKS

There are differing theories on the condition called gastric dilatation-volvulus complex (GDV), which involves bloating and stomach torsion. The most popular explanation suggests that strenuous exercise (jumping and running) after a large meal may compound the risks of the stomach twisting in the abdomen, blocking the flow or absorption of gastric material. Large breeds are especially prone to GDV, which can be fatal. Dividing daily portions into smaller, more frequent meals, preferably fed during rest periods on the trail or in camp, can help prevent GDV.

Feeding Your Dog

Puppies are generally fed three or four smaller meals per day. Just as smaller, more frequent meals are healthier for humans, adult dogs should be fed at least twice a day. To do this, divide their total daily portion into two smaller meals (morning and evening). Small meals are beneficial for active dogs too. Exercising on a full stomach is uncomfortable because most of the body's blood supply is busy helping with digestion rather than supplying oxygen to the muscles and the cardiovascular system.

It is not necessary to increase your dog's amount of food for a day hike. Instead, supplement his diet at snack breaks. Pack dog biscuits, jerky treats, and a pouch of semimoist food or extra dry kibble. Some dogs like carrots, apples, and melon pieces as much as any canine treat. (Never feed chocolate to dogs. It is toxic.)

In cold weather, bring higher-protein dog snacks. Look for real liver, turkey, chicken, or egg as the first ingredient and avoid products with sugar and fillers.

Plastic Resealable Bags

The airtight, self-sealing invention is in the top five essentials for the trail. These bags are great for carrying food, treats, medication, and first-aid necessities, and they can easily be converted into food and water bowls. Their "sealing" quality comes in handy for disposing of dog waste.

Water

Water is as essential to your dog as it is to you. Do not skimp on bringing water or count on finding it along the trail. Dehydration can result in sluggishness, kidney problems, and heat stroke. Both humans and dogs are vulnerable to dehydration in the heat and at high elevations.

Do not let your dog drink from standing water in puddles, ponds, lakes, or swimming holes in slow-moving creeks and rivers. That's where different forms of bacteria and algae breed, and small dogs and puppies have been known to get very ill and in some cases die from drinking contaminated water. Be especially wary of areas where cattle graze.

Both dogs and humans are susceptible to the intestinal parasite *Giardia lamblia,* which can cause cramping and diarrhea, leading to serious dehydration. Giardia can be present in all sources of untreated water.

How Much Water Do I Need?

Carry at least eight ounces of water per dog per hour of hiking. Consider that an average walking pace on level ground is about 3 miles per hour. Fill plastic water bottles three-quarters full and place in the freezer the night before. Your dog will have a source of cool fresh water as the ice melts along the way. Two frozen water bottles can also keep her cooler if you place one in each pouch of her dog pack.

Offer water to your dog frequently (every half hour or more on hot days). It is easier to regulate hydration with regular small intakes of water.

Snow may keep your dog cool, but do not believe that a hot, thirsty dog will instinctively know to eat snow to quench her thirst. One hiker reported that her Southern California–born-and-raised dog was almost delirious from dehydration after she took him on a summer hike up a mountain where she thought the abundant snow would make up for the lack of water.

Bowls

Weight and encumbrances are the main concerns when packing for a hike. There are plenty of ways to create inexpensive doggie dinnerware on the trail. Paper or plastic picnic plates and bowls are lightweight and adequate for food and water. A plastic resealable bag can store the kibble and convert into a food dish or water bowl (you'll need to hold the bag while your dog drinks from it). Pet supply stores and mail-order and online outlets have several doggie gadgets for carrying and serving food and water on the trail, from canteens to collapsible bowls.

First-aid Kit

Although you cannot prepare for all mishaps, it is best to have a few first-aid items. See the First-aid Kit Checklist sidebar later in the appendix.

Backpacking Gear

Maybe it's the thought of retreating deeper into the solitary beauty of the wilderness with your four-legged companion that draws you. Or perhaps you're satisfied with setting up camp a few miles up the trailhead to share an easy, idyllic overnight in the great outdoors with him. Whichever appeals to you, backpacking with your dog requires some extra necessities and additional planning. Your goal is to travel light while considering emergencies, outdoor dining pleasures, and sleeping comforts for both you and your dog. With good planning and careful attention to gear, backpacking can heighten the pleasures of the trail for you and your dog.

Add the following things to your list for a backpacking adventure:

Permits

Permits are generally obtained from ranger stations of the government agency that manages the land you wish to hike on (e.g., national or state park and forest, Bureau of Land Management). Permits are usually required for overnights in wilderness areas and in other heavily used recreation areas. In some places, registering or obtaining a permit can be required even for day hiking. In popular areas where use is strictly regulated, you may have to apply for a permit several months ahead of time.

Food

Make a list of the number of meals and snacks per hiking day for you and your dog. Package your dog's meals and snacks (preferably dry or semimoist) individually in resealable bags for convenience and to keep food smells from attracting bears.

DAY HIKE GEAR CHECKLIST

- ☐ Flea and tick treatment application prior to hike
- ☐ Bug repellent in sealed plastic bag
- ☐ Health and vaccination certificate
- ☐ Collar and bandanna or colorful harness with permanent and temporary ID tag and rabies tag
- ☐ Leather leash or expandable leash
- ☐ Plastic water containers full of water: thirty-two-ounce bottle for half-day hike (under 4 hours) and two-quart bottle for longer hikes
- ☐ Eight ounces of water per dog per hour or 3 miles of hiking, in addition to water for you, to be carried with you
- ☐ Water purifier for full-day hikes
- ☐ Snacks for you and your pet
- ☐ Collapsible dish or resealable bag
- ☐ Plastic bags for cleaning up after your dog
- ☐ Sunscreen for tips of ears and nose
- ☐ Booties for pooch and comfortable, sturdy, waterproof boots for you
- ☐ Wire grooming brush to help remove stickers and foxtails from your pet's coat at the end of the hike
- ☐ Extra clothing (sweater or coat for thin-coated dog, sweater and windbreaker for you)
- ☐ Extra-large, heavy-duty plastic garbage bags (good to sit on and makes a handy poncho in the rain)
- ☐ Flyers for a lost dog
- ☐ Pocketknife (Swiss Army–type knife that includes additional tools: fork, scissors, pliers, file)
- ☐ Flashlight and extra batteries
- ☐ Matches or cigarette lighter and emergency fire starter
- ☐ First-aid kit
- ☐ Telephone number and address of closest veterinarian

You can safely supplement your dog's dry kibbles with most human food you would bring for yourself, except sugar and chocolate (remember, chocolate is toxic to dogs as well as cats). Plan to take one extra cup of human food per day to supplement your dog's dinner in camp. Pasta and rice are lightweight and easy to cook in camp and can be prepared creatively for extra taste and nutrition.

Meat eaters can add canned tuna or chicken, as well as any freeze-dried meat sauce or soup mix. Either way, your dog will appreciate the added flavor to her kibbles and will benefit from the energy fuel. (***Note:*** Introduce her to new foods at home gradually before going on an overnight trip.)

Cutting your dog's regular dog food with puppy food will add the extra protein and fat needed for higher calorie-burning backpacking excursions. Begin mixing in small amounts of puppy food about three days before the hike so your dog's digestive system can adapt gradually.

Setting up Camp

1. **Pick your campsite in daylight, taking into account exposure, water, mosquitoes, and other features that might affect your dog's comfort.**
2. **Put your dog on her tie-out line, where she can curl up to rest, and give her water while you set up camp (sleeping and cooking quarters). Keep her water bowl full, within easy reach but out of the "step and spill" zone.**
3. **Get enough water to boil or filter for cooking dinner and breakfast, and enough drinking water for you and your dog for the evening and following trail day (eight ounces per mile per dog).**
4. **Prepare dinner for you and your dog.**
5. **Wash the dishes and burn or seal garbage in plastic bags for pack-out, to remove any food smells from camp. Be sure to use the bear-proof metal food storage bins whenever provided, and consider buying your own small bear-proof canisters for your aromatic goods.**
6. **Walk your dog before bedtime, tidy up camp, and snuggle up for the night.**

Breaking Camp

1. **Walk your dog and clean up any of her waste.**
2. **Share a hot breakfast with her (instant hot cereal or scrambled eggs over her kibble, with a hot drink for you and warm water for her).**
3. **Clean up and pack up. Leave your campsite cleaner than you found it.**

THREE REASONS WHY YOUR DOG SHOULD BE ATTENDED IN CAMP AT ALL TIMES

1. He would be vulnerable to wild predators otherwise.
2. It would be unkind to cause him the stress of being separated from you in unfamiliar surroundings.
3. Separation anxiety is often expressed through barking, whining, and howling, which ruins the wilderness experience for other campers. Do not forget that separation anxiety could also bring on a chewing rampage that might leave you with a shredded tent, sleeping bag, or backpack.

BACKPACKING GEAR CHECKLIST

Be sure to pack all items on the day hike checklist, plus the following:

Dog Necessities

- ☐ Extra leash or rope
- ☐ Dog pack for your dog and backpack with internal frame for you
- ☐ Doggie bedroll (foam sleeping pad)
- ☐ Dog's favorite chew toy
- ☐ Dog food (number of days on the trail times three meals a day)
- ☐ Additional water in a two-quart bottle
- ☐ Water purifier
- ☐ Dog snacks (enough for six rest stops per hiking day)
- ☐ Nylon tie-out line in camp (expandable leash can be an extra leash and tie-out rope)

Human Necessities

- ☐ Tent with rain fly (large enough for you and your dog to sleep inside)
- ☐ Clothing (raingear, gloves, fleece or knit hat, long pants, wicking top, fleece top, socks)
- ☐ Camp stove and fuel bottle
- ☐ Iodine tablets (backup water purifier)
- ☐ Food (lightweight, nutritious carbs and proteins—instant oatmeal, dried fruits and nuts, pasta, rice, canned tuna, dehydrated backpacking meals, tea bags or cocoa packets
- ☐ Extra garbage bags
- ☐ Bear-proof food canisters
- ☐ Pepper spray (if hiking in bear country)

Water

You need to take enough water for drinking (for you and your dog) and cooking. If you are sure of the availability of water, consider carrying less and boiling, filtering, or chemically treating the water in camp. Several water purification systems are available at outdoor recreation stores, but be aware that some dogs will not drink chemically treated water.

Bedding

For yourself, choose a sleeping bag rated to keep you warm in the region and season in which you are backpacking.

For your dog, carry a piece of foam and a towel, which you can roll up with your sleeping bag. Or try a lightweight dog bedroll, designed to be cuddly on one side and durable on the side in contact with the ground; dog bedrolls are available in pet supply stores and through mail-order and online outlets.

If you choose to sleep under the stars, make sure your dog is staked on a line (6-foot radius from a stake or tree) short enough to keep him away from the campfire but long enough to allow him to have physical contact with you. Physical contact gives your dog the security that will help keep him quieter if the sounds of the dark outdoors are new to him. It enables you to hush him at the first hint of a growl, keeps him warmer on cold nights, and lets you know when he's on alert.

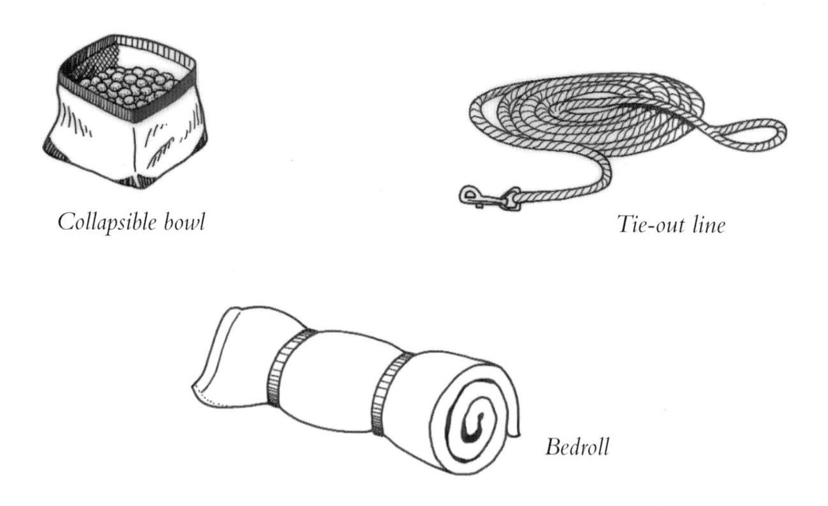

Collapsible bowl

Tie-out line

Bedroll

Appendix B: Medical Emergencies and Treatment

Planning, a common-sense approach, and a leash will help prevent most mishaps on the trail. Keep your dog on leash when:

- Hiking in territory known for its higher concentration of specific hazards (bears, mountain lions, snakes, skunks)
- Crossing fast-moving streams
- Negotiating narrow mountainside trails
- Hiking in wind and snow (dogs can become disoriented and lose their way)

If your dog gets into trouble, here are some basic first-aid treatments you can administer until you can get him to a vet.

Bleeding from Cuts or Wounds

1. Remove any obvious foreign object.
2. Rinse the area with warm water or 3 percent hydrogen peroxide.
3. Cover the wound with clean gauze or cloth and apply firm, direct pressure over the wound for about ten minutes, to allow clotting to occur and bleeding to stop.
4. Place a nonstick pad or gauze over the wound and bandage with gauze wraps (the stretchy, clingy type). For a paw wound, cover the bandaging with a bootie. (An old sock with duct tape on the bottom is a good bootie substitute. Use adhesive tape around the sock to prevent it from slipping off. Be careful not to impede circulation.)

Frostbite

Frostbite is the freezing of a body part exposed to extreme cold. The tips of dog's ears and footpads are the most vulnerable.

1. Remove your dog from the cold.
2. Apply a warm compress to the affected area without friction or pressure.

Heatstroke

Heatstroke occurs when a dog's body temperature is rising rapidly above 104°F and panting is ineffective to regulate temperature.

1. Get your dog out of the sun and begin reducing body temperature (no lower than 103°F) by applying water-soaked towels on her head (to cool the brain), chest, abdomen, and feet.
2. Let your dog stand in a pond, lake, or stream while you gently pour water over her. Avoid icy water—it can chill her. Swabbing the footpads with alcohol will help.

Hypothermia

Hypothermia occurs when a dog's body temperature drops below 95°F because of overexposure to cold weather.

1. Bring your dog indoors or into a sheltered area where you can make a fire.
2. Wrap him in a blanket, towel, sleeping bag, your clothing, or whatever you have available, or place warm water bottles in a towel next to him.
3. Hold him close to you for body heat.

Insect Bites

Bee stings and spider bites may cause itching, swelling, and hives.

1. If the stinger is still present, scrape it off with your nail or tweezers at the base, away from the point of entry. (Pressing the stinger or trying to pick it from the top can release more toxin.)
2. Apply a cold compress to the area and spray it with a topical analgesic like Benadryl spray, to relieve the itch and pain.

FIRST-AID KIT CHECKLIST

- ☐ First-aid book
- ☐ Muzzle—the most loving dogs can snap and bite when in pain. Muzzles come in different styles and sizes to fit all dog nose shapes.
- ☐ Buffered aspirin—older dogs in particular may be stiff and sore at the end of a hike or a backpacking excursion. Consult your vet on the appropriate dosage.
- ☐ Scissors (rounded tips) to trim hair around a wound
- ☐ Hydrogen peroxide (3 percent) to disinfect surface abrasions and wounds
- ☐ Antiseptic ointment
- ☐ Gauze pads and gauze
- ☐ Clingy gauze wraps and elastic bandages
- ☐ Sock or bootie to protect a wounded foot
- ☐ Duct tape to wrap around a sock used as a bootie
- ☐ Tweezers to remove ticks, needles, or foreign objects in a wound
- ☐ Styptic powder for bleeding
- ☐ Rectal thermometer
- ☐ Hydrocortisone spray to relieve plant rashes and stings
- ☐ Lemon juice for a quick rinse if your dog is skunked; recipe for de-skunking shampoo mix
- ☐ Your veterinarian's telephone number and the telephone number of the veterinary clinic closest to the trailhead
- ☐ National Animal Poison Control Center phone number: (888) 426-4435

3. As a precaution, carry an over-the-counter antihistamine (such as Benadryl) and ask your vet about the appropriate dosage before you leave, in case your dog has an extreme allergic reaction with excessive swelling.

Skunked

When your dog gets skunked, a potent, smelly cloud of spray burns his eyes and makes his mouth foam. The smell can make you gag, and contact with the spray on your dog's coat can give your skin a tingling, burning sensation. Apply de-skunking shampoo as soon as possible.

De-Skunking Shampoo Mix:

1 quart hydrogen peroxide
¼ cup baking soda
1 tablespoon dishwashing detergent

Put on rubber gloves and thoroughly wet your dog, apply mixture, and let stand for fifteen minutes; rinse and repeat as needed.

Sore Muscles

1. Rest your dog.
2. Apply cold-water compresses to tight muscle areas to reduce inflammation.
3. Administer buffered aspirin (check with your vet on dosage for your dog's breed and weight).

Venomous Bites

1. Keep your dog calm (activity stimulates the absorption of venom).
2. Rinse the area with water, and transport your dog to the nearest vet.

Cardiopulmonary Resuscitation

Check with your veterinarian or local humane society for pet CPR classes.

Appendix C: Wildlife Conflicts

Most hikers with dogs come to the natural world "in peace," to retreat and absorb the beauty. Nevertheless, you are still an uninvited guest at best. Respect the animals whose home you are in, and trespass lightly.

Protecting Wildlife

Leashes are mandatory in many outdoor recreation areas primarily to protect the wildlife that lives, breeds, migrates, or nests there. Even in areas where your dog is allowed offleash, do not let him chase wildlife or livestock for sport. It stresses and depletes the animal of survival energy and can cause a serious injury that leads to a cruel, agonizing death.

In the spring nesting birds are very vulnerable to free-roaming dogs in meadows and low brush. Young deer can be separated from their mothers and fall prey to your dog's primal but inappropriate impulses.

Your companion is more likely to chase wildlife at the beginning of the hike, when he is fresh out of the starting gate. Keep him on leash for about thirty minutes while he walks off some of his excess energy and gets used to his surroundings.

If you have any doubts about your dog's behavior, keep him leashed.

Preventing Encounters

The potential for being injured or killed by a wild animal is extremely low compared with many other natural hazards. Information and preparedness is the safest way for hikers with dogs to enjoy their time on the trail. Although there is no absolute rule to wild animal behavior, there is sufficient knowledge to trust some established guidelines. When given the opportunity, most wild animals are more than happy to avoid humans; unfortunately, people often feed wild animals because they look cute and cuddly. Once a wild animal gets a taste of human food, it becomes habituated to that food and will not forget that humans are a source of food. Wild animals that have grown accustomed to human food and garbage can become brazen, posing a threat to human safety. In bears these bad "human-engendered" habits identify them as "problem" bears, which sadly leads to their eventual and inevitable destruction. If you love wild animals, respect them, admire them from a safe distance, and please do not feed them.

Be informed about where you plan to hike and what lives there. Contact the region's fish and game, park, or forest headquarters. Keep your eyes open and learn to identify tracks, scat, and concealed kill sites. Keep your dog on a leash in questionable surroundings.

Bears and Bear Safety

Development encroaching on habitat and more hikers in remote wilderness areas have increased the bear's exposure to humans, their food, and their garbage. It is more important than ever to know how to minimize the risk of an encounter and what to do if one occurs.

BEAR FACTS

Bears can run, swim, and climb trees.

Bears have good vision, excellent hearing, and a superior sense of smell.

Bears are curious and attracted to food smells.

Bears can be out at any time of day but are most active in the coolness of dawn and dusk and after dark.

Bears and wild animals in general prefer anonymity. If they know you are out there, they will avoid your path.

There is no scientific evidence that dogs are "bear bait." But a loose dog in bear country runs more of a chance of surprising a bear and antagonizing it with barking and other antics. Even if your dog gets lucky and runs back to you unharmed, your problems are just beginning if the bear follows.

Stay on the trail, where there are fewer chances of surprising a bear snacking in a berry patch. Make your presence known with noise that is distinctly man-made, such as talking, singing, or humming a tune. The slight jingle of a metal ID tag against the metal rabies tag on your dog's collar or harness acts like a bell and can help notify bears of your presence. A small bell on the dog collar and one on your belt, walking stick, or boot lace is an even stronger statement in bear country.

Bear cub

When it comes to odor, in bear country the motto is "less is safer." Pack all food items (human and dog) and any other odorous items in airtight resealable bags. Dispose of all items with food smells in airtight bags or in bear-proof storage containers. Clean your dishes and pet bowls as quickly as possible so food smells do not float through the forest as a dinner invitation to the local bears. Some national forests and wilderness areas require that campers use portable "bear-resistant food canisters." These plastic canisters (some collapsible) are available for sale and rent at sporting good stores and some ranger stations.

If you see a bear in the distance, stop, stay calm, and don't run. Keep your dog close to your side on leash. You should feel awe rather than panic. Walk a wide upwind detour so the animal can get your scent, and make loud banging or clanging noises as you leave the area. If the bear is at closer range, the same principles apply while you keep your eye on the bear. If the terrain doesn't allow you to negotiate a detour, back down the trail slowly. Avoid sudden movements that could spook or provoke the bear. Be cool, slow, but deliberate as you make your retreat.

Mountain Lions

There are fewer mountain lions than bears in the wilderness, and the mountain lion population is concentrated in the western United States and Canada. As with bears, development and human intrusion are at the core of encounter problems. Know what to do to avoid and manage an encounter.

- Keep your dog on leash on the trail.
- Keep your dog in the tent at night.
- Seeing doesn't mean attacking. If you come across a mountain lion, stay far enough away to give it the opportunity to avoid you.
- Do not approach or provoke the lion.
- Walk away slowly and maintain eye contact. Running will stimulate the lion's predatory instinct to chase and hunt.
- Make yourself big by putting your arms above your head and waving them. Use your jacket or walking stick above your head to appear bigger. Do not bend down or make any motion that will make you look or sound like easy prey.
- Shout and make noise.
- If necessary, walking sticks can be weapons, as can rocks or anything you can get your hands on to fight back with.

MOUNTAIN LION FACTS

Mountain lions are elusive, and preying on humans is uncharacteristic.

Mountain lions are most active at dawn and dusk and usually hunt at night.

They are solitary and secretive and require a vegetated habitat for camouflage while they stalk prey.

Their meal of choice is big game (deer, bighorn sheep, and elk). In the absence of game, however, they can make a meal of domestic livestock and small mammals.

They prefer to feed on what they kill. An unattended dog in camp is far more appetizing than his kibble.

Other Animals

Bobcats: Smaller than mountain lions, these wild cats are no threat to humans and would prefer climbing a tree over confronting your dog.

Coyotes: In spite of their ability to survive persecution in healthier numbers than their wolf cousins, coyotes are not a threat on the trail. Hikers are more fortunate than some homeowners, though. In some neighborhoods of Southern California and the Southwest, loss of habitat to housing developments has increased the incidence of unattended pets turning into a meal for a coyote.

Skunks and porcupines: Skunks and porcupines are primarily nocturnal and will fend off the curious with a spray or shot of barbed needles, respectively. It's a good idea to carry lemon juice concentrate and a pair of disposable latex gloves (available in hardware store paint departments) in your pack in case your dog gets sprayed by a skunk. A lemon juice rub and stream water rinse will tone down some of the fumes until you can give your pooch a full spa treatment—with a de-skunking shampoo mix—at a pet wash location, groomer, veterinarian, or in your own backyard. Always carry a couple of dog towels or old sheets in your car to wrap your dog and protect your upholstery. In a pinch large plastic trash bags and duct tape come in handy to create a barrier between the seats and a damp, stinky dog.

A dog pierced by a mask of porcupine quills is a pitiful sight. Few dogs can withstand the pain of having barbed needles pulled out of their faces by inexperienced, nervous hands without any anesthetic. Take your dog to a vet as quickly as possible.

Snakes: Most dogs have an instinctive aversion to lizards and snakes. Dogs will bound away at the first sight, sound, or touch of a slither. Snake bites are usually a result of stepping on a snake unknowingly rather than conscious provocation. Most snake bites occur on the nose or front legs and can be lethal to a small or young dog. If taken to the vet quickly, larger adult dogs will survive most bites. Ask your veterinarian if the recently developed rattlesnake vaccine would benefit your dog. Also ask your vet or local dog club about snake avoidance classes in your area. If the dog is bitten, first keep the dog calm (as activity stimulates the absorption of venom). Then rinse the area with water and transport your dog to the nearest vet.

Spiders: Most spider bites cause mild irritation and swelling, but in the case of black widow spiders, their venom can be more lethal than snake venom. Seek veterinary attention if your dog is bitten by a black widow spider.

Bees, wasps, hornets, and yellow jackets: A leash is the best preventive measure to protect your dog from her own curiosity. Insect nests can be in trees or on the ground.

Hike Index

Alberta Peak: Continental Divide National Scenic Trail, 211
Bear Peak, 78
Big Dominguez Canyon, 236
Black Mountain (West Summit) Trail, 154
Blue Lake, 72
Cascade and Portland Loop, 251
Coyote and Squirrel Trails, 143
The Crags Trail, 183
Dawson Butte Ranch Open Space, 34
Devil's Backbone Nature Trail, 66
Devils Canyon, 159
Devils Creek and Lake, 220
Dome Mountain Trail, 63
Edna Mae Bennett Nature Trail, 51
Eldorado Canyon Trail, 88
First Fork and Red Creek Loop, 263
Granite Lakes Trail, 112
Heil Valley Ranch/Lichen Loop, 75
Homestead Trail, 22
Horsethief Falls, 192
Jud Wiebe Memorial Trail, 247
Kelly Lake, 125
Lory State Park Loop, 56
Lower Barr Trail, 199
Marshall Mesa, 85
Marvine Loop, 148
Middle Frisco Trail, 206
Mount Audubon, 69
Mount Cutler Trail, 175
Mount Thomas Trail, 108
Newlin Creek Trail, 178
North Mount Elbert Trail, 97
Notch Mountain, 102
Pass and Coal Creek Loop, 257
Pawnee Buttes, 46
Picket Wire Canyonlands, 28
Ptarmigan Lake, 230
Red Rock Canyon Trail, 202
Reilly and Levsa Canyons, 195
Rocky Mountain Arsenal National Wildlife Refuge, 40
Seven Lakes, 129
Silver Creek Trail, 118
Spanish Peaks Traverse, 187
Storm King Fourteen Memorial Trail, 137
Susan G. Bretag/Palmer Loop, 166
Thompson Mountain, 170
Upper Roubideau Area Loop, 241
Walker Ranch, 82
Washington Gulch Trail, 225
Wheeler Trail, 92
Williams Creek Trail, 215